BLACK DIAMONDS!

BLACK GOLD!

BLACK DIAMONDS!

BLACK GOLD!

THE SAGA OF TEXAS PACIFIC COAL AND OIL COMPANY

DON WOODARD

TEXAS TECH UNIVERSITY PRESS

This book was set in Berkeley Oldstyle ITC, Copperplate Gothic BT, and Snell BT and printed on acid-free paper that meets the guidelines for permanence and durability of the committee on Production Guide- lines for Book Longevity of the Council on Library Resources.(∞)

Design by Rob Neatherlin

Printed in the United States of America

Library of Congress Cataloging-in-Publication Data
Woodard, Don.
     Black diamonds! Black gold! : the saga of Texas Pacific Coal and Oil
Company / Don Woodard.
        p. cm.
     Includes bibliographical references and index.
     ISBN 0-89672-379-8 (alk. paper)
     1. Texas Pacific Coal and Oil Company—History. 2. Coal trade—Texas—
Fort Worth—History. 3. Coal mines and mining—Texas—Fort Worth—
History. 4. Petroleum industry and trade—Texas—Fort Worth—History.
5. Businesspeople—Texas—Fort Worth—Biography.
I. Title.
HD9549.T49W66 1998
338.7′66262′097645315—dc21   97-47669
                                         CIP

98 99 00 01 02 03 04 05 06 / 9 8 7 6 5 4 3 2 1

Texas Tech University Press
Box 41037
Lubbock, Texas 79409-1037 USA

800-832-4042

ttup@ttu.edu

To
Wanda
Have I told you lately that I love you?
Well, darling, I'm telling you now.

and to

Don, Jr. and Blake
My beloved sons in whom I am well pleased.

CONTENTS

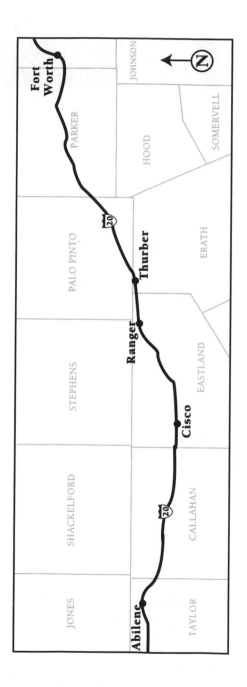

I have witnessed the comings and goings of many of the legends in Fort Worth's pantheon of oil who were on the scene in the last half of the twentieth century. Consequently, it was natural that in 1990 I would be involved in a project of the Fort Worth Petroleum Club to compile a volume entitled *Oil Legends of Fort Worth,* a history of all the oil companies and operators who had ever had offices in Fort Worth.[1] Since I had been a landman for Texas Pacific Coal and Oil Company from 1952 to 1964, the chairman of the project, Jack Tunstill, Fort Worth independent oilman, asked me to write a synopsis about Texas Pacific. "It won't take you but a few days," he said. True, but this book, inspired by that summary, took more than seven years.

Despite having spent twelve years in TP's Fort Worth headquarters, I did not know "come here from sic'em" about the origins of the company in the 1880s or its ensuing saga through the 1890s and the first half of the 20th century. In pursuit of the full story, I unearthed a vast trove of Texas Pacificana. There were many books and articles concerning isolated bits of the history, but no one had ever assembled all the pieces into an integrated whole.

At first my research turned up very little about W. W. Johnson, who had opened the first coal mine at Thurber. He was a shadowy figure. Then one day my son, Don, Jr., handed me a black, typewritten manuscript titled *William Whipple Johnson,* written by Robert W. Spoede as a thesis for a Master of Arts Degree from Hardin-Simmons University. It had been loaned to Don, Jr. by his friend Don Crawford of Mineral Wells. The book contained a wealth of information pertaining to W. W. Johnson, gleaned from letters and documents which Spoede had found scattered on a barn loft floor on Johnson's ranch north of Gordon, Texas. These papers had lain undisturbed, except by rats and mice, for more than fifty years. That barn was a literal time capsule.

On field trips to the Strawn-Mingus-Thurber region in the summer of 1967, Spoede and his wife Nancy encountered many people who mentioned Will Johnson, but the amount of hard information he gleaned from his interviews was scant as more than half a century had passed since the death of Johnson and his wife, Anna. The Spoedes found many people in the area who had seen the Johnsons, but none who had known them well enough to give specific information about them. They were told that there were no surviving heirs, and that Donald Crawford, Sr. of Strawn owned the Johnson ranch.

Upon inquiry by the Spoedes, Crawford said that as a boy playing in the loft of one of the Johnson barns, he had seen ledgers and other papers scattered about. Several years previously, he added, one of the barns had been struck by lightning and had burned, but he did not remember if that was the barn in which he had seen the papers. He offered to take them out to the ranch to see what they could find.

Arriving at the ranch the next day, Crawford and the Spoedes found the material providentially had not been in the barn that had burned. To say that Will Johnson left a paper trail is an understatement. The excited explorers found a wooden box overflowing with letters and documents. It aggregated seven thousand pages of manuscript, about 60 percent letters and the remainder legal and financial documents and miscellaneous materials. Only a relatively small amount had been destroyed by rats and insects. Don Crawford, Sr. later gave the papers to the Southwest Collection at Texas Tech University in Lubbock.

John Wilson, who as a boy lived on the Johnson Ranch, made an exciting find in 1994 when he and his wife Sue happened upon a 1903 issue of the *Gordon Weekly Courier* that neatly unlocked the door to a century-old mystery that no writer or researcher had been able to solve: Where did W. W. Johnson bury his brother and business partner, Harvey Johnson, a hundred years ago?

Then there was the fortuitous discovery that was triggered when I attended a funeral in Fort Worth's Greenwood Memorial Park in August 1992. On that hot afternoon I came upon the headstone of Hunter McLean, a friend and political associate of mine for many years. It had been Hunter McLean, close friend and adviser of Lyndon B. Johnson, who in October 1963 had stopped me at Houston and Seventh streets in Fort Worth and told me that plans were afoot to have President John Kennedy visit Fort Worth on November 22nd.

Returning to my office from the cemetery, I retrieved from my files Hunter McLean's obituary notice. To my astonishment and delight, the story related that Hunter had written a genealogy entitled, *From Ayr to Thurber; Three Hunter Brothers And The Winning Of The West.*[2] Thurber! Hunter! As long as I had known McLean, I had never associated his name, Hunter, with that of the founder of Texas Pacific, Colonel Robert D. Hunter.

Attorney Edgar H. Keltner, Jr. had been a Texas Pacific vice-president during the 1963 sale of the company to Joseph E. Seagram & Sons, Inc. As such, he had worked closely with TP Chairman H. B. Fuqua. Keltner loaned me a bound volume containing every document pertaining to the Seagram sale.[3] Until then I had found absolutely no record of just what had transpired in the sale.

H. B. Fuqua's long-time secretary, Pat Woods, was a veritable ware-house of information, furnishing many letters, photographs, and memories. John Roby Penn, Jr. and Chissa and W. K. Gordon, Jr. rolodexed through their memories to contribute vignettes, facts, and artifacts of the dynamic Gordon-Penn era. Enthusiastic, gloriously garrulous octogenarian George B. Studdard, who had been hired by TP at Ranger and lived in Thurber throughout the 1920s, staying with the company until after its sale, gave invaluable eyewitness testimony.

I had been fairly well satisfied with all of the TP facts my seven years of research had unearthed. But one missing piece of the puzzle made me vaguely discontented. Who was H. K. Thurber for whom Colonel Hunter named the mining town? His identity had remained shrouded in the mists of time. At the last minute, Billy Joe Moore, a TP landman in the 40s, 50s, and 60s, walked into my office on the afternoon of December 20, 1996. He asked me what I knew about H. K. Thurber. "Very little," I replied. Moore had just returned from a trip to New York City and the morgue of the vaunted *New York Times*. With a broad grin across his face, he said, "Well, I know everything!" and handed me a sheaf of news items from the *New York Times* published in the 1890s. Among them was the obituary of Horace Kingsley Thurber, containing a thumbnail biography of that entrepreneur from birth to death.

And there were many others who contributed: Sally Still Abbe, Harold Achziger, Don Addison, John Andreatta, Barbara Arends, John T. Bailey, Ellen Barnes, Willard Barr, Perry Bass, David O. Belew, Joe Bell, Leo Bielinski, Lee Bigelow, Marvin Blum, Bill Bogle, Patrick Bopp, Henry Boykin, Jim Bradshaw, Walker Brents, Jr., Rita Bridges, Roger Brooks, Bob Browder, Charlcie Bullard, Robert O. Burford, Frank Burkett, Joyce Butler, Chris Callaway, Kay Capps, Sheila Carter, Gladys Carver, Bob Cass, Aaron Cawley, Margaret W. Chambers, Doug Clarke, Ernest Closuit, Jr., Dave Corbin, Ann Corkery, Bobbie Corzine, Karen Coulson, Jud Cramer, Don Crawford, Troy Crenshaw, Wiltie A. Creswell, Jr., Judy Cross, Ralph Dahlstrom, Mrs. Price Daniel, Bill Daniels, Jack Daugherty, Art Dickerson, Claude W. Dodgen, Jr., Glenn Dromgoole, Jack Earp, Jim Eagle, Irvin Farman, Ben Feemster, Cantey Ferchill, John C. Ferris, Jr., David Fielding, Mike Fitzgerald, Ben Franklin, Carl Freund, Bayard Friedman, James Fuqua, Lawton Gambill, Taylor Gandy, Darlene Garrett, Jenkins Garrett, John B. Garrett, Phil Garrett, Jim Getz, Lillie Gibson, Rogers Gideon, Burton Gilbert, Alton Goodrich, Mr. and Mrs. W. K. Gordon, Jr., Gordon Gray, Howard Green, Harmon Greene, Bill Gupton, Linda K. Hanson, Betty Harland, Bill Harris, Joe Harris, A. D. Hartline, Tommy Helm, Keri Henderson, Charlie Hillard, Bob Hines, Nolan Hirsch, Dwayne Holden, Rosemary Horan, Neal Hospers, Ruth Howard, Al Hrubetz, Mark Jacoby, J. Lee Johnson, III, Jerry Johnson, Robert H. Johnson, Worley Jones, John Justin, Bob Keasler, Dee Kelly, Bud Kennedy, Randall Kressler, Roger

Latham, Debbie LaHood, Tom Law, Bonnie Lindly, Walter Littlejohn, Ben F. Looney, Don Looney, Bill W. Lucas, Joe Lydick, Bob McCamey, Jon McConal, Scott McDonald, Thurman McGaugh, John McMackin, Lew McNeil, Ralph Manoushagian, John Margolies, Robert C. Marston, Sandra Mauney, Vernon Mayfield, Joe Menefee, Leroy Menzing, Bob Millwee, Mike Moncrief, Doug Morgan, J. W. Morgan, Larry Morrell, Francine Morrison, James M. Moudy, Lucille Moudy, Griffin Murphey, John H. Murphy, Jr., Steve Murrin, Maurine Nailon, Odessa Nelson, Beth Newberry, Jim Nichols, Clif Overcash, Robert Parten, Robert Peet, Roman Pena, W. Frank Pendleton, J. Roby Penn, Jr., Viola Pitts, Bryan Poff, David Poindexter, Jeane and Elzie Pruett, Dick Pruitt, Bill Pumphrey, Gordon Ramsey, Bob Ratts, Mike Reese, Fred Rehfeldt, Rick Rehfeldt, Edd Riddle, Charles Ringler, Alan C. Roberts, Lesbia Roberts, Ted Roe, Hamilton Rogers, Mary Rogers, Ray Rohlfs, Nick Rose, Carole Rylander, Ted St. Clair, Bill Scales, Ruby Schmidt, Jerry Sherrod, Alver Simmans, Jerry Simmans, Judie K. Smith, C. Glenn Smith, Preston Smith, Stephen D. Smith, Lola Spearing, Katherine Stell, Sterling Steves, Perry Stewart, Glenda Stone, R. M. (Sharky) Stovall, Lester Strother, George R. Studdard, Roger Summers, Basil Taylor, Joe Taylor, Guy Thompson, Jr., Georgie Birch Thurber, James Thurber, Rice Tilley, Jr., L. C. Tomlinson, Lambuth Tomlinson, Scott Tomlinson, Barbara Tomme, Jean Traster, Ron Traver, William E. Tucker, Tommy Vandergriff, Jerry Vandever, Dennis and Marie Veit, Myrt Vititow, Jon B. White, David A. Williams, Mack and Madeline Williams, Mary Ellen Williams, Roger Williams, Bill Wood, Bill Woodard, Jewel Woods, Brad Wright, Charles E. Yager, Jr., Wes Yarbro, and Dan Zurovetz.

I want to thank Anna Ferguson, Sue Sledz, Susan Wiggins, Ken Wimberly, and Doug Frazier for their technical assistance in producing the manuscript. Without Blake Woodard, a computer genius, this book would never have seen printer's ink. And thanks to Wanda Woodard, who knew Babe Fuqua and a great many of the TP men and women of his era. Her close editing of the manuscript is responsible for the elimination of countless errors and typos.

I also thank Troy Ainsworth, Fran Kennedy, and Marilyn Steinborn of Texas Tech University Press for the care and effort they provided throughout the publication process. And most of all, I thank Carole Young, Director, who not only edited and suggested, but inspired and encouraged, and I might say cajoled. Her commitment during the three years it took to go from draft manuscript to finished book never flagged.

Texas Pacific Coal and Oil Company

1

In the beginning of the 1880s, there was a man in the small town of Strawn in Palo Pinto County, Texas, whose name was William Whipple Johnson. Although Will Johnson has become part of the lore of Strawn, Mingus, Gordon, and Thurber, little was known about his life. From material gathered by Robert Spoede, mentioned in the preface, the character of William Whipple Johnson has begun to emerge from the shadows. Among the papers found by Spoede was Penn Mutual Life Insurance Policy No. 55748, dated 15 December 1888, insuring the life of W. W. Johnson. The application for the policy states that he was born in Ionia, Michigan, on October 11, 1845, the son of Ethan S. and Jane Whipple Johnson.

Ethan S. Johnson, appears to have been a businessman of better than average education and high aspirations. Jane Whipple Johnson was admired by the people of Ionia. She was a devout Baptist, literate and cultivated. She was the granddaughter of William Whipple of New Hampshire, one of the fifty-six signers of the American Declaration of Independence. His copperplate signature appears immediately above those of Samuel Adams and John Adams. Will always took pride in the similarity between his signature and that of his great-grandfather.

Will had six siblings, three sisters and three brothers. Barbara Arends and Karen Coulson in 1996 visited the Highland Park Cemetery in Ionia, Michigan, and recorded the names and years of birth and death of all members of the Johnson family except Will and Marion. Will is entombed near Gordon, Texas. Marion Johnson Faulkner is probably buried in or near Los Angeles.

Alice married Oscar H. Dean and Celia married E. Byron Miller. They remained in Michigan. Marion married E. G. Faulkner and moved to Los Angeles, California. Ethan B. and Stephen F. spent their lives in institutions for the mentally ill.[1]

Will Johnson attended school in Ypsilanti, Michigan, and there became enamored of a girl named Anna Fatzinger. According to Anna's cousin, Cornelia Crocker, Will would walk round and round an apple tree looking for the best apple to give to his childhood sweetheart.[2]

Name	Born	Died
Ethan S. Johnson	1813	1883
Jane Whipple Johnson	1823	1902
Alice Johnson Dean	1843	unknown
William Whipple Johnson	1845	1914
Ethan B. Johnson	1847	1920
Harvey Johnson	1850	1888
Marion Johnson Faulkner	1852 (? est.)	unknown
Stephen F. Johnson	1854	1915
Celia Johnson Miller	1857	1928

In 1861, Will, then only sixteen, began to dabble in real estate. In 1867 he jumped headlong into lumber and land speculation and development.[3] His activity in the lumber industry of the northern portion of the lower peninsula of Michigan was fairly profitable. One reason was the cheap and efficient water transportation that was readily available. The rivers of Michigan were used to float logs to the saw mills, and the finished lumber was easily transported to market on the Great Lakes. Another reason was the cheap land that could be obtained either by borrowing the purchase price or by a simple promise to pay—normally at 10 percent interest.

Sometime around 1870, presumably after Harvey finished school, Will, Harvey, and their father formed a family partnership to provide general merchandise to the citizens of Ionia. The partnership did not limit itself to selling calico and buttons and bows, but also looked for any opportunity to capitalize on the general prosperity that prevailed in the years following the Civil War. The war had inspired an increased demand for the agricultural products and the lumber, copper, and iron of Michigan. The railroads were building their webs of tracks across the state, and immigrants, particularly from Germany, were pouring in.

The Johnsons, enthusiastic over the potential for Ionia's growth after it became linked to the outside world with a railroad, developed a residential addition to Ionia known for years as the Johnson Addition. Young Will traveled Michigan extensively in those days, seeking investment and speculative opportunities. Things seemed to be progressing well for the Johnson partnership of father and sons.

Investors, even the small ones like the Johnsons of Ionia, were banking their futures on a continued run of good luck. They risked both natural and economic catastrophe. Many a small lumber operator was wiped out by a forest fire or a mill fire. However, it was the Panic of 1873 that caused the ruin of the Johnson enterprises in Michigan. The panic began on

William Whipple Johnson, courtesy of Robert W. Spoede. This illustration was made from a glass negative belonging to Don Crawford, Sr. of Strawn.

September 19, 1873, when the New York Stock Exchange reported numerous failures. The economic depression that followed in the wake of that Black Friday suppressed the business activity of the United States for several years to come. It was not only small business men whose enterprises collapsed—many of the great houses of finance crumbled into the economic chasm. The failure of Jay Cooke & Company and the George Opdyke & Company banking houses was like the breaking of a great dam. Because so much investment was based upon speculation, the collapse of these two houses caused a tightening of the money market, and those who had borrowed more than they could pay were ruined. This included the Johnsons. As their debts became due, and the 10 percent interest continued to rise, their creditors closed in on them. The court suits that ensued were too numerous for the Johnsons to keep track of as the months turned into years. Will Johnson, individually and jointly responsible with his father and brother, owed over one hundred creditors a total of twenty thousand dollars (approximately $700,000 in 1990 dollars).[4]

Deluged with debt, Will and Harvey saw no way out of the morass except to leave Michigan. Around 1875, they fled to New York to live a life of concealment and evasion. Presumably, Ethan remained in Michigan to face the clamoring creditors. In New York, somehow they were able to obtain a large store of dry goods. This apparently occupied Will's time as he thought about new beginnings. In any event, New York was the East, while it was the West that writers such as Horatio Alger and Horace Greeley, contemporaries of the Johnsons, were extolling. In the 1860s and 1870s,

Alger wrote a famous series of rags-to-riches books for boys. His heroes always rose from tattered poverty to riches and respectability. Greeley advised young men that the best business they could go into would be on their father's farm or in his workshop but: "If you have no family or friends to aid you and no prospect opened to you there, turn your face to the great West and there build up a home and fortune."

Heeding the call of "Go West, Young Man!" Will and Harvey packed up their few possessions, bade farewell to New York and went West. By 1878 they had arrived in Corsicana, Texas, where they engaged in land speculation. One of Will's acquisitions, presumably paid for with the funds obtained from sale of the dry goods in New York, was a 960-acre farm in Houston County, some one hundred miles southeast of Corsicana.[5]

Texas offered many attractions to the man who had been ruined by debts and was looking for a place to begin again. Not the least of these was the protection of a statute of limitations on inactive old debts. Any debt that had been dormant for ten years was unenforceable under Texas law.[6]

In 1876, two years before Will and Harvey arrived in the Lone Star State, the Texas & Pacific Railway (T&P) had reached Fort Worth. Due to the lingering effects of the 1873 panic, Fort Worth would remain the western terminus of the railroad for nearly four years. On January 20, 1880, New York broker and railroad promoter, Jay Gould, was elected to the T&P Board, and the clang of sledge hammers against steel was once again heard as the twin rails began their race across the prairies. Telegraph lines were strung simultaneously. On November 1, 1880, railway mail service was initiated to Strawn, seventy-five miles west of Fort Worth.[7]

Prior to 1885, the railroad used wood to generate power for its locomotives. Wood was also needed for posts to fence right-of-way and as crossties. The railroad's appetite for wood undoubtedly inspired the land- and lumber-wise Johnson brothers to leave Corsicana and move to Strawn. Within a year, the Johnsons traded for a 380-acre farm ten miles north of Strawn, complete with a small house.

Meanwhile, Anna Fatzinger, Will's childhood sweetheart, had married a man named W. C. Campbell who at one time was engaged in sheep ranching near San Antonio, Texas. They had one child, a daughter named Fannie born in the early 1870s. They were divorced on February 21, 1880, in Chicago. Anna was awarded custody of Fannie, but full visitation rights were granted the father, who remained on his Texas sheep ranch. However, the child lived with neither mother or father, but with her maternal grandmother and aunt Mattie in Chicago. About 1883 it appears that the father spirited the child away to his family in Guelph, Ontario, Canada, and apparently Anna never saw her again.[8]

Prior to Anna's divorce from Campbell, Will had conducted an extensive correspondence with her sister, Mattie Fatzinger. But it was Anna that he was really interested in. By April 24, 1880, only two months after her divorce, Anna was writing to Will as her future husband. On May 6, 1880, she wrote: "I thank God that I lived to receive that sweetest of all blessings that could be bestowed upon me—the love of a true and noble heart."[9]

Their debt problem continued to plague the brothers, for if their creditors in Michigan discovered their whereabouts before the ten year dormancy law took effect, they would be wiped out by the execution of the various court judgments against them. To protect themselves against the threat of discovery, they signed practically all their property over to Anna Fatzinger Campbell, on August 30, 1880. Will also had been married for a short while around 1878, but he, too, had divorced. Now Anna came to Texas where she and Will were married in 1880, presumably subsequent to the August 30 property transfer. The marriage to Anna brought additional capital to Will and Harvey in their enterprises in the Strawn area, for within one year she received her share of her father's estate. The amount of money that became available was in the thousands, small in comparison to some of the figures that Will would deal with in the future. But for the Johnson brothers, hard pressed for capital, it was warmly welcomed. Even more welcome was the safe haven that Anna provided for Will and Harvey's assets from the ever present threat posed by the old Michigan debts.[10]

On September 13, 1880, Harvey Johnson was appointed postmaster of Strawn, six weeks before the T&P Railway and the U.S. mail reached Strawn on 1 November. On January 4, 1881, Will Johnson became assistant postmaster.[11]

The railroad continued building westward at a furious pace. On December 15, 1881, only a little more than a year after it had reached Strawn, the T&P was completed to Sierra Blanca in far West Texas where its rails joined those of Collis P. Huntington's Southern Pacific, which had been building eastward from California. On December 16, 1881, transcontinental service via El Paso was inaugurated. The dream of a southern route across the continent had come true.[12]

Back in Strawn, Will and Harvey Johnson operated a commissary in a large tent on the south side of the tracks that catered to the wants and needs of hundreds of gandy dancers (railroad track workers). In addition, the enterprising brothers had secured from the T&P a contract to furnish crossties for the railroad. They were also marketing thousands of cedar posts used in fencing the railroad right-of-way and the vast cattle ranches that were springing up along the iron pike.

Palo Pinto County cedar furnished the Johnsons with a steady income. They hired men to cut posts from the land to which they held the rights and they also purchased posts from settlers in the area and resold them. On September 23, 1906, the *Gordon Weekly Courier* saluted the beneficial role played by the Johnsons in Palo Pinto County: "We remember that in 1886, when gaunt famine stalked abroad in this part of the land, when hundreds of people had left and others were preparing to leave to seek work and food, this couple came to the rescue. They advertised for men to work the cedar brakes near Strawn. The laborers flocked there, and the great cedar post industry had its beginning in this county, and to some extent the necessities of the people were relieved. Many years later, huge piles of cedar bark could be seen at Strawn, where the posts had been prepared for market."[13]

One day in 1880, while riding through northern Erath's hills, Will stopped at a farmhouse for a cool drink of water. He told the farmer that he was looking for timber for his fence post-and-crosstie operation. The sodbuster replied by telling of the hard time he was having digging a well. "Black rock makes it hard to dig," he allowed, scuffing at a small pile that had been chiseled from the shallow hole. "For a little bit, I'd sell this place and move to somewheres that wasn't so rocky." Johnson became excited—he knew instantly that the black rock was coal. As he gazed intently at the substance, visions of black diamonds danced in his head.[14]

Given that coal was in place, would it be found in commercial quantities? Would it be economically recoverable? Although many questions had to be answered, there could be little doubt that the most logical purchaser of the coal would be the Texas & Pacific Railway whose main line ran a little over two miles north of the most likely site for a mine. Its coal-burning locomotives racing over his crossties would devour all the coal he could dig, thought Johnson. And what is more, the T&P could reach the mine simply by laying a short spur jutting south from its tracks. He would sound out the T&P.

In early 1881, Anna's brother, John Jacob Fatzinger, paid a visit to the Johnsons in Strawn. He had graduated from the Pennsylvania Military College in June 1879, with an engineering degree. As Johnson showed his brother-in-law around the Strawn area, Robert Spoede speculates that young Fatzinger, with his engineering background, could well have reinforced and confirmed Johnson's intrigue with the commercial potential of coal in the area.[15]

Will Johnson approached officials of the Texas & Pacific Railway in late 1882. The railroad was most interested in the tantalizing prospect of securing coal from a source so close to its main line.[16]

In 1882, a daughter, Marion, was born to Will and Anna, named quite probably for Marion Faulkner, one of Johnson's sisters who lived in Los Angeles. But their joy in their daughter was short lived—on November 7, 1885, the baby died of croup. Afflicted by claustrophobia (he once panicked after descending only a few feet into a mine), Johnson could not bring himself to bury the child in the ground. He built a wooden mausoleum in their backyard. Alienated from her first daughter Fannie, Anna now had lost her second daughter. She was devastated. According to legend, she went daily to the mausoleum and changed her little girl's dress.[17]

William and Anna Johnson, circa 1905. The only known picture of Anna. Courtesy John Wilson.

W. W. Johnson's sorrow was not at an end. The next year, 1883, his father, sixty-nine, died, and was buried in the Ionia cemetery. In all likelihood, Will and Harvey, because of distance and debts, did not go home for the funeral.

But life goes on. Will Johnson continued with his coal mine obsession. Before he could dig and sell coal, however, he had to acquire the coal lands. The tract that seemed to offer the best and easiest prospect of profitability was the 2302.5-acre Pedro Herrera Survey, located about eight miles southeast of Strawn. A major problem faced Will and Harvey in proving title to the land, for it had passed through many ownerships since Pedro Herrera had been granted an unspecified tract of land by the State. Ownership was traced through the original assignees of Pedro Herrera— J. S. Hood and William Steele—to the rightful owners of their day. In October 1886, the Johnsons bought the survey from F. T. Jowell and wife for twenty-five hundred dollars (approximately $60,000 in 1995 dollars). Acting as a partnership, they paid the Jowells three hundred dollars in cash and gave them their note, payable in three months with interest at 10 percent per annum, for the balance.[18] After acquisition of the Pedro Herrera Survey, the Johnsons continued to buy up large quantities of land. Their holdings came to exceed twenty thousand acres.

In October 1886, immediately after purchasing the Pedro Herrera Survey, the Johnsons sank a shaft sixty-five feet to the coal seam—measuring twenty-eight to thirty-two inches in thickness—in a broad, lonely valley in the low hills of northwestern Erath County.[19] Black diamonds were mined for the first time in Erath. Will Johnson's dream had come true.

This became the No. 1 mine of the fledgling Johnson Coal Company, and was located about one-half mile southeast of what would be Thurber. Originally, however, the camp was known as Johnson's Mine or Johnsonville, consisting of five buildings clustered around the mine shaft with numerous tents and shacks—homes to miners—scattered about the property.[20]

Where did Johnson get his miners? They came from Coalville, a town located some two miles north of Gordon. When the first surveyors passed through southern Palo Pinto County, they discovered outcroppings of coal on the west side of Clayton Mountain. With the coming of the Texas & Pacific Railway in 1880, the coal deposits assumed great importance. Early in 1881, James, Cowan and Nolton Company opened a mine in the area. A second soon followed, and the little mining camp became known as Coalville.

Later the railroad bought the Coalville mining operation, and it became known as the Gould Mines or the Railroad Mines. The miners were organized by the first Knights of Labor local in Texas, No. 135. The Knights of Labor was one of the most important early labor organizations in America. It was the first to organize all workers into a single union, rather than into separate trade unions. Its official name was The Noble Order of the Knights of Labor. Anyone except bankers, stockbrokers, professional gamblers, lawyers, and those who sold or manufactured liquor could become members. In 1884 the miners went on strike for higher wages. The railroad refused and the mines were closed. Elsewhere, however, the strike was successful and when the railroad was forced to meet the union's demands in 1885, the Knights of Labor became powerful and its membership zoomed from one hundred thousand to seven hundred thousand in a year's time. However, the Knights lost a second strike against Gould's railroads in 1886. That defeat, added to the antilabor sentiments that followed the 1884 Haymarket Riot in Chicago, caused the group's membership to decline. And it caused Coalville's demise.

When Johnson opened his mine eight miles to the southwest, many of the Knights of Labor miners moved there. The Union purchased ten acres of land adjoining the Johnson claim on the east, located on the site of present day Big Lake. The Coalville meeting hall was moved from its former location and reconstructed in the center of the plot. By hiring these Knight of Labor miners, Johnson took on a nagging, persistent headache, for the men were a rough collection, restless and poverty-stricken, and demanded wages close to those received at Coalville.

The Johnsons did little to relieve the tension among the workers. They promised to erect dwellings to house the men and their families, but because of financial difficulties, were unable to do so. However, each individual employee was allowed to construct his own shelter on the company's property. These structures were often nothing more than tents or leaky shacks.[21]

In December 1886, the T&P Railroad agreed to construct a spur from its line to the mine, although a contract was not signed until the following May—and no wonder—both parties had their problems.[22] The Johnsons, as has been seen, had to take care of a myriad of details inherent to starting up a coal operation; i.e., tending to legal matters, obtaining financing, buying land, curing title, recruiting miners, dealing with recalcitrant workers and the Knights of Labor Union, providing housing, arranging for supplies, excavating down to pay dirt, digging the coal, and transporting it to the surface.

And the railroad? Well, for one thing, Texas railroads were literally fighting a running gun battle with organized bandits. Several train robberies in North Texas, between December 1886 and September 1887, were blamed on the two Burrows brothers, Reuben and James, starting with the holdup of the Fort Worth & Denver on December 1, 1886, at Bellevue in Clay County. This was the very month that the T&P Railroad had agreed to construct the spur to the mine. The bandits' next target was the T&P, in Johnsonville's own back yard. On January 23, 1887, a seven-man gang stopped a T&P train near Gordon and escaped with two thousand dollars.[23] The spur from the T&P mainline down to Johnsonville was put on hold until the robberies had been dealt with. But holdups were not the only problem.

A second matter of business concerned a piece of legislation in Congress. Less than two weeks after the Gordon train robbery, the Interstate Commerce Act was enacted on February 4, 1887. The Act was designed to prevent discrimination and abuses by railroads. Until then, railroads enjoyed, for the most part, freedom from government regulation. The Interstate Commerce Act forbade price-fixing and discrimination in rates. Its most important feature was the establishment of the Interstate Commerce Commission to administer the law. The ICC was the federal government's first regulatory agency.

Eventually, the Johnson contract worked its way to the top of the pile and was signed on May 7, 1887. Under the terms of the contract, the Johnsons agreed to sell the railroad all the coal it could use and they could produce at cost plus fifty cents a ton "but not to exceed, at any time, $2.75 per ton."[24] They agreed to keep the coal free of slate and clay and to deliver five hundred tons per day and to increase the output of the mines as rapidly as possible. The T&P agreed to lay the spur to the mine and grant free railway passes to the Johnson brothers.[25]

In 1913 Thomas R. Hall (who joined Texas & Pacific Coal Company in 1889 and was eventually promoted to cashier and pay master) wrote of those days: "In 1886 I was in the engineering department of the Texas & Pacific Railway Company, and it was my party which was ordered to make the survey for the spur. This was done without delay and the track was completed sometime during the following year. When the track was completed, there were some fifty cars of coal piled on the ground around the mouth of the opening, which had been hoisted by horse power. This represented all the coal taken out up to that time. This coal was loaded onto cars and shipped. A tipple was erected, machinery installed and work seemed to begin in earnest."[26]

The new mining venture and the contract with the railroad ignited great expectations on the part of the Johnsons. Up until this point, their activities had been carried on as the Johnson Brothers Partnership. Remembering their earlier somber experience in Michigan, they decided in the summer of 1887 to incorporate their Texas coal mining venture. By incorporating, they could insulate their fortunes from economic ill winds. It would also enable them to raise badly needed capital. The name of the new entity was The Johnson Coal Company. The directors were W. W. Johnson, H. E. Johnson, and William M. Allen. Will Johnson acted as Chairman of the first meeting held on July 13, 1887, in Strawn. The management of the company consisted of Will Johnson as President, Harvey Johnson as Vice-President and Secretary, and H. P. Hilliard of Weatherford as Treasurer.

The division of the shares of capital stock of the new company furnished a clear indication of the unique relationship of trust and confidence that existed between the two brothers: "Although the mining company was a partnership and jointly shared in, the land was in the name of Harvey. When the company was incorporated, Harvey received all the capital stock of 10,000 shares, except two shares, or 9998 shares. One of these two shares went to Will Johnson and the other to W. M. Allen. Legally, this placed Harvey in complete and almost total control of the mine, but there was never any doubt that he submitted to the judgment of his older brother who was after all the president of the company. This arrangement speaks distinctly of the mutual trust of the two men in one another."[27]

The new company immediately authorized management to borrow one hundred thousand dollars for a term of twenty years at 6 percent interest, and to issue one hundred bonds of one thousand dollars each. The company would secure the bonds with a first mortgage on all its lands and improvements, tools, machinery, and franchise. Trustee for the bonds dated August 1, 1887, was The Central Trust Company of New York. Unfortunately, the bonds sold poorly.[28]

With the birth of their new corporation, there was another birth that year that brought joy to Will and Anna—a new son. The baby was given the names of the two brothers, William Harvey.[29]

But even though future prospects for the mine looked promising, start-up costs of the operation soaked up capital. In an effort to stay afloat, the Johnsons cut the price paid to the miners from $1.75 to $1.50 per ton in the spring of 1887. The unhappy miners struck. After two months, the company acceded to their demands and raised the price to $1.95 a ton. By August 1887, the Johnsons were deeply in debt, needing fifty thousand dollars (equivalent to $1.2 million in 1997) to remain solvent. Their attorney, H. M. Taylor, went looking for capital. He found his financial savior in a St. Louis businessman by the name of Colonel Robert D. Hunter. Hunter and Taylor met in Denver that August where a loan agreement was reached. The mine was saved—for the present. In the not too distant future, Will Johnson would find that Hunter would become a problem. Give Robert D. Hunter an inch and he would take a mine.[30]

2

Robert D. Hunter had a full head of hair, gray and short-cropped. He had a walrus mustache and a goatee that hung down like an icicle. Arched by heavy brows, his piercing eyes could stare down any adversary bold or foolish enough to challenge him. His right eye bore mute witness to some long-forgotten barroom brawl. Having spent his life in the wild west of the last half of the nineteenth century, he sat tall in the saddle. Many legends have grown around him.

William Hunter McLean, in his excellent genealogy, *From Ayr To Thurber*, gives a prideful account of his great uncle, Robert Dickie Hunter, born in Ayrshire, Scotland, on April 5, 1833. His parents were Adam and Janet Dickie Hunter. The family emigrated to the United States in 1843, when Robert was ten years old. They settled near Bunker Hill, Illinois. In 1858, when Robert was twenty-five, he married Janet Webster. Janet was born in Scotland on Christmas Day, 1836. Her family came to America in 1838, also settling near Bunker Hill.[1]

In 1859, a year after their wedding, the Hunters, together with Albert G. Evans, departed Illinois for the mining areas of Colorado. In 1860, just before the outbreak of the Civil War, Hunter, apparently without Evans, went to Arizona to try his luck at prospecting in the Superstition Mountains. Whether he found no gold or whether it was because the Apaches under Cochise were on the attack, Hunter soon returned to Colorado. In late spring 1863, three weeks before the Battle of Gettysburg, Hunter and his wife Janet, great with child, decided to go back home to Missouri. As their covered wagon caravan reached Manitou Springs at the foot of Pike's Peak, Indians suddenly appeared. On June 12, 1863, while the skirmish was underway, a daughter, Jennie Colorado Hunter, was born under a covered wagon. The Indians were driven off and the wagons with the new babe continued on their journey back to Missouri.[2]

There were several siblings in the Hunter family, full and half. Robert D. Hunter was most closely associated with brothers William and David. Although of the right age and certainly temperament, Robert did not serve in the Civil War. The title of "Colonel," by which he is best known, is honorific—how he got it is unknown. His brother David served as a Union officer in the Civil War—he had been with General William Tecumseh Sherman on his historic march to the sea. With the cessation of hostilities, David Hunter returned home to Missouri to join Robert and William in the cattle business.[3]

Early in 1866, about the time that Will Johnson was entering the real estate picture in Michigan, Robert D. Hunter started driving cattle from Texas to the southwest corner of Missouri. Here these herds were combined with other herds for the final push to Kansas City. William and David were probably along, because the trail driving, watering, grazing, and night patrolling of two thousand cattle in each herd required a number of drovers. It is probable that the 1866 drive first introduced the Hunters to Fort Worth, a village of some three hundred persons, back then a cattle trail gateway via the Chisholm Trail, which passed along its east side.

When the cattle reached Missouri, the residents of Vernon County, who did not fancy the passage of large herds over their farms and range lands, prevailed on the sheriff to arrest Hunter and impound his herd, together with ten thousand head of cattle in other droves. Hunter convinced the sheriff that he would make bail for himself as well as the other owners if the sheriff would accompany him to Nevada, the county seat. The sheriff agreed to the plan, and they set out for the county seat thirty-five miles to the east. When out of sight, and as prearranged, the drovers pointed the immense herd of cattle toward Indian Territory, a safe haven to the Southwest. Upon arriving at a saloon in Nevada, Hunter plied the naive lawman with libations until he was totally incapacitated. He then took leave of the helpless sheriff and mounted his horse to meet his companions with their herds in friendly territory.

Hunter returned to Texas in 1867, and annually for the rest of the decade, to drive herds to market or to be sold to government contractors obliged to supply meat to Indian tribes.[4]

In 1870, a second daughter, Maude Lee, was born in Missouri to Colonel and Mrs. Hunter. But hard on the heels of prosperity came hardship, for in the winter of 1870-71 cattle prices were depressed. In view of the sobering financial experiences of 1870 and 1871, the Hunter brothers decided to give up the hazards and demands, both physical and fiscal, of cattle drives in favor of more civilized and sedentary cattle trading and livestock management, operating out of Kansas City and Chillicothe, Missouri. Their entry into this phase of the business was propitious. Citizens of Abilene, Kansas, were up in arms. They had had their fill of the shoot-'em-up rampages of trail driving cowboys. In 1871-72, they launched a crusade to rid their town of the uncouth, unwelcome visitors. This action greatly distressed railroad impresario Jay Gould of New York because Abilene, which later would become famous as the boyhood home of Dwight D. Eisenhower, was the point where cattle from Texas were loaded onto Kansas Pacific Railroad cars for transport to the packing houses of Chicago.

In the late 1860s, Gould made millions by manipulating Erie Railroad stock. He then tried to corner the gold market. His operations caused the Black Friday panic of September 24, 1869, and Gould became the most hated man in America. After gorging on the Erie, his insatiable appetite turned to western railroads. Among those he came to own or control were the Union Pacific, Kansas Pacific, Denver Pacific, Missouri Pacific, Central Pacific, Texas & Pacific, St. Louis Southwestern, and the Wabash. He owned about one of every ten miles of railroad in the United States by 1880.

Jay Gould, born in 1836, was only thirty-five in 1871 when he hired the thirty-eight-year-old Hunter and Shanghai Pierce, a colorful Texas rancher, to establish a new shipping point at Ellsworth, Kansas, seventy-five miles west of Abilene up the Smoky Hill River. From this development began a long friendship and business association between Hunter and Gould.[5]

Hunter and Pierce proved to be a dynamic duo. Hunter became the superintendent of the enlarged stockyards at Ellsworth, while Pierce, who owned expansive spreads in Wharton and Matagorda counties, returned to the Lone Star State in 1871 to funnel new droves of cattle onto the trail that wound its way up to Ellsworth. Soon thousands of Texas cattle were coming into Ellsworth where the patronage of Texas cowhands caused hotels, saloons, and brothels to do a thriving business. Having fulfilled their contract with Gould, the Colonel and Shanghai rode off into the sunset. Hunter settled in Dodge City.

Hunter contacted Texas and New Mexico ranchers, romancing them with the beauties and prospects offered by Dodge City. When the ranch owners had, with a traditional western handshake, committed themselves to drive their herds to the Dodge railhead, Hunter hurried back to arrange a welcome for the cowboys when they reached trail's end. A band, complete with drum major, greeted the cowboys as they entered the town, and city officials were on hand to extend hospitality. Saloons, dance halls, brothels, and gambling flourished in profusion to entertain the trail-weary cowboys. After a night of wild carousing, many of them awoke the next morning to find that their hard-earned dollars had disappeared.

John Chisum, owner of the famous Jinglebob Ranch, unlike many of the cattle barons of the west, was not a man "whose word was as good as his bond." He had carved his cattle empire out of the barren lands of New Mexico Territory, but in so doing had made enemies through some questionable business deals. Chisum had purchased cattle throughout West Texas, giving promissory notes as payment. Many of these notes he had failed to redeem. On his trips to Texas, Colonel Hunter, always alert for a good business opportunity, purchased scads of these notes for 10 percent of their dollar value. He then arranged with Chisum for delivery of a herd to Dodge City. When the cattle arrived and were safely corralled and counted, Hunter swaggered forth to make payment, but instead of cash, he carried a saddle bag of Chisum's notes and a court order. For John

Chisum, it was like looking down the barrel of a cocked Colt six-shooter. What could he do? He grinned and accepted the payment. Apparently, neither cowman was one to bear a grudge, for Hunter later saved Chisum from bankruptcy by becoming a partner in the vast Jinglebob holdings.[6]

In the meantime, Colonel Hunter's prospecting partner and longtime friend, Albert G. Evans, had joined Edward W. Pattison in the formation of the livestock firm Pattison and Evans of Kansas City, Missouri. R. D. Hunter joined the partnership in 1873, and its name was changed to Hunter, Pattison and Evans. In 1874, upon disassociation of Pattison, the name of the firm was changed to Hunter, Evans and Company, with Hunter being resident partner in St. Louis. In 1876, the firm's headquarters was moved to East St. Louis, with branches in Kansas City, Chicago, Kansas, and Texas. In that year the firm established the first beef canning company in St. Louis.[7]

R. D. Hunter was the major and dominant partner, who conceived and directed cattle marketing and ranching ventures for the Hunter brothers or the firm of Hunter, Evans and Company. William Hunter was the cattle buyer in Texas and sometimes Mexico, an assignment imposing a nomadic existence between St. Louis and a half-dozen towns of Texas until settling in Fort Worth for the last years of his life.

David Hunter managed diversion ranches, where trail cattle were collected in Nebraska and Montana, including the family-owned H3 Ranch, on the Niobrara River of Nebraska. The firm, for itself or as managing partner of syndicated financiers attracted by substantial profits in cattle trading, owned ranches in the Texas Panhandle, Colorado, Kansas, Nebraska, and Montana, and, in addition, leased federal land running into millions of acres. The firm's eastern investors and immense patronage of railroads brought it early into association with banker and railroad tycoons of the era. One of these eastern magnates was Jay Gould.

Hunter, Evans and Company grew to associate other partners of prominence in the cattle business and to receive much commendation for its reliability and success. *Parsons Memorial and Historical Library Magazine* noted: "Among cattle commission firms none is more notable as being composed of substantial, practical, clear-headed businessmen than that of Hunter, Evans and Company. Each member of this firm is a successful livestock man of long experience, which coupled with their individual responsibility, renders their house one reliable and safe."[8]

In the centennial year of 1876, about the time that Hunter, Evans and Company had moved its headquarters to East St. Louis, war clouds appeared in the West. On June 25, 1876, Lt. Colonel George Armstrong Custer[9] and his regiment of 650 men attacked an Indian force on the Little Bighorn River in southern Montana. Custer had estimated Indian strength at one thousand. As it turned out, there had been between twenty-five hundred and five thousand Indians. About 225 soldiers including Custer

Advertisement on plat of Fort Worth, circa 1880. Courtesy, Fort Worth Public Library.

were killed. When news of the unmitigated disaster reached the East, a pall of gloom and fear was cast over the entire country. Because Hunter's firm had ranches in Montana, the dispatches from the battlefield would have caused him and his investors great concern.

The 1880 census of St. Louis shows the R. D. Hunter family as: Robert D. Hunter, age forty-six, born in Scotland; Janet Hunter, wife, age thirty-nine, born in Scotland; Jennie C. Hunter, daughter, age sixteen, born in Colorado; Maude L. Hunter, daughter, age ten, born in Missouri; and Sarah J. Rhodes, niece, age nineteen, born in Colorado. Sarah was the daughter of R. D. Hunter's sister, Isabella Rhodes. It is not known how Sarah came to live with her uncle.[10]

✦

In 1882 the census would be decreased by one when notorious outlaw Jesse James was killed. It is quite probable that Robert D. Hunter met Jesse James. At the zenith of Hunter's career as a cattleman, Jesse James in late 1881 moved to St. Joseph, Missouri, where he went by the alias of Tom Howard and posed as a cattle buyer. On April 3, 1882, with his confederate, Robert Ford, looking on, he climbed upon a chair to adjust the picture on the wall of his new home. His only thought had been to straighten the picture, but Ford had another idea. After all, the governor of Missouri had posted a five thousand dollar reward for Jesse James, dead or alive. Ford shot him in the back. The famous outlaw was buried on his family farm near Kearney, Missouri. In 1902 his remains were moved to Mount Olivet Cemetery in Kearney.[11]

✦

Soon after the end of the Civil War, longhorn or range cattle brought three to five dollars a head. By 1884, prices for such cattle crested near twenty-five dollars a head. The intervening years had seen brief but sharp fluctuations in prices, but on the whole, those years had been prosperous ones for cattlemen, especially for middlemen like Hunter. In July 1882, the *St. Louis Republican* reported that Colonel and Mrs. Hunter, with daughter, Jennie, and niece, Sadie Rhodes, were in New York for the summer at Rye Beach on Long Island Sound. No mention is made of twelve-year old Maude. Early in 1883 Hunter began construction of an imposing mansion in St. Louis at 3650 Lindell Boulevard. Society news articles spoke of its grandeur. The house was barely finished before it saw the wedding of niece Sarah J. Rhodes to B. W. Zallee.[12] It was in this period that the reputation of Hunter, Evans and Company as a reliable and financially trustworthy house was established. Ominous factors had crept into the picture, however, occasioning wide concern in 1884.

The explosion of railroad construction in the west and southwest, cross-threading the vast area with means of access, had brought with it farmers, homesteaders, and grangers, who erected fences necessitating cattle drives to be pushed ever westward into country of longer trails and less water. The Goodnight-Loving Trail, for instance, began at Fort Belknap near Graham, Texas, and followed a westerly route to the Pecos and then northward into Colorado. Even though the trails were long, tedious, and dangerous, they nevertheless persisted because of the high cost (about six dollars a head) of shipping cattle by rail from Texas to Chicago.

Improved breeds of cattle were introduced on the farms and small ranches whose owners, hostile to the competition of longhorns or stock cattle, added their voices and influence to rumors (not without substance) of cattle carrying ticks and "Texas fever." Territorial Indians protested the leasing of their ranges for cattle grazing. In response, the federal government abruptly changed its policy of grazing leases, canceling them suddenly and without notice in areas where pressures were felt and offering only short-term leases in distant areas. The combination of these influences on cattle-managing entrepreneurs discouraged eastern speculators in large grazing ranches. With sources of capital severely restricted and without accessible federal lands for grazing, firms such as Hunter, Evans and Company adroitly side-stepped to the cattle commission business. The year 1884 saw an economic decline so adversely affecting cattle sales and prices that cattlemen groused that the railroads got more for hauling a cow to market than they got for raising it. Faced with so bleak a picture, Colonel Hunter lent his support to calling a convention to be held in St.

Louis in November 1884 to find solutions to the problems plaguing the industry.[13]

But before that great conclave convened, Colonel Hunter had other more important business to attend to—the wedding of his twenty-year-old daughter, Jennifer Colorado Hunter, to twenty-four-year-old Edgar Lewis Marston.

Edgar L. Marston was born in Burlington, Iowa, on March 8, 1860, to the Reverend Sylvester W. and Susan Hodson (Carpenter) Marston. The minister father, earlier identified with prominent educational institutions in the South and then the Middle West, moved his family from Iowa to St. Louis in 1868. Young Marston graduated from La Grange College and Washington University School of Law in St. Louis. He practiced law briefly and in 1882 went into ranching in Fort Worth.[14]

Colonel Hunter's new mansion on Lindell Boulevard was completed, decorated, and resplendent on June 4, 1884, for the wedding that was to create a dynasty. Upon their return from a European honeymoon, the couple lived for a short while in the big Hunter mansion. The bridegroom then joined his father-in-law's firm, Hunter, Evans and Company in St. Louis as its representative to eastern financial interests.

With the big wedding concluded, Hunter turned his undivided attention to the 1884 National Convention of Cattlemen in St. Louis. Unfortunately, the summit failed to find a solution to the economic woes plaguing large cattle and ranch managing firms. Congress, failing to respond to their entreaties, was more attentive to the complaints of Indians, homesteaders, and midwest cattle feeders, leaving cattle shippers to work out as best they could differences with railroads. Cattle collector ranches on federal lands were driven ever farther to the north into country hazardous for cattle in the winter.

In the midst of his economic worries, Hunter was once again moving his place of residence. The home that he had just completed the year before on Lindell Boulevard was an immense structure requiring a retinue of servants. It was far too big for Colonel and Mrs. Hunter. Their niece, Sarah, and daughter, Jennie, had both married and departed and their other daughter, Maude, was away at school. Society columns of the *St. Louis Republican* reported that on December 31, 1885, Colonel Hunter and Janet resided at 3031 Washington Avenue and on July 24, 1886, at 2720 Pine Street.[15]

With the arrival of the autumn of 1886, the prospects for cattlemen were bleak. The bitter winter of 1886-87 brought unmitigated gloom to Colonel Hunter and his associates. Subfreezing temperatures for more than a month froze streams, lakes, and water holes and buried grass under ice and snow in the midwest. Millions of cattle died. Bankruptcies among ranchers and cattle companies were rife. Hunter, Evans and Company lost twenty thousand cattle, but somehow avoided disaster. With drastic

Robert Dickie Hunter, circa 1895. Courtesy Nita Stewart Haley Memorial Library, Midland, Texas.

changes in family, dwelling places, and a dour economic picture, Colonel Hunter was clearly at a mid-career fork in the road.[16]

In August of 1887, he took the fork that led down to Johnsonville to have a look at the mine that was serving as collateral for the loan he had made to Will Johnson. He returned to St. Louis and on November 25, 1887, wrote a letter to H. M. Taylor, Johnson's attorney who had met with him in Denver to arrange the loan:

> In answer to your inquiry as to the Johnson Coal Company's property in Erath County and Palo Pinto County, Texas, I would state that I inspected the company's mine in August, 1887, going down the shaft into the mine, which I examined with care. I found the vein of coal to be about 30 inches in thickness, covered on top with slate and underlaid with mining fire clay. The coal was about 57 feet below the surface of the ground, and that it was free from water. I regard the coal as of superior quality, suitable for steam and domestic purposes. I have considerable experience in coal mining, and, owing to the fact that this mine produces the only merchantable coal as yet found on any railroad in Texas, I regard the property as very valuable. With necessary capital to sink additional shafts, and put on the market the coal which could readily be sold, I am satisfied that the mine could be made to pay a profit of $1000 [1997 = $24,000] a day.[17]

Someone else who was impressed with the Johnson operation was John C. Brown, the Receiver of the Texas & Pacific Railway. On December 15, 1887, Brown wrote to Will Johnson: "I am very much pleased with the prospects of your mines. I think they are very flattering, and if you can secure the amount of money necessary to develop them to their utmost capacity, it will undoubtedly be exceedingly profitable. The quality of the coal is entirely satisfactory to us, and it is much better than the Indian Territory coal. We have tried it for steaming purposes and domestic use, and find it, as I say, entirely satisfactory. I believe that next to Pittsburg, Kansas, it is the best coal that has been used in Texas."[18]

What happened to cause Jay Gould's Texas & Pacific Railway to fall into receivership? In 1884 and 1885, the same catastrophes that plagued Hunter's cattle empire affected the T&P Railway. Monsoon floods in Louisiana and East Texas swept away tracks and bridges wholesale. The railroad in southern Louisiana was described as "two streaks of rust." In Central and West Texas, drought was the devil. A scorching sun burned off the grass and dried up rivers and watering holes. Gaunt cattle wandered aimlessly in search of pasture and water and died by the thousands. During the freezing winters that followed, thousands more perished in the deep snow. Shipments of cattle out of the afflicted areas were greatly reduced or stopped altogether. The railroad sustained heavy financial losses. The general business depression throughout the nation in 1884-85 also contributed to the financial difficulties of the railroad. Unable to meet its financial obligations, the line went into receivership on December 15, 1885. It would not be returned to Jay Gould's control until May 1, 1888.[19]

Just as the clouds that had for so long lowered over the Johnson brothers seemed to be lifting, tragedy struck again. As the new year of 1888 arrived, Harvey Johnson, Will's indispensable partner, died on 30 January, after a short illness. The love between the two brothers was demonstrated by the constant attention that Will gave the dying younger Harvey. On the day of his death, Harvey wrote out a bill of sale to Will for all his possessions in return for a consideration of one dollar.[20]

Will Johnson wanted with all his heart to take the body of Harvey back to their home in Ionia, Michigan, for burial, but was dissuaded from doing so by their Michigan attorney, Albert Williams. Although Will was protected in Texas by the statute of limitations on inactive old debts, he could still be prosecuted in Michigan where his creditors awaited his return. Unwilling to leave his beloved brother in a grave on the lone prairie, he placed Harvey in the family mausoleum with Marion.[21]

With the death of his brother, the fire and desire went out of Will's belly. Harvey had been the one who had overseen the routine day to day business of the mine. He was the one who had the common touch. He enjoyed his dealings with the miners and farmers, whereas Will kept his distance from them. With no enthusiasm, no partner, and no capital, little coal was brought to the surface. The lack of sufficient capital made it impossible to obtain the equipment, machinery, and other paraphernalia that would have maximized coal production and minimized cost, such as a screen that would separate clay from coal. Consequently, the coal delivered to the railroad was contaminated with clay and other impurities, which seriously retarded the ignition of the fuel and increased the difficulty of maintaining steam in locomotive boilers.

The high cost of coal, its poor quality, and the small amount that was produced caused the management of the railroad to become dissatisfied. In March 1888, T&P Receiver John C. Brown sent a letter to Johnson expressing his dissatisfaction. Brown pointed out that the Johnsons were failing to meet their obligations to the railroad as spelled out in the May 7, 1887 contract by which the T&P had laid the spur to the mine at no cost to the mine owners. He quoted a provision from the contract to the effect that if the quantity, quality, price, or amount of traffic for the railroad failed to justify the continuation of the spur, the T&P would have the right to remove it. Brown complained that the mines had rarely exceeded an output of one hundred tons a day when five hundred tons a day had been stipulated in the contract. He pointed out that the Johnsons had promised to furnish quality coal but in fact had furnished inferior coal. Brown opined that the coal itself was of excellent quality, but the Johnsons had failed to remove the slate admixture. He criticized the cost of the coal, which had remained at the maximum of $2.75 per ton, stating that the fair price would have been $1.50 per ton. Having stated his grievances, Brown then threatened to take up the spur track "unless we can make other and better arrangements with you." Brown assured the mine owners that the T&P did not desire in any way to "embarrass you in your enterprise, but that the T&P wanted to encourage the operation of the mine."[22]

It is difficult to understand why the railroad would even consider taking up the spur track. The expense of laying the track had already been incurred. Taking up the track would only involve more expense with no possible return. If the track were left in place, the T&P could simply cease buying coal from the mines and still hope for some revenue on coal shipped to other purchasers. But remember that Hunter was a personal friend and business associate of Jay Gould. On May 1, 1888, control of the T&P Railway was returned by the court to Gould, whereupon the spur track to the mines was summarily ripped up. It is likely that Hunter and Gould wanted to force Johnson into relinquishing the mines. This action would not be out of character for Jay Gould. Undoubtedly he saw great opportunity for profit in owning a coal monopoly in an area where coal was the main commercial fuel. By May, Johnson was ready to quit.

During the month of May 1888, Johnson and Hunter and their attorneys met in Denver, at which time Hunter offered to buy the mines. On 21 May, Hunter received a ninety-day option to buy the Johnson Coal Company. Before the sale was finalized, Johnson granted Hunter two more options, Hunter paying for each.[23]

Johnson wanted to retain an interest in the mines, serve as a director, and have the mines retain the name of Johnson Coal Company. There were indications that Hunter at first seemed agreeable to the proposals, but subsequently he changed his mind. Perhaps he thought it was more politic for the new coal company to be the namesake of its obviously most important prospective customer, the Texas & Pacific Railway.

Between May and the September expiration date of Hunter's option, the situation at the mine became tense. Drinking in the camp became a serious problem. By the middle of September, Johnson increased miner unrest by announcing that he would be unable to meet his payroll for the month of August. Nevertheless, the miners, unaware of the impending sale of the property, agreed to work and defer receipt of their pay—$1.95 a ton—until 22 September.

At the end of the agreed time, no pay being received, the men quit the mine. Beset by a growing mood of anger, antagonism, and frustration, some sold their statements of earnings for half their value. Some moved away and others sat above ground and waited, wondering how they could feed their families.[24]

On the same day the Johnson miners walked out of the mines, an event of note occurred in Fort Worth. At the Mansion Hotel, a group met to incorporate the Texas & Pacific Coal Company. The charter was issued by the State of Texas on October 4, 1888. The incorporators were: R. D. Hunter of St. Louis, Missouri, and Edgar L. Marston, M. B. Loyd, J. Y. Hogsett, and S. P. Greene, all of Tarrant County, Texas. The amount of capital stock was set at two million dollars. In October 1888, Hunter, through the financial house of Blair & Co., 24 Broad Street, New York, obtained five hundred thousand dollars in capital secured by twenty-year first mortgage bonds on the new company's assets and property.[25]

An organizational meeting was held on October 6, 1888. The names and residences of directors elected for the first year were: R. D. Hunter, St. Louis, Missouri; Edgar L. Marston, Fort Worth, Texas; Horace K. Thurber, New York, New York; John J. Knox, New York, New York; John Greenough, New York, New York; J. Y. Hogsett, Fort Worth, Texas; M. B. Loyd, Fort Worth, Texas; A. M. Carter, Fort Worth, Texas; and S. P. Greene, Fort Worth, Texas. Hunter was elected President and General Manager.[26] He had gained control of the Johnson Coal Company even before it was transferred to the new company. By agreement dated October 27, 1888, he received 8,888 shares of the 10,000 outstanding shares in the Johnson Coal Company. Will Johnson received $48,750 in cash, 250 $1000 bonds, and 834 shares of the fully paid capital stock of the Texas & Pacific Coal Company.[27]

In the space of only three years, Johnson had lost his daughter, his father, his brother, and now his mine. With Hunter bailing Johnson out of his financial woes, it might be assumed that a warm and cordial relationship would have been built up between the two. Not so. Johnson came to loathe the man who bought the mine. Although Johnson emerged from the sale of his mine with a fortune, plus a sizable stake in a promising new venture, he always believed that he had been cheated by Hunter.[28]

Cheated or not, Johnson, who had fled Michigan ten years before as an impoverished debtor, was now rich. He and Anna built an impressive two-story house in 1889 that stood in splendid contrast to cabins that predominated in Strawn. The *Palo Pinto County Star* in May 1889 gave a glowing description of the home: "The magnificent residence of Mr. W. W. Johnson is nearing completion. It is the finest residence in Palo Pinto County, and so far as we have seen, west of Fort Worth. In its appointments it is complete in every particular, while the inside finish is perfection itself."

◆

Despite popular misconception, there was never a corporate connection between the Texas & Pacific Railway and the Texas & Pacific Coal Company. Such a misconception was understandable, especially after Hunter made the coal company the namesake of the railroad. Then, too, the railroad was the raison d'être of the coal company. It bought all the coal its iron horses could eat and hauled all the rest. Both sets of the coal company founders had close associations with the railroad. It was what brought Will and Harvey Johnson to Strawn in the first place. Just how high up in the railroad hierarchy the Johnsons' contacts went can only be guessed at, but they must have gone nigh to the top, considering the fact that they had negotiated contracts to supply crossties and coal to the railroad and had even induced the T&P to lay a spur track to their mine at no cost to them.[29] What is more, they held VIP railroad passes. As for Robert D. Hunter, there can be no doubt that his contacts went to the very top, for he was a longtime friend and associate of the railroad's president, Jay Gould. Hunter McLean surmises that Gould could well have played a key role in Colonel Hunter's decision to turn from St. Louis and cattle to Texas and coal.[30] Gould, who held a profound respect for the Colonel's proven enterprising abilities, was vitally interested in developing the Texas coal fields through which his railroad ran. Not only would the coal be a traffic producer, but the coal was needed as fodder for his voracious iron horses. The Johnsons, because of their labor problems and lack of proper equipment, had not been able to furnish a steady and dependable supply of high-grade coal required in the locomotive boilers, much less become a valuable shipper funneling traffic revenues into the railroad's coffers.

In addition to these economic reasons, Gould and the swashbuckling Colonel had been friends since the Ellsworth episode of twenty years ago. After the mining operation was in full swing, he would on occasion visit Hunter in Thurber, where his private railroad car was a star attraction to the miners. That railroad car can be seen today, enshrined in the small East Texas town of Jefferson as a tourist attraction.

◆

On November 12, 1888, Hunter took possession of the mine and immediately set about to make it abundantly clear that he would brook no insolence from either the rabble or the rabble-rousers in the camp. He adhered to the cardinal rule of diplomacy: Be sure you know your own mind and make sure your adversary knows it, too. His moves stirred resentment in the idle miners. Their disgruntlement became intransigence and that in turn became confrontation. A committee of miners asked to meet with him. Hunter was visibly irritated and determined to impress upon the hostile miners in no uncertain terms that he was Lord of the land. He eyed the miners coldly. "Before I'm through with you, a dollar will look as big as a wagon wheel to you. I will run my business or run it to hell!"[31]

Hunter announced his conditions of employment. First, there would be no union, Knights of Labor or any other. Second, $1.15 would be paid per ton of coal, a 40 percent pay cut from the $1.95 provided by the Johnson contract. Third, the "screen method" would be introduced so that only large chunks of coal that did not pass through the apertures would be paid for; there would be no pay for lumps that fell through the screen. The miners looked upon the Colonel as the man from hell. They would remain idle rather than yield to his fiat. Provoked by their hostility, Hunter erected a barbed-wire fence around the camp and began an all-out effort to remove the recalcitrant miners from the company's property. Hunter alone decided what he would pay the miners for their humble abodes, and called on the sheriff to evict forcibly any who refused his offering price.

Driven from their homes, the dispossessed, discouraged, and dispirited workers moved their families into tents and crude shelters on the Knights of Labor land outside the camp, and established what became known as "Striker Town." Hunter sent his son-in-law, Company Treasurer Edgar L. Marston, from New York to Pittsburgh to recruit new miners. Marston quickly discovered his assignment was daunting. Some of the miners from the old Johnson mine launched a counterattack by rushing east and passing out propaganda on the streets of Pittsburgh which, according to the *Fort Worth Gazette,* conveyed the impression that they were on strike against Texas & Pacific Coal Company. This was not true because Hunter, following his purchase of the Johnson properties, had not hired any employees. The miners had worked for Johnson, not Hunter. Still, these former Johnson miners were successful in scaring off new recruits.[32]

If Marston's recruiting efforts in Pittsburgh were nothing to write home about, the news from back home in St. Louis brought joy. His first born son, Edgar Jean Marston, arrived on November 10, 1888, two days before his grandfather took control of the Johnson coal mine. The baby would one day become President of Texas & Pacific Coal Company.[33]

The year 1888 had brought some other exciting developments to the booming Lone Star State: the formation of the Texas & Pacific Coal Company, and the majestic new $3.7-million State Capitol Building in Austin.

✦

In 1882, while Will Johnson was engrossed in start-up operations for a coal mine, the Texas legislature appropriated three million acres of public land in the High Plains to a private contractor to finance the construction of the Capitol Building. Spread over ten counties in the Panhandle, this land became the XIT Ranch.[34]

✦

While Marston, the happy father, hunted for coal miners in the east, violence erupted at the mine back in Johnsonville. On the evening of December 12, 1888, several of his miners were severely beaten by "rowdies"—Hunter's word for them. The lone deputy sheriff stationed at the mine could not cope with the situation. Hunter fired off a message to Sheriff N. J. Shands at Stephenville, county seat of Erath County: "There has been a constant firing of guns and pistols, several hundred rounds having been fired, and a few moments ago they shot into our storehouse and assaulted our office."[35]

Hunter's message was received in the sheriff's office on December 14. As it happened, the sheriff had left Stephenville a day earlier for the coal mines with eviction orders against the miners who had refused to vacate their homes. *The Dallas Morning News* reported that County Judge J. L. Humphries, "guessing that the situation was deteriorating, telegraphed Adjutant General W. H. King in Austin, and requested military aid in keeping the peace and protection of life and property."

King wired back to Judge Humphries, advising him to ask the sheriff to return to the coal mines immediately to ascertain the facts of the situation. It is not clear whether Sheriff Shands, who felt his deputy on the scene was sufficient, made this return trip to the mine. Besides, the sheriff had little enthusiasm for settling Hunter's labor problems. After all, Hunter was an outsider and a business tycoon, whereas the strikers were the sheriff's own people. In any event, Shands sent a reply to King, informing him that no help was needed.

The Adjutant General in Austin, however, concurred with Judge Humphries. It sounded like the camp had been taken over by a mob. If so, it was a job for the Texas Rangers. King telegraphed Captain S. A. McMurry, Frontier Forces of the Texas Rangers, Company B, stationed in Quanah: "Go in person to the coal mines in Erath County. Investigate trouble and report in writing to this office. Have your company join you if necessary." Upon McMurry's arrival at the mine, he received a letter from the Adjutant General. King told McMurry about the sheriff's note and suggested that "a show of force might have a good moral effect. Do not keep the detachment at the mines any longer than is absolutely necessary to restore peace and good order." Captain McMurry took the T&P to Fort Worth where he telegraphed Quanah for ten Rangers to meet him there on 21 December. On the following day, the Ranger detachment left for Johnsonville with orders to guard the miners whom Marston had finally been able to import from Pittsburgh.[36]

The National Labor Tribune, official publication of the Knights of Labor, sent a committee from Pittsburgh to Johnsonville to look into the situation. The committee arrived in Fort Worth the same day as did the Rangers from Quanah. The group, headed by William Rennie, promised a fair evaluation of conditions at the mine. They left Fort Worth on the same train as the Rangers and arrived at the mine on December 22, 1888.

Six days later, the Rennie committee completed its report to the national organization. Rennie stated that working conditions at the mine were better than those of Pennsylvania coal fields. He further stated that the trouble was caused by unreasonable men demanding excessive terms. He said the strike was not sanctioned by the national organization of the Knights of Labor. Rennie wrote: "I know of no camp where a miner can enjoy more advantages than at the mines of the Texas & Pacific Coal Company."[37]

Captain Sam A. McMurry.
Courtesy Dick Smith Library,
Tarleton State University.

With the sheriff and the county judge filing conflicting evaluations of the situation from Stephenville, who was the Adjutant General to believe? He decided to go in person to the camp to see for himself. On January 1, 1889, he questioned a group of miners who met with him about the lawless actions of December 12, 1888, demanding an explanation of the shootings and the names of those involved. He was told that it was not the miners, but gamblers and rowdies who were harassing the company. The miners promised that there would be no more violence. King, satisfied that order would be maintained, prepared to leave for Austin. Before his departure, he told representatives of the Knights of Labor that the Rangers were there to keep the peace, that anyone who wanted to quit work could do so, but that he intended to see that the strikers in right-to-work Texas should not prevent others from working who wanted to.[38]

On January 2, 1889, Hunter changed the name of Johnsonville to Thurber, in honor of Horace Kingsley Thurber of New York City, a substantial investor in the enterprise. Thurber, about four years older than Hunter,

A group of Captain Sam McMurry's Company B Texas Rangers at Thurber in 1889. The lady, center, is wife of Ranger Sam Platt, fifth from left. Courtesy of Western History Collections, University of Oklahoma Library.

was born in Delhi, Delware County, New York, on December 27, 1828, the son of Abner Gilmore and Lucy Dunham Thurber. Abner Thurber was a founder and one of the first deacons in the Second Presbyterian Church built in Delhi in 1831. Horace was raised and grew up in this church. In memory of his father who died in 1860, Horace in 1865 gave a ten-foot-high stained glass window to the church depicting Daniel in the Lions' Den, which still graces the main chancel. During the years leading up to the Civil War, the Thurber home in Delhi was a station for runaway slaves on the underground railroad. Young Horace received his education at the Delaware Academy, a private school then but public now, from which he graduated about 1846.

Horace began his business career as a clerk in the Delaware Bank (to-day known as Delaware National Bank). In the early 1850s he came to New York and entered the wholesale grocery business as a bookkeeper for Henry Harms, at 286 Washington Street. In 1858 he entered into partnership with John F. Pupke, under the firm name of Pupke & Thurber, doing business at 173 and 175 Chambers Street. The firm soon became one of the most important in the trade but dissolved in 1866. Thurber continued the business under the name of H. K. Thurber & Co. His younger brother, Francis Beattie Thurber and Stephen L. Bardash were junior partners.

The business soon outgrew the premises in Chambers Street, and in 1874 acquired property at the junction of West Broadway, Reade and

Hudson Streets, erecting a building which was still standing at the turn of the century. Here under the name of H. K. & F. B. Thurber & Co., the firm became one of the leading food products concerns in America, with branch houses in London and Bordeaux, France, and doing business in all parts of the world. In 1884, owing to failing health, H. K. Thurber retired from the active management of the business, remaining in the firm, however, as a special partner. The firm name then became Thurber, Whyland & Co. In 1890 he withdrew entirely from the business. The concern was then incorporated under the title of the Thurber-Whyland Company.

H. K. Thurber did not remain idle, but became interested in several enterprises. Among them were the United States and Brazil Steamship Company, the Trow Directory Company, and the Texas & Pacific Coal Company. He acquired a large amount of land and livestock in the west. He met with financial reverses in the panic of 1893, and went west to look after his interests there. For the rest of his life he made his home in Hailey, Idaho, where he died on July 20, 1899. He was survived by his wife, Nancy MacLaury Thurber. The couple had no children. His remains were returned to his birthplace, Delhi, New York, for burial in Woodland Cemetery.[39]

Back in Thurber, while the Rangers kept the peace at the mine, Hunter brought in more men to work in the idle shaft. Some came from Pittsburgh, but twenty-five of the new men hailed from Chihuahua, Mexico. Pressure from the strikers immediately hit the new arrivals. Dan McLauchlin, a hot-headed Irish strike leader, cursed the Rangers, the men they protected, and the coal company: "You see, they had the Rangers and they had to get something for them to do. They failed at getting Pittsburgh miners for them to guard, and they have done the next best thing, brought Mexicans here. We know that the Mexicans cannot dig this coal, and we are as determined as ever to win this fight."[40] Threats by McLauchlin and others must have influenced the Mexicans, for at midnight on January 5, 1889, they silently stole away.

Although the atmosphere about the camp appeared to be peaceful, only 177 tons of coal were mined during the months of November and December, 1888 and January, 1889. The Rangers found themselves standing between the infuriated, determined mine owner and angry miners.

Early in February, 1889, new labor from Pennsylvania and Indiana began to flow into Thurber. On February 19, 1890, Hunter wrote in his *First Annual Report* to shareholders: "It was February before we succeeded in securing the services of a body of miners. During this month, I shipped 172 white and black miners from Brazil, Indiana, at the expense of the company. Of this number, 54 of the white men on arrival at the mines, refused to work and joined the lodge of the Knights of Labor, which held their daily meeting about one mile from our headquarters. The black men remained faithful to their word, and experience has shown they give less trouble and are easier to please than the foreign element which predominates among the white miners. We continued shipments of men under like conditions until our mines were equipped. This has cost the company a total loss of $10,883.64 for transportation."[41]

On 4 February, Captain McMurry went to Fort Worth to escort a train-load of workers to the mine. On 11 March, two Rangers escorted another load of miners from Fort Worth. As the number of incoming workers increased, they were carefully guarded by the Rangers. Hunter now stiffened his determination to remove the dwellings of the miners from company property. He again called upon the sheriff in Stephenville to evict those who refused to move. To Sheriff Shands this was a distasteful task and he put off action as long as possible.

As 1889 ended, the strength of the Knights of Labor waned and the strike was called off. The strikers moved away or became employees of the 100 percent nonunion Texas & Pacific Coal Company. The Texas Rangers quietly returned to Quanah and Colonel Hunter was left as the power in Thurber.[42]

The period of peace and quiet following the strike proved to be short-lived. Early in July, 1890, Hunter again requested protection from the Rangers. He stated the town had grown in population to about fifteen hundred, of which eight hundred were Negroes. He feared that some of the old strikers, who had lingered in the vicinity, were trying to incite a race riot. In response, Adjutant General King sent Captain McMurry once more to Thurber. Arriving on July 10, 1890, McMurry consulted with Hunter. He wrote King that there was considerable disorder and a very "hard set" in the town. He recommended that two or three Rangers be sent to Thurber for two or three weeks. No serious trouble occurred, and by the end of the month, the Rangers left Thurber and calm reigned for the next four years.

There was, however, one Ranger, Ed S. Britton, who remained in Thurber. Colonel Hunter took a shine to Britton and offered him a position he couldn't refuse–weighmaster of a new mine. Years later, Britton told his secretary, George B. Studdard, that Hunter one day asked him to come to his office and said: "Monday morning we are going to start sinking a shaft for the No. 3 mine just a little way west of town, and if you will resign from the Texas Rangers, I will put you on our payroll starting tomorrow at ninety dollars per month, and you don't have to furnish a horse and saddle. When the shaft is finished, and the main entries driven, I want you to go out there as weighmaster." As a Ranger, Britton had been making seventy-five dollars a month and had to furnish his own horse and saddle. His reply to Hunter was quick: "Colonel, you've just hired yourself a man."[43]

After the miners had been evicted from the company's property and their old shacks either removed or dismantled, Hunter began a furious building program. "We have spent $56,494.29, which represents one large general store with warehouse attached, drug store, hardware store,

Hardware store, circa 1895. Courtesy Dick Smith Library, Tarleton State University.

Drug store under construction, circa 1900. Courtesy Dick Smith Library, Tarleton State University.

Typical shotgun-style Thurber house. Courtesy Dick Smith Library, Tarleton State University.

boarding houses, offices, stables, shops, school houses, churches and over two hundred two, three, four and five room houses."[44]

Thurber's first housing development extended eastward from the downtown area to the motor line from the brickyard to Shale Pit Mountain, south to the edge of New York Hill and northward for two blocks past Park Row. It was in the south portion of this area that the black miners lived. Poles and Italians were concentrated on hills to the west. The rest of the neighborhoods were more mixed.

The first houses to be built were of shotgun (named because the layout was such that a shot fired through the front door would exit the back door) or box construction. They were built with walls of one-by-twelve pine boards. The roofs were wood shingled. An occupant had a choice of colors: red or green. The houses were generally surrounded by a picket fence, also red or green. On the inside, a clothes closet or kitchen cupboard was built diagonally across one corner of each of the three fourteen-by-fourteen-foot rooms. Each room had one or two small windows and a door. Many housewives, using flour paste, covered the pine walls with old newspapers. A coal-burning stove provided heat to warm the house and cook the meals. Because the houses had no indoor plumbing, an outhouse was always found at the back of each lot. At the rear of many of the houses stood small buildings commonly known as wash houses. It was here that

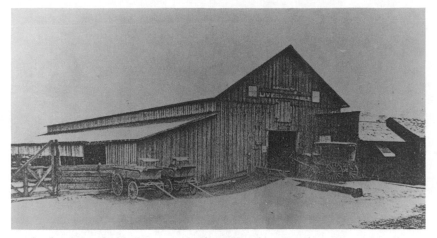

Thurber livery stable. Courtesy Dick Smith Library, Tarleton State University.

the housewife did the family wash and the miner washed the black of the coal pits from his body after a day's work.[45]

Only a few of these early houses had porches, although in later years porches were added to most of the dwellings. Yards were likely to be hard-packed dirt and needed to be swept regularly. Mesquite thorns, dead leaves, sticks, clods, pebbles, and rusty staples that had popped out of the fence had to be picked up. Yards were swept over and over until they were slick as slate.[46] The absence of grassy lawns with shrubbery and shade trees gave the residential areas a barren look, although most residents cultivated flowers in their yards. If the tenant owned a horse or other livestock, he had to build a barn to shelter it.

Many of Thurber's miners were either unmarried or had families back home. Consequently, boarding houses were among the first buildings constructed. Most of the single mine workers lived in these structures with five or six men sharing the same room. Meals and laundry were furnished by the keeper of the boarding house at a cost of twenty-five to thirty-five dollars per month.

Many of the men, especially foreigners, would form a group of six or seven, rent and furnish a house and set up bachelor quarters, each man performing his share of the household chores. Called a "batch," this type of living was more economical than living in a boarding house.[47]

When Hunter purchased the Johnson Coal Company in 1888, there was a saloon on the property. Johnson had leased the saloon to John L. Ward, and this lease was still in effect when Hunter took over the

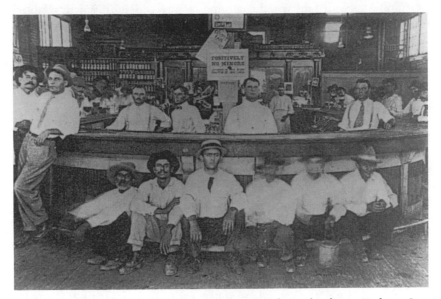

Horseshoe bar of the Snake Saloon. Courtesy Dick Smith Library, Tarleton State University.

property. After the barbed-wire fence went up, Ward's saloon was the only establishment within the enclosure that was not under Hunter's control. Hunter purchased Ward's interest for the sum of twenty-seven hundred dollars.

Queasy about the legality of the coal company's operation of a saloon, Hunter leased the bar to a friend, Thomas Lawson, granting him the exclusive right to sell alcoholic beverages within the town. Lawson opened the saloon for business on May 20, 1889. Within a year, however, the legal doubts having been dissolved, Hunter moved to break the lease. Texas & Pacific Coal Company would run the bar as well as the mines. He took possession of the saloon and filed suit, alleging that Lawson had failed to carry out the terms of the contract. A lengthy legal battle ensued. The case went all the way to the Texas Supreme Court, which declared Lawson's contract void as being in restraint of trade.

The saloon soon outgrew the building that housed it. A new saloon was built just west of the livery stable. This two-story red brick building housed the saloon on the ground floor. The second floor was used as a lodge hall. This saloon was dubbed "The Snake" by the miners. It was famous for its massive horseshoe-shaped mahogany bar. Later, a saloon was built on the hill to the west to serve the Polish and Italian miners living in that area. It became known as "The Lizard."

Unlike the wild and woolly saloons featured in Fort Worth's fabled Hell's Half-Acre, Thurber's saloons had no gambling tables or dance floors. There were no dance hall girls or female entertainers. The Snake and The Lizard, always crawling with miners, were off limits to women. No seating was provided. Consequently, the long bars were always crowded.

Thurber's saloons were always well-stocked with all types of alcoholic beverages, both foreign and domestic. Liquors and wines were in abundant supply, but beer was always the most popular beverage. Thurber's miners preferred keg beer, and a large refrigerated warehouse stood adjacent to the saloon for beer storage. This beer was not pasteurized, and it was necessary to keep it under refrigeration from the time it was brewed until it was consumed. It was shipped from Fort Worth Brewing Company to Thurber in refrigerated railroad cars, and rolled down a ramp into the cold storage vault. Another ramp delivered the kegs to the bar, where it could be purchased by the glass, pitcher, bucket, or keg. In addition to furnishing liquid refreshments to the miners, the saloons also furnished ice to the townspeople.[48]

Despite all the labor and housing problems in 1889, Hunter was still able to open Mine No. 2 at a depth of seventy-five feet. This mine was located almost one mile northwest of Mine No. 1. If you stop today on the road that runs between Thurber and Mingus and peer through the brush, you can see the slag pile of the No. 2 mine. In his *First Annual Report,* Hunter wrote: "Mine No. 2, when we took possession, was a shaft sunk to the coal without any opening or entries. You now have a mine with a capacity of five hundred tons per day."

In 1889, the year after Hunter took over the Johnson mine, a twenty-seven-year-old engineer named William Knox Gordon made his debut upon the Thurber stage. W. K. Gordon was born in Spotsylvania County, Virginia, on January 26, 1862, the son of Cosmo and Adelaide Gordon. After completing high school, he studied engineering in Fredericksburg, Virginia. Upon graduation, he worked in 1881-83 as a civil engineer on the Virginia and Caroline Railroad, later called the Seaboard Air Line. In 1883-1885 he was with the Georgia-Carolina & Northern Railroad, and in 1885-88 he was with the Raleigh and Gaston Railroad, the Carolina Central, and the Georgia Pacific. In 1889, his work brought him to Texas to help survey the proposed Coal and Mineral Railway line from Thurber to Dublin.[49]

Hunter outlined to the stockholders a plan to build a thirty-seven-mile railroad south from Thurber to connect with the Texas Central at Dublin: "If this is built, the attention of the promoters will be called to the inducements offered to extend the road south of the Texas Central to the famous iron mines of Llano, Mason and San Saba Counties, which are the richest in the United States. The distance is 150 miles, and the nearest coal property to these iron deposits is your own. Should this road be built, an unlimited amount of coal can be sold, and all the railroads of southern and southwestern Texas would be supplied by the mines of the Texas & Pacific Coal Company." It was in surveying for this proposed railroad that Gordon became acquainted with Hunter. The impresario was so impressed with the young man that upon completion of the railroad survey, he hired him as mine engineer for his Texas & Pacific Coal Company. He was soon promoted to superintendent and general manager. For more than three decades, Gordon's commitment, skills, creativity, and vision were unmatched.

Mines are a dangerous place to work. Explosions can be caused by ignition of airborne coal dust or methane, an odorless, colorless, highly flammable gas given off by coal. Thurber's poorly ventilated and unsafe mine offered a challenge to Gordon, and he immediately set about the dual task of making the black hole safer and devising means of getting coal to the surface at the lowest possible cost.[50]

Gordon's efforts on both counts were successful. No death occurred in a TP mine because of fire or explosion. As for the second goal, he began to devise ways and means of improving production. Testifying to his effectiveness are two patents issued by the United States Patent Office to W. K. Gordon for his inventions: patent no. 594736 issued November 30, 1897, covered automatic dumping cages; and patent no. 851512, issued April 23, 1907, covered a saw-operating mechanism.

Reporting to his stockholders Hunter enthused: "I feel confident of the success of the company for the coming year and that your stock will become a dividend payer."[51] Hunter's enthusiasm might have been colored by the results of the election of 1888 in which the Republicans defeated Democrat Grover Cleveland and put Benjamin Harrison in the White House. Cleveland was vehemently detested by cattlemen for policies that had driven many of them, including Hunter, out of the cattle business.

Sometime between 1887 and 1889 the family moved to Texas. Hunter's wife, Janet, and daughter, Maude, preferred living in Fort Worth rather than in the mining town of Thurber. In the early years of Thurber's development, the Colonel provided temporary Fort Worth residences for Janet and Maude, and infrequently for himself, on the west side of Summit Avenue. In 1889, they rented the home of Judge Robert E. Beckham at the southwest corner of West Daggett and Summit Avenue.[52]

Soon after the family arrived in Fort Worth, Maude met a young man named John Clemens Phelan, a native of New Orleans, the son of Patrick and Ophelia Eseneault Phelan. He was born 1 July 1860, in St. Charles Parish, Louisiana. Educated in the Jesuit College of New Orleans, by 1884, he had moved to Texas where he joined the wholesale mercantile firm of

Town band lines up in front of Little Lake. Baptist Church and New York Hill in the background, circa 1900. Courtesy Dick Smith Library, Tarleton State University.

Martin-Brown Company as secretary. Maude and John became friends and romance blossomed.[53]

Meanwhile, business in Thurber picked up speed. In 1891, Mine No. 3, located three quarters of a mile west of Thurber was opened at a depth of 105 feet. Now there were three mines in operation.

In 1892, No. 4 and No. 5 were placed in production. No. 4, located less than one mile north of No. 1, was opened at a depth of fifty-two feet. No. 5, located a mile west of Thurber, was opened at a depth of 103 feet. Mine No. 1, having produced 129,552 tons over three years, was abandoned in 1892. In operation now were four mines: Nos. 2, 3, 4, and 5.

◆

Thurber boasted the first public library in Erath County, with an initial endowment of five hundred volumes, donated by H. K. Thurber, and an allotment of fifteen dollars a month for a librarian's salary, furnished by Hunter.

Several private academies were operated at various times in Thurber's history. Most were of short duration, with the exception of the Catholic Academy, which existed from the early 1890s until 1923. With both day and night classes, it was run under the supervision of the Sisters of the Incarnate Word of San Antonio.[54]

◆

Although there was coal everywhere in Thurber, there was precious little water. The Johnson miners hauled water from ponds and stock tanks in the area. Colonel Hunter in his *First Annual Report* stated that a diamond drill had been acquired to test for deeper coal veins. If deeper veins were not found but an abundance of water was, it would be more than worth the expense of the drill. But no water was found, so Hunter contracted with the Texas & Pacific Railway to bring in water in tank cars. As the camp grew, however, this proved to be not only expensive but inefficient. To eliminate this ongoing worry, Hunter decided in 1892 to build a lake. According to W. K. Gordon, who designed the reservoir, the dam was built three times as strong as necessary, because the lake was located upstream from the town, and a broken dam could flood Thurber. Later known as the Little Lake, this body of water covered twenty acres of land and impounded thirty million gallons of good water. The lake can still be seen from the New York Hill Restaurant. Two large cypress tanks were installed on the hill at the west end of the dam, and a small steam pumping plant, situated near the tanks, lifted the water from the lake. Water was piped from the tanks to various locations in town.[55]

On November 24, 1892, Maude Lee Hunter married John Clemens Phelan. The wedding was detailed in the *Fort Worth Gazette:*

> For dainty tastefulness for the absolute lack of formality, it is questionable if a wedding ever occurred in Fort Worth that excelled that which last night was celebrated at Ye Arlington Inn, when John C. Phelan and Miss Maude Lee Hunter were united in matrimony's holy bond.
>
> The elite of Fort Worth was present to lend their encouragement to the launching of this new barque on the sea of matrimony. The bride and groom left for a brief trip to New York, Chicago and other northern cities. Mr. and Mrs. Phelan will be at home after December 20 at Ye Arlington Inn. [56]

✦

1892 also marked the four hundreth anniversary of Columbus's landing in the New World. Inspired by President Benjamin Harrison's call for patriotic exercises in schools to celebrate the historic event, Francis Bellamy of *The Youth's Companion* magazine, wrote the Pledge of Allegiance to the Flag.[57] In the election of November 1892, there occurred a result never seen before nor since—the election of a former president as the new president. Grover Cleveland, who had been defeated in 1888 by Benjamin Harrison, now four years later unseated Harrison. This put Cleveland in the record books as both the twenty-second and twenty-fourth president. Reflecting on the demise of his cattle enterprise in Cleveland's first administration, Hunter undoubtedly took little joy from the Democrat's return to the White House.

✦

In 1893, Mine No. 6, located one mile south of No. 5, was opened at a depth of ninety-five feet. Five mines were now in operation: Nos. 2, 3, 4, 5, and 6.

In the five years since he sold his mine to Hunter, Will Johnson continued to be an active player in many enterprises—ranching, lumber, banking, coal mines, and railroads. Although some of the enterprises succeeded and others did not, he and Anna prospered out on the vast frontiers of the burgeoning Lone Star State. But now in 1894, tragedy came again into their lives. Their hopes and dreams were centered upon their small and frail son William Harvey. Remembering the illness that took the life of their daughter in 1885, the couple was determined to guard their heir zealously. He was not often permitted to play with the other boys in Strawn—he might catch something, or he might be hurt. To compensate for keeping him in virtual quarantine, they pampered him with gifts—even a pony. On May 18, 1893, U.S. Marshal P. B. Hunt wrote to Johnson: "I ship today Quebie. I hope he will reach you safely. Feel quite sure he will be all your little boy can wish as a pony."[58] Despite their zealousness, the boy died on June 24, 1894. Will and Anna had now lost two children. Babies on the Texas frontier died from such illnesses as bacterial infection, polio, mumps, smallpox, diphtheria, croup, measles, diarrhea, typhoid, scarlet fever, and whooping cough.[59] In the funeral procession for the little boy, Quebie, with empty saddle, was tied to the hearse. But the procession did not wend to the cemetery. Once again it ended in the Johnson back yard. The Johnsons dressed their little son in a fairy costume he had worn in a school play and placed him in the home mausoleum beside his sister and Uncle Harvey.

In 1894, Mine No. 7, located one mile north of No. 5, was opened at a depth of 135 feet. In the same year, Mines Nos. 3 and 4 were abandoned. Mine No. 3 had produced 210,103 tons over three years. Mine No. 4 had produced 80,021 tons in its two year life. Four mines remained active: Nos. 2, 5, 6, and 7.

In June 1894, labor unrest again came to Thurber. The unpleasantness stemmed from animus between Hunter and a saloon operator named Jimmie Grant. Grant opened a saloon east of the townsite in 1888. His bar soon became a favorite watering hole for the miners, as well as ranchers and farmers in the area. At the Colonel's instigation, the saloon was frequently raided by Erath County officers. Arrests were made on charges of gambling, drunkenness, disorderly conduct, and carrying and discharging firearms. Finally, in 1893, Grant decided he had had enough. He moved his cantina to a spot just over the Erath-Palo Pinto county line. Bradford's Dry Goods Store and a grocery store soon were established nearby. The little settlement became known as Grant Town. Soon after, Grant sold his business to Messrs. Bruce and D. W. Stewart.

Bruce and Stewart's Saloon quickly became a popular hangout with the Thurber miners, even though they continued to call it "Jimmie Grant's." There they could air their grievances without fear of interference by the company security force who frequented Hunter's Snake and Lizard saloons in Thurber. Their gripes always found a sympathetic ear, because a number of the Johnson miners had remained in the area, some working at various jobs, others working in the Lyra coal mines. "Walking delegates" from the mines in Indian Territory appeared from time to time to rouse the rabble. These interlopers proceeded to sow the seeds of unrest among Hunter's malcontents. Then there was the lawless element, omnipresent in western frontier towns, always ready to disrupt peace and concord.

Hunter believed that drinking was a serious threat to the safety and well-being of the Thurber miners. He cited the danger of a possible explosion if men were drunk or recently had been on an alcoholic spree. Should such an explosion occur, lives could be lost and a mine severely damaged. Hunter issued orders through W. K. Gordon that no man could enter the mines while under the influence of alcohol. He also warned bartenders at the company saloon not to serve those who appeared to be intoxicated. When the miners were refused service by the Texas & Pacific bartenders, many went to Bruce and Stewart's hospitable haven. In response, Hunter declared the Palo Pinto bar off limits to his men and closed a private company wagon road that led past its swinging doors. The road paralleled the spur tracks connecting the mines with the main line of the Texas & Pacific Railway at Thurber Junction. A new road was constructed some distance from the railroad tracks. Hunter maintained that relocation of the wayfare was done to keep the public out of harm's way. Horses, frightened by locomotives, tended to bolt, endangering passengers in their buggies and wagons.

Closing the road also made it more difficult for miners to reach their forbidden oasis and brought immediate protests from Bruce and Stewart. The old road had passed within a few yards of their saloon, but the new one was some distance away. They filed suit against Hunter and the coal company, charging that a public road had been closed. They lost. The court determined the road was privately owned by the Texas & Pacific Coal Company and they could close it if they wanted to. As a counter, D. W. Stewart distributed circulars in Thurber that promised free beer on the following Saturday at the Bruce and Stewart oasis in Grant Town. Discovered in Thurber by vigilant company guards, the enterprising Stewart was severely beaten and dragooned from town.

Now Hunter moved again. He reduced wages from $1.15 per ton to $1.00 per ton. Radicals among the miners urged a strike. But the miners had no supporting organization to give aid and succor. There was no strike. But through these actions, Hunter made many enemies. Unknown individuals on May 27, 1894, sent the following:

COL. R. D. HUNTER: We have started an organization of Avengers to kill tyrants, and if you do not open the road to Jimmy Grant's saloon we will kill you, you son of a bitch. And we have been chosen by the goodness of God to put down all monopolies, and if you do not discharge W. K. Gordon and that son of a bitch, Bob McKeinan, and that gray haired bitch, Ben Mathews, we will kill you anyway. Open the road to Jimmy's and discharge the three sons of bitches and we will not hurt you.

Avengers

P.S. We are called by the Supreme Ruler to remove R. D. Hunter, F. Cronk, W. K. Gordon, Bob McKeinan [sic], Ben Mathews [sic] and Andrew Remage.

Of granite determination and quite unaccustomed to fear, Hunter reacted quickly by posting a two hundred dollar reward notice for the arrest and conviction of the coup-plotters:

I, Colonel R. D. Hunter, hereby offer a reward of $200 for the arrest and conviction of the party or parties guilty of writing the following letter. The letter was dropped into the post office at Thurber about May 27, 1894. Parties were too cowardly to sign their names to same.

The threatening letter was reproduced at the bottom of the reward notice. The letter writers were arrested and tried in federal court in Waco on charges of sending threatening material through the United States mail.[60]

Six years had passed since the Texas Rangers under Captain S. A. McMurry had ridden into town in 1888 to maintain law and order. Now in 1894, Hunter believed the Rangers were needed again. In a letter to Adjutant General W. H. Mabry, he appealed to the state for help: "Although our men have not struck, and are still at work, the striking miners from the Territory and elsewhere are sending their walking delegates in here in a clandestine manner and are trying to create a strike. Three of the rascals have been arrested and put under bond, but they keep sending more, and while our people are trying to work, they have been terrorized to a great degree."[61]

Upon receipt of his letter in Austin, Mabry dispatched Captain William (Bill) McDonald to Thurber to investigate the situation. After talking with all parties involved, McDonald reported to Mabry that although wages had been reduced, the consensus among the miners was that Thurber was a good place to work and live, and they could still earn a decent living at the new pay scale. Moreover, their wages were always paid on time, which was not the case under the Johnson regime. McDonald also reported that the prices of goods sold in the company stores were reasonable. In fact, the only dissatisfaction he was able to discern emanated from Bruce and Stewart's saloon at Grant Town.

Those who had continued working in the pits were threatened by men who suddenly appeared out of the dark. The marauders threatened to

Mine guards hired by Texas & Pacific Coal Company, circa 1894.
Courtesy Dick Smith Library, Tarleton State University.

dynamite the mines if the miners did not stop work. Many reported to McDonald that they had been called out of their homes at night and given similar warnings. One evening a mass meeting of miners was held outside of town. Captain McDonald attended and listened to the speaker who, in fiery oratory, told the crowd that they should dynamite the mines and dispose of the Colonel.

Mingling with the miners, McDonald slowly worked his way toward the speaker. When the harangue had stopped, he mounted the large log that was being used as a podium: "As you all know, I'm Captain Bill McDonald of the Texas Rangers. The acts that you men are contemplating are unlawful, and I will jail any man who carries out this criminal action!" The crowd dispersed and went home. The next morning, McDonald was informed that a crowd of miners wished to see him. Not knowing their feelings, he picked up his Winchester and walked out to confront the men. He was informed that the men were ready to go to work, and asked if they would be protected if they went to the mines. On his assurance that they had nothing to fear, the men went back to work. Those in Thurber at that time have opined that of all the Rangers who were sent there, McDonald most

The company's first General Store, Texas Pacific Mercantile and Manufacturing, circa 1894. Courtesy Dick Smith Library, Tarleton State University.

epitomized the renowned peace keepers. The situation was dangerous, and it was due to his fair-handed firmness that it was settled in a peaceable manner.[62]

While the Johnsons operated the property, they ran a general store, drug store, and a saloon for the village. These facilities were small and provided only the bare necessities for life in the camp. Hunter, on the other hand, established a large well-stocked general store with meat market and groceries, drug store, and hardware. Hunter's emporiums were the forerunners of twentieth-century supermarkets. In 1894 these merchandising facilities were placed under control of a separate corporation, the Texas and Pacific Mercantile and Manufacturing Company.

The Knox Hotel, built in 1894 at the northwest corner of the square, became the main gathering place in Thurber. It was here that most of the social events took place—dinners, grand balls, or other social gatherings. A half-page advertisement in the local newspaper proclaimed the Knox Hotel as: "Best Hotel West of Fort Worth. This Hotel is first class in every respect; lighted throughout by electricity; hot, cold and mineral water baths at all hours, free; a home for the traveling man; rates $2.50 per day, with special rates to opera troupes. First class Livery Stable in connection. Where Good Teams can be Hired at Reasonable Rates. Concord Stage meets all trains at Thurber Junction. Flowing Mineral Water in Knox Hotel Yard."[63]

Payday in the mines was the third Saturday of each month. Texas & Pacific Coal Company missed honoring payday only once. On November 16, 1894, on the Friday before payday, a Texas & Pacific train was robbed near the place where bandits struck in 1887 during the Johnson era. Thomas R. Hall, cashier and paymaster, told about the robbery in a souvenir bulletin published in 1913 to commemorate the company's twenty-fifth anniversary:

It was known that the funds for meeting the miners payday were being shipped on that day, and the robbers stationed themselves about one and a half miles east of Gordon, captured a section gang and had them take up a rail and flag the train. There were four of them, and when the train stopped, two of them boarded the express car while the other two stood guard and kept the passengers inside the coaches. The express messenger convinced them that he could not open the safe, so they undertook to dynamite it, with the result that the door was sprung so badly that they could not open it, and were compelled to abandon the attempt.

They took all the money that was kept outside of the main safe, which was considerable, it being cotton season, and much money was being shipped to the local stations for the purpose of buying cotton. This money was kept in an iron box and was convenient for the express messenger to open upon its arrival at stations. This they appropriated. The Texas & Pacific Coal Company's pay fund, in the safe, amounted to $33,000. Owing to the damage done to the safe, it could not be opened for several days, and as a result payday was postponed until the following Wednesday, when the company shipped other funds from Fort Worth.

As soon as Colonel Hunter was advised that the train had been robbed, he started a posse in pursuit, headed by Captain William Lightfoot, Grude Britton and Lit Williams. The robbers went north from where they undertook to rob the train, cutting fences and keeping as straight a course as possible, heading for mountainous country fifteen miles away.

The robbery occurred at one o'clock in the afternoon, and at three o'clock the same afternoon, the posse started by Colonel Hunter took up their trail, and followed it until dark. On resuming their chase the next morning, they found where the robbers had camped the night before and divided their loot; a number of money bags and other papers scattered about on the ground indicated this. This occurred in a cave in the mountainside at a place called Board Tree Springs. From there, the robbers scattered and all trace of them was lost; however, the hunt was kept up, and Colonel Hunter always thought, and I believe he was right, that Ben and Jim Hughes, two notorious characters who formerly lived in Palo Pinto County, planned the robbery.

Ben Hughes lived in what was then known as the Indian Territory. In the course of eight or nine months, the officers heard that he had a gang around him there, who were supposed to be the men who robbed the Texas & Pacific train.

Colonel Hunter sent Captain Lightfoot, Britton, Williams and Sam Farmer, formerly a policeman at Fort Worth, to Hughes's place in the Territory; upon their arrival at the nearest railroad station, they secured an Indian policeman to help, as a guide and to make the arrest. They went at night to the house kept by Ben Hughes, nine miles from the station, and surrounded it, thinking to wait until daylight. However, a dog discovered the presence of the men and was so vicious that Sam Farmer had to shoot it. This stampeded the men in the house and they came out shooting their Winchesters, and the fight commenced in the dark.

When daylight came, it was found that the Indian policeman was dead, having been shot through the head, and Ben Hughes with his right arm broken from a bullet, was lying behind a log, begging the boys not to shoot him. His wife, however, who had come to his relief, stood over him with a Winchester and refused to let the officers near him until they promised to let her go with him. The other men who were in the house, four in number, escaped.

The boys loaded the dead Indian and Hughes, with his wife, in a farm wagon and took them to the station. Ben was brought to trial in Dallas, in the United States District Court, and acquitted by proving an alibi. We afterwards learned that the men who were in that house that night were the men who robbed the Texas & Pacific train on November 16, the year before, and we think were then making plans to come to Thurber and rob us on payday.

Colonel Hunter, right in the beginning, started the custom of sending a heavy guard to receive the funds for payday, and it has been kept up to the present time, and this has perhaps saved us from being robbed a number of times.[64]

Back in Fort Worth, Colonel Hunter had moved his domicile yet again. In 1894 he rented property owned by John R. Hoxie, President of Farmers and Mechanics National Bank, on the west side of Summit Avenue at the west end of El Paso Street. Those older homes were soon to be replaced by the magnificent mansions on Summit, to become known as "Quality Hill" or "Cattle Barons Row."[65]

In 1895, Mine No. 8, located one-half mile west of No. 7, was opened at a depth of 217 feet. In the same year, Mine No. 2 was abandoned. It had produced 452,707 tons over six years. Four mines were still in operation: Nos. 5, 6, 7, and 8.

Thurber was an amazingly self-sufficient town. It was one of the first cities in West Texas to have an electric light plant. The first electric generator was small in size, with its armature and field coils wound on wooden cores. It was built in 1895 at the company's machine shop. Most of the beef and pork eaten by Thurber's population was home grown. The company had several thousand head of cattle in its various pastures. Between

Thurber and Ranger was a large pasture known as the P.O. Ranch, replete with ranch house, bunkhouse, barn, and corrals. The meat was processed in a slaughterhouse built north of town. In about 1895, the company also established a dairy near the northeast corner of what is now Big Lake. The dairy supplied all of the milk consumed in Thurber.[66]

✦

Seemingly everybody has heard of Thurber. Everyone has a story or anecdote to tell. Most of the stories have the ring of authenticity to them and can be readily admitted into the repository of Thurberana. Such a story-teller is Harmon Greene, the barber of Fort Worth's Colonial Country Club during the 1980s and 1990s. Apocryphal or not, here is the tale of the barber:

The summer of 1895 had been as usual hot and dry in Thurber. The dog days of July and August had come and gone. So had September. Still no rain.

But things were about to change. By mid-afternoon of October 2nd, dark clouds began forming in the west that would bring upon Thurber a veritable gully washer. A day to remember. That was the day Jed Coleman was to be buried.

Jed and his beautiful young wife Fannie had arrived in Thurber the year before from Tennessee by covered wagon. He had been given a job in the Texas Pacific blacksmith shop. On September 30th, Jed was shot and killed by an enraged miner when he was found at midnight with the aggrieved Italian's wife in the livery stable. News got around town that his body was nude when found by the constable who had gone to the stable to investigate the loud gun shot.

At Jed's funeral, an itinerant preacher, Peter Van Horn, delivered a fire-and-brimstone sermon, saying that there are some things that immortal, invisible God only wise will not allow a man to get away with. Now while the rites were proceeding in the little church, the gathering storm began to roll in from the west. As though some heavenly hearer wanted to add an hearty amen to the preacher's words, an occasional boom of thunder punctuated his homiletics. The sermon finally concluded and the hymns sung, it was time for the funeral cortege to form.

But while the funeral procession was under way, other forces were at play. A cattle drive from the west had arrived, bringing a herd of longhorns destined for the Thurber slaughter house. The cattle corralled just north of town, trail boss Big Jim Tucker, together with two of his cowboys, were in the Snake Saloon drinking straight whiskey.

The horse-drawn hearse carrying Jed Coleman, followed by his wife, Fannie, and friends, was proceeding down Railroad Avenue to the Thurber Cemetery. It was hoped that Jed could be buried before the lowering storm hit. But too late! Jagged flashes of lightning staccatoed, crackled and crinkled down the sky. Thunder rolled like echoes from a ponderous bass drum.

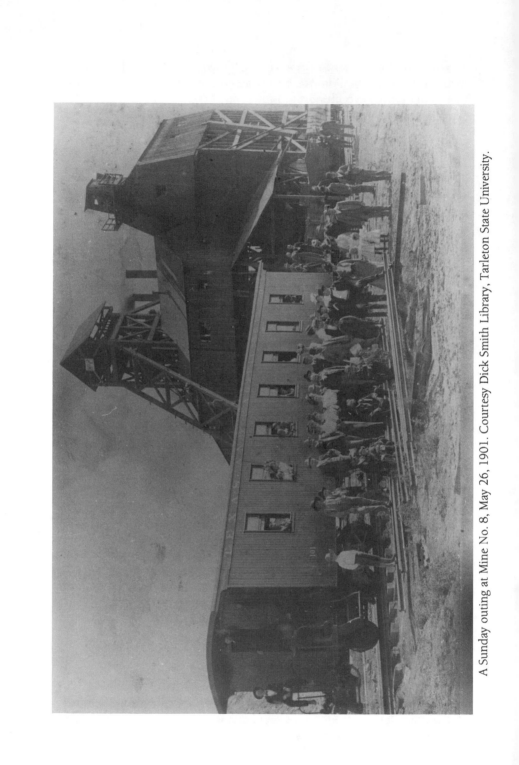

A Sunday outing at Mine No. 8, May 26, 1901. Courtesy Dick Smith Library, Tarleton State University.

Mine No. 9. Courtesy Dick Smith Library, Tarleton State University.

Heavy gray skies parted and torrents of rain poured down. Jim Tucker's restless, bawling cattle became spooked and began to stampede. It was Hell on hoof.

A mighty herd of red-eyed cattle came roaring down Railroad Avenue, meeting the cortege head on, completely destroying the hearse and the two buggies following. The horses were injured. Jed's coffin was demolished. Fannie and Jed's friends, as well as the driver of the hearse, jumped from their buggies, barely making it to the safety of the Snake Saloon. It was said they all promptly ordered a double whiskey to settle their nerves. Big Jim Tucker, looking from the saloon and seeing his cattle sweep by, hoped that what he saw was not happening but was the result of too much bourbon, and that his cattle were safe in the corral where he had left them.

After the storm and stampede, the men from the Snake surveyed the damage and started looking for poor Jed, finding him with his feet sticking out from underneath the wrecked hearse. Old man Wells, the undertaker, quickly found another box, and after cleaning Jed up, stuffed him in and nailed it shut. The next day, the 3rd of October, Jed stylishly re-hearsed, the cortege bumped up the rough and rocky hillside road to Thurber Cemetery where he was laid to rest.

And what about Jed's widow, Fannie? Well, a few days later she was caught in bed with naked Reverend Peter Van Horn, the preacher who had officiated at Jed's funeral. Colonel Hunter drove them both out of Thurber's garden.[67]

◆

Was Thurber imbued with Victorian principles? "Everything about the place forms a part of one harmonious whole. Order reigns and law is respected. Law breakers are not wanted in Thurber and cannot stay there. The town has its own code, which is more rigorous than the statutes, and when that is violated a writ of ouster is served and rigidly enforced."[68] One of the most called for books in the Thurber Library was Nathaniel Hawthorne's, *The Scarlet Letter*.

The twenty-acre lake built in 1892 was called Little Lake after 1896 when a much larger lake was built. This lake would be known as Big Lake or Thurber Lake. It was located southeast of town on Gibson Branch. W. K. Gordon designed the lake and supervised its construction. George Carter recalled the lake's construction: "Fifty men were used on the job, as well as one small steam shovel, four one-mule dump carts and two dump-board wagons with mule teams. Two big mule teams with long, heavy chains and two men to each team, were used to tie onto big logs and rocks to be dragged away. They were a busy lot of men with axes, cross-cut saws and dynamite. It was hard work getting rocks and dirt to the dam, but the work was finished in the fall of that year."[69]

Big Lake, 1901. Courtesy Dick Smith Library, Tarleton State University.

Big Lake cost $21,138.45 to construct and covered over 150 acres, compared to twenty acres for Little Lake. In six months the lake had filled with water and was stocked with channel cat, crappie, bass, and bream. A mile-long pipe line was laid from a pump station at the northwest corner of the dam to a large cypress water tank on Cemetery Hill. Thurber now had a plentiful supply of water that was transported by tank wagon to the homes of residents at a cost of ten to twenty-five cents per barrel. Later the water was piped to the houses.

In addition to Big Lake, in 1896 the company built a seventeen-ton ice plant that supplied all the ice used in Thurber and surrounding communities. Surplus water was sold to the Texas & Pacific Railway.

For entertainment, Colonel Hunter decreed the building of the Thurber Opera House. Built in 1896, it offered the most up-to-date entertainment facilities of its day. The interior was brilliantly illuminated by 136 incandescent lights and heated by steam. A large frame structure, it could seat over six hundred people in elevated seating areas that would give everyone a clear view of the thirty-by-fifty-foot stage. Seats in the center section of the lower floor were removable, providing space for diners and dancers on the occasions of many grand balls and other social events. This section of the opera house replaced the ballroom of the Knox Hotel as the scene of social activities for company executives and their friends. During the period from 1896 to 1910, most major dramatic and operatic troupes touring

The Opera House, built in 1896, quickly became the center of Thurber's cultural life. Grand Balls, opera companies, and theatre groups frequently filled the building. Courtesy Dick Smith Library, Tarleton State University.

Texas played in the Thurber Opera House, their private railroad cars being parked nearby. It was usually the only stop these shows made between Fort Worth and El Paso. In between road shows, many local musical and singing groups performed on special occasions. The daughter of an Italian miner would sing the score from *Aida,* Mr. Peterson, manager of the Opera House, would perform his feats of magic, or the girls from the Catholic Academy, marching in precision drill, would recite "The Charge of the Light Brigade." Each year, junior and senior classes of Thurber High School presented their annual plays in the Opera House.[70]

◆

In 1896, the Republicans in their national convention in St. Louis nominated William McKinley for president. One wonders whether Colonel Hunter and his son-in-law, Edgar L. Marston, attended the convention in their home town.

Miner demonstrating position in which they had to dig coal. Courtesy Dick Smith Library, Tarleton State University.

Whether or not they did, there can be little doubt that their attention and interest were centered on that event. The Democrats, meeting in Chicago, nominated thirty-six-year old William Jennings Bryan.[71] Bryan represented labor, farmers, and the West and advocated the free coinage of silver at a fixed rate with gold. McKinley on the other hand, represented big business and stood for a high tariff and the gold standard. During the campaign, Bryan made more than six hundred speeches in twenty-seven states. McKinley, out of concern for his invalid wife, campaigned mostly by sitting on his front porch and letting the politicians come to him. Although Bryan carried the South and West, McKinley, with running mate Garret A. Hobart, won by more than six hundred thousand votes. The electoral vote was 271 to 176.

✦

Mining in the 1890s and early twentieth century was not an easy life. At 6:00 A.M., dressed in work clothes made of heavy, tough material, their caps with carbide lamps on their heads, the miners boarded the Black Diamond, a company train that took them to those mines that were remote from town. The miners assigned to nearby mines walked to their work. Upon reaching their mine, the miners would ride the elevator down to the bottom of the pit where they would spend the day.

Miner lying on his side in mine. Courtesy Dick Smith Library, Tarleton State University.

Because the coal beds dipped to the west, the deepest mine, at 327 feet, was the westernmost mine, New No. 2 (not opened until 1909) located about five miles to the northwest of town. The shallowest mine at fifty-two feet below the surface was No. 4, located northeast of town. Coal mining at Thurber was a far cry from the coal fields of Pennsylvania. In these eastern fields miners often can stand upright to wield their picks, shovels, and electric drills. Because the coal face at Thurber was never more than thirty inches thick at any point, the miner had to lie on his side in a narrow tunnel. From this cramped position, he would swing his pick until noon. He brought his lunch pail so he ate his noon meal where he dug and was quickly back to work, because the more coal he dug, the more he was paid. He would continue his back-breaking labor until the day-end whistle blew at 5:30 P.M. Back in the fresh air at the surface, he would board the Black Diamond, which returned him to the point from which he had departed twelve hours previously. Before he reached home, however, he might stop in at the Snake or Lizard for a couple of beers and camaraderie.

As the coal was dug out of the vein, it was loaded in carts that were pulled to the elevator by mules that lived out their lives at the bottom of the mines. When the carts reached the top of the tipple, the coal was dumped onto a twelve-foot-long inclined screen into a railroad car below.

The one and one-quarter-inch screen filtered out the noncommercial pea-sized coal or slack— about an eighth of each load. Because it reduced their tonnage, and consequently their wages, the screening process engendered much strife and resentment among the miners.[72] One possible use for the pea coal would have been to pulverize it into coke. Gordon wrote of such a conversion effort: "In 1895, a small coke manufacturing plant was established to produce a grade of coke from the screening. The percentage of ash in this coke was finally reduced to about 16%, and for a while, the demand for the product was greater than the output. However, the smelting plants in Arizona which were users of this coke finally canceled orders and declared that the percentage of ash was so high that they could not use it profitably in their smelters. At a later date the ovens were demolished."[73]

Although the T&P mines were among the best equipped and safest in the country, nevertheless accidents did occur. One of those accidents occurred on February 17, 1897, when a raging fire destroyed Mine No. 5. The *Thurber Journal* on February 20, 1897, graphically described the action:

THE TIPPLE AND ENGINE HOUSE LICKED UP BY THE FIERY FIEND. THE NIGHT SHIFT AT WORK IN THE MINES BROUGHT OUT BY COURAGEOUS FRIENDS— ELEVEN MULES SUFFOCATED.

It was 5:29 A.M., Wednesday, at that hour when sleep is sweetest, at that hour which, when one is aroused, one feels he would exchange his dearest treasure for "just another nap" when the appealing shrieks of the steam whistle at No. 5 shaft was heard, and at a glance in that direction showed the heavens lighted by reflection from a raging blaze.

While those in the vicinity of the shaft, one and a half miles from town, were hurrying to the scene, the townspeople were none the less active, for night watchman Singleton was busying himself giving the alarm and arousing the company officials and other employees, who responded with the promptness so characteristic of our people in answering distress calls.

In a remarkably short time, the livery stable was emptied of horses and vehicles, and an army of determined men were on their way. Determined, if possible, to rescue and preserve the lives of men whom they felt sure were entombed in the bowels of Mother Earth, doubtless unaware of their danger. Scores of men followed this cavalry on foot. And soon one of the locomotive engines was thundering over the hill, drawing a number of coaches filled with miners and others anxious to risk their own lives for those of their friends and comrades. On this train was Col. R. D. Hunter, President and General Manager, who at the first alarm, though unwell, hurriedly prepared to go. Not knowing the nature of the trouble, he felt his presence was needed, feeling, too, solicitous of the welfare of his employees.

It was the tipple over the main shaft on fire, which soon spread to the engine and boiler houses and fan house, the blaze originating in top of the tipple in the weigh room, and it is supposed, from a torch, carelessly placed by one of the slate-dumpers too near the cinder-like woodwork.

It was within fifteen minutes of time to sound the whistle for a change of shift, when night engineer Brewster discovered the fire, and immediately ran up in the tipple, but so rapidly had the flames taken hold, he could do nothing, and he at once realized the place was doomed, and hurried to give the alarm by putting all the power that steam could exert into the huge steam whistle, and with remarkable presence of mind started his pumps going, setting every fire-fighting apparatus at hand to play on the flames.

At the first glance of those rapidly arriving, the picture of certain death and destruction sprang up, more vividly than can be described, and the fate of those fifty human souls in various portions of the mine, ignorant of the death-dealing flames raging above them, which threatened to shut off their every means of escape, was problematical.

Every structure on top was doomed. The flames were shooting high into space, and seemed with demon-like hilarity to mock the very efforts of those who would attempt to check them. But the fan-house over the air-shaft and man-way adjoining the engine room was the last to ignite from the intense heat, and this, as the only means of escape for the entombed miners, must be saved even at the sacrifice of the lives of those who would attempt it. The fan-house was the only salvation and the fire fiend was rapidly eating its way into it.

Assistant Superintendent J. H. McLure was among the first to arrive, Superintendent Gordon being out of the city. The heat about the structure was so intense that it was almost beyond human endurance to stand it, but Mac, standing at the man-way, shouted out: "This fan-house must be saved! Those men in the pit must be warned! Who'll follow me to deliver this message of life or death?"

To this responded the voices of Robert McKinnon, Ben Matthews, Robert Beveridge, James McCleary, Tom Coulson, Ben and Harry Brookman, James Blackwell and Jimmie Nickol, who said, "We'll go!"

The crowd, by this time numbering several hundred, was paralyzed by their admiration for the courage of the daring men who were taking one chance in a thousand for their lives, but the thought of those poor souls underground urged them to sacrifice. These men gathered around the man-way, and Mac called out to the crowd, "Men, save the fan-house or we perish . . . God help us!" And then they were lost to view, and the prayers from hundreds of hearts went up in their behalf. While the demonstration of human endurance from the fire fighters was admirable, it seemed as though it was a fight against Fate.

Colonel Hunter was in the midst of the workers and his encouraging words urged them to superhuman efforts. Piece by piece the burning woodwork was torn away, and as the pumps and fan had stopped, a bucket brigade of a hundred or more was quickly formed from the tank, and a deluge of water was hurled down the air shaft and thrown upon the burning fan-house, this water down the air shaft being the only means of forcing air and keeping it fresh throughout the pit for the salvation of the men therein.

The woodwork of the main shaft was burning to the bottom of the pit and none save those on the bottom knew the extent of the fury, and this apparently insurmountable condition of things confronted the brave little party of rescuers who had gone down.

The miners were scattered at various places throughout the mine for a distance of three-quarters of a mile in different directions, and no intimation of their peril could reach them until the lack of air warned them, unless the rescuers could reach them. To go through this fiery furnace was apparently certain death, and to go around was over 1,000 feet one way and three-quarters of a mile the other. To act, and to act quickly was imperative. McLure, McCleary, Beveridge and Coulson decided to go through, and placing sponges in their mouths, they did so, while the others, taking a southern route went on their errand of mercy. The air was yet good, but smoke was filling the roadways, and the rescuers had to grope their way as best they could until they were far back in the entries, where the miners were peacefully digging away, and were loathe to believe that peril was so near. Most of them being foreigners, it was difficult to make them understand the situation, as the smoke and lack of air had not reached them. They were corralled, about forty of them, and the journey, and a difficult one it was, was taken up by an old "return" way, not shorter than three-quarters of a mile, and finally the "bottom" was reached, and the miners formed into a line at the mouth of the man-way. But the rescuers, almost exhausted, knew not the condition of things above, knew not whether the fan-house had been saved, or whether, now that they were at the mouth of the man-way, they were doomed not again ever to see the light of day. For had the fan-house burned, the man-way and air shaft would have been filled with burning debris, shutting off their only means of escape.

At this time, the encouraging voices of another party composed of Captain Eddy, John Murphy, Thomas Armstrong and others whose names we have been unable to get, were heard descending the man-way, through smoke and heat, which told to the now almost exhausted party of fifty or sixty that life was yet in reach, but that an effort was necessary to obtain it, and soon the slow process of ascent was begun, only two or three being allowed to proceed at a time.

The scene at the top can't be described. As the smoke begrimed miners emerged from the manhole, they fell exhausted upon fathers, mothers, wives, brothers, sisters and friends, and were borne away in love's arms, and not until the last one was safe on terra firma did the rescuers come up. By many, who perhaps had never before called His name in reverence, the words "Thank God" were uttered.

During the entire time the bucket brigade worked heroically, and right here we must mention a scene seldom witnessed on an occasion of this kind . . . the fact that 15 or 20 young ladies were in the line, working with a determination. Among the entombed men were their fathers, brothers, sweethearts and friends, and their devotion to the effort to save their lives was admirable.

On the bottom there were 22 mules, and of this number, 11 died of suffocation. Their quarter is near the main shaft, and so dense was the smoke and heat that those nearest could not survive it. This gives the reader an inkling of what the rescuers and miners were compelled to pass through.

While everything on top was destroyed, except the fan-house, and much damage resulted to the timbers in the main shaft and near the pit bottom, it will in no way interfere with the output of coal, for No. 8, the new shaft which the company has been holding in reserve for a year, was at once put into operation.[74]

The eleven mules that survived the fire and most of the tools and equipment in Mine No. 5 were removed with portable hoisting apparatus, but the mine, opened in 1892, was almost worked out and was never reopened. Its total production in its five-year life was 432,280 tons. After the fire, greater precautions were taken to ensure the safety of the miners. Most of the newer mines had alternate escape routes, tunnels driven to another mine.[75] For their acts of heroism during the conflagration, Colonel Hunter presented each rescuer with a gold medal, appropriately inscribed. Among the honorees were Robert McKinnon and Ben Matthews, who had been maligned by the "Avengers" over the Grant's saloon incident.[76]

About 1897 a use was found for the pea coal or slack that had no commercial value as locomotive fuel because it would not burn as efficiently as lump coal. Because pea coal could not be sold, the company gained no profit and the miners gained no wages. Hunter's Scottish heritage instilled within him a deep dislike for this conspicuous waste.

Hunter began to look for a way to use the pea coal and became interested in the shale deposits on the coal company property. With the idea in mind of using it for manufacturing brick, he decided to explore the concept further. But in 1897 Colonel Hunter's robust health began to wither. With failing health, it would seem unlikely that he would have on his own commenced a new, enormous, and risky venture. According to W. K. Gordon, Jr., it was not Hunter but the younger Gordon's father who was the impetus behind making brick from the shale. "When my father first came to Texas, he got off the train at Gordon and even before going to his hotel he started walking the hills. He was always interested in geology and terrain. He was always thinking about what the land would produce. He walked the rest of that first afternoon around the hills to see what the country was like. After he was hired by Colonel Hunter, he kept walking

Brick plant, built in 1897, located southeast of town. Courtesy Dick Smith Library, Tarleton State University.

around, surveying the area to see where to dig a coal mine. It was said that you could show him a ledge of rock in the Thurber area and he could tell you within a few feet the exact depth from the surface to the coal at that point. While he was walking one day after a rain, he got mud on his boots. Then an idea hit like a ton of bricks! He studied the mud and burned it. It looked as if it would make brick. He or Colonel Hunter sent a sample to a laboratory in St. Louis. The report came back positive."[77]

Hunter and Gordon quickly realized that Thurber's gray shale could be turned into red rubies. The wasted pea coal was more than suitable to fire furnaces in a brick-making factory and would cost nothing because the miners were not paid for pea coal that fell through the screen. Also, there was a practically inexhaustible mountain of raw material—the shale that the technicians said was perfect for the manufacture of drain tile, roof and floor tile, and dry-pressed and vitrified brick. Their imagination was aided, no doubt, by the fact that to the east at Rock Creek, in the southwest corner of neighboring Parker County, George Bennett had started making brick in 1891 in a factory that survives today as the Acme Brick Company.[78]

Because Texas & Pacific's charter did not provide for the manufacture of brick, in March 1897, the Green and Hunter Brick Company was incorporated with capital stock of one hundred thousand dollars. By the end of summer, the best equipped brick plant of its kind west of the Mississippi was producing dry-pressed building bricks. In 1898 a paving brick department was added. The brick plant was located less than one-half mile southeast of Thurber's business district, just east of the company's first mine shaft. To furnish draft for its kilns, a 160-foot-high red brick smokestack was constructed in 1898. (This stack is not to be confused with the one that was raised ten years later for the power complex, which is the stack still standing today).

America was in the last decade of the nineteenth century. The twentieth century, which would see great corporations rising with worker migration across the country, was fast approaching. Those corporations seeking a new locale for a plant or office would always be interested in the school system that a prospective city offered. Hunter and Gordon were ahead of the times, because after taking over the camp and encircling it with a fence, they not only built homes for the workers, but they also built schools for them and their children. They recognized that while feeding the mind, the spirit—the soul—must also be nourished. So along with the homes and schools, they also built churches. All were owned by the company.

A baby could be born in a company house with a company doctor in attendance, swaddled in clothing from the company dry goods store, nourished by food from the company grocery store, attend school in a company-owned building, and upon reaching adulthood be employed in one of the company enterprises. He could be married in a company church building and move his bride into a company house furnished with furniture and fittings purchased from the company store. At death, his body would be prepared for burial by the company undertaker, placed in a coffin purchased from the company and buried on the company's Cemetery Hill.

The company's stores did their greatest volume of business after 4:00 P.M., as the miners returned from work or the children were coming home from school. Due to the crowded condition of the grocery store and meat market, a customer would often face an hour's wait for service. To ameliorate this problem, "order wagons" were introduced. They would travel about the town each morning, taking orders for supplies to be delivered in the afternoon.[79]

Company officials maintained that the stores were solely for the convenience of the residents, but Thurberites looked upon the barbed-wire enclosure as a devil's device to ensure a lucrative monopoly for the company marts. Gatekeepers were stationed at each entrance to bar enterprising peddlers from bringing their wares into town. Purchases of returning residents were confiscated. Although the company might have achieved some success in keeping peddlers out and miners in, there was one potent force it could not inhibit or intimidate—the U.S. mail. By 1898 mail order catalogs were being delivered to Thurber.

✦

In 1886, Richard Sears was a twenty-two-year old railroad agent in North Redwood, Minnesota. Having on his hands an undeliverable consignment of watches, he discovered that he could sell such merchandise to agents down the line, who sold it in their towns. Sears paid the manufacturers when the agents paid him, so he needed no capital. He made five thousand dollars in six months, quit his six dollars a week railroad job and working with Alvah Roebuck, by 1898 was sending 583-page catalogs into the prairie.

Sears, Roebuck's path had been blazed by another Midwestern merchandizing genius, Aaron Montgomery Ward. As a traveling salesman of dry goods, Ward had discovered what railroads and the Homestead Act had wrought: a vast, thinly settled inland empire of lonely farm families.

Sears, Roebuck prospered with the help of Rural Free Delivery, which made the Big Book as central to many rural lives as the Good Book. Indeed, in an oft-told story, a boy who was asked by his Sunday School teacher where the Ten Commandments come from replied, "Sears, Roebuck." In 1907, Sears mailed three million fall catalogs.[80]

✦

A more rigid and efficient method of compelling a resident to patronize company stores was permitting charge accounts with settlement by deduction from wages on payday. A system of scrip, called "check," was later

Scrip used at Thurber stores. Issued in books with values of $1 to $10, individual coupons, came in denominations of five, ten, and twenty-five cents. Courtesy Dick Smith Library, Tarleton State University.

instituted. This ensured that the worker would spend his earnings in town, because the scrip was good only in Thurber. Before the miner had dug the coal and earned his money, he could obtain coupon books on credit at the pay office. Coupons were accepted as cash in the company stores as payments for goods. Scrip, like credit cards of the future, was addictive. Come payday, the amount owed for the scrip was deducted from wages before the miner received a cent. As the lyrics of the song so aptly put it, "I owe my soul to the company store." Once each month, the check that had accumulated in the store office was taken to the brickyard and burned in one of the kiln fireboxes. Transportation to the brick plant and the actual burning was carried out under the supervision of armed guards.[81]

Now with a decade of growth under its belt, Thurber's housing began to take on a somewhat more subdued and bourgeoisie appearance compared to the original red or green shotgun houses. New housing was of frame construction, with weather-boarding on the outside and interior walls of shiplap (wood boards grooved so the edges overlap adjacent boards to make a flush joint). These houses were finished on the inside with paint and wallpaper. Outside, they were painted gray with a white trim.[82]

Although Hunter was diligent in building houses for the miners, it does not appear that he was overly concerned about where he slept in Thurber. He apparently maintained quarters in one of the public buildings before the Hotel Knox was built in 1894 after which that likely would have been his Thurber address.[83] The Colonel more than compensated for his modest Thurber digs by the elegant home he built in the Quality Hill area of Fort Worth.

In 1866, Fort Worth was only a small settlement of some three hundred. (According to Colonel Hunter, Thurber's population reached three hundred in 1888.[84]) Following the arrival of the Texas & Pacific Railway in 1876, the small village began to blossom and bloom so that, during the Gay Nineties, incredibly beautiful ranch and Victorian mansions were popping up all over. With its playhouses, concert halls, churches, and social clubs, Fort Worth was called the "Queen of the Prairie."[85] By 1996 the city's population was in excess of five hundred thousand; Thurber's was five.

Noah Harding, cashier of Fort Worth National Bank, erected the first of the imposing mansions along Summit Avenue in 1890. Colonel Hunter followed suit seven years later in 1897 when he built an impressive residence at the northeast corner of Summit and El Paso.[86] The next-door neighbor to Colonel Hunter was cattle baron George T. Reynolds. This beautiful home with oak doors, stained-glass windows, and walnut paneling was built in 1901 and stood until 1992, when it was demolished after a protracted battle between preservationists and a group of doctors. Other mansions built on Summit were those of Samuel B. Burnett, Dan Waggoner and son W. T. Waggoner, and Winfield Scott. Almost a century later, Scott's magnificent home, Thistle Hill, built in 1903-04, is still looking north across Pennsylvania Avenue down Summit.

After completion of his home in Fort Worth in 1897, Hunter's health began to decline. During the year of 1898 he suffered a long illness.

✦

Colonel Hunter was not the only one to suffer a restriction upon his activities and movements in the year of 1897. In Eastland, ten miles west of Ranger and forty miles west of Thurber, a strange experiment took place. News of the event swept over the entire region and became the talk of Texas. Texas's most famous horned lizard (more commonly referred to as a horned frog or horny toad) Old Rip was buried alive in a cornerstone of the Eastland County Courthouse. He was entombed by a county clerk who was curious about old timers' claims that these lizards can survive for years without light, water, or air. The outcome of the clerk's experiment would not be revealed until that court house time capsule was opened three decades later.[87]

✦

The year 1898 year marked the beginning of the march of the United States to superpower status. The first European power that would be bruised by the new colossus would be Spain. In Havana harbor the U.S. battleship Maine exploded on 15 February. It was said that Spain was the culprit (although later it was proven to be a defective boiler). The cry rang out in the town of Thurber as it did all over America: "Remember the Maine!" Colonel Teddy Roosevelt—a man right out of the mold of Colonel Robert D. Hunter—led his Rough Riders up San Juan Hill, and six hundred Marines landed at Guantanamo where a makeshift band played "There'll be a Hot Time In The Old Town Tonight." In the treaty signed at the end of the war, Spain granted Cuba its freedom and ceded to the U.S. the Philippines, Puerto Rico, and Guam. America was now recognized as a world power.

◆

In 1899, Mine No. 9, located one mile south of No. 8, was opened at a depth of 190 feet. In operation now were four mines: Nos. 6, 7, 8, and 9. Hunter McLean wrote that No. 9 was known as "Warfield" in honor of Mary Joseph Warfield Ward, wife of attorney Robert Henry Ward, Assistant General Manager and house counsel of Texas & Pacific. Ward left Thurber in 1899 and was replaced as Assistant General Manager by Hunter's son-in-law, John Phelan.

Hunter's health improved somewhat and hope flickered that he might soon be able to resume his vigorous life style, but at the time of the death of his brother William in November 1899, he was bedridden at his palatial home and unable to attend the funeral.

In December 1899, Hunter relinquished his position with Texas & Pacific Coal Company. Hunter's other son-in-law, Edgar L. Marston, known for his dapper-attire and fashionably trimmed mustache, was at the time living in New York. Marston was chosen to succeed Hunter as President. W. K. Gordon, Superintendent and General Manager, was left in charge in Thurber.[88]

In 1900, Mine No. 6 was abandoned. It had produced 372,817 tons over seven years. Mine Nos. 7, 8, and 9 continued to produce. Total lump coal mined in 1900 was 323,534 tons. Disposition of this output was as follows: Texas & Pacific Railway 292,084 tons; Southern Pacific Railway 21,916 tons; Fort Worth & Rio Grande Railway 593 tons; commercial sales 8,346 tons; used at Thurber 440 tons; donated to sundry causes 155 tons.[89]

In 1900, for a consideration of $91,233.21, 1,820 of the 2,000 shares of Green and Hunter were transferred to Texas & Pacific, which had amended its charter to permit the manufacture and sale of bricks. Despite launching into the brick-making business, the company did not change its name to Texas & Pacific Coal and Brick Company.[90]

Hardly had the brick plant been completed when contractors for Galveston County, Texas, came calling in Thurber to buy bricks—lots of bricks. On September 8, 1900, a disastrous hurricane struck Galveston, killing about six thousand people. It was one of the worst disasters to date in North America. The county subsequently built a huge concrete, granite, and sandstone seawall to guard against future hurricanes. Along the base of the wall, ten-mile long, four-lane Seawall Boulevard was constructed with millions of vitrified Thurber brick. Two months after the Galveston hurricane, President McKinley was reelected, again defeating Democrat William Jennings Bryan. Elected vice president was forty-two-year-old Rough Rider Theodore Roosevelt.

The new twentieth century was only ten days old when a well being drilled by Captain Anthony F. Lucas at Spindletop, near Beaumont, blew in on January 10, 1901. It proved to be one of the world's greatest gushers and a portent of events that would soon begin in West Texas.

In 1901, Mine No. 10, located one-half mile northwest of No. 8, was opened at a depth of 235 feet. Four mines were active: Nos. 7, 8, 9, and 10.

✦

About the time that Mine No. 10 was opened in 1901, a twenty-six-year-old Italian miner by the name of Giovanni Sartore died. Although it is relatively easy to trace the history of Thurber's founders like Colonel Hunter and W. K. Gordon, what do we know of those men like Giovanni Sartore who toiled and sweat in the mines? What happened to them? Many of them found their final resting place in the picturesque 9.1-acre mesa-like cemetery that crowns the hill just north of Thurber. The burial ground, reached by a rugged, rocky road, is diagonally bisected by the Palo Pinto-Erath County line. The oldest grave is that of an African-American baby girl, Eva Chapman, infant daughter of W. T. and A. C. Chapman, who was born and died in 1890. More than one thousand people are buried in the cemetery, but through the ravages of time and the elements more than two-thirds of the graves today are unmarked.[91]

Jon McConal wrote about Giovanni Sartore's grave:

Forgive Gino Sartore if he seemed excited as he drank coffee in Thurber's New York Hill restaurant. After all, he was about to see for the first time the grave of the first member of the Sartore family to be buried in this country.

The grave is that of his uncle, Giovanni Sartore, who came to this country in the late 1800s to work in the Thurber coal mines. Those mines attracted thousands of immigrants. Many had left behind families they would never see again except in fading photographs.

The fact that any of the Sartore family would be able to see the grave is due in large part to chance and in another part to the meticulous work of the Thurber Cemetery Association in restoring the cemetery during the last year.

"There were over 1,000 people buried up there," said Leo Bielinski, who has helped in that effort. "But so far we have only identified 300 of the graves."

The grave of Sartore's uncle is one of those 300. His uncle was the oldest in a family of four boys and three girls.

"My father [Lorenzo] was only 7 when he [Giovanni] came to America. But as far as we can tell, my uncle worked in the coal mines near Pittsburgh before coming here in about 1897," Sartore said.

Apparently, soon after his arrival he joined the company band, called Hunter's Band. He played the trombone. Bielinski, who has done tons of research on the area, showed a copy of the picture of Giovanni in his band uniform. He is dressed in a fancy uniform and has a lock of dark hair falling across his forehead.

Sartore said he heard his father talk about his uncle for most of his life. So when Sartore was attending a Dallas convention about 14 years ago, he rented a car and drove here for the first time. He tried unsuccessfully to find his uncle's grave. "The cemetery was so overgrown," he said.

But he told Les Mullins of Hereford about his efforts. One day Mullins stopped and made a two-hour unsuccessful search of the cemetery. He left his card at the nearby Mingus City Hall. Somebody gave it to Bielinski.

"My hair stood up on my neck," Bielinski said. "We had just dug up a broken tombstone and was putting it back together. It apparently belonged to Gino's uncle."

After confirmation, Sartore returned last week to look at his uncle's marker. We drove past foothills clotted with mesquite and the site of some of the old coal mines where Giovanni could have worked.

We went to the Thurber Cemetery on top of a mesa and stopped at the Sartore marker, which was engraved in Italian. Sartore translated the words: STAR OF ITALY Born June 20, 1875; Died March 29, 1901.

"We think Star of Italy must have been some lodge."

Lettering on the bottom is broken. But Sartore knelt, felt it and finally said, "I've got that. It's 'Pray for his soul.'"

He stood up. Tony Sico, his associate, took his photograph. Sartore, 72, is lanky. The wind caught his hair, dashing it onto his forehead. It looked just like that falling into his uncle's face with one difference. Gino's hair is white.[92]

Under a hot sun on June 12, 1993, before perhaps a hundred Thurberphiles, a gray granite monument was unveiled in the cemetery by W. K. Gordon, Jr. Engraved on the rock are the names of Giovanni Sartore and all others known to have been buried there.

◆

The small electric plant that was built in Thurber in 1895 was replaced in 1901 by a large direct current dynamo, and the town became completely electrified. Several years later, an alternating current generator was installed capable of generating twenty-three thousand volts, and Thurber became the only city in the state, or perhaps the world, having two complete sets of electrical wiring in every house. The two systems became known as "day current" and "night current" with the DC (direct current) being used during daylight hours and the AC (alternating current) after nightfall.[93]

On June 1, 1901, the Colonel and son-in-law John Phelan executed articles of incorporation for Hunter-Phelan Savings and Trust Company in Fort Worth. This company was located at the corner of Houston and Eighth Streets, where later one of Fort Worth's first skyscrapers, the W. T. Waggoner Building, would be built.[94]

◆

On September 6, 1901, President McKinley went to Buffalo, New York, to attend the opening ceremonies for the Pan American Exposition. As the handshaking throng filed past the president at a reception in the Temple of Music, Leon Czolgoz, carrying a revolver wrapped in a handkerchief, approached McKinley, who, thinking the man's hand was wounded, reached for his left hand. As he did so, Czolgoz fired twice. The president sank back, wounded twice in the abdomen. He lingered several days. The twenty-fifth president of the United States was the third to be assassinated. He would not be the last.

Forty-two-year-old Theodore Roosevelt entered the White House. The new president was a man after the Colonel's own heart. Although neither was born in the West, both adopted and then went on to nurture a life-long love of the West. Like Hunter, he was a man of immense self-confidence and firm conviction. His motto: "Speak softly and carry a big stick!" The hero of San Juan Hill observed only half of his motto, for he was not one to speak softly. He did, however, most definitely carry a big stick. Without a doubt, Hunter admired the charismatic young president.

◆

In 1902 Swift and Armour opened packing houses in Fort Worth rather than ship the cattle from Fort Worth to northern points for slaughter. Colonel Hunter, who had made his first fortune in the cattle business, surely observed this new development with intense interest.

Although 1902 was a very good year for Fort Worth, the same could not be said for Thurber. In the pre-dawn hours of 25 February the company's big general store and bakery were destroyed by fire, leaving the town of five thousand without food. Ed S. Britton, who was then in charge of the Mercantile Department, took the early morning train to Fort Worth to obtain supplies. A warehouse was quickly converted into a grocery store, and by 1:30 P.M. of the same day, provisions were arriving and the employees were being served over the counter with supplies.[95] By 1 March, only four days after the fire, the Thurber newspaper carried a front page story advising that everything was back to normal, that stocks had been replenished and that the grocery and meat market were staffed by clerks who spoke English, Italian, Polish, and Spanish.[96]

The year 1902 ended on a sad and somber note. On 7 November, Colonel Robert D. Hunter died at his Fort Worth residence on Summit Avenue and El Paso. He was sixty-nine years old when he died, four months shy of his seventieth birthday. A 33rd Degree Mason and active member of the Shrine, Hunter was buried in St. Louis's beautiful Bellefontaine Cemetery. Originally buried on the lot of his deceased brother William, he was reinterred in 1903 on the large R. D. Hunter family plot.

◆

Historic Bellefontaine Cemetery is the final resting place of many who contributed conspicuously to the westward growth of our country. A few of note: Thomas Hart Benton, Missouri's first United States Senator, stalwart champion of the West, advocate of hard money, and defender of the Union; Captain James B. Eads, who, in 1874, completed the Eads Bridge–the first steel bridge to span the Mississippi River; General William Clark of Lewis and Clark Expedition fame; Adolphus Busch who with his father-in-law Eberhardt Anheuser established St. Louis's most famous brewery; Sara Teasdale, who, in 1918, won the first Pulitzer Prize for Poetry ever awarded; James S. McDonnell, founder of the great McDonnell Aircraft Company; Captain Henry M. Shreve, who built the first practical boat for use on the Mississippi, and whose name is immortalized in Shreveport, Louisiana; and William S. Burroughs, inventor of the mechanical calculator which made the Burroughs Corporation known throughout the world.[97]

Colonel Hunter on horseback, circa 1895. Courtesy Nita Stewart Haley Memorial Library, Midland, Texas.

3

In his *First Annual Report*, Colonel Hunter had estimated the 1890 population of Thurber at thirteen hundred. Upon his death in 1902 it had grown to approximately five thousand, most of whom were foreigners. From the dismal mining camp of Johnsonville in 1888 to the electrified city that Thurber had become at the advent of the twentieth century, Robert D. Hunter and W. K. Gordon had truly made a silk purse out of a sow's ear. Upon Hunter's retirement in 1899, local control of the company had passed into Gordon's hands. Now with the old Scotsman dead and buried in St. Louis and President Edgar L. Marston far off in New York, Thurber became known as "Gordon's Kingdom." The miners both feared and revered him, calling him the "Bigga Boss."

To fill its manpower needs the company maintained employment offices in New York, New Orleans, and Galveston. When a man who could not speak English was hired at one of these offices, a tag showing his destination was attached to his clothing and he was placed on a train for Thurber. Around the turn of the century, the nation's immigration laws were more liberal than those of later years. To attract settlers and give every immigrant an opportunity to become an American citizen, the district court for each county was empowered to grant citizenship certificates to those of foreign birth. Each applicant for U.S. citizenship was required to file with the district clerk three forms: (1) a Certificate of Arrival, naming the country of origin, the name of the vessel transporting the applicant to the United States, the port of entry, and the date of arrival; (2) a Declaration of Intention, stating that it was the applicant's desire to become an American citizen, renouncing any allegiance to a former government; and (3) a Petition for Naturalization, containing the same information as the Declaration of Intention, together with the names of the immigrant's spouse and children and the applicant's occupation. When the Petition for Naturalization was signed by the applicant, a witness, and the district clerk, citizenship papers were issued. Most of the immigrants arriving in Thurber lost little time in fulfilling these obligations—becoming an American citizen was a long-cherished dream of many. The fee for becoming a citizen was one dollar, one-half of which went to the state.[1]

As immigrants arrived from their native lands, they segregated themselves according to nationality. The Italians settled for the most part south of the railroad line leading to the mines, on No. 3 Hill. This became known as Italian Hill. Polish immigrants settled on the north end of the same hill and their section was called Polander Hill. Each nationality brought from its native land not only the language, but customs and practices strange to the inhabitants of western America. Eventually, all blended into one harmonious community.

Because the Italians were in the majority, their customs became better known than those of other foreign-born people. Each Italian home had a backyard oven where homemade bread was baked. A fire would be lighted in the oven and allowed to burn until the bricks reached the desired temperature for baking. The fire was then removed and the loaves placed in the oven by means of a long-handled wooden shovel and allowed to bake until done. This bread, called *pang*, had a heavier texture and thicker crust than American bread, and was preferred by Italians over the bread baked in the company bakery. Bread was baked twice weekly and on baking days a delicious aroma of fresh baked bread hung over the entire community. Many of the Italian homes also had wine cellars. These were usually walled and floored with brick and provided storage for the family's wine, cheese, and meats. Almost every event of importance was celebrated with a dance. The Italians had their own dance hall and danced their traditional dances as well as new ones they learned in America.

The Polish population also had a dance hall. It was here that the three-day wedding dances were usually held. Polish wedding celebrations were gala affairs in Thurber. On the day of the wedding, the groom would drive his bride to the church in a buggy, followed by the bride's attendants and friends of the couple. An accordion player accompanied the procession to the profusely decorated church where the wedding vows were solemnized. On the wedding night, dancing began at dusk either in the home of the bride's parents or the Polish dance hall, and continued for three days and nights. Guests who wished to dance with the bride would first have to break a dinner plate by throwing a silver dollar or half dollar at it. The ammunition became the property of the happy couple.[2]

Mexicans living "on the hill," had their own holidays and fiestas, chief among which were Septiembre diez y seis (September 16) and Cinco de Mayo (May 5). September 16 is Mexican Independence Day. It was on that day in 1810 that a fatherly parish priest named Miguel Hidalgo rang church bells in the little town of Dolores, summoning his congregation of peasants to revolt against the intolerable injustices imposed upon them by Spanish rule. Cinco de Mayo celebrates the victory of Benito Juarez over the French at the Battle of Puebla in 1862.

Christmas was observed by the Mexicans from December 16 to January 6. The high point of the celebration was the breaking of the piñata, a gaily decorated pastel papier-mache figure, often of a toro (bull), filled with gifts and candy. It hung by a cord from the ceiling. The children were blind-folded and took turns trying to break the piñata with a stick. When it broke, gifts and candy scattered to the ground, and the children scam-pered after them.

For women, the Mexican holiday costume consisted of a full red and green skirt decorated with sequins and beads, an embroidered short-sleeved blouse and a silk shawl. The men wore the traditional costume of the matador, a bolero and tightly fitting pants ending just below the knee. A wide brimmed sombrero completed the holiday attire.[3]

In 1903 all Thurber was feasting from a bountiful supply, the brick makers on a mountain of shale, the miners on an underground mountain of coal. On February 25, 1903, W. K. Gordon married Fay Kearby of Dal-las. The Hotel Knox was the social center of Thurber, and it was there that a grand ball honoring the newlyweds was held. The Gordons continued to live at the hotel until they moved into an executive home on Marston Ave-nue.[4] Less than a week after his wedding, another event occurred that was to loom large in the life of W. K. Gordon. On 3 March of that year, South-western Life—an insurance company—was born. The company had its home office in Dallas and was to become the premier life insurance com-pany in Texas. On May 1, 1903, Gordon became one of its original stock-holders and during the years increased his holdings until at the time of his death, nearly half a century later, he was its largest single stockholder.[5]

✦

For fifteen years, the body of Harvey Johnson had lain moldering in his brother Will's backyard mausoleum. At the time of his death in 1888, it had been deemed unwise because of old debt problems for Harvey to be taken back to Michigan for burial. When his mother died in 1903, Harvey's remains were finally sent home. A front page story in the *Gordon Weekly Courier* of May 28, 1903, explains:

Strawn, Texas

The Ionia, Michigan *Standard* contains the following obituary of Mrs. Jane Whipple Johnson, who was well known and highly respected by the people of Strawn who had the pleasure to know her. Mrs. Johnson often visited her son, William W. of this place, and her Christian character and kind disposi-tion made her a universal favorite, and our people sympathize with her fam-ily in their sad bereavement.

Died in Los Angeles, California, December 8, 1902, Mrs. Jane Whipple Johnson, widow of Ethan S. Johnson of Ionia, Michigan.

Mrs. Jane Whipple Johnson was a daughter of Zebulon and Phoebe (An-drews) Whipple and was born in Ridgeway, New York, September 17, 1823, and came to Michigan with her parents when a child; was married to Ethan S. Johnson in Ionia in 1840 and had resided in Ionia many years.

The famous Hotel Knox built in 1894 and destroyed by fire in 1907. Courtesy Dick Smith Library, Tarleton State University.

At the time of her death she was visiting her daughter Marion (Mrs. E.G. Faulkner) in Los Angeles. Mr. and Mrs. Oscar H. Dean went to Los Angeles upon the receipt of the telegram announcing to Mrs. Dean the serious illness of her mother. They did not reach there in time to see her alive. Mrs. Johnson's son William W. who resides in Strawn, Texas was present at her death bed. Mrs. Johnson's body was embalmed and placed in the family mausoleum, with that of her son Harvey (who died in Texas many years ago), until Mrs. Dean, who was in poor health and remained at her brother's home for treatment, should be able to return home. Mrs. Dean returned to Ionia on April 23rd, with the remains of her mother and brother Harvey for burial beside her father Ethan S. Johnson.

Mrs. Jane Whipple Johnson was a granddaughter of William Whipple, one of the signers of the Declaration of Independence. As a daughter, wife and mother, Mrs. Johnson's life was an exemplary one and worthy of a descendant of the illustrious Revolutionary ancestors who were prominent in the great struggle for liberty and the founding of the great Republic. At the time of her death, she was the oldest communicant of the First Baptist Church of Ionia.

✦

In 1903, two things happened in the brickmaking end of the enterprise. First, Gordon put in place facilities for the manufacturing of vitrified brick.

Second, a better grade of shale was discovered on a hill one mile to the north. For the first six years of operation, the shale used in brickmaking had been taken from the hill adjacent to the brickyard site. Today one can stand on the site of the plant, which was located south of present day Interstate 20, and to the north see evidence of how the hill was scalped to provide shale to feed the plant.

Through the first eight months of 1903 everything in Thurber, on the surface, was serene and productive. But there had been ominous and disquieting signs that the situation was about to change. The company had enjoyed peaceful labor relations since 1894 when Hunter with the help of the Texas Rangers had put down the insurrection of the "Avengers" who had vowed to kill him. Now, a decade later, Hunter was dead, and in September 1903, labor strife again would crackle through Thurber. The United Mine Workers (UMW) came to unscab an old wound.

On September 17 and 24 and October 1, 1903, the *United Mine Workers Journal* published a description of conditions it said prevailed at the mines. The acidic bitterness that had been directed towards Hunter now splashed on Gordon:

> This tyranny has been going on from the time the mines were opened, and the only way we can account for its existing so long is by reason of Thurber being an isolated village and miners being largely foreigners, Italians, Slavs, Poles and Mexicans. For 14 years, there was a reign of terror in Thurber, and the miners were compelled to obey blindly the rules of the company.
>
> As an illustration of the power of this man Gordon, King of Thurber, we have but to mention a prohibition election that was held there not long ago. Three commissioners were appointed, and at the request of King Gordon, two commissioners decided that Thurber, in Erath County, should be exempt from the Erath County election, and this over the strenuous objection of the third commissioner. The election was held and the county went dry. But Thurber is wet today. And all of this in the great State of Texas. However, for years Thurber has not been reckoned as a part of the State, but a little kingdom all by itself. It is a common expression, when some particular outrage committed became known, to say, "Oh, that's Thurber."

In 1890, the Knights of Labor merged with the United Mine Workers of America. Both unions had been steadily losing strength, but having combined, brought notable order into the chaos of the national industry. For the next several years, the organization concentrated its efforts in the eastern coal fields of Pennsylvania, West Virginia, and Kentucky, finally moving into Illinois, Indian Territory, Arkansas, and Texas. By 1900, strong unions dominated the mines in Indian Territory and in Texas at Lyra, Rock Creek, Bridgeport and Alba. In 1903, the United Mine Workers turned its attention to Thurber.

Union organizers had filtered into the town on frequent occasions but had met with little success. Upon being discovered by the company officials, they were escorted out of town by company guards and usually severely beaten in the process. In early August 1903, a Mexican organizer disappeared and a few days later the body of a murdered Mexican was found in the hills south of the brickyard.[6]

William M. Wardjon, an organizer from Illinois, secured employment in a Thurber mine. On being assigned a place to work, Wardjon worked quietly for three days, fearing that he might be watched. On the fourth day he injured a hand, rendering him unfit for work. The day following the accident he appeared at the mine, holding his well-bandaged hand carefully in front of him, and reported for work. After being lowered to the bottom of the shaft, he made his way to his place, but instead of working, spent that day and several more wandering about the mine talking with leaders who were in favor of organization, and laying plans for concrete action.

A few men from Lyra had quietly slipped into town and were working in various locations about the mines, spreading the word among those whom they felt could be trusted. With all preparations in readiness, the move was scheduled for Labor Day.[7]

Gordon defied the union-minded miners by posting two notices on the company bulletin board. His action signaled a growing exasperation with the miners. It indicated a switch on his part from calm diplomacy to overt brinkmanship in an effort to prevent a UMW incursion. The first notice, as reported by the *Fort Worth Star-Telegram* on September 11, 1903, read: "To Mine Employees: In accordance with instructions received last July from our President, Edgar L. Marston, the following rates and changes will be in effect commencing October 1, 1903: Price of mining $1.05 per ton instead of $1.00. A bonus will be paid miners who have to their credit at the end of the month more than 30 tons. The minimum bonus 2 cents a ton; maximum 10 cents a ton for production of 70 tons or more a month. Trains for mines will leave Thurber at 7:00 A.M. instead of 6:30 and nine hours will constitute a day's work." The miners paused before the bulletin board and read the concessions that had come down from Marston in New York.

Then Gordon posted his second notice. It was succinct and to the point: "For the information of all employees notice is given that Thurber will remain a non-union camp. Those who are unwilling can get a settlement at any time."[8]

On Labor Day, September 7, 1903, still hoping for a chance to cool the embers, Gordon prepared for an elaborate company-wide barbecue and celebration at Big Lake. Free food! Free beer! Everyone invited! Thurber was going to have fun! At the same time, Gordon foresaw unrest when the miners would be standing around the barbecue pit, awash in grappo and beer, magnifying their grievances, real and imagined. He communicated his uneasiness to Governor Sam Lanham. The governor, familiar with the situation in Thurber because his home town was neighboring Weatherford, responded by ordering Adjutant-General John A. Hulen[9] to dispatch Captain John H. Rogers and a company of Rangers to Thurber.

Gordon's fears were justified. He could not have known that UMW District President Pete Hanraty had camped recently and surreptitiously for two days and nights in the cedared hills around Thurber. On the third day, Hanraty, disguised with fake beard and mustache, made his way to the employment office and was hired to work in the brick plant. He straightway busied himself with sowing the seeds of discord and discontent and the tares of unionism.

With miners and brickmakers working different shifts, they did not often have the opportunity to come together in one combined aggregation. Gordon's big Labor Day picnic was their chance. Harry Connors, the teenage son of a miner, was given a saddle horse and instructed to ride among the crowd of more than eleven hundred with the message that they were to leave the picnic and march five miles north to Lyra, where an organizer for the United Mine Workers would tell them how wonderful the union could make their lives. Most of the miners followed Harry and a beer wagon out of the picnic grounds.[10]

About sixty men joined the union at Lyra on that Labor Day. They were instructed by William Wardjon to work quietly among the other miners and "set the camp ablaze with the fires of unionism." Wardjon, hell-bent upon organizing the Thurber miners, declared in an interview with the *Fort Worth Star-Telegram:* "Before the miners could ever return to work under any terms other than unconditional surrender, I will let the grass grow over Thurber streets." The new union members returned to the mines and began a whispering campaign. "They found that a majority of the miners were ready to organize. On September 9, union officials presented demands to the company that the scale of wages be raised, that the work day be shortened to eight hours and that the United Mine Workers be recognized as the bargaining agent for the miners."[11]

When these demands were refused by management, one of the most dramatic scenes in American labor took place on Thursday, September 10, 1903, at the little one-lane bridge at Rocky Creek in southern Palo Pinto County. "About 300 miners from the United Mine Workers Local at Lyra marched four miles eastward to Rocky Creek to meet a thousand miners and other workers from Thurber who had marched four miles northward through Thurber Junction to this midway meeting place."[12]

The battle lines were drawn. *The Dallas Morning News* reported on 11 September: "On one side of the creek, Mexican mine workers stood with bared heads and uplifted hands and repeated the oath of the United Mine Workers, as it was administered to them in Spanish by one of their number." On the other side of the creek, Wardjon preached unionism to about five hundred men, using interpreters to reach those who did not understand English. He ordered the men not to go to the mines and not to get their tools or draw their pay until they were told to do so by District President Pete Hanraty.[13]

W. K. Gordon's reaction to the strike was recorded in the *Fort Worth Star-Telegram* on September 11, 1903.

> We offered this advance, thinking that we could double the output and thereby afford to cut our profit in two. The miners have demanded $1.35 a ton straight and an increase in the wages of other employees, the whole amounting to about 33 per cent advance. The company cannot pay this scale. We were told that if we did not pay it they would tie us up. If we should agree to pay it we would be tied up through bankruptcy, so we might as well be tied up now.
>
> In the 14 years that this company has been in existence we have had no trouble with our men. Some of them belonged to the union, but we made no objection. When there was trouble elsewhere we permitted collection for relief to be taken up in the camp, and the company generally contributed $50 or $75 to the fund. Our people during these years have been happy and prosperous. Some of them have saved considerable money and have deposits in the company bank; others have sent their earnings to Italian banks in New York. Now the men have joined the union. The union leaders tell them to make this demand upon us. They say that the company can afford to pay the scale, as the advance will cost it nothing, since we can raise the price of coal on the railroads and the public. We cannot do this, however. We are forced to compete with the mines of Indian Territory and Alabama, where the veins are thicker than here, and which mines enjoy interstate freight rates, often more favorable than those of the Texas Railroad Commission. If we were to ask the railroad people to share this advance with us, even to bear one-fourth of it, they would laugh at us, and tell us they would get their coal from Indian Territory.
>
> These men will not believe that we are obliged to do business on an exceedingly close margin. Nevertheless, we are now getting 85 cents a ton less for our product than we received 14 years ago, and yet the scale which we announced to take effect October 1st was the same as the scale we paid at first. [Almost, but not quite. In 1888 the starting wage was $1.15 a ton. In 1894 this was reduced to $1.00. Now on 1 October 1903, it was to be increased from $1.00 to $1.05.]
>
> I am sure the company will never grant the demand, that it will go out of business first, as it cannot operate at such prices.[14]

After a conference with company officials, Pete Hanraty gathered the miners together and in his speech assured them that they had no cause to worry about the welfare of their families or themselves. He promised that food and shelter would be provided by the union and that work was available both at Lyra and other areas of the country. He advised them that they should first vacate their houses and then draw whatever pay they were owed by the company. The miners made plans to quit the premises.

The company announced that it would pay off the single men first as they had no household furnishings to move and no houses to vacate. On Friday morning, 11 September, the men began lining up in front of the pay windows and withdrawing the pay due them. This continued until noon on Sunday, 13 September. Every miner had severed his connections with the Texas & Pacific Coal Company. During the three days, the company paid out approximately thirty thousand dollars in wages.

Gordon volunteered to run the train to the mines so that the men could retrieve their tools and announced that the company would purchase any of their equipment that they did not wish to take with them. Accordingly, on Saturday morning the Black Diamond with seven coaches rolled slowly out of the station and mournfully whistled through the hills, carrying about five hundred men to the four working shafts, mine Nos. 7, 8, 9, and 10. Captain Rogers and his Texas Rangers were on board. They were not needed. There was no mob.[15]

All industrial activity ceased in Thurber and an eerie quiet settled over the town. Brickmakers and miners went about the streets with sad faces and fearful hearts—this was not your ordinary work stoppage or strike. The men of Thurber had given up not only their jobs, but now they must say goodbye to their homes.

The exodus from Thurber began. Families loaded their household goods onto whatever conveyance was available—wagons, hacks, carts, or buggies. All day and into the night the roads leading out of the village were lined with creaking, groaning vehicles of all types. Sans rowdiness or disturbance of any kind, the entire population picked up and left. This tactic was in sobered contrast to the one fifteen years earlier involving the Knights of Labor that was accompanied by violence and destructiveness. This time the atmosphere was funereal. Families were being uprooted and long time friends were tearfully parting. Over the years they had shared joys and heartaches, hardships and good times with one another. Many of the miners personally sought out Gordon to tell him good-bye. Some embraced him and with tear-filled eyes spoke their profound sorrow. Locked in a deadly fight, both sides respected the other. Although Gordon was always the "Bigga Boss" who lived in the big white house, he had not lived in splendid isolation, but rather had always been easily accessible to all the miners. Consequently, most of the men bore him no malice or ill-will. Gordon shared these feelings, saddened by the departure of his friends and concerned for the future of the company.

A majority of the miners moved their belongings the few miles to the mines at Lyra and settled in the tent city provided by the union. Work was available there as the Lyra mines were called upon to replace the coal formerly supplied by the Texas & Pacific Coal Company. However, many of the miners left the area altogether, some going to the Illinois coal fields and some returning to their native countries.

By 14 September—one week following the Labor Day picnic—Thurber was an abandoned town. The brick plant as well as the mines was closed and silent. The omnipresent pall of coal smoke lifted. Bored Texas Rangers, who had been sent by General Hulen in response to Gordon's request, found themselves with nothing more exciting to do than pitch horse shoes, play mumblety-peg, and clean their revolvers.

Gordon thought it was due to William Wardjon's wise counseling that the miners evacuated the town in an orderly withdrawal, for that paragon of a labor leader had urged the men to do no wrong and to respect the company officials and its property. Most of the credit for the non-violent nature of events, however, belonged to the entire Thurber family. They were not accustomed to violence or destructiveness, and many of them did not understand the extreme go-for-broke tactics ordered by the union.

Gordon then attempted to recruit workers from other sections of the country but was unsuccessful because union leaders met the trains and persuaded potential scabs on board from continuing on to Thurber.

The United Mine Workers called a conference in Fort Worth, to be held on 23 September, to discuss the developments at Thurber. W. K. Gordon told the union that he would not attend. Advised by Gordon of the ominous turn of events, President Edgar L. Marston thought it was time for him to look over the situation in person. He arrived in Fort Worth on his private railroad car No. 111.[16] Recognizing the importance of public opinion, he issued the following statement, which appeared in the *Dallas Morning News* on September 18, 1903:

> The present condition of affairs at Thurber, according to what I have heard, has been caused not so much by the recent demand by a committee of miners for an increase in wages, or for an eight-hour day, but a demand that the United Mine Workers of America receive official recognition in the management of the Texas & Pacific Coal Company.
>
> To fully appreciate the condition at Thurber, one must recall the experience of 1888, at which time Colonel Hunter and myself organized this coal company for the development of the Texas coal fields. We found a coal shaft with a capacity of 150 tons per day, and operated under the auspices of the Knights of Labor. This organization dictated the wages paid, the hours of work per day, the number of men employed and to whom work should be given. They objected to or excluded all men not belonging to their association. They denied the right that a man has by the Constitution of the State of Texas to sell his labor in a free market, thereby sacrificing the rights of a non-union man. They opposed the introduction of labor saving machines, and, in

fact, sought to limit the supply of labor and to control the fuel supply of the country.

The owners prior to our purchase had no control over this property, and while receiving from the railroads $2.75 per ton, lost money on every ton mined. Under such circumstances, we thought it best at the inception of our operations to enforce the authority of the operator and have the same recognition of each employee.

At no time has there ever been a refusal on the part of the officers to meet each and every employee and discuss the difference of opinion or adjust grievances which might affect the operation of the mines. Mr. Gordon has always been ready to meet one and all. There has been no dissatisfaction, grumbling, no upheaval nor strike between 1888 to September 1903.

Without any demand from the employees, the working day last fall was reduced to nine and one-half hours, and without any suspicion or intimation of discontent, the management, during the present summer, having secured a broader market for its production during the coming fall and winter, published two weeks ago a new schedule of increased wages and a reduction to a nine-hour day, to take effect October 1, 1903.

In the manner of leaving Thurber, the miners have set an example to all other laboring men; they have left quietly, orderly and without disturbance, recognizing the ownership of property. This feature is very gratifying, but one acquainted with the beautiful spirit of citizenship predominating at Thurber would expect nothing else.

Marston's rhetoric then hardened: "Our employees left us after making demands which meant bankruptcy of the company. It is now the duty of the officers of the company to man our mines and continue operations, as we have done in the past."

Marston went on to explain that the company did not oppose unionism per se, but because of conditions peculiar to Thurber, it was felt that a nonunion milieu would better serve the interests of both management and labor:

The company does not oppose trade unionism or organized labor, nor has it discriminated against its employees on account of membership. We have, however, always maintained that owing to our location and surroundings, and the number of men employed, that the interests of both parties could and would be best served by a personal meeting or a direct control between the employer and the employees. I can see where this is impractical in many instances and, owing to the nature of employment, individual meeting with employees is impractical. But at Thurber we have always encouraged the cultivation of an independent spirit.

I do not look for any interference from the members of the United Mine Workers of America in the operation of the Thurber mines, provided the company secures men who are willing to work for the wages offered and nine hours a day as proposed by the company.[17]

While his message was being read and digested by the public, Marston requested a conference in Fort Worth with the UMW leaders, W. M. Wardjon and Pete Hanraty. The result of the meeting was that Marston capitulated to the union demands. The coal company president and the coal union leaders shook hands. The troika agreed that they would go together to Thurber to tell the miners about the armistice.

On September 20, 1903, the first union meeting was held in Thurber. (During the 1888-1889 strike, meetings were held at the Knights of Labor Hall outside the company property.) On that final summer afternoon, over one thousand men marched from Lyra and assembled in the Thurber Opera House. At the appointed hour, a private railroad car bearing Marston, Wardjon, and Hanraty was shunted onto a siding near the Opera House.[18] The miners were told that an agreement on wages and working conditions had been reached, and that a contract would be signed in Fort Worth next week at a meeting of operators and miners.

The Fort Worth meeting, held at the Worth Hotel on 26 September, was captured for history in a photo that now hangs on the wall of the New York Hill Restaurant in Thurber. Across the face of the photo appears the legend: "Worth Hotel Fort Worth September 1903 Meeting. Coal Operators and Miners Negotiating First Working Agreement in Texas." In the picture W. K. Gordon is shown standing against a wall. President Marston is seated at the table with another participant who in future years would loom large in the labor movement in America.[19] That man was twenty-three-year old John L. Lewis, destined to become President of the United Mine Workers. Lewis was to amass great fame and power as a UMW leader, so much so that he would be able to stand up against President Franklin D. Roosevelt.[20]

The contract, signed by Edgar L. Marston, George E. Bennett and W. H. Aston for the operators, and Pete Hanraty, William Wardjon, and J. R. Edwards for the United Mine Workers of America, granted an increase of ten cents per ton above the offer made by the company before the strike. This restored the wage to the $1.15 per ton scale originally paid when Hunter took over the mines in 1888. Although a hefty increase, it was still twenty cents below the $1.35 per ton that the union had demanded at the outset of the strike and eighty cents below the $1.95 per ton that W. W. Johnson had paid.

The contract provided that twenty-six working days of eight hours each should constitute a working month; that the miners would be paid bimonthly, on the first and third Saturdays of each month; all union dues would be collected at the company pay office and deducted from the miners' earnings; and the union would pay the wages of a check weigher for

Texas & Pacific Coal Company and United Mine Workers sign pact. Conferees include W. K. Gordon (standing, and second from left), John L. Lewis (seated at table, right), and E. L. Marston (seated at table, second from right). Worth Hotel, Fort Worth, 26 September 1903. Courtesy Dick Smith Library, Tarleton State University.

each mine. The mine operators agreed to keep the mines dry and in safe working condition; provide blankets, bandages, first aid supplies, and ambulances at each mine. A life insurance provision stated that in case a miner was killed on the job, a death benefit would be paid to his survivors, consisting of a twenty-five dollar contribution from the company and a fifty-cent assessment from each member of the United Mine Workers employed at the same mine. Leaving the meeting, a glum-faced Gordon summed it all up in his remark to some of the miners: "Boys, you now own the mines."[21] But as time would prove, the miners had on that day won but a Pyrrhic victory.

With the union business out of the way, the Thurber Opera House returned to its raison d'être—staging traveling plays, dress balls, and Grand Opera. But the highbrow stuff was not the only bill of fare in Thurber. Over at the Thurber Athletic Club there was badger fighting.

✦

Badger fighting? What was that? Upon entering the Athletic Club, the uninitiated—sometimes a naive New Yorker who had traveled with President Marston on his private car down to Texas—would see on stage an enraged bulldog, straining at his master's leash. The object of the dog's ire was a barrel turned on its side from which trailed a rope. Inside the barrel, so the gullible easterner was told, a vicious badger crouched, ready to spring. Anticipation grew as the capacity crowd of miners placed their shouted bets on either the dog or the badger. When the time came for the fight, it was always discovered that the only person present who was qualified to pull out the badger was someone who wasn't prejudiced by having made a wager. Invariably this was the newcomer. Filled with the excitement, the gull would mount the stage and take the free end of the rope. When the signal was given, he would give a mighty yank that produced from the barrel not a badger but, to his surprise and chagrin, an innocent chamber pot. The visitor's humiliation invariably elicited hoots of laughter and applause from the audience.[22]

✦

C. W. Woodman, Secretary of the Texas Federation of Labor, came to Thurber at this time. He organized all company employees other than the miners. On November 16, 1903, the sixth annual convention of the Texas State Federation of Labor met in Fort Worth. A. C. Woodall, representing the Thurber local of the United Brick and Clay Workers of America, spoke to the assembly concerning the organization at Thurber:

This brings me down to the organization of the unions outside of the miners and the work of Brother C. W. Woodman, and right here I wish to say that I never saw a more untiring and ceaseless worker than he. He worked with and for the boys both day and night until now it is safe to say that he has the unique distinction of being the only man in the United States that has thoroughly and completely organized every branch of labor of an entire city, barring the one exception of the miners. Thurber has a population of 5,000 inhabitants, of which there are something like 1,400 on the payroll. There are seven labor organizations in our little city: Clerk, Miners, Federal Labor, Meat Cutters, Carpenters, Bartenders and Brickmakers.[23]

After the strike, and probably for the first time in America, the union put its symbol on each brick: an impressed triangle with a letter "B," a "T" and another "T" at each apex of the triangle. The "BTT" stood for Brick, Tile, and Terra-cotta workers.

The first paragraph of the contract renegotiated in 1914 was not about working conditions or wages. It provided that the union retains the right to imprint its logo on each brick. That was considered of the utmost importance, because that symbol told the world that this was the finest brick made anywhere.[24]

In September 1903, the storms of labor strife were rolling at Thurber. In the same month, storms of nature were rolling over North Carolina. Because of those storms, plans of two brothers had to be delayed until December. And so it was that on December 17, 1903, Orville and Wilbur Wright at Kitty Hawk demonstrated that heavier-than-air flying machines were possible.

While Edgar L. Marston, Colonel R. D. Hunter's son-in-law, was preoccupied with labor problems in 1903, what was his other son-in-law, John C. Phelan up to? In October 1903, a year after Hunter's death, Phelan incorporated the Independence Mining Company of Fort Worth to develop a lignite coal property in Bastrop County, Texas, and founded the mining community of Phelan, southeast of Austin, from whence he operated his mines, some two hundred miles from Fort Worth. In 1904, ownership of the Hunter-Phelan Savings and Trust Company, incorporated in 1901, passed to Otho S. Houston, Felix Bath, Winfield Scott, W. L. Smallwood, and D.C. Cogdell.

Both the trust and mining companies under John Phelan's management suffered early financial reverses, jeopardizing investments of his wife and mother-in-law. Maude and her mother worried about his demands upon, and management of, their estates. Early in 1906 John and Maude Phelan separated. In April 1907, Maude sought a divorce, which was granted in October. Maude Phelan and her two children, Hunter Clemens Phelan and Janet Webster Phelan, thereafter resided with or near Maude's mother, Janet, who had returned to Colorado and pleasant memories of her early married life there with Colonel Hunter. Janet, Maude, and her children would live a short while in New York City, then move permanently to Pasadena, California.

Mine No. 11, circa 1905. Courtesy Dick Smith Library, Tarleton State University.

Janet Webster Hunter married Howard Church Chapin. Although the date of the wedding is not known, certainly it would not have been prior to 1904. She died in Pasadena April 8, 1935, as Janet H. Chapin. She was ninety-eight years old, surviving the Colonel by thirty-three years.[25]

✦

On June 3, 1904, fire completely destroyed the tipple of Mine No. 8 and spread to the woodwork of the shaft. The flames were not extinguished until 19 June.[26] Unlike Mine No. 5, which had been destroyed by fire in 1897, Mine No. 8 did not have to be abandoned. In fact, it would become the second largest producer of all the mines. Also in 1904 a new mine, No. 11, opened one-half mile south of No. 10 at a depth of 194 feet. Five mines were now in operation: Nos. 7, 8, 9, 10, and 11.

The year 1904 was a vintage year for lovers of opera. In that year Giacomo Puccini's *Madame Butterfly* was first presented in Milan. Because the Thurber Opera House was in full swing at that time, no doubt Puccini's new opera played there before a packed house of enthusiastic Italian miners.

On October 10, 1904, joy came to the Gordon household with the birth of a daughter, Margie Kearby Gordon. In November of that year, Theodore Roosevelt was elected president in his own right. On April 8, 1905,

Roosevelt became the first U.S. president to visit Fort Worth. He was on his way to a wolf hunt with Burk Burnett and Tom Waggoner, who had made their fortunes on cattle ranges in North Texas and Oklahoma Territory and who maintained homes in Fort Worth. When he arrived at the T&P depot, he was greeted by twenty thousand people. Thousands more lined downtown streets to cheer the president as he rode in an open carriage accompanied by cavalrymen who were uniformed like the Rough Riders.[27]

W. K. and Fay Gordon's world was shattered with the death of their eight month-old daughter, Margie. The baby died on June 15, 1905. She was interred in a family on-premises brick mausoleum.

✦

That same year, a twenty-six-year-old German physicist named Albert Einstein published three seminal papers in physics. One of them developed the epochal mass–energy equation $E=mc^2$, a component of his special theory of relativity.

✦

Some seventeen years had now passed since Will Johnson sold his coal operation to Colonel Hunter. Will and Anna, now that they had no living children did not need such a large house and moved from Strawn to a ranch four miles north of Gordon. With them, they carried the caskets of their son and daughter. Outside the new ranch house, they built another mausoleum and covered it with ornamental shingles. The building was seven by ten feet with a door and three windows. The bodies of their children were placed inside and the parents continued to visit them every day. Johnson improved his forty-two hundred acre ranch with new fences, a large lake, deer park, and many barns and outbuildings. The ranch comprised a large part of the John Bird Survey that was surveyed in 1850. The survey was the first legal paper recorded in Palo Pinto County after its organization in 1857.

In 1906 the great San Francisco earthquake and fire occurred. Bad fortune of a different kind threatened the lifestyle of the miners in Thurber—the voters of Erath County, in a local option election held on June 11, 1904, voted 1,890 to 928 for the county to be dry.[28] The company responded to this development by building a new and bigger saloon across the county line in 1906.

This new Snake, 120 feet long and 40 feet wide, featured a bar as long as two train cars and could accommodate several hundred men at a time. It became famous as the largest and busiest saloon between Fort Worth and El Paso. Thousands of dollars slid across the mahogany bar each week. On week days, four bartenders were needed to serve the thirsty miners. Saturdays and holidays required six, eight, or even ten men. No seating whatever was provided in the old Snake, but after the move to Palo Pinto County, this restriction was relaxed. Several sheds were built on the saloon grounds, each with tables and benches. In warm weather, the men gathered here in small groups. Each member of the group would pitch in toward the price of a keg of beer. Sometimes one of the group would be sent to the meat market for barbecue or a Dutch lunch, consisting of a variety of sausages and cheeses. Fist fights were common occurrences, blamed mostly on the Irish, but shared by every nationality represented in Thurber.

Colonel Hunter from the outset had ordained that Thurber would have a school and library. In 1906, when the old Snake saloon closed, Gordon converted it into a school. Classes were held there while the new school building was erected just south of the town square. Separate educational facilities were provided for black students. Texas & Pacific Coal Company paid no school taxes, but provided the school building and supplemented the state per capita appropriation so that the salaries of its teachers and its educational standards exceeded those of many larger school systems.[29]

In 1906, Mine No. 12, located one mile south of No. 11, was opened at a depth of 110 feet. In the same year, Mine No. 7 was abandoned, having produced 1,183,073 tons over twelve years. Mine No. 7 had the distinction of being the first mine in Texas to replace the mule with electric power for hauling purposes. From that year, mules no longer lived out their lives in the dark below with never a sight of the sun. It was also at this mine that Gordon's patented dumping cages were first installed. Shortly thereafter, these cages were used in all the Thurber mines.[30] As a result of these innovations, Mine No. 7 became the first of the mines to produce a million tons. With the closure of No. 7, five mines were still active: Nos. 8, 9, 10, 11, and 12.

In 1907 fire destroyed the Hotel Knox. A new hotel—the Plummer—was built west of the mine office to replace it. The new twenty-room hotel was far superior in construction and elegance to the first hotel, but those who had lived at the original always fondly remembered the happy hours they had spent within its portals.[31]

On November 1, 1907, Fay and W. K. Gordon rejoiced in the birth of their new baby daughter, Louise Kearby Gordon.

In 1896 the company built a seventeen-ton ice plant for Thurber. Now a dozen years later—in 1908—this ice plant was enlarged and modernized. A new brick building housed the power plant. To furnish draft for the complex's four coal-fired boilers, a 148-foot tall smokestack was constructed. The tall smokestack carried the black, dirty smoke high into the air to keep it from settling on the town.[32]

On September 29, 1908, twenty years from TP's birth, President Edgar L. Marston in New York obviously took great pleasure in writing a sentimental letter to Corporate Secretary S. Mims in Thurber:

A little foolish sentiment, but you will appreciate the remembrance, for you are the oldest employee of the T&P Coal Company. I send you by express the pen holder and pen used in signing the check to pay the bonds and secure the release of the $500,000 mortgage of the T&P Coal Company issued October 1888. I commit this pen and holder to you as Secretary of the Company, which I wish you would keep in the office as a souvenir of 1888-1908.[33]

◆

In November 1908, William Howard Taft was elected twenty-seventh president of the United States. The voters gave Taft a plurality of more than a million votes over William Jennings Bryan, who suffered his third loss as the Democratic nominee.

◆

In 1909, two new mines were opened. There was something different about these new mines—their numbers. The miners in Thurber, particularly those from southern European countries, entertained certain superstitions—one of them being the fear of the number thirteen. Mining, at best, was a hazardous proposition without going down into a black hole whose number was thirteen. So although the new mines were indeed the thirteenth and fourteenth, out of respect to the superstitions of the miners, they were christened New No. 1 and New No. 2. New No. 1 was located one mile south of No. 12 at a depth of 155 feet. New No. 2 was located about five miles west of Thurber at a depth of 327 feet and was reached by a railroad spur from near Mine No. 10, three miles in length, which crossed Palo Pinto Creek on a steel bridge. The bridge and track were constructed and owned by Texas & Pacific Coal Company.[34] Seven mines were now in operation: Nos. 8, 9, 10, 11, 12, New No. 1, and New No. 2.

About 1909, Thurber's newest housing was built with brick. The fashionable houses on Marston Street were bungalow-type in shape, whereas those to the east on Church Street were square structures with flat roofs. Dwellings on both of these streets were equipped with modern plumbing and bath facilities and plastered interiors. They were enclosed with gray picket fences. Marston Street was often referred to as "Silk Stocking Row," as most of the company executives lived in that area.[35] According to W. K. Gordon's memoirs written in 1913, this would represent the last building brick that the company manufactured: "Prior to 1903, when organized labor first gained a foothold in Thurber, Thurber Brick was known throughout Texas to be the best brick made in the state, but after Union Labor secured its foothold, obtained increased wages and a reduction in working hours, it was found impossible to manufacture building brick and meet Open Shop prices. For this reason the Building Brick Plant was put out of commission in the year 1909."³⁶ Because Thurber's dense, vitrified paving bricks were impervious to water, a heavy demand would continue for them into the 1930s. Unlike building brick, they had no peer.

By the summer of 1910, the Gordons' daughter Louise was two and one-half years old. On July 9, 1910, a son was born. He was named W. K. (William Knox) Gordon, Jr. and would be called Billy.

In 1911, New No. 3 Mine, about one-half mile west of Thurber, was opened at a depth of 122 feet. It was the fifteenth T&P mine that polka-dotted the Thurber landscape. George B. Studdard went down into New No. 3 mine several times in the 1920s: "The shaft to a mine was straight down. The mines were not slope mines. The cage would be lowered straight down. In the case of New No. 3 mine, which was located on the western edge of Thurber, it was 122 feet to the bottom. At the bottom of the shaft, it was hollowed out sufficiently that a man could stand upright. This is where the spraggers and trappers worked."³⁷

◆

Spraggers? What did they do? By 1906, mules had been replaced by electric locomotives. "When a motorman brought in a string of loaded cars to be hoisted, he stopped his train several yards away from the cage (elevator), uncoupled the motor and moved it onto another track, out of the way. The spragger would uncouple one car at a time so that it could roll down a slight incline to the cage. Before a car could gather speed, the spragger would insert a steel rod (sprag) between the spokes to prevent it from running away and crashing into the cage."³⁸ One of the spraggers was A. A. Daniels, who had lost his right hand in an industrial accident in Seattle. His handicap did not keep Texas & Pacific from giving him a job. He became the best left-handed spragger in the mines.³⁹

And trappers? What did they do? When a car of coal was loaded onto the cage to be hoisted, the trapper touched the toe of his shoe to a trigger which threw a trap, thus holding the car of coal securely so it would not roll off the side of the cage enroute to the surface.

When a car was ready to be hoisted to the surface, a whistle was sounded. One blast signified coal was in the car. Two blasts signified dirt, shale and waste matter. Three blasts meant miners were on the elevator. When the car down in the mine had been loaded with coal, a blast of the whistle apprised the operator, and the car was hoisted on the elevator to the tipple, where the mine car was turned upside down, dumping the coal into the waiting railroad car below. Each time a load was dumped into the railroad car, the weighmaster would make a notation as to the increased weight of the car. Thus, he knew how much coal had been in the mine car.

When the miner had finished loading his car in the mine, he would affix a brass tag with his number to the car. This tag would be removed by the man in the tipple and dropped down a one-inch pipe to the weighmaster. The weighmaster had a columnar pad with numbers printed across the top. The weighmaster would enter

Thurber Square, Dec, 1910, 1—mine offices, 2—Plummer Hotel, 3—Hunter Academy and Catholic Church, 4—Methodist Church, 5—Grocery Store, 6—Dry Goods and Furniture Stores, 7—Bandstand, 8—Drugstore, 9—Post Office, 10—twin wooden water towers, 11—Opera House, 12—Hardware Store, 13—Power Plant Smokestack built in 1908, 14—Billboard sign advertising a play at the Opera House Friday, December 23 which occurred in the year 1910. Courtesy Dick Smith Library, Tarleton State University.

Executive house on Marston Street. Courtesy Dick Smith Library, Tarleton State University.

on the pad the pounds of coal that came out of the car identified by the number on the brass tag.

If a car contained dirt, shale and waste material when it reached the tipple, it would be shunted off in another direction, where it was emptied into cars two or three times larger than the mine cars, which would transport it to a dump. At the dump the car ran up an incline to the top, where both sides of the car opened and the contents spilled out. Great mounds were thus created and may be seen even today, although erosion and removal by manufacturers of hollow building blocks have diminished their size.

Texas law mandated the sinking of an emergency escape shaft. This shaft was also utilized as a passage for fresh air to be blown into the mine by a huge fan at the surface.[40]

✦

Mine No. 9, having produced 948,621 tons over twelve years, was abandoned in 1911. Because New No. 3 was opened in the same year, a total of seven mines continued to operate: Nos. 8, 10, 11, 12, New No. 1, New No. 2, and New No. 3. In 1888, the one mine in operation was located on the only line of railroad from Thurber Junction, some two and one-half miles distant. Now in 1911, over twenty miles of railroad were required to reach the various mines.[41]

✦

During the night and early morning hours of April 14-15, 1912, the luxury liner *RMS Titanic* struck an iceberg in the cold North Atlantic and, although billed as unsinkable, sank just the same. In November 1912, Woodrow Wilson was elected the twenty-eighth president of the United States.

✦

In 1912 W. K. Gordon built himself a palace. Although all but one other of the original houses of Thurber have vanished, this splendid, imposing white house, like the towering smoke stack, still stands.

Many religious denominations were present in Thurber and the company built churches for them all. Although Catholics predominated, Methodists, Baptists, Presbyterians, and Episcopalians were represented. In 1908 in addition to a church and pastor, the Methodists supported a Wesley House staffed by two lady missionaries and a teacher. The women lived in Marston Hall and made detailed annual reports to church superiors that furnish charming first-hand accounts of what life was like in the missionary field of Thurber when the twentieth century was young.[42]

> The people of Thurber have been very kind to us, and they seem to realize the importance of the work. We have 186 members in our Temperance Society for Children. They take a fourfold pledge against intoxicants, tobacco, profanity and gambling.[43]

> Thurber is a coal mining camp; everything is owned and operated by the Texas & Pacific Coal Company. The company furnishes our building (which they remodeled two years ago) with water, coal, wood, electric lights, all free of rent. They cooperate with us in everything that is for the betterment of the camp.

> Marston Hall is well equipped for settlement work, and is the social center of the community. The public library is in our building. It was given by Mr. Marston, the president of the mines. It is well patronized, as is the reading room in connection with it, which is well supplied with many of the best magazines, current periodicals and several of our Church organs.

> The largest brick plant in the State is located in Thurber. These two industries (mining and brickmaking) furnish employment for all. Good salaries are paid. There are almost no cases of real destitution.

> Thurber has a population of between eight and ten thousand, about three-fourths of which are foreigners. Two thirds of the foreigners are Italians. Our day school for foreign children opened on September 18, 1911, with six pupils, but the school grew so rapidly that we had to have more room. The company kindly consented to put up a new building, and on November 5, we moved into the new building. We now have an enrollment of 64.

Formerly the foreign Sunday school was held at Marston Hall, but as the school building is located in the center of the foreign population, we felt that the attendance would be increased if we met there, and the attendance has increased from about 12 to 52.

The night school for the Italian men is a new feature of our work. This is held three nights of each week. The men are so interested and eager to learn that it is a great inspiration to teach them. I have a class in kitchen garden, which the little Italian and Mexican girls enjoy very much. I also have charge of the library and reading room. Our library, which contains fifteen hundred volumes, was given to us by the company, and the President, Mr. Marston, sends us a number of new books each year. The work here is very interesting and we enjoy it.[44]

Our foreign Sunday school continues to grow, and the attendance is splendid. Many of the children who attend the Catholic day school are regular attendants at our Sunday school. The Christmas entertainment was a source of great pleasure, being the first Christmas tree many had ever seen. We had a good program, after which the presents were distributed. The presents for each class were provided by some Sunday school in our district. The treat, consisting of apples, oranges, nuts and candy, was furnished by the mining company, and the tarlatan sacks for these were furnished by one of the classes in our American Sunday school. The night school for Italian men offers about the only opportunity we have to come in contact with the hundreds of men of this nationality. Those who attend are very much interested and are doing good work. There are a number of Protestants among the Mexicans, and as we have no pastor for them, the Baptist Board of Missions sends a Mexican minister here to preach for them twice a month. These services are held in our school building, and we assist all we can.[45]

I have found Thurber a very attractive field. If ever there was an open door, surely this is one, especially as regards foreign work.[46]

In the ten-year period from 1903 to 1913, prosperity reigned. With the company operating seven mines simultaneously for much of the span, coal production doubled from 337,041 tons in 1903 to more than seven hundred thousand tons in 1913. At the same time, Thurber's population doubled to ten thousand, a fourth of whom worked in the mines. By 1913, Thurber—the largest city between Fort Worth and El Paso—was jumping.[47]

It was the blend of the population, rather than the size, that gave Thurber its uniqueness. Though some reached Thurber by way of the Pennsylvania coal fields, most of them came directly from Poland, Italy, Wales, Ireland, and Mexico. The Thurber melting pot comprised three thousand Italians, one thousand Poles, and one thousand Mexicans. A dozen other nationalities furnished about three thousand. Some two thousand natural-born Americans, both white and black, rounded out the total.[48] The

Parade, circa 1900. Courtesy Dick Smith Library, Tarleton State University.

residents of this racially and ethnically diverse community felt enriched by its diversity. The variety of customs, languages, and talents were woven together into a democratic tapestry of many colors. Regardless of their origin, all became confirmed, dyed-in-the-wool Thurberites, boastfully proud of their city. Their civic pride was manifested in their holidays, parades, civic clubs, and pennant-winning baseball team. But above all, they were thrilled, elated, and honored to be Americans. They learned to speak English; they raised families and prospered.

The Fourth of July and Labor Day, as well as several holidays observed by the European and Mexican families, were occasions for lavish celebrations. Everyone, regardless of nationality, would turn out to honor the holiday queen, participate in the sporting events, and dance to the music of the American, Mexican, or Italian band.[49]

Mine No. 8 was abandoned in 1914, leaving six active mines: Nos. 10, 11, 12, New No. 1, New No. 2, and New No. 3. In its nineteen-year life, No. 8 gave up 1,940,292 tons of coal. Despite the disastrous 1904 fire that nearly did it in, No. 8 would be surpassed only by No. 10 in total tonnage produced.

◆

While all the work and play was going on in Thurber, events were heating up in Europe, from which continent most of the Thurber miners had come.

Fire and Mine Rescue Service, top row: left to right: Severio Passoni, Mario Andrei, Renaldo Contri; bottom row: Lee Americo, Cesare Piacnza and Lorenzo Fiorenga "Baddi," circa 1913. Courtesy Mrs. John Franks.

On June 26, 1914, six young men were poised in Sarajevo, Bosnia, to throw bombs at the car of Archduke Franz Ferdinand. Five of them, intimidated by the crowds or unwilling to hurt the archduke's wife, did nothing. However, one asked a police officer which car was the archduke's. The police officer identified it and the boy threw his bomb, which bounced off the archduke's car and exploded under the following car.

One of the other five, Gavrilo Princip, went off disconsolately for coffee at a corner cafe, where he loitered. Later, the archduke, going to a museum, decided to visit the people injured by the bomb. His driver, confused about the route to the hospital, stopped in front of the cafe where the astonished Princip sat. Princip leapt up and shot the archduke and his wife, thereby lighting Europe's fuse.[50]

◆

In the year that World War I started, life ended for Will Johnson, the man who first had seen the glitter of black diamonds in Erath County. He and Anna lived for only eight years on the ranch north of Gordon to which they had repaired in 1905. In 1913 they moved to Mineral Wells. Here they once again had a large colonial-style home, where they lived for the rest of their lives. Sadly for Will Johnson, that would not be long. It is supposed that they moved to town for reasons of health, as the couple had a maid and a nurse in Mineral Wells.

In the early fall of 1914, the Johnsons went to the coast of Texas in a private railway car to enjoy the ocean breezes. While there, Will contracted typhoid fever, and the couple, together with Mrs. Johnson's younger cousin, Cornelia Crocker of Geneva, New York, returned quickly to Mineral Wells. There, Will Johnson died in his upstairs bedroom on October 19, 1914. He was interred in the family mausoleum back at the ranch where his daughter and son rested.[51]

✦

Among the papers that Robert William Spoede found on the floor of the Johnson barn a half century later was a beautiful philosophical essay that Johnson had written early in his life, before his marriage to Anna Fatzinger. Its language indicates the author was not unacquainted with Psalms, Ecclesiastes, and the Song of Solomon:

WHAT IS LIFE?

Is it life to breathe the pure air of Heaven and never once think of Him who formed our frames in such sublime and complete workmanship and gave me powers to inhale its fragrance? Is it life to inhabit this house of clay like a bird caught within its cage, our hearts' desires perfectly satisfied in pursuing our worldly pleasures, never aspiring to that which is pure and high, never exercising those Godlike powers given us by our Creator which constitute that divine spark, the soul?

Has life no higher and nobler aim than this? Are we placed here for no better than to rise and pursue from morning till night the ceaseless round of toil, never allowing ourselves a moment of recreation, nor one short hour for meditation? A soul like this looks abroad and beholds no beauty because there is none within the recesses of his own hardened heart.

The sun, the dew, the vernal rain, the promising season, the abundant harvest are all instruments to aid his avarice, assist him in acquiring untold wealth of earthly gold, and thus destroy all the feelings of benevolence, justice, mercy and truth that were once attributes of his immortal mind; and he now regards them as things of minor worth.

This is not life. This is not the blessing given man by God to prepare the soul to enjoy the bliss of heaven, nor should we live as taught by earthly creeds, awaiting with fearful hearts, the coming of the dreadful messenger of death. For when we are prepared to live as mortals should, we are ever prepared to die.

Let us cherish and nourish every pure impulse thus germinating in the fruitful soul of religion, and behold in every human being a brother endowed with powers, feelings, and frailties like our own, and let us strive with an awakened heart to lessen his griefs and to increase his happiness.

Thus we shall receive the blessings of the good and secure our own happiness on earth. As the beauteous flowers receive the sun, let the gentle influence of joy and chastening grief prepare our hearts to welcome whatever may be our lot, till this life on earth shall pass to that above. Our life on earth is beautiful and fair if we improve the means to make it so and ever strive to gain instruction from every source however humble.

Earth is our Master's vineyard and we may touch and view its flowers, and inhale their sweet fragrance, while cheerfully performing our high duties and patiently awaiting the joyful period when all shall feel the pure ecstatic joy of the realization of fond anticipating, of long cherished hopes then consummated, all desires for happiness satisfied, all deep and bitter sorrows kindly healed, and the dim imaginations of earthly bliss lost in boundless rapture and full perfection.[52]

So William Whipple Johnson's long, long trail that had led from Michigan to Texas had come to an end.

4

"THERE'S OIL IN THE MCCLESKEY!"

In 1915 war was raging in Europe and in the North Atlantic Ocean. On 7 May the Cunard liner *Lusitania* sank in eighteen minutes after it was torpedoed by a German U-boat off the Irish coast. One thousand, one hundred ninety-eight lives were lost. In that year, Texas & Pacific mine New No. 2 was abandoned, having produced 175,155 tons over six years. Five mines were now left in operation: Nos. 10, 11, 12, New No. 1, and New No. 3.

In 1916, the year that Woodrow Wilson was re-elected president, two sisters, Elsie and Lola Morton, about sixteen years old, came to Thurber from Eastland and were employed by Texas & Pacific Coal Company to teach in the company school. Elsie's daughter, Lola Spearing, told a tale of those days: "Mother and Aunt Lola roomed and boarded with a woman who each day prepared a box lunch for them to take to school. The woman had made a quantity purchase of Vienna sausage, and, consequently, there was always a can of that delicacy in their lunch boxes. After a few months of this treat, Elsie and Lola were not able to look another Vienna sausage in the eye. Elsie later told her daughter: 'She must have gotten a hell of a deal on that Vienna sausage!'"[1]

✦

On August 11, 1916, a woman was buried in Thurber Cemetery. That event was revisited some three-quarters of a century later in a piece by *Star-Telegram* columnist Jon McConal:

> O. B. "Buttercup" Bridier's emotions were jolted like somebody had tied a high-voltage electrical wire to them recently in Thurber.
>
> He found a piece of a toy train that had once marked his grandmother's grave in the Thurber Cemetery. The grave had no other marker. And Bridier, of Willow Park, had not seen the little iron train since 1934.
>
> Bridier and his wife, Fay, stood in the cemetery of this almost ghost town about 75 miles west of Fort Worth.
>
> Mesquite trees are abundant around the nine acre cemetery. Bridier remembers coming to the cemetery as a youngster and looking at his

grandmother's grave. He had a picture of her. It showed a strong-looking woman with short black hair who was wearing a formal black dress.

"She died of a heart attack and was buried here on August 11, 1916," he said. "I can remember seeing her grave and that little train and telling my dad how much I wanted it. But he always said No."

Bridier moved away in 1943. But he never returned here until he read a column I had written about Leo S. Bielinski, who was also reared here, and who was cleaning up the cemetery.

"Leo and I were friends as kids," said Bridier. "I hadn't heard from him in all of these years. But I called and asked if I could come out with him with my metal detector and look for my grandmother's grave.

"I realized the chances of finding that little train were very remote," he said. But he kept looking. And, one day the metal detector began that high accelerated whine that indicates something metallic.

So he began to dig. One inch. Two inches. Three inches. At four inches, his fingers felt something.

"I yelled at Leo," he said. "I told him he was not going to believe what I had found."

It was the coal tender of the small train. It's made of cast iron and is about two inches in length.

He is still looking for the tiny engine and believes it is still here. And when he finds it, then he will erect a fitting marker for his grandmother.[2]

One is made to wonder at the mute significance of the only part of the little train that Bridier found in this cemetery of coal miners: a coal tender!

◆

In 1917, the company sank its sixteenth and last coal shaft. New No. 4 was located over one mile southwest of New No. 2, and about the same distance westerly from New No. 1. The site was south of present day Interstate 20 and near the foot of Ranger Mountain. However, the demand for coal was on the decline by this time and the mine was never put into operation.

As World War I convulsed Europe, U.S. policy-makers began to worry whether America's petroleum reserves would be sufficient to meet the needs of an expanding economy and at the same time fuel the army and navy should America be drawn into the conflict. Waiting in the wings however were wildcatters—hardy optimists willing to pay any price, bear any burden, meet any hardship, take any risk—who would discover enough oil to supply all of the nation's needs.

The terms "wildcat," describing a well exploring for oil in any area where it has not been found, and "wildcatter," describing the explorer, go so far back no one is quite sure how they originated. Perhaps oilmen adopted the word because the characteristics of the animal itself were

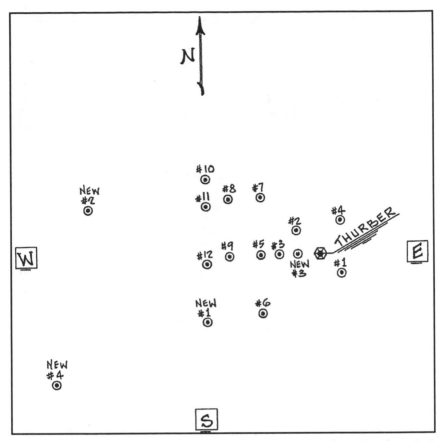

Plat of Texas & Pacific Coal mines plotted by Ben Franklin from data furnished by W. K. Gordon to Weldon Hardman found in *Fire in a Hole,* pages 63-64.

those required by an oil hunter—audacity; patience in stalking prey; sight so acute that the ancients believed a wildcat could see through a stone wall; and above all, a fierceness and independence that defies taming.[3]

W. K. Gordon, who was to become a legendary wildcatter, discussed with Texas & Pacific's President Edgar Marston the possibility that oil might be found on the company's coal lands. Marston sent a geologist from New York to study the area. His report was negative, but Gordon, who Thomas R. Hall believed "knew more of the geological formations of this section of the country than any living man,"[4] continued to urge his views with such fervor upon Marston that he dispatched other geologists to the scene. All reported adversely. Gordon's was only an illusive dream. There was no black gold there.

Still, Gordon persisted. The only way to prove or disprove the presence of oil was to drill. Consequently, in 1915, he drilled a well on coal land that the company had purchased some fifteen years before. It was located approximately nine miles northwest of Thurber, eleven hundred feet east of the west line and 250 feet north of the south line of the Thomas Court Survey on the north fork of Palo Pinto Creek in Palo Pinto County. The drilling commenced on January 7, 1915, and was completed a week later on 14 January at a total depth of 830 feet. Initial production of the well was sixty barrels of oil and three million feet of unmarketable gas per day. The limited production of the well did not arouse a great deal of enthusiasm with Marston, but Gordon had caught the bewitching scent of oil. He began testing other areas.[5]

W. K. Gordon was not the only one who had smelled oil. So had the union organizers. In a letter to the citizens of Ranger in 1927 Gordon wrote: "In the late fall of 1916, the United Mine Workers of America, with its local headquarters in Thurber, Texas, led by one Patrick Singletonio, a renegade who had more than once taken the life of his fellow man, assisted by one Jack Tarver, a thug and prize-fighter, had by threats and intimidation, organized the Oil Field Workers of the T & P Coal Company."

The union leaders proposed a closed shop contract to the company. But Gordon remembered the lessons of 1903. He was determined there would be no oil union in Thurber. In his letter, Gordon told Rangerites that if the company had agreed to the contract:

> It would have taken from you, your sons and your sons' sons the right to work as oil field employees even on your own farms and ranches without first paying tribute to the United Mine Workers of America.
>
> To defeat the unionization efforts, it was vital that free-born, independent young Texans be found to take the strikers' places so that field operations would not be suspended.
>
> It was an interesting picture, that crispy Monday morning, when on a little mesquite knoll in West Palo Pinto County, the strikers stood aside, baffled and disgruntled, as carload after carload of husky young men from Ranger arrived upon the scene and quietly, but with stern determination, took charge of operations, thereby sustaining the open shop for the oil fields of Texas. The man to whom all credit is due, and the one whom Ranger should not forget, is Luther M. Davenport.[6]

Gordon now was fighting a battle on two fronts. While holding the unionists at bay at Thurber, he had another battle to fight in New York. He must once again preach his unwavering belief in the riches of Thurber-area oil to a skeptical Edgar Marston. He took the train to New York. "There he argued so convincingly, that President Edgar L. Marston finally threw up his hands and said, 'Well, go ahead.'"[7]

Gordon returned to Thurber and employed Luther Davenport, who was widely acquainted with farmers and ranchers in several counties, to drive over the territory in a buggy, call on the land owners and obtain mineral leases at a nominal figure. On February 27, 1917, Gordon sent a telegram to company headquarters in New York, giving a progress report on the leasing situation. President Marston, concerned at the ballooning expense, replied by wire: "Do not think we should take on any unnecessary leases, but if you think advisable that we have the property mentioned for two years at 25 cents an acre, suggest doing so."

Marston followed up his telegram with a letter to Gordon:

> I think it unwise to load up with any more acreage and I think if we have not sufficient gas and oil in two years our position will be weakened. If we were getting out 2000 to 4000 barrels of oil a day, the situation would be different.
>
> The little Coal Company is not in the position of The Texas Company or the Magnolia Company; therefore, we must commence to realize that we have our limitations.
>
> Now as to allowing the Miners' Union to get control of our oil field, I think it would be a great mistake. I certainly would fight any attempt to unionize our employees in the oil field.[8]

The average annual rainfall in the Ranger area is about twenty-three inches. But beginning in hot July 1916 a dry spell descended upon Eastland County with a vengeance. In the last half of the year only six inches fell. Thirsty farmers, eyeing the cloudless skies and surveying their parched fields, were worried. They well had cause to worry—only ten inches of rain would fall in all of 1917.

A committee of Ranger civic leaders met to discuss the dry, dire, and dreary prospects facing the sere countryside. Knowing that Texas & Pacific Coal Company was buying oil and gas leases in the area, it was decided that W. K. Gordon should be approached to try to convince him to begin testing immediately around Ranger. John M. Gholson, Ranger's leading merchant drove over to Thurber, some sixteen miles east as the crow flies but, in those days of poor and roundabout roads, nearly double that distance.[9] Gordon and Gholson struck a deal. In exchange for a block of thirty thousand acres around Ranger, Gordon, backed by Marston, agreed to drill four deep wells and to risk up to two hundred thousand dollars of Texas & Pacific Coal Company's money.[10]

Through the efforts of Davenport and Gholson, Gordon eventually held oil and gas leases on three hundred thousand acres in Eastland, Stephens, Throckmorton, and Palo Pinto counties. Executives in oil centers heard of the activity but, knowing the unfavorable reports of the geologists as to petroleum, supposed the land was being leased for coal and dismissed the subject from mind.

Now it was time for Gordon to put his theory to the test. Surely somewhere on that vast block of acreage there was an oil field waiting to be found. But where to drill? In March rig timbers were unloaded on the Nannie Walker farm, half a mile north of Ranger. Gordon himself chose the location.[11] He also chose the drilling contractor, Warren Wagner.[12]

As drilling operations were underway on the Nannie Walker farm, President Woodrow Wilson, pledging to make the world safe for democracy, led the United States into World War I. The date was April 6, 1917. Heavy demands would be placed on the American oil industry. Wildcatters everywhere intensified their search for petroleum. W. K. Gordon proceeded to drive a stake for another well, this time on the John McCleskey farm, about a mile southwest of Ranger.

The No. 1 J. H. McCleskey was spudded on July 2, 1917. Time passed. The hole became deeper with each passing day as the bit inched its way through the rocks. Hot August arrived, and then all hell broke loose. But not on the McCleskey—the action came a mile and a half north on the Nannie Walker:

> At 3,200 feet, gas was struck and 10,000,000 cubic feet a day came roaring forth. But gas was not oil and there was no market for this flow. So the well was left in solitude to hurl the gas into the air.
>
> The McCleskey hit the same stratum but the rush of gas did not prove as great and, after the boiler had been moved back to lessen the danger of fire, drilling was resumed, slowly however.
>
> When the drill went through the gas sand without finding the hoped-for oil, the faith of the inhabitants of Ranger ebbed. The president of a major oil company, a visitor in Marston's New York office, shook his head as he remarked, "The well's too deep; you'll never find anything."[13]

The nervous Marston, indecisive and vacillating, had now seen one hundred thousand dollars of black diamond money poured down a hole in search of black gold. He reached a decision. He sent a telegram to Gordon: "Think we have made a mistake. Better quit."

In response, Gordon fired off a telegram to Marston in New York. The argument conveyed in that telegram was sufficiently convincing that Marston relented and sent another message countermanding his original telegram. Gordon was authorized to use his own judgment, although a limit was placed on additional expenditures. Gordon's steely persistence caused him to keep drilling even after Marston's limit was reached, using, so legend has it, mine commissary funds to pay the drilling crew.

Gordon directed Warren Wagner to continue drilling. To husband resources, crews were reduced. Drilling was in open hole. Oil well casing—steel casing run down the hole and cemented to seal off water and to prevent cave-ins—was adjudged a nicety that could be dispensed with.

John H. McCleskey and second wife, Cordie, circa 1915. They married on July 24, 1911. His first wife Sarah Ann died April 27, 1909. Courtesy of Jeane Pruett.

No. 1 J. H. McCleskey, discovery well of the Ranger Field, blowing in on October 22, 1917. Courtesy Mrs. W. K. Gordon, Jr.

Ironically, the building of any storage facilities to contain the oil if it was hit, was also omitted.

On October 22, 1917, about the time that Bolsheviks were storming the Czar's Winter Palace in Petrograd to capture control of the Russian government, Frank Champion, a thirty-eight-year old driller on the afternoon tower, came to work at noon, relieving Jack Walters, driller on the morning tower. Champion began his career by dressing tools in Corsicana in 1900 and was a veteran of a dozen districts—Spindletop, Bartlesville, and other fields in Texas, California, Kansas, and Colorado.[14]

The crew that had been relieved drove away in the only car on the lease, and Champion and his helpers proceeded with the task methodically, though the driller had little expectation that the McCleskey would hit pay because the gas level had been drilled through and nothing found.

Drilling had been going on an hour and a half when there came a faint rumbling far down in the earth, growing into a growl as it came nearer. From the mouth of the well, dirt and rock were flung on the floor of the derrick. An instant later there was a spray of oil.[15]

Outlined against a blue-gray October sky, the first gusher at Ranger blew in. For Texas & Pacific Coal Company the whole world changed that day. Immediately, the flow increased—a beautiful sight with the late autumn sunshine glinting on the broad column of greenish gold—the color of dreams—that skyrocketed over the top of the eighty-four foot derrick.[16]

Although Gordon was not present in person to see his dream come true, figuratively his head was on that day anointed with oil. His cup ran over.

Earl Root, the water pumper, came running up from the earthen tank and for a moment, Frank Champion and Harve Wells, the tool dresser, stood gazing in amazement, heedless of the drenching of oil they were receiving. Then Champion raced to shut off the fire, for the glistening drops were beginning to shower upon the boiler.

There was no equipment to control the well, so lightly had its chance of production been regarded. The men nailed two boards across the top of the open casing to check the flow as much as possible and the oil, pouring against the bull wheel, rushed into the gulch. Soon the workers had thrown up a dam and the improvised reservoir captured most of the petroleum.

Then leaving the tool dresser at the well, Champion and Root walked to town. Unnoticed as yet, they stopped at the telephone office and the driller informed Warren Wagner, who was at Strawn, that the McCleskey was an oiler. When Champion emerged from the telephone office and turned the corner into the view of the lounging groups around the stores, they eyed him without curiosity, not realizing what his glistening garments meant. "It's an oil well, boys," he remarked laconically.

Hearing the ensuing cheers, John Gholson and banker Cull Moorman rushed forth. Charlie Gholson, the merchant's brother, sprang into his touring car and drove furiously up and down the two blocks of the business section, shouting, "There's oil in the McCleskey!"[17]

The storekeeper, the banker, and the driller piled into a Model-T Ford—tin lizzie—and sped to the well. They found the McCleskey flowing steadily at a rate estimated at more than a thousand barrels a day.

✦

On April 23, 1994, I went to Ranger for the town's 75th anniversary of incorporation. That day Elzie Pruett escorted Chissa Gordon and her son, Bill, Jack Tunstill and me to the site of the McCleskey well. We drove one mile west of Ranger and turned south on a graveled county road for one mile. We crawled through a barb-wire fence and followed Elzie up a cedar and mesquite infested grade. We noticed several grass-covered indentations in the ground, much like buffalo wallows, which stair-stepped down the hillock. Elzie informed us that these indentations were made by mule-powered go-devils which dug pits to catch the oil flowing down from above. As one pit was filled, another pit was hurriedly dug a few feet below the previous one. Thus most of the McCleskey's oil was saved. As we continued up the slope, we observed every few feet outcroppings of a black rock that Tunstill said indicated the existence of an underground structure. This was undoubtedly the clue that W. K. Gordon, with experienced hunches and educated guesses, followed seventy-seven years before.[18]

◆

News of the McCleskey's storybook ending raced across Texas—indeed across America—like a prairie fire. There was no radio in 1917—the first commercial radio broadcast did not air until 1920—so word was spread by telegram, newspaper, and word of mouth.

The Nannie Walker—which had been gassing for months, unnoticed and all but forgotten by the townspeople—now emitted a roar that caused hundreds to come running. The Walker had blown itself into an oil well and was gushing at a greater rate than the McCleskey, proof positive that Ranger was for real.[19]

With two wells flowing prodigious volumes of oil, W. K. Gordon and the Texas & Pacific Coal Company continued oil exploration with gusto. Among the wells that T&P began to drill soon after the McCleskey discovery was a test on the Floyd Brewer farm in the Merriman community, four miles south of Ranger. In June 1918, the Brewer hit the pay sand for one thousand barrels a day. Four other wells on the Brewer lease followed in rapid order.

Although T&P Coal had leased most of the surrounding land, there were a few scattered tracts that had not been bought. One of these was the Merriman school grounds. Warren Wagner, the contractor on the McCleskey well, scurried to lease it for himself. In only thirty-seven days, his cable tools thumped and thudded thirty-two hundred feet to bring in a well flowing five thousand barrels a day. From its one-eighth royalty, the Merriman school district became the wealthiest, per capita, in the world. Former Texas Governor Oscar. B. Colquitt declared in 1918 the fund was sufficient to give every child in the district a high school education and then four years in college.[20]

Another tract which had not been leased by TP was the Merriman Cemetery. One company offered the cemetery's trustees one hundred thousand dollars for a lease. The trustees refused the offer with the declaration: "Merriman is not for sale."[21]

The fame of Ranger swept over the land and the black gold rush was on. With several wells having initial productions up to five thousand barrels a day, activity in Eastland, Palo Pinto, and Stephens counties became feverish. Two years after the discovery, TP was operating, solely or jointly, 214 drilling rigs on its properties in the Ranger Field. Total production of all operators in the field was then 120,000 barrels per day.[22]

The McCleskey's initial production was sixteen hundred barrels of oil and 3.5 million feet of gas per day. During a two and a half year period, Big Mac produced approximately 250,000 barrels of oil. And the price was right! A considerable part of the Ranger production brought a bonanza of four dollars a barrel, compared to a miserly ten cents at Spindletop in 1901 and East Texas in the early 1930s.

Because of Gordon's aggressive lease acquisition program, most of the oil belonged to Texas & Pacific Coal Company. With black gold spilling over the tops of T&P's tanks, Gordon may have smiled when he remembered Marston's wistful remark in his letter of February 27, 1917: "If we were getting out 2,000 to 4,000 barrels of oil a day, the situation would be different." Not only Texas & Pacific Coal, but Ranger and all the drought-stricken country round about, prospered and flourished. The T&P discovery opened exhilarating new vistas for the oil industry, and it fed the petroleum-hungry armies and navies of World War I.

The No. 1 J. H. McCleskey segued a coal company into an oil company. On April 17, 1918—less than six months after the discovery—the name Texas & Pacific Coal Company was changed to Texas Pacific Coal and Oil Company.[23]

The McCleskey discovery touched off a frenzy of activity. Prospectors poured into Ranger and the surrounding countryside in search of black gold. Tent cities and derrick forests sprang up. Ranger's population exploded to thirty thousand. Geologists, lease hounds, suppliers, teamsters, roughnecks, laborers, cooks, and bakers came—as well as the unsavory and unwelcome.

Because Ranger was connected to Fort Worth by the Texas & Pacific Railway, the ensuing boom made "The City Where the West Begins" a veritable oil capital. The Gordon bonanza catapulted Fort Worth into the ranks of America's major cities. Wildcatters, geologists, landmen, brokers, ranchers, and farmers descended upon the city. The caravansaray in Fort Worth for the treasure hunters was the luxurious Westbrook Hotel where, according to historian-newspaperman Mack Williams, one and all paused to pay homage to the Golden Goddess, a larger than life marble nude. All that was necessary to produce gushing oil wells or to make a fortune in lease trading was but to rub her derriere.[24]

With the discovery of oil at Ranger, the decision was made in 1918 to move the general offices of the company from New York to Thurber, although the Executive Offices would remain in New York City for five more years. To accommodate the Yankee invasion, new homes were built on the hill south of the Quadrangle. It is not surprising that the new residential area came to be called New York Hill. Today, curious travelers on Interstate 20 as they pass that location might wonder why, deep in the heart of Texas, a roadside cafe would be called New York Hill Restaurant.

The houses in this area, many of them two-story structures, were built of brick with interior walls of wallboard and hardwood floors. Brick sidewalks lined the streets and a brick walk led to the entrance of each residence. New York Hill's lawns were well landscaped, with grass, shade trees, shrubbery, and beds of brightly blooming flowers.[25]

While things were booming in Thurber in 1918, the booming in Europe stopped. At the eleventh hour of the eleventh day of the eleventh month, the guns became silent. Armistice! The World War had ended. Along with the rest of the nation, Thurber celebrated the cessation of hostilities with joy and thanksgiving.

As the year 1919 dawned, the country was only days away from bidding a sad farewell to Theodore Roosevelt. The indomitable, ebullient, charging Bull Moose, always an inspiration to the nation, died on 6 January.

Three weeks after Roosevelt's death, at 7:30 on the morning of January 24, 1919, following a night of heavy rain, Big Lake dam broke at the northeast corner, flooding the valley between the Big Lake and Mingus. The long drought had ended and 1919 would prove to be a very wet year. A small army of men soon manned the barricades and managed to save a third of the lake's water. Dirt, rock, and cement were hauled across the dam from the west side to the break on the east side. Electric power came from the nearby brickyard and the dam was quickly repaired. Come hell or high water, Thurber's can-do spirit and teamwork were never found wanting.[26]

A few miles away, Ranger's dirt streets became quagmires. In 1940, the movie *Boom Town,* starring Clark Gable, Spencer Tracy, and Claudette Colbert, depicted the scene with Model T Fords, wagons, horses, and people floundering in a sea of mud. Conditions were the same in other towns in the area, but the rain did not stop the rush for oil. Hundreds of eager people possessed with black gold fever continued to descend on the area. A young man, thirty-one years old, who hailed from San Antonio, New Mexico, appeared in Cisco in 1919 with hopes of striking it rich by buying the local bank. But the bank was not for sale. Worse than that, he could not even find a place to sleep. So great was the demand, the rooms in Cisco's Mobley Hotel were being rented to four guests at a time. An idea

Home on New York Hill, circa 1919. Courtesy Dick Smith Library, Tarleton State University.

turned on in the young man's mind. If he couldn't buy a bank, he would buy a hotel. Upon making inquiry, he was told by the Mobley's owner that he would sell the hotel to him for fifty thousand dollars. The young man's name was Conrad Hilton. Within forty-eight hours he managed to raise the funds, and the little Mobley Hotel in Cisco, Texas, some thirty miles from TP's No. 1 J. H. McCleskey, became the first hotel in the fabulous Hilton empire.

In 1919, tragedy struck the W. K. Gordon family. June 30 was a warm summer day in Thurber. The temperature reached near ninety. The Gordon children asked if they could go swimming. W. K. Gordon, Jr. recalled: "Rocky Rhodes was secretary and chauffeur for my father. I was nine and my sister, Louise, was eleven. Rocky drove us and Louise's little friend to a spot on Palo Pinto Creek between Strawn and Mingus. All of us had been in the water and had gotten out. The girls went back in. They got out too far in the stream and apparently fell in a deep hole. They began to struggle and shout for help. Louise's friend was saved but Louise drowned."[27]

Alver A. Simmans, who was born in Thurber in 1906, and whose father, Luther, worked in the TP machine shop, filled in additional details of the tragedy. Alver was thirteen at the time:

> Billy and Louise Gordon and Hope Corbett, driven by Rocky Rhodes, stopped at the store in Mingus and invited my sister, Vivian, and me to go

swimming with them in Palo Pinto Creek. We lived on the creek, and since Mama knew it was up and muddy, she would not let us go with them.

So they went on to a spot about three miles from Mingus, where the road crosses the creek. Just to the right of the bridge is a place called Blue Hole. After they had been in a while, they all got out and Rocky and Billy went into some trees to put their clothes on. While they were changing, the girls decided they would go back in. That's when Louise drowned. God! How dreadful! How it must have killed Rocky Rhodes to bring this awful news to Mr. Gordon![28]

The Gordons interred Louise in the on-premises family mausoleum where they had placed their infant daughter Margie in 1905.

◆

In October of 1919, the attention of baseball-crazed Thurber, like that of the rest of the country, was riveted on the World Series, featuring the Chicago White Sox and the Cincinnati Reds. That series has gone down in history as "The Black Sox Scandal." Eight Chicago players were accused of plotting to lose the series to Cincinnati in return for payments from gamblers. Baseball club owners quickly appointed Federal Judge Kenesaw M. Landis as commissioner of baseball. They gave him unlimited power to control the game. Landis banned the accused players from baseball for life.

◆

The sad year of 1919 brought two more farewells to Thurber: mine Nos. 11 and 12 were closed. Mine No. 11 produced 1,445,417 tons over its fifteen-year life and No. 12 produced 1,146,879 tons in thirteen years. These closings left only three mines to provide jobs for the Thurber miners: No. 10, New No. 1, and New No. 3.

Rich as the McCleskey was, that million dollar well merely primed the pump. Lurking below the surface were oceans of oil, not only in the Ranger area but in the regions beyond. The flow from the monumental McCleskey lit the imagination of wildcatters everywhere. The McCleskey was plugged and abandoned May 30, 1920, 956 days from the day of discovery.[29] No one knows exactly how much oil came out of the Ranger pool between 1917 and 1920. Nor can it be known with any great degree of certainty how much black gold remained when the well was plugged. According to some engineering calculations, as much as 86 percent of the oil was left in the ground. This was because billions of cubic feet of gas, for lack of a market, was flared into the air. No gas, no pressure. No pressure, no oil. Young Ranger died years before its time.[30]

Oil changed the poor into millionaires and if a well went bust, millionaires could again be poor. A case in point: The Morton sisters came to Thurber to teach school in 1916. One of them, Lola, married George

McCleskey home (left to right): Daniel Edward McCleskey, George H. McCleskey, and John Hill McCleskey, circa 1903. Courtesy Frances McCleskey Rock.

McCleskey, called Top, son of John McCleskey. Lola McCleskey's niece, Lola Spearing, recalled: "Top and Lola went to Chicago. They traveled extensively. They bought a yellow Mormon automobile half a block long, jewelry and sterling. They spent money like it was water. They thought the Niagara of black gold would flow forever. Then the well was plugged. In 1923 or 1924, someone set their house on fire. It burned to the ground, a total loss. They lost everything. They did not have two nickels to rub together."[31]

In 1920, after a World War and two terms of Democrat President Woodrow Wilson, the nation elected Warren G. Harding twenty-ninth president of the United States. Ahead lay the Roaring Twenties, with gangsters and prohibition and Teapot Dome scandals, culminating at the end of the decade in the great stock market crash of October 1929.

Following the Ranger discovery, President Edgar L. Marston decided it was easier to get oil out of a pipe than to dig coal out of a thirty-inch seam two or three hundred feet below ground. After having been led from its beginning by the all-in-the-family leadership of Hunter and Marston, an outsider would be installed as president. The president would be not a coal man, but an oil man who would lead the company into the uncharted oil milieu of the future.

5

When Texas & Pacific Coal Company was born in 1888 as strictly a coal mining company, motorized vehicles were still in their infancy, but Henry Ford and his engineers, among others, would change that in short order. Between 1903 and 1908, Ford created nineteen models, designating each by a letter of the alphabet. Some of the cars were experimental and never reached the public. In 1908, the Model T was born, and for years to come, America heard the clatter of its engine and the imperious "aoouga" of its horn. By 1910, there were 458,000 cars and 10,000 trucks in the United States. Thanks to Ford's revolutionary process of industrial production, which made cars affordable for the masses, cheap fuel, and highway building programs, the 1920 census reported for all types of motorcars, a leap in one decade from one-half million to over ten million vehicles.[1] By 1927, Ford had sold more than fifteen million Model Ts.[2] Texas Pacific Coal and Oil Company was poised to reap rich dividends from this burgeoning automobile industry. When Ranger was in flower proration was nonexistent and there was a market for every drop of TP oil.[3] Furthermore, Thurber bricks would help pave the way.

About 1919, following the bonanza discovery of the Ranger oil field, President Edgar L. Marston, then fifty-nine, and General Manager W. K. Gordon, fifty-seven, turned their thoughts to who would lead Texas Pacific Coal and Oil Company in the 1920s. The most obvious candidate was Marston's son, Edgar J. Marston, but at thirty-one, his father felt the young man ought to have about ten more years of on-the-job training. What was needed now was an oil man young in years but rich in experience who could run the company until young Marston gained sufficient maturity and experience to assume the mantle of leadership. The elder Marston went head hunting. His search for a new Texas Pacific president led in 1919 to Casper, Wyoming, to forty-four-year-old John Roby Penn, vice-president of Midwest Refining Company.

John Roby Penn was born in Reno, Pennsylvania, on August 11, 1875, to John Roby and Clara Darnell Penn. The elder Penn was a banker and an accountant. The son, John Roby, attended public schools in Oil City, Pennsylvania, about twenty-five miles down the Allegheny River from Titusville, site of Edwin L. Drake's first oil well in America. He attended

Edgar L. Marston, circa 1920. Courtesy Sheila Carter.

Amherst College, at Amherst, Massachusetts, in 1895-96. A bob-sledding accident during his second year made it impossible for him to continue his education at that time. Living in the heart of the nation's nascent and burgeoning oil country, it was natural that the young man would look towards the oil industry as a possible career. He became a petroleum landman in 1900 for the Ohio Oil Company of Findlay, Ohio, working mainly in Ohio and Illinois. In 1917 he moved to Midwest Refining Company as vice-president.

✦

Landmen are known as the ambassadors of the oil industry. They negotiate the purchase of leases from landowners and make trades with other oil companies. They have the patience to spend endless hours in courthouse records rooms; the endurance to drive hundreds of miles into rural America, searching for long-lost heirs; and the charm needed to get along equally well with a widow who has two acres of land and a tycoon who has ten thousand. They are just as at ease with the bank president in his carpeted office as with the farmer on his tractor in the field.[4]

✦

Landmen are like traveling salesmen. Back at the turn of the century, there were few hotels or restaurants to be found in the rural towns that these travelers visited. The best a man could hope for would be overnight bed and board at a farm house. Penn spent many a night in such accommodations. John R. Penn, Jr. told about an idiosyncrasy of his father in those days: "After bargaining with a farmer for a night's lodging, Dad would see the farmer's wife chasing a chicken to kill for dinner. Dad did not like to think about the chicken cackling and running for its life only two hours before it was being eaten. Dating from that time, he would never eat freshly killed chicken."[5]

Marston wanted a man who had had experience with a major oil company, preferably one of the Standard Oil of New Jersey companies. The Ohio Oil Company, with whom Penn had gotten his start in the business, had been one of the earliest members of the Standard Oil of New Jersey family. In 1906 the federal government, under the Sherman Antitrust Act, brought suit against Standard Oil of New Jersey. In 1911, the Supreme Court of the United States ordered Standard to dissolve under the provisions of the Sherman Act. This action forced thirty-four companies of Standard Oil of New Jersey to operate as independent units.

Marston found Penn and brought him to New York in 1919 as assistant to the president. The Board of Directors, of which Gordon was a member, was quick to ratify the move. In 1920 Marston became Chairman when Penn was named President. Marston continued to live in New York, while

Penn was transferred to Fort Worth, where he made his home. He never lived in Thurber, the site of the general offices.

✦

In 1920, when J. R. Penn moved from New York City to Fort Worth, another man moved from Boston to New York. For the general populace of baseball-minded Thurber, this was a more noteworthy event. His name was Babe Ruth. Ruth's total of fifty-four home runs in 1920 and fifty-nine in 1921—more by himself than almost any entire team had ever hit before in a season—brought a new dimension to the game and earned him the title Sultan of Swat.[6] But the best was yet to come for the Babe and the Yankees. Under Penn, the best was yet to come for the Texas Pacific Coal and Oil Company. Sadly, the same could not be said for Thurber.

✦

As activity in the Ranger area began to simmer down, the company sent Gordon to Patagonia in South America in late 1920 to scout out the possibilities of another oil bonanza. Accompanying him was his eleven-year-old son Billy. Unlike his early days in Thurber when he tramped over the hills studying terrain and geology, his exploration in Patagonia revealed nothing to excite his interest. "After the absence of about a year," said W. K. Gordon, Jr., "we returned to Texas. Dad then spent another year investigating petroleum prospects in other areas of the United States. On one occasion we were in Odessa. When we got off the train, we spent the day riding around in a car which he had rented. When we got back on the train, he said, 'Billy, one of these days they are going to find a sea of oil from here to the Canadian border.'"[7]

On April 8, 1920, some seven weeks before the No. 1 McCleskey was plugged and abandoned, seventeen-year old George B. Studdard commenced working for Texas Pacific in the Ranger office. His first job was as stenographer to Purchasing Agent F. D. Bostaph. He would work forty-eight years, retiring in 1968 as Tax Commissioner.[8] While Gordon was in South America, Studdard transferred from Ranger to Thurber on January 16, 1921. Working close to top company officials, the young man learned all about coal, oil, and brick. Although brick never made it into the company's name, it was profitable not only for TP, but for others downstream from the plant—bankers, railroads, truckers, brickyards, contractors, and bricklayers.

Studdard enthused about the lasting qualities of Thurber brick:

> Going west on I-20, have you ever looked to your right, just as you were getting to Thurber, and seen that hill? We always referred to it as Shale Mountain. You can see it's stripped. You've heard of making a mountain out of a molehill. In Thurber they almost made a molehill out of a mountain.

There was a lot of shale extracted and hauled to the brick plant. They first started using shale from a deposit near the plant southeast of town, but they found that the one to the north had a much better grade of shale. A lot of people refer to it as clay, but it was not clay. It was shale, and whenever processed into brick and run through the brick kiln and finished, it would have a vitrified surface, that is, a surface like a pane of glass window. It would not absorb moisture and so was ideal for paving streets. . . .

When I moved to Thurber, I lived at first in Marston Hall. After I married, I lived on Church Street. Most of the houses on that street were built of brick. They used No. 2 brick. These No. 2 bricks, for some reason or other, were rejected as pavers, and they were used as building bricks. You have traveled in places where you would see old brick buildings which looked like they were literally rotting down, just decaying. That was caused mainly by cold weather. Rain water seeps into cracks and crevices where it freezes and expands. Those brick buildings that you see in Thurber have lasted through all the years, and you don't see the brick sloughing off.[9]

But how did the whitish, grayish, or yellowish shale become the red ruby brick that emerged from the Thurber kilns? The red color in brick comes from the iron oxide (Fe_2O_3) in Texas shale. The firing process changes the mineralogy of the shale so that the color changes from the unfired colors (ranging from buff-yellow to gray) to a red color. The higher the firing temperature in the kiln, the deeper the red color of the fired brick.[10] The shale was turned into a slurry; squeezed into molds; thrust into a hot, fiery furnace heated seven times over, and baked until redder than a chili pepper; then taken out and left to cool before being shipped to some distant construction site.

✦

Dwayne Holden, Lockheed Martin Senior Configuration Management Specialist, told about his boyhood home that was built of indestructible, used Thurber brick: "In 1942, my parents, Woodie and Ruth Holden, built a house in Abilene, Texas, in an area known as ACC Hill. Their contractor, a Mr. Lambert, insisted on using bricks made in Thurber because they were bigger and stronger. He was able to find used brick in Thurber and trucked them to Abilene. His brick mason used them to make a beautiful red brick house. Fifty years later the house is still standing, a tribute to the brick makers of Thurber."[11]

✦

Some time after the end of World War I, the building brick plant was destroyed by fire. This was of no great consequence, as it had stood idle since 1909 when the company had discontinued the manufacture of building brick, choosing to concentrate on paving brick. At that time, black Model T Fords began to multiply in Texas like jackrabbits. Unlike jackrabbits, the Model T could not bound and jump and zigzag through the brush and briars. They needed a track to run on.

Streets and highways in many parts of the state were paved with Thurber brick. In 1913 Gordon wrote: "The Paving Plant has been in operation since its construction in 1898, and now has an annual capacity of 10,063,500 brick. The quality of these brick is second to none made in the United States, and so widely has this fact become known, that there is not a city in Texas of any size that has not some of its streets paved with Thurber Brick."[12] As mentioned, Thurber bricks were used in the construction of Seawall Boulevard in Galveston. A Texas historical marker at the intersection of Vanderbilt and Clinton streets in Stephenville states that many streets in that city are paved with Thurber brick. Rita Bridges, a student at John Tarleton when it was a Junior College in 1945-1947, remarked that one of her classmates told her that the reason she picked Tarleton was because she fell in love with "the red cobblestone streets of Stephenville."[13] Sixteen-foot-wide Ranger-Eastland-Cisco highway, the longest stretch of brick pavement in the state, was paved with Thurber brick. The road led straight to the front door of Conrad Hilton's Mobley Hotel.[14] Congress Avenue in Austin was paved with Thurber brick. So was Camp Bowie Boulevard, a main thoroughfare in Fort Worth's historic Arlington Heights.

The 1908 smokestack that still stands at Thurber was also built of Thurber brick. The smokestack came up in the middle of the power plant complex. The town generated its own power and had an ice plant there. One of the restaurants at Thurber now is called the Smokestack.[15] The building housing the Smokestack restaurant was, in Thurber's heyday, the drugstore. Every Christmas, the entire second floor of the building became a wonderland of toys. Alver Simmans recalled how he would go there and spend hours watching the toy trains, wishing mightily that Santa would bring one to him.[16] The building was destroyed by fire on January 15, 1992, but its walls of imperishable Thurber brick stood until 1996 when the remains were bulldozed. In future days, the salvaged bricks will doubtlessly fetch a pretty price for some new home, wall, fence, or building. The owner, Randy Bennett, moved the restaurant across the street to the old Dry Goods and Furniture Store, which is also constructed of indestructible Thurber brick.

◆

On May 10, 1921, nearly a year after the No. 1 J. H. McCleskey was plugged and abandoned, the drilling contractor on that historic well, Warren Wagner, was himself, so to speak, plugged and abandoned. Wagner, thirty-eight at the time, was shot to death on the streets of Fort Worth by Floyd Holmes, President of Planet Oil Company. Wagner had accused Holmes of being involved with his wife.

Holmes, maintaining that Wagner had threatened him, argued self-defense. He was acquitted.[17]

✦

What was the physical layout of Thurber in the 1920s? George Studdard remembers:

> Rather than having a single large commissary, Colonel Hunter decided at the outset to have separate stores for different services and commodities built around a quadrangle. During the 1920s, the Opera House was located at the northeast corner of the Quadrangle. Next to it was Marston Hall, a large T-shaped two-story building. A lot of the employees lived there. So did I when I transferred from Ranger in 1921.
>
> Coming on around to the west was the grocery store, which was a wooden two-story building. Upstairs was the Masonic Lodge. Edgar L. Marston sent a Mr. Creighton down from New York to manage the grocery store. He spoke with an English accent.
>
> On the west side was a large brick building that housed the Dry Goods-Furniture Store. This building today is the Smokestack Restaurant. The Undertaking Department was located in the north wing of that building. Embalming was done where the restaurant kitchen is now located. Mr. Wells was the mortician. He would meet me on the street and take me by the hand and say in a solicitous yet sympathetic manner, "You look a little peaked. Are you feeling well today?" A man-powered elevator ran to the second floor where the caskets were on display. One day some kids rode up on the elevator. Unnoticed by his cohorts, one of them slipped into a casket. By and by the other boys, seeing a body in the casket, edged up for a closer look. Then the prankster opened his eyes and, calling the boys by name, said, "Hello." No Halloween was ever scarier.
>
> Coming south across the street were the old offices of what originally was the Texas & Pacific Coal Company, occupied mostly by W. K. Gordon [later by Ed S. Britton] and Cashier and Paymaster Thomas R. Hall. Judge W. J. Oxford and the Legal Department were on the second floor. The people who worked in the offices were on the private pay roll. Everyone else was on the mine payroll.
>
> Coming on from there were other offices. Then a drugstore. Next to it was a two-story building. Actually, it was two buildings, but connected by a steel stairway that led up to the center. You would turn to the right at the top of the stairway. That was where some of the doctors had offices. Also, the switchboard was there. All the telephones in town, whether residence or office, went through that one central switchboard. You didn't have a separate switchboard for just the office. That was the switchboard for the entire town. Texas Pacific owned the exchange and had connections with Southwestern

Bell if you wanted to call long distance. Turning to the left at the top of the stairway, you would enter the engineering offices.

Then there was a large two story brick building. The ground floor was the Meat Market and Hardware Store. The second floor was occupied by the General Offices.[18]

The company owned all the churches—Baptist, Methodist, Episcopal, Catholic—and paid for any necessary repairs. All utilities—gas, water, and electricity—were furnished by TP. Today, the New York Hill Restaurant occupies the site of the former Episcopal Church. W. J. Ochiltree was an influential member of the church, and as a consequence, the church was often called Bill Ochiltree's Church.

Coal, brick, oil. Texas Pacific Coal and Oil Company was, at least in the eyes of the miners, rich! If you have an excellent product with a competitive price, chances are that your company will prosper and grow. Texas Pacific benefited from such a formula from its formation through the first two decades of the twentieth century. Thurber in 1921 attained its brightest magnitude. After that year, as the T&P and other railroads steadily converted their coal burning locomotives to the plentiful, less expensive, and more versatile oil, the coal town began its mournful and melancholy descent into oblivion.

The conversion from coal to oil started before the turn of the century. Edward L. Doheny in 1895 convinced the Santa Fe Railroad to convert one of its locomotives into an oil burner, one of the first of its kind.[19] The U.S. Navy also decided to switch from coal to oil. The battleship USS Texas, a twin-stack coal burner, was launched in 1914—in time for her fourteen-inch guns to speak in World War I. The trend continued when, in 1925, she was converted to oil-fired boilers with a single stack.

It had been eighteen years since W. K. Gordon in Fort Worth's Worth Hotel remarked to the miners, "Boys, you now own the mines." In hopes of regaining its market for coal, the company in 1921 canceled its contract with the United Mine Workers and announced a reduction in the scale of wages. The miners recalled the dire pronouncement that Gordon rendered in 1903 that a higher wage scale would force the company out of business. Failing to appreciate the vastly different economic conditions prevailing in 1921 as compared to 1903, the miners struck. This time their demands had no chance.

During this year, one of the last three operating mines was closed—New No. 1. Located some two miles southwest of Thurber, the mine's slag pile can be seen today from the access road on the south side of Interstate 20. The mine produced 1,328,959 tons during its twelve-year life.

As in 1903, hundreds of families, with union encouragement, left Thurber. A tent city was established just outside the Texas Pacific Coal and Oil Company property, which resembled an army camp, as World War I army

NOTICE

HAVING EXHAUSTED EVERY MEANS IN ITS POWER TO REACH AN AGREEMENT WITH THE U. M. W. OF A. AND FAILING TO DO SO, THE COMPANY HAS DECIDED TO OPERATE ITS MINES INDEPENDENTLY, AND OFFERS THE FOLLOWING SCALE FOR A PERIOD OF TWELVE MONTHS:

		Per Ton
Mining Rate	. . .	$2.00
		Per Day, 11¼ Hours
Engineers, Day	. .	$7.08
Engineers, Night	. .	$6.26
		Per Day, 8 Hours
Top Men	. . .	$4.36
Bottom Men	. .	$5.00
Spraggers	. .	$3.65
Trappers	. .	$2.65
Road Cleaners	. .	$4.75
Face Men	. .	$5.29
Blacksmiths	. .	$5.51
Blacksmith's Helpers	.	$4.77
		Per Yard
Entry Yardage	. .	$1.68
Back Brushing	. .	$1.47
Straights	. .	$ .68
		Each
Cribs	. . .	$1.00

The whistle will be blown at Mine No. 10 Monday morning, September 19, and Check Numbers can be obtained either at the office or at the mine.

TEXAS PACIFIC COAL AND OIL CO.

By W. K. GORDON, Vice President.

Thurber, Texas, September 17, 1921.

Notice of reduction of wage scale. Courtesy Dick Smith Library, Tarleton State University.

surplus tents were purchased by the union to shelter the strikers. The striking miners received grocery allotments from the union. Little violence accompanied the 1921 strike, though company officials, fearing the worst, arranged to have Texas Rangers and United States marshals on the scene. Thurber and Mingus became armed camps due to a simultaneous strike by the miners and railroad workers. Armed guards patrolled the railroad shops and yards at Mingus. Scab miners were protected by shotgun-carrying company guards to and from the last two mines in operation, No.

10, located about two miles northwest of Thurber and the closer New No. 3.[20]

Lawrence Santi, UMW legislative representative, was a delegate to the Conference of Southern Coal Operators, convening in Fort Worth, during the strike. W. K. Gordon attended for the company. After the union and operators failed to reach an agreement, the two men traveled together to Mingus on a train. Although Gordon was sympathetic toward the plight of the miners, he stood firm on the company's decision to carry out the ultimatum that had been presented to the union. His attitude had crystallized: if the miners want to go, let them.

Meanwhile, the miners, living in their tent city, waited in vain for an agreement between union and company officials that would send them back to the coal pits. They could not believe that they were no longer needed in Thurber or that the need for coal had dwindled. The triumph and victory of UMW in 1903 was not repeated in 1921. As time wore on, the miners began to drift away. Some went to the coal fields of Illinois, Colorado, or other states. Some moved away and began new careers in other fields. Some remained in the Thurber area, working in oil fields, on pipeline construction, or other projects.

When President John R. Penn transferred to Fort Worth from New York City in 1920, he was accompanied by thirty-two-year old Edgar Jean Marston, son of Edgar L. Marston. About a year after their arrival, the Fort Worth Chamber of Commerce rolled out the red carpet to welcome the corporate blue chips to the city. An invitation was sent out for a reception and banquet honoring the two newcomers to be held on July 28, 1921, at the plush River Crest Country Club. The toastmaster for the event was W. M. Massie. Delivering toasts were Amon G. Carter, food and beer distributor Ben E. Keith, and attorney W. B. Paddock.

◆

At the time that the chamber of commerce was entertaining Penn and Marston, Franklin D. Roosevelt was vacationing on Campobello Island in Canada. Several days later on 10 August, as he returned from sailing, he and his sons fought a forest fire. The next morning, he could not stand. He was hospitalized in New York City until October. The diagnosis was polio. Even when he returned home, he was able to sit up only with assistance. Although elected President of the United States four times, unknown to the general public, he never walked again.[21]

◆

On June 22, 1922, the last survivor of the original company founders, Mrs. William W. Johnson—Anna—died. She was the last of the Johnsons who had started it all in Thurber before Thurber was Thurber. Death had taken her daughter, Marion, in 1885, her brother-in-law Harvey in 1888,

Thurber early 1920s: Edgar J. Marston, Edgar L. Marston, John Roby Penn, and W. K. Gordon. Courtesy John Roby Penn, Jr.

her son William Harvey in 1894, and her husband Will in 1914. And in 1902 she had also seen the death of "that damned villain," Colonel Robert Dickie Hunter.

✦

For a year following her death, Anna's body lay with her husband and children in the small family mausoleum located at the ranch house north of Gordon. Her will, however, directed that another mausoleum be built on a high hill overlooking the ranch. Under the supervision of her executor, Judge E. B. Ritchie, the new mausoleum was constructed of native reddish brown sandstone found in abundance on the ranch. The eighteen-by-eighteen-foot square enclosure has walls two and one-half feet thick, with a stone turret at each of the four corners. The mausoleum was dedicated on July 2, 1923. "The mausoleum is located a few miles north of Gordon, east of Highway 919 and west of Lake Palo Pinto. There is no company, even of other graves or mausoleums. Other than the occasional curious, spurred possibly by some newspaper article, the only visitors to the site are the owner of the land, his ranch hands, the birds, the rattlesnake, the deer, the rabbit, the chaparral cock and the ever-moving winds of west Texas."[22]

After seven decades of alternating blazing Texas summers and fierce winter blizzards, the old edifice is beginning to show its age, pieces of crumbled rock and

Johnson Mausoleum. Courtesy *Fort Worth Star-Telegram.*

mortar having dropped here and there like overripe fruit. On a cornerstone are the names and dates of death of each member of the family. Engraved on another stone is this inscription: "Residents of Palo Pinto County from the year 1880. Pioneers in the development of our natural resources. Leaders in all matters of material and moral progress. Their works do follow them."

✦

Colonel Robert Dickie Hunter sleeps among heroes and the great and famous in St. Louis's green Bellefontaine Cemetery. William Whipple Johnson, his wife and children sleep in splendid isolation on the lone prairie deep in the heart of Texas.

On November 29, 1922, TP incorporated a subsidiary, Thurber Pipe Line Company. The company built two pipelines. The first was one of approximately twenty miles in length, running from the Robberson Oil Field in Garvin County, Oklahoma, to TP's refinery it was building at Wynnewood. The second pipeline ran through several large producing areas in Texas where it was a major operator. The north end of the pipeline started with a few gathering lines in southwestern Young County, crossing into Stephens County near Eliasville where the trunk line started. It continued southward near Caddo where it veered to the southeast in Palo Pinto County. Its southern terminus was the Illinois Pipe Line Company tank farm at Mingus which it reached in 1926. From there the oil was transported through their facilities to the new TP refinery in Fort Worth, also completed in 1926.[23]

Following the 1921 strike morale was low. Hundreds of miners left for other locations, and the future of the disillusioned remaining miners was uncertain. The future of Thurber was suspended as Gordon spent much of 1921 and 1922 investigating oil prospects in other areas. In the increasingly conspicuous and disquieting absence of their leader, miners, brickmakers, machinists, carpenters, electricians, plumbers, printers, butchers, store clerks and all other blue collar workers, along with white collar General Office personnel, went soberly about their every day routine, trusting that when Gordon returned prosperity, security, and contentment would again reign. On December 11, 1922, Ed Stephens, wrote to Gordon:

My dear Mr. Gordon:

We feel so rejoiced over the change that will take place soon at Thurber that it prompts me to write you. If it is true that you will take charge again of Thurber and its holdings, it has made the hearts of many a poor man, woman and child glad. Of late I made a trip to Arkansas and Oklahoma, and in meeting so many people, I would be asked is it so that Mr. Gordon will take charge again at Thurber. My answer would be, "May God have it so." And I hope so. I hope that God will bless you and keep you in his loving care. You have done many a wonderful good thing for the poor people in Thurber.

When you return to your old stamping grounds, the tears of many a man, woman and child will be made dry. The two years of sorrow will be forever forgotten. Those that you have been a father to for 20 years who are now in Arkansas, Oklahoma, Ohio, Pennsylvania and many other places will return with a glad heart. The image of your face is imprinted on the hearts of those poor people of Thurber and continually before their eyes.

May the Father of Mercies support you and pour into your bosom the rich consolation of his grace, and preserve and strengthen you for your family.[24]

Stephens added a postscript to his letter. Although only six words, it spoke volumes: "Not a member of any union." Sentimental Gordon was touched by the letter. He kept it in his desk the rest of his life.

On December 1, 1922, Charles E. Yager, Jr., twenty-three years old, with a degree in geology from the University of California at Berkeley, began his employment with Texas Pacific. Although small in stature, he would cast a long shadow over the company. Yager was born in Stillwater, Indian Territory, on February 14, 1899, a day so cold, Yager recounted, "the Mississippi River froze. My mother's family nicknamed me Mickey Dooley after a then popular cartoon character. Mickey got dropped and I was Dooley the rest of my life."[25] Yager treasured a 1917 Abilene High School Yearbook, *The Flashlight,* that gave some insight on young Dooley: "Dooley is an artist, a wearer of the green, a ladies man, a driver of a Maxwell, a jolly Senior Sun. He shines in English like the interior of an ink well on a dark night. His chief pleasure consists in explaining some scientific principle while his classmates stand around in open-mouthed wonder. His ambition is to be a great architect or a first-class English teacher."[26]

Although Yager held a degree in geology and would make his mark in life as a geologist, it was as an architect that he was first hired by Texas Pacific. After graduating from Abilene High School, he went to Texas A&M for one year, 1917-18. Then he went into the Army. When he was released, he returned to Abilene:

> All these geologists had come out to Abilene to do surface work all through the country. I told my family I was going to study geology. They said, "What in the world is that?"
>
> Then I went to the University of Texas, after the army, and was there two years. You had to have a foreign language before you could graduate from Texas. I took Spanish. But the Spanish teacher must have been blind, for even though I attended class religiously for about a month, he sent me a notice saying "You have never been to class, so we are dropping you from the rolls." In my second year at Texas, I realized I could not graduate there without a foreign language. I searched the books and found that this was not a requirement at the University of California at Berkeley, which, incidentally, had one of the top geological departments in the U.S. I transferred there and finished in 1922.
>
> But I could not get a job as a geologist. I even went to Houston in search of employment. My family had moved to Lubbock. I had a great uncle who lived in Thurber and had been with TP from the beginning. He, like W. K. Gordon, was from Virginia. He called up one day and said TP was getting ready to build a refinery in Wynnewood, Oklahoma, and perhaps I could get a job up there helping to design the refinery. The only architectural course I had taken was in my freshman year at Texas A&M, but I had spent summers working in an architect's office. I called the contractor at Wynnewood and told him of my background. He said, "Come up." So I was hired to do architectural duties.
>
> When the refinery came on stream in June, 1923,[27] I then found myself in the Geological Department and was there for about two years. In 1924, I married Gilcy. When she was born in Pauls Valley in 1903, they gave her the Chickasaw name Hyahwahnah. The doctor came to see her the next day. She weighed only three pounds. He said that was too long a name. "She is just the size of a gill." She has been called Gilcy [pronounced Jilcy] ever since.[28]

Although Yager never called Thurber home, about six or seven months after his employment, he was sent down from Wynnewood to Thurber on an assignment which lasted for only a few weeks. Once there "Dooley" furnished first-hand witness of the good times had by all to his sweetheart Hyahwahnah Rennie, back in Oklahoma in the form of a tabloid newspaper *The Yager Daily News*. On August 3, 1923, under a headline "Big Dance Given at Club Last Night" was the following item:

All of Thurber's best society attend a rotten dance. Several couples dead drunk. One guy from Ranger nearly hit by R.R. Thompson, Chief Geologist for the Company. Mrs. Creswell lost the diamond out of her ring. (Note: Editor doubts she had one in it.) Many flappers attended but Editor couldn't handle them all. Punch was spiked. Editor had to lay off after first drink. The windmill style of dancing seemed to be in vogue. Everybody but the jelly-beans danced that way. The dance closed about 2 A.M. but Editor got tired and quit about 12:30 A.M.

A second item from *The Yager Daily News:*

Revenue agents raid beer bar, capturing one still, 500 bottles of beer, ten quarts of grappo (TNT). Louie the owner put in jail for fourth time. This causes the hot weather to be a lot more disagreeable to a bunch of the old beerhounds of the company. The Editor wishes to state that he is not in this crowd.[29]

After that one issue, *The Yager Daily News* folded. But that is not to say that young Charles (Dooley) Yager was not heard from again, for he would become President of Texas Pacific.

✦

Cub reporter Yager was so obsessed with the society doings in Thurber on August 3, 1923, that he missed the national scoop of the decade, for at the very hour that the big Thurber party was breaking up, fifteen hundred miles to the east in the State of Vermont, Vice President Calvin Coolidge was awakened from sleep and informed that President Warren G. Harding had died a few hours before in San Francisco. Coolidge dressed and knelt in prayer, then walked downstairs to the dining room where his father, by the light of a kerosene lamp, administered the presidential oath at 2:45 A.M.

✦

Baseball was always popular in Thurber during the summer months. The town's first baseball park was located at the end of Park Row. Later, a park was built on Cemetery Hill, complete with a grandstand, and was enclosed by a high board fence. In the 1920s, a new park was constructed at the original ball park site on Park Row to accommodate larger crowds. Teams representing the miners, the brickmakers, and the high school played almost every summer afternoon. A high school cheer from the class of 1922 is displayed at the Smokestack Restaurant in Thurber:

> Bean soup, pea soup, pumpkin pie
> Ach der leber, my, my, my!
> Hit 'em in the eye-ball, sock 'em in the jaw!
> Hospital, cemetery. Rah! Rah! Rah![30]

In the 1920s, Thurber boasted one of the finest semi-pro teams in the state. The Thurber team was a member of the Oil Belt League, composed of teams from Thurber (Texas Pacific Coal and Oil Company), Ranger, Breckenridge, Parks Camp (Texaco), Olden (Magnolia Petroleum Company), and Cisco. Large crowds of enthusiastic fans from Thurber and the country round about poured into the Thurber ball park to watch Sunday afternoon games.

✦

The 1923 baseball season was one talked about for a long time in Thurber and the other towns of the Oil Belt League. It began with the infamous Black Sox Scandal of 1919. In 1921 Baseball commissioner Kenesaw Landis banned eight Chicago White Sox players from organized baseball for their conspiracy to throw the 1919 World Series. One of the players banned was Chicago star pitcher, Eddie Cicotte. During the 1919 season, Cicotte had won twenty-nine games and lost only seven. He was believed to be the finest pitcher around. Cicotte tearfully admitted to a Chicago Grand Jury that his price for betrayal of duty and honor had been ten thousand dollars. He declared he was through with baseball and would start life over again.[31] But did he?

One day after the [Oil Belt League] 1923 season had gotten well under-way, a fellow got off a freight train in Ranger and made his way up Main Street. He stopped and inquired the way to the baseball park. After being directed there, he casually walked in about the time batting practice started. The Manager, Red Snap, saw him standing back to one side and walked over to him. After a few minutes conversation, the man asked Red's permission to go to the outfield and shag some flies. Red allowed him to do so, and the man gave a good account of himself. The man soon asked if he could pitch to batting practice, and Red again consented. The guy began cutting loose with pitches which hardly anyone was able to hit solidly. Of course, Red signed him up right away.[32]

After the 1923 season had ended, the stranger left as unceremoniously as he had come. Something always bothered Red about this fellow.

Red and Joe McKinnon, Thurber's [team] Captain, had been friends for many years and frequently discussed where they had seen this guy's picture. One day an article showed up in the *Sporting News* discussing some of the players who were mixed up in the Chicago Black Sox scandal of 1919. There were pictures and names of the players who had been thrown out of organized baseball and barred for life from ever participating again. There was the man—Eddie Cicotte, star Chicago pitcher. He had played for Ranger under an assumed name![33]

✦

Texas Pacific Coal and Oil Company often seemed to be at the crossroads of events in the oil world. When John Roby Penn left Midwest Refining Company in 1919 to come to Texas Pacific, the President of Midwest was Henry M. Blackmer. In 1923, some four years after Penn's departure, Blackmer was identified as a key player in the Teapot Dome scandal.

✦

A Senate investigation in 1923, as well as subsequent testimony in court trials, revealed that Secretary of the Interior Albert Fall had persuaded Secretary of the Navy Edwin Denby to transfer government oil reserves at Elk Hills, California, and Teapot Dome, Wyoming, to the Department of the Interior. Fall then leased the reserves to private oil producers Edward L. Doheny and Harry Sinclair. These leases were made without competitive bidding. In both cases, Fall received large sums of money for helping to arrange the transfers—one hundred thousand dollars from Doheny for Elk Hills and three hundred thousand dollars from Sinclair for Teapot Dome.

The scandal forced Fall to resign in 1923. He was later convicted of accepting a bribe and sentenced to prison. Denby resigned in 1924. Sinclair, one of the richest men in the country, also served a short sentence. Doheny avoided prison, but his reputation as a philanthropist remained sullied for the rest of his life. Blackmer, who had received a million dollar kickback in a scheme that had provided the funds to pay the Teapot Dome bribe, fled the country.[34]

✦

In 1923, Gordon resigned from Texas Pacific and moved to east Fort Worth. Since his new home at 2624 Edgewood Terrace was just outside city limits, he encountered no restriction on reinterring his daughters Margie and Louise in his backyard. Their caskets had been preserved in his family mausoleum in Thurber.[35] Although no longer a TP employee, he remained on the Board of Directors until his death.[36] Ed S. Britton, who had come to Thurber as a Texas Ranger thirty-five years earlier and stayed to become Weighmaster of No. 3 mine, succeeded Gordon as General Manager in Thurber.[37]

In 1923, Texas Pacific's executive offices moved from 20 Broad Street, New York City, to Fort Worth. Home in Fort Worth was Suite No. 1511 in the new twenty-four-story Farmers and Mechanics National Bank Building. Chairman of the Board Edgar L. Marston remained in New York City. The TP chiefs in Fort Worth were John R. Penn, President; Edgar J.

Ed Britton came to Thurber originally as a Texas Ranger. He became Superintendent in 1923 when W. K. Gordon resigned and moved to Fort Worth. Courtesy Dick Smith Library, Tarleton State University.

Marston, Vice President; John Hancock, General Counsel; Herman W. Knox, Corporate Secretary; Rudolph Seibel, Assistant Secretary and H. O. (Andy) Anderson, Assistant Treasurer. Richard K. Howard was in charge of stock-holder records. There were few rank and file employees in Fort Worth, because the general offices remained in Thurber.

In 1924 Texas Pacific bought Valiant & Toomey Paving Contractors of Fort Worth and merged it into Thurber Construction Company. Thurber Brick Company manufactured the bricks and sold them to its sister company, Thurber Construction Company, which did the paving. Jess I. Norman, an official with Valiant & Toomey, joined TP at the time of the acquisition and remained with the company for the rest of its existence. He later became Corporate Secretary.

In 1924, Katherine Stell, seventeen and fresh out of high school, came to work for Texas Pacific in the Fort Worth offices as a receptionist and PBX operator. The day she was hired, Edgar J. Marston was in New York. She was told by other women in the office that Marston had two idiosyncrasies. One was that whenever he went to New York, he wore a derby. The other was that he would never speak to you, that he hardly ever spoke to anyone. One day not long afterwards, Stell looked up from the PBX desk to see a man walking down the hall. He wore a derby. Stell smiled at the man and greeted him cheerily. He smiled back but never said a word. As time went on, a bond was apparently created between the laconic Marston and the loquacious Stell. At any rate, he gave her a $20 gold piece at Christmas and told her to go buy herself a hair ribbon. The twenty-dollar gold piece at Christmas became a tradition. Stell does not think any other woman in the office other than possibly his personal secretary, Gladys Barrett, was the object of this generosity.[38]

One of the shining stars that Penn brought into TP was David Donoghue. Coming to TP as Chief Geologist in 1925 after stints with Gulf and Marland, Donoghue played an important role in TP's acquisition of leases in the vast West Texas region beyond Ranger. Donoghue left TP to become an independent consultant. He became an expert witness for the Texas Railroad Commission on spacing, unitization, drainage, and other related problems of the oil industry.[39]

While the changing of the guard was going on in the executive suites in New York and Fort Worth, and in spite of the strike that reduced the town's population by half, life went on in Thurber pretty much as it had done for thirty years. Brickmakers made brick and miners dug coal. After January 16, 1920, when the Eighteenth Amendment ushered in the Roaring Twenties to America, they also engaged in bootlegging by distilling grappo, a white lightning drink known throughout the area.

Geno Solignanni, 81, who was reared here, remembers those days. "Everything in here was bootlegging . . .. But that was the only way folks could make a living after the coal mines shut down. . .."

And the residents, comprising mainly Polish and Italian immigrants who had come here to work the Thurber coal mines, made a wide variety of booze. That included peach and apricot brandy and grappo. "Grappo was 180 proof," said Solignanni. "You used raisins."[40]

After the passage of several decades, a discrepancy exists as to the formula for grappo. Solignanni stated that grappo was an Italian whiskey made from raisins. When asked about this divergence of testimony, an indignant George Studdard stoutly maintained that the source was grapes: "Why else would it be called grappo? Had it been made from prunes, undoubtedly it would have been called prunella. Or if from raisins, then just as certainly it would have been called raisin'ell!"

Mostly the Italians—some of the Poles—would get together and pool their money and buy a railroad refrigerator car of grapes from California. The car was brought up the main line to Mingus. They would unload the car and make their wine from the grapes. After the wine was made, they took the refuse, such as the hulls that were left after the juice of the grapes had been squeezed out. They would put this mass in barrels where it would ferment. Then they distilled it. That was grappo. It was like bootleg corn whiskey. Only it went down *much* easier.[41]

Remember Yager's report to his fiancee on the effects of grappo on those attending a dance at the Thurber Club? During the twenties, the Thurber Club—open to the public—was the hot spot in town. The club's Dance Committee was responsible for finding entertainers to perform in Thurber.

The company furnished the club a big building which had formerly been a pool hall and domino parlor. A little addition was built on the back of the building into which a table and billiard table were moved. That created room for the dance floor. And what a floor it was! It was the most popular dance floor between Fort Worth and El Paso. The flooring was three quarter inch maple, just as smooth as a mirror. Nice and hard.[42]

The Dance Committee hired Lawrence Welk and his six-piece band to play. Welk had come to Dallas for the State Fair and then drove out to Thurber for a Halloween dance. "While old Lawrence was there," said Studdard, "we signed him up for our big annual New Year's Eve party."[43] Welk commented on his Texas tour:

In 1926 West Texas was still wide-open, rip-roaring frontier territory, crowded with people swarming into oil towns like Odessa, McCamey and Midland, looking for a quick fortune. A good many of them found it, too, and overnight oil millionaires were common. I went to Texas where I had been asked to lead a six-piece band for the summer. Right away this farm boy found himself in deep trouble! West Texas was something else, and I spent almost the whole summer in a state of shock. For one thing, my new band and I didn't see eye to eye on a number of things. I hadn't been with the group very long before I realized something funny was going on. A few of the fellows kept disappearing from the bandstand all during the evening, and when they returned, they looked progressively glassy-eyed. I couldn't imagine what they were doing, until my new drummer took me aside and patiently explained that they were out in the back smoking marijuana. Even after he explained it to me, I didn't know what it was. Between the marijuana smokers who kept ducking outside for a smoke and the drinkers who just sat on the bandstand until they fell sound asleep, I often wound up the evening playing all by myself. I really didn't mind too much. I strolled around the dance floor playing requests much of the time anyway, and it wasn't at all unusual for one of those big-hearted Texans to tip me with a twenty- dollar bill. I always made more in tips than I did from my regular salary all the time I played in West Texas.[44]

When the band played in Thurber, it probably was not marijuana that produced glassy eyes for Welk's musicians. Without a doubt, it was grappo!

The New Year's Eve parties were the high point of the entertainment calendar. Studdard remembers the great energy, enthusiasm, and imagination that went into decorating the club for the occasion:

We would go down there and put a network of wires suspended from the ceiling and line it with smilax. TP owned a large tract of fee land near Longview in East Texas.[45] The old man who was in charge of our operations there would have his helpers gather a lot of smilax, a vine which grows profusely in East Texas. He would roll it in burlap and ship it to us by express, and we would decorate the Club with it. We had a huge papier mache moon we would put over on one wall to add a romantic touch—sort of a Moon over Miami theme.

The annual New Year's Eve party was our only formal dance we had through the years. Each member of the club was allowed two invitations. One of them had to be for a guest who lived more than fifty miles away from Thurber. Everybody wanted to come to that dance. Members would submit the names of their guests to the Dance Committee for approval. Guests were not charged admission.

The dance was always led off by a vice president, or whoever was the ranking officer in town. We would go through a series of drills and steps. It was really nice. It was uptown stuff. It was really beautiful.[46]

Because of Prohibition, the drink du jour of the Thurber Club at these New Year's Eve extravaganzas was Bevo—a near beer that tasted like beer but contained no alcohol and was, therefore, legal.

While fun and games were going on in Thurber, Penn and Gordon were engrossed in thought as to how to maximize profits from the sale of the company's windfall of oil. Two years after Penn's arrival in Fort Worth, construction had been commenced on the Wynnewood, Oklahoma refinery. Now with that refinery in operation, plans were begun to build a second refinery in Fort Worth at 3428 Denton Road (now Deen Road) about one mile north of NE 28th Street. The plant today is owned and operated by Southwestern Petroleum Corporation. Crude to feed the new TP refinery would be transported through the company's pipeline running from the Ranger area. On April 30, 1926, the *Fort Worth Press* informed its readers as follows:

> Opening of the TP Coal and Oil Company refinery on the Denton Road near Diamond Hill with a daily production of 2,500 barrels of gasoline is scheduled for June 1, TP Vice President E. R. Lederer announced Monday.
>
> Nearly $600,000 has been spent in remodeling the plant which was formerly the Montrose Refinery. Aside from modernizing the machinery in use by the plant, new machines have been installed, a new power house, boiler plant, pump house and tanks have been built. Crude oil will be pumped from the Ranger district to the refinery, where the newest process of dewaxing, filtering and blending of lubricating oils will be carried on. Three hundred men will be employed at the plant.[47]

Despite the fact that the railroads retired many of their coal-eating locomotives for oil burners, the company sustained its coal operations to give employment to the miners until 1926, when a third strike occurred after Penn and Gordon stood steadfast against any wage increase. That was the proverbial straw that broke the camel's back. The weakened coal market could not withstand this third assault. Oil, more accessible and cheaper, captured the combustion market during the era which saw the advent of the automobile and the airplane.[48]

The company immediately closed mine No. 10—the grand champion of the Thurber mines, both in length of life and in coal produced. It opened in 1901 and operated for a quarter of a century, producing 2,617,158 tons. It was the only one of the fifteen mines to reach the two million ton mark. For all practical purposes, the company was now out of the coal business. However, out of consideration for those miners who remained and were willing to work in an open shop mine, New No. 3 mine was left to operate for a short while longer.

In 1927, some forty years after W. W. Johnson sank his first mine, time had run out for coal at Thurber. Last in, last out. New No. 3, which in 1911 had been the last mine opened by the company, was the last one closed in 1927. It had produced 372,729 tons in sixteen years. The Thurber mines, a victim of economics and a final labor strike, have been sealed ever since.

Throughout the company's thirty-eight-year coal-producing history, it operated fifteen mines for a total production of 12,835,763 tons. Whereas the McCleskey's 250,000 barrels of black gold was gone in less than three years, remaining coal reserves in the area are estimated to be 127 million tons.[49]

The final Thurber diaspora commenced. The last of the miners along with all their possessions piled high atop their Joad Family look-alike flivvers, began their exodus from the town.

> While the miners were gone, the brickmakers, members of a different union, stayed. Highway construction was booming. The Texas State Highway Department had been created in 1917, and Good Roads groups sprang up in well-populated counties to discuss plans to link 256,000 square miles of the state with a network of paved roads. A larger dream was the Bankhead Highway (later U.S. 80), which would cross the nation by way of the Southern states, Texas, New Mexico, and Arizona to California. Brick highways were the best. Contractors purchased millions of Thurber bricks for the state highway system.
>
> When the Great Depression broke in the fall of 1929, the demand for brick fell sharply. The following year, the Thurber brick plant closed down, and several hundred men lost their jobs. Since no labor dispute had been involved at the plant, the Texas Pacific Coal and Oil Company performed a remarkable act of paternalism. It allowed the idled plant men to remain in their company houses rent free and to receive thirty dollars' credit in the company store each month. This apparently continued for several years.[50]

After the last mine closed, the company began selling the vacant houses. For a decade thereafter, house movers often could be seen on Highway 80, moving houses to various points.

✦

> Lola Spearing and her family lived in Abilene at the time. She remembers one trip they made to visit her aunt in Fort Worth in the early thirties. Their car suffered numerous flats as a result of nails falling out of the houses onto the highway. "My dad had to fix the flats. He was a little less than a happy camper by the time we got to Fort Worth. It also did not sit well with this small child."[51]

Nails on the highway were not the only traces left by the houses moved out of Thurber in the 1930s. Under one house, workers found several three-inch toy rabbits apparently molded from shale at the brick plant. So, not only red brick came forth from Thurber's Shale Mountain, terra cotta rabbits did also. In 1995 one of them found a home in my office, a gift from Young County rancher Chief Noka-homa Pumphrey.

✦

In October 1927, the citizens of Ranger commemorated the tenth anniversary of the discovery of the Ranger Field with a two day celebration. The Texas Pacific band led the parade followed by company officials in decorated floats. W. K. Gordon, in a speech on October 21, deflected credit for the discovery from himself by lavishly and generously remembering his old friend, landman Luther Davenport, who in 1916, was instrumental in keeping the union out of the TP oil fields, and who had later spearheaded Gordon's campaign that resulted in leases covering some 300,000 acres and ensuring for Texas Pacific a dominant role in the new field.[52]

It had been ten years since "oil" had oiled its way into the corporate name of TP. Now another dramatic change was about to occur, this time in the company's top management. The baby born when the company was born would now become President.

6

In 1927–the year that Hoagy Carmichael wrote "Star Dust,"–John Roby Penn stepped down as TP President. He remained on the Board as Chairman of the Executive Committee. He was succeeded in the presidency by Edgar J. Marston, thirty-nine-year old son of Edgar L. Marston. This had been the plan from the outset. The elder Marston in 1919 had thought his son needed on-the-job training before he assumed the leadership mantle of the company. Penn had been brought into TP not only to be president, but to be a schoolmaster for young Marston. Now with the closing of the last coal mine in 1927, the elder Marston apparently felt that the time was propitious to finalize his plan. But with the Great Depression looming, the move would turn out to be the beginning of an historic and troubled five-year period for Texas Pacific Coal and Oil Company.

Shortly after young Marston's assumption of the TP presidency, Charles Lindbergh became the first person to fly non-stop across the Atlantic Ocean. A crowd of one hundred thousand swarmed about his plane, *The Spirit of St. Louis,* when he landed at Le Bourget flying field in Paris on May 21 after a 33½ hour flight from New York City. When he returned to America, President Coolidge pinned the Distinguished Flying Cross, first ever awarded, on his lapel. A few weeks after decorating Lindbergh, the President took his family to the Black Hills of South Dakota for a summer vacation. On August 2, 1927, he called newsmen to his office in the Rapid City High School. He handed each reporter a slip of paper on which appeared the words: "I do not choose to run for President in 1928."

Following his visit to the White House, Lindbergh had gone to New York City where four million people welcomed him with a confetti parade. With the entire country literally intoxicated with Lindbergh and his flight, the U.S. Department of Commerce urged him to make a nationwide tour in his plane to promote the new air age. Lindy did so, and at 1:57 P.M. on Monday, September 26, 1927, he flew over downtown Fort Worth, circled the municipal airport three times, and landed the *Spirit of St. Louis* to immense applause from one of the biggest crowds in the city's history. That night a banquet was given in his honor at the Texas Hotel.[1] There can be little doubt that civic leaders Marston, Yager, Penn, and Gordon were all in attendance.

TP Aero trademark

If Marston was indeed present, it is quite likely that as he listened to the twenty-five-year-old hero, new ideas flashed in his mind. The Age of Flight had flown in, and with it a ravenous thirst for aviation fuel. With cars running to and fro upon the earth and airplanes flying through the skies, Marston undoubtedly saw fabulous markets opening for the petroleum industry. Gasoline refined by Vacuum Oil, later Socony-Vacuum, still later Mobil, was what made Lindbergh's flight possible. If Vacuum could refine and sell gasoline, why not TP? After all, the company had boundless petroleum reserves. It had two refineries: No. 1 at Wynnewood, Oklahoma, and No. 2 at Fort Worth, completed only last year. It had pipelines to both refineries. The company's gasoline was being sold wholesale to others. Why should TP not jump into the profitable marketing arena with its own filling stations? And in the Age of Flight, what better name for the company's gasoline than TP Aero?

✦

Meanwhile, December 1927 came and Thurber was getting ready for a traditional holiday season. Thirty-five miles down the red-brick road in Cisco the holidays would be anything but traditional. In the lobby of the First National Bank the nationally acclaimed but ludicrous Cisco Melodrama was presented by four inept actors on December 23. The plot called for Santa Claus to rob the bank. But this was no play. It was real life. Marshall Ratliff, attired in a Santa Claus suit, accompanied by three accomplices, walked into the First National Bank across from Conrad Hilton's Mobley Hotel and said, "Stick 'em up!" Santa and his "elves," leaving two fatally wounded Cisco officers, ran out with twelve thousand dollars. They ran, but spotlighted by a red Santa Claus suit, they could not hide. In a shoot-out, one of the robbers was slain and the money recovered. Three days later, the other three were captured. One died in the electric chair. One received a life sentence. The third—Ratliff—killed a guard in the Eastland jail, whereupon he was lynched by irate citizens.[2]

◆

The seeds planted in Marston's mind during the Lindbergh visit now began to sprout. The company's first TP Aero filling station opened in 1928 in Fort Worth at the busy intersection of West Seventh, University Drive, and Camp Bowie Boulevard. With borrowed money, some five hundred stations were built in the next few years. Thurber, although reduced in population, got its fancy station, too. George Studdard wrote that a new brick filling station (circa 1929) was built in the company's birthplace. The bandstand that had stood in the center of the square was moved to the south end in order to give the station a prime location. "I recall that Charles Hamilton laid the brick driveway in a herringbone pattern. It was really a work of art."[3] The TP Aero trademark soon became a familiar one throughout North Texas and Oklahoma. At the turn of the century, some motorists would get a large barrelful of gasoline from an industrial depot, bring it home, and store it. Often these barrels had a spigot at the bottom; the gasoline was transferred to a spouted can, and then poured through a chamois filter into the tank. This entire process was smelly, time-consuming, and dangerous.

The first retail outlets for gas were blacksmith shops, hardware, and grocery stores. The same process of getting the gas into the tank prevailed, with the safer alternative of not storing the fuel at home offset by the bother of having to go some place else to get it. Sometimes gas was sold from a barrel on wheels brought to the car, while horse-drawn tanks made house calls.

◆

As gasoline, formerly a useless by-product of the refining process, became a necessity, a pump was developed to pump gas from a fifty-gallon container. In 1905, Jack Gumper of Fort Wayne, Indiana, installed this contraption in an outside wooden cabinet. He described the apparatus as a "filling station" and painted these words in bold lettering on the outside of the cabinet. This perhaps was the first gas station.

Curbside pumps, usually in dense downtown locations, became a very common way to get gas, but they had their disadvantages: street traffic became congested by lines of people waiting to get gas; and it was hazardous to locate a pump right beside the road. A car could swerve and crash into a pump, resulting in a catastrophe. Local ordinances were passed banning these curbside outlets.

In 1907, Jon McLean opened a "drive-through" station in Seattle for Standard Oil of California. Inside a little building off the street, McLean rigged up a tank on a platform with a glass measuring device and a hose. The motorist drove in one side, got a tankful, and drove out the other side.

All of the early pumps were known as "blind pumps" because the consumer could not see the product as it was being purchased, and this led to suspicion and mistrust by motorists. This problem was allayed by the next great advance in gas pump design—the introduction of the visible or gravity pump in the late teens. These huge (ten to eleven feet high) devices featured a five or ten gallon glass cylinder at the top, with markers mounted inside. The gas was hand-pumped into these cylinders, and then gravity-fed into the tank. Since consumers could now see the product they were buying, gas companies began to dye the gasoline to establish product identity—Texaco was green, Esso was red, and Sunoco was blue.[4]

Early in 1928 another item from the region captured national attention. Remember the horned frog that had been incarcerated in the cornerstone of the Eastland County Courthouse thirty-one years previously? On 28 February after the courthouse was demolished and the cornerstone pried open, a horned frog materialized, alive and kicking. A crowd of two thousand citizens was on hand to witness the unbelievable. The horned frog was immediately christened Old Rip after Rip Van Winkle. Had it really been there thirty years? It didn't take long for tales of a hoax to surface, but most Eastlanders became steadfast believers that Old Rip had slept for thirty-one years in the cornerstone. Witness after witness said a metal seal and several layers of brick were on top of that cornerstone.

Old Rip made headlines across the country, and Will Wood, son of the county clerk who in 1897 placed a horned frog into the cornerstone, took the animal on an extended tour, including a brief visit with President Calvin Coolidge. It is not recorded what transpired between president and resurrected horned frog. It can be assumed that the conversation was brief, with Rip saying about as much as Silent Cal.[5] Coolidge's taciturnity was proverbial. In probably the most famous tale told about his penchant for silence, a woman supposedly told him that she had bet she could get him to say more than two words at a dinner one night. "You lose," the president is said to have responded.

Within a year of his emergence from the cornerstone, the horned frog died. He was embalmed and his body—or that of an impostor—can still be seen in a courthouse window. Eastland, never much of a tourist attraction before, pulled out all of the stops and used horned frogs as a marketing ploy. Local gas stations— including, of course, TP Aero stations—gave complimentary horned frogs to customers who filled up their tanks.

✦

With young Marston in the cockpit, the company was quickly and firmly wedded to the age of aviation. On July 5, 1928, the National Air Tour consisting of twenty-four planes arrived in Fort Worth from Tulsa. One of these planes was a Ryan Brougham belonging to Texas Pacific Coal and Oil Company. All of the visiting pilots were the guests of TP at a dinner that night in the Fort Worth Club.[6]

On August 20, 1928, the *Fort Worth Press* carried a story about the inauguration of air-train service between Chicago and Fort Worth which would commence on January 1, 1929. Passengers would leave Chicago by rail at midnight. They then would fly from Kansas City to Fort Worth. The return trip would be by air from Fort Worth to Kansas City, thence by train to Chicago. TP Coal and Oil Company held a financial interest in the enterprise.[7]

A presidential election was held that year. Calvin Coolidge having chosen not to run, the Republicans nominated Quaker Herbert Hoover, a prohibitionist. The Democrats nominated Governor Alfred E. Smith of New York, a Catholic who opposed prohibition. In the campaign, Hoover spoke hopefully about wiping out poverty. Eventually, he promised, Americans would have "two chickens in every pot and a car in every garage." Hoover carried 40 of the 48 states, and became the thirty-first president, defeating Smith by an electoral vote of 444 to 87.

Presidential politics out of the way, the country's attention quickly returned to airplanes. In November 1928 the Fort Worth Association of Commerce sponsored an Aerocade into West Texas, the first organized commercial air tour over Texas. Fourteen commercial planes and six Army planes made the trip, carrying a total of sixty-two passengers. The trip covered a total of 1055 miles. The cities of Wichita Falls, Vernon, Childress, Amarillo, Plainview, Lubbock, Big Spring, Midland, San Angelo, Abilene, and Ranger were visited. The trippers were given big dinners and celebrations at each of the stops. A TP plane went over the route of the trip several days before the Aerocade. With the company heavily involved in and identified with aviation, there can be little doubt that Marston felt he had a winner in Aero as the brand name of his gasoline.[8]

Out in California in December 1928, a tri-motor Fokker army plane named *Question Mark* flying with a crew of five had set a record of 150 hours of continuous flight. The veteran pilots on the *Question Mark* were Major Carl Spaatz and Captain Ira Eaker, both of whom would become World War II air force generals. The flight crew and the ground force had the best equipment that money could buy. The experiment had been carefully planned. The best military aeronautical engineers had mapped the flight.

Some time in the following April, a couple of Fort Worth aviators, believing that records are made to be broken, paid a visit to Texas Pacific
Coal and Oil Company. The aviators were Reg Robbins and Jim Kelly.
They knew of TP's interest in aviation because the company kept its plane,
a Ryan Brougham like their own, hangared at Municipal airport. In the
conference in the TP executive offices, E. J. Marston, Roby Penn, W. K.
Gordon, John Hancock, and Dr. E. R. Lederer listened attentively as the
men told of their dream of breaking the record set by the *Question Mark*.
The fliers asked if the company would support the endeavor by donating
oil, gas, and grease for their flight. The plane the two would use was a Ryan
monoplane like Lindbergh's *Spirit of St. Louis,* but where Lindbergh's was
new, Robbins and Kelly's was second hand with fifty thousand hours on
it. Despite their doubts, the executives decided to take a chance and provide them all the gas, oil, and rocker arm grease as long as the plane remained aloft.[9]

On Sunday, May 19, 1929, Robbins and Kelly took off in their plane
named *Fort Worth* from Municipal airport (later named Meacham Field) at
11:33:24 A.M. The event rated first page headlines for an entire week, not
only in Fort Worth, but across the nation. The two fliers took turns pilot-
ing the plane and catnapping in a hammock. Refueling was accomplished
by a second plane, with pilot K. K. Hoffman and co-pilot H. S. Jones, flying
twenty to twenty-five feet above the *Fort Worth* and dropping a hose down
to refuel the endurance plane with TP Aviation gasoline and TP Aero Motor Oil. Robbins later would tell his second cousin, Lee Barnes, about the
hazards of the refueling process. "Whenever we were taking on gas and I
was trying to keep the hose in the intake spout, it would some times suddenly be jerked out of the tank as the planes bobbed up and down
through the rough air, and gas would spill in my face. When that happened, I drank a lot of TP gasoline."[10] In 1997, octogenarian Robert C.
Marston, son of the TP President, told of looking up as a fifteen-year old
lad and watching the refueling process as the planes passed about a thous-
and feet or so over the airport. "You could see the TP logo on the upper
plane with the hose hanging down."[11] Food, mail, and newspapers, were
also passed to them. Every twelve hours, Kelly would climb out of the
cabin onto a catwalk to the front of the plane. Swinging below to a specially constructed perch beneath the nose of the ship, he anointed the
rocker arms of the Wright Whirlwind engine with Dr. Lederer's patented
TP Aero Lubricant. While so engaged in harm's way on the second day of
the flight, his belt buckle nicked the spinning propeller, but thankfully it
was only a nick, and the plane perservered—day and night—through blue
skies, sunshine, clouds, and rainstorms. David Poindexter was ten years
old and lived in Arlington Heights at the time of the flight: "You could
wake up all hours of the night and hear the plane flying over."[12] On Saturday, May 25, at 7:13:48 P.M., the record was broken. On the ground loco-

motives and factory plants blew whistles so that persons without radios would know of the achievement. But Robbins and Kelly flew on. The *Star-Telegram* reported:

> Texas Pacific Coal and Oil Company, headquartered in Fort Worth, helped make the flight possible. The oil company kept an official of the firm at the airport throughout the flight to see that nothing was lacking which the two fliers might need. TP gasoline, TP Aero Motor Oil, and TP rocker arm grease were used throughout the record-breaking flight. Company officials were delighted Saturday night. "Rocker arm trouble was what caused the *Question Mark* to come down," they pointed out, "and those fellows didn't use our grease." They showed a note from Robbins to Airport manager William Fuller which said, "That rocker arm grease of the TP Company sure does stay in there." "Rocker arm grease! Rocker arm grease!" company officials chanted delightedly. "If Robbins and Kelly stay up there a year, we'll still pour oil and gas into their plane."[13]

To the great glee of the TP, the decision to land on Sunday afternoon was not caused by the failure of a rocker arm but because of a split propeller, the result of its having come in contact with Jim Kelly's belt on day two.

When the wheels of the *Fort Worth* touched down at 4:05:25 P.M., Robbins and Kelly had reached their unreachable goal—a new world record of 172 hours, thirty-two minutes, and one second was on the books. It bested the *Question Mark* record by more than twenty-two hours. Headlines would proclaim the feat second only to Lindbergh's. Before the plane had come to a stop, twenty thousand cheering people surged out onto the muddy, rain-drenched field and mobbed the intrepid pair as their feet touched earth for the first time in a week. A police motorcade took them downtown to the Fort Worth Club where they spent the night after Amon Carter served them juicy steaks. The following Saturday, the Chamber of Commerce gave the heroes a fifteen thousand dollar purse at a banquet for the public at the Texas Hotel. Edgar J. Marston and J. R. Penn were two of the members of the Chamber committee which raised the money. The Mahoney-Ryan Aircraft Corporation gave them a new Ryan plane. Representing TP at the banquet, Vice-President John Hancock said, "Those boys went up to stay, not to stunt. They went about preparations in a simple, practical way. Their sound business judgment and care in handling a plane were largely responsible for their success."[14] The record-setting flight was used extensively by TP in its future advertising touting the merits of TP products.

On April 16, 1929, a subsidiary known as Thurber Tank Line was incorporated in Delaware and fifty railroad tank cars were purchased. The identification painted on each was TTX. TP gasoline and other refined products were routed to destinations throughout the forty-eight states, as well as points in Canada and Mexico. The Thurber Tank Line's Traffic

Lake Worth frozen, January 1930. From left to right: Jewel Lowe, Helen Bamber, Lillian Miller, Virginia Gulledge, Robbie Martin, Pearl Patton, and Pat Woods. Courtesy Pat Woods.

Manager was Edward A. Starr, who was licensed to practice law before the Interstate Commerce Commission. Starr had been instrumental in securing a downward adjustment of freight rates on the movement of oil field equipment.[15]

In 1929, Sybil Woods, a recent high school graduate, began her TP employment at the refinery on Fort Worth's North Side. Sybil was always known as Pat. At the refinery, her job was to type reports on wide typewriters. Top personnel at the refinery were J. Von Carlowitz and Dr. E. R. Lederer. After several weeks at the refinery, she was transferred to the downtown office. The office manager was Rudolph Seibel, "a German to whom the slightest detail was of paramount importance." It was said that he inspected desk drawers of clerks and secretaries to be sure that pencils were arranged just so. Pat was elated to work downtown, even though her desk amounted to a shelf on the wall behind the steno desks and her job was typing statistics. "I beat the typewriter hard and fast with the vigor of youth, which naturally attracted Seibel's attention." When the steno assigned to the assistant sales manager, M. (Farney) Farnsworth, resigned, Farnsworth asked that Pat be assigned to him. She was given a desk and a buzzer to answer when Farney wanted her. "I enjoyed work in the Sales Department and soon familiarized myself with oft-repeated sales terms."[16]

The Hoover Administration had hardly begun when the stock market suffered the worst crash in its history. On October 29, 1929, frantic speculators sold 16.4 million shares. It was indeed Black Friday. The country entered the Great Depression.

In January 1930, it was not only the economy that was suffering the big chill. The weather, too, was North Pole cold. Starting on January 7 extending to January 26, the temperature remained below freezing except for the 12th and 13th. On the night of January 18, the temperature fell to one degree below zero. On the morning of the 19th, Lake Worth, Fort Worth's water supply, was frozen solid. The next day, Pat Woods and seven other Texas Pacific women drove out on their lunch hour to see for themselves what the Siberian Express had done to the lake.

But spring came, then summer. In June, 1930, Thomas R. Hall died while on a vacation trip to Mississippi. It was Hall who preserved the account of the 1894 train robbery that caused the only pay delay that the coal company ever experienced. Hired in 1889 as a carpenter, he later transferred into the office and eventually became Cashier and Pay Master, "the most important and highly responsible position in the gift of the Texas Pacific Coal and Oil Company to bestow."[17]

The company had gotten out of the coal business in 1927. In 1930 it would get out of the brick business. Throughout the Roaring Twenties, the brick plant's eighteen kilns poured forth eighty thousand paving bricks a day. With money tight, the market for paving brick vanished. Paving contracts were cancelled and the company soon found all of its storage space filled and no demand for its product. The plant was shut down in January of 1930. It reopened for a brief two-month run in 1931 and then, like the coal mines, closed forever.[18]

One of the last big orders for Thurber brick was from the City of Fort Worth in the boom year of 1928. Two and one-half inch vitrified bricks were used to pave West Seventh Street and Camp Bowie Boulevard from the Clear Fork of the Trinity river to Sanguinet Street, a distance of 2.7 miles. The brick can still be seen today in many sections along this important esplanaded west side thoroughfare.[19]

✦

In July 1992, workers were doing maintenance work on the historic street. Frank Burkett of Fort Worth commented about the project in a letter to the *Star-Telegram*:

> How come you don't have one of your reporters check into the two types of work now causing barricades on Camp Bowie Boulevard?
>
> On the east end, you have lanes closed briefly here and there so bricks can be replaced where utility digs or accidents made them come out. These are in stretches where the bricks were all re-laid five to 10 years ago.
>
> Out in Ridglea, they scraped all the hot top off the bricks which had been covered for 30 or 40 years, and now they're covering them up again.

I liked the old bricks just scraped off. They rode pretty smooth, and it was nice to see them again after all these years, except where the scrapers chopped their tops off.

If they've got to keep covering them up, couldn't they have the decency not to wreck 'em so future generations with a little more sense can some day use the bricks to restore the boulevard to its former grandeur from one end to the other?

The last two decades have proved that brick roads are: cheaper because they do not wear out; easier to maintain because when you have to make a hole or fix a bump, you just get a couple of guys and a barricade and put the bricks back; safer because you can't hot rod on bricks, and they're soothing to the spirit; prettier because they remind you of how classy things used to be.

We ought to have a city wide policy to get the old bricks back up into view all over town, wherever they are.

Nothing lasts like bricks and we could take our time about it. Most of them are down there, safely waiting—unless somebody scrapes down and ruins them all.[20]

✦

Before the summer was over, calamity would befall TP and Thurber. Fire—the scourge of Thurber! Fire had wreaked havoc in Thurber many times: the terrible No. 5 mine fire in 1897, the general store fire of 1902, the No. 8 mine fire in 1904, the Hotel Knox blaze in 1907, the building brick plant following World War I, and now in 1930, fire destroyed the General Offices.

> The General Offices were located on the second floor above the Market Department and Hardware Store which had been built in 1917. Shortly after midnight on September 14, 1930, the General Offices were destroyed by fire originating in or near a freight elevator shaft. With the shaft causing a draft, the entire building was engulfed in flames in a few minutes. TP's three Reo trucks quickly responded. Strawn and Ranger also sent trucks.[21]

Sixty-four years later, Alver Simmans spoke of the fire: "Harmon Shaw was my boss. I was his assistant in the Accounting Department. Almost before the fire had been brought under control, he and I left for Fort Worth to make copies of various reports, letters, and personnel records that had gone to Fort Worth from Thurber. These would be needed to set up new offices. We decided to drive by Mr. Marston's home to give him an eye witness account of the disaster. When we arrived at Mr. Marston's big house in Arlington Heights, it was still early morning. The door bell was answered by the maid, who informed us that Mr. Marston was asleep and could not be disturbed."[22]

The fire was on Sunday morning, and representatives of Adressograph, Underwood, Burroughs, Monroe Calculating Machine, Globe-Wernicke and others were requested to be in Thurber as soon as possible Monday morning. Each received orders for machines and desks and other material necessary to reopen the office as quickly as possible. The Dry Goods Store's merchandise and furniture and fixtures were moved out of their building [today the Smokestack Restaurant] on the west side of the square and consolidated with other stores. Saw-Horses and lumber were hauled from the lumber yard and set up in the Dry Goods building, which would serve as the home of the General Offices until they were moved to Fort Worth in 1933. The saw-horses served as makeshift desks pending the arrival of new furniture and office equipment.[23]

Only three weeks after the Thurber fire, a fire of frenzy and excitement flared in East Texas. On October 5, 1930, Columbus M. "Dad" Joiner brought in the Daisy Bradford No. 3 well to open the vast East Texas oil field. The standard gauge for an oil field to qualify as major is one hundred million barrels of oil. East Texas held five billion barrels of reserves in a field measuring forty-six miles in length, with a width of three to twelve miles. The number of wells drilled in the field would exceed ten thousand. Unfortunately, there was little demand for petroleum in 1930. The whole country was absolutely flooded with oil. Unlike Ranger in 1917, when World War I created a demand for oil that brought premium prices, oil in depression 1930 dropped to ten cents a barrel.

The quadruple whammy of the depression, ten-cent oil, heavy bank debt occasioned by borrowing to finance construction of the Fort Worth refinery and five hundred service stations, and the Thurber fire that destroyed the General Offices sent the company into a tail spin. The company's balance sheet at the end of 1931 showed notes payable of $1,800,000 (which is more than 12 million 1997 dollars). Ominous forebodings of bankruptcy loomed all around. Only one thing saved TP from that calamity, and that was the large tract of land in East Texas that W. K. Gordon bought for timber to be used in the coal mines. The tract was located west of Longview and with the discovery of nearby oil was now quite valuable. Penn authorized the selling of the tract for a large consideration which was used to reduce the company's debt.[24] The serendipitous purchase in 1907 of a tract for timber that in 1932 proved to be rich in oil is another instance of the magic touch seemingly possessed by Gordon.

Former TP landman Billy J. Moore added more details to the East Texas sale:

> A special meeting of the Board of Directors was called. Mr. Penn was authorized to go to New York and sell the mineral rights in the East Texas timber properties. The property had become very valuable due to the fact

that it was in the East Texas Field. Penn left by train immediately for New York and closed the sale for an amount sufficient to forestall the foreclosure proceedings which had been instigated against the company by New York bankers. The deal was finalized only hours before the foreclosure was to take place."[25]

Penn had been a landman. This fact fits tidily into Moore's account of this crucial incident in the company's history, because landmen are the ambassadors and traders of the industry, and this was, without question, a task that called for superb horse-trading.

The sale was reported in the *Fort Worth Star-Telegram.*

TEXAS PACIFIC SALE IN EAST TEXAS REPORTED

Sale of the Texas Pacific Coal and Oil Company's 183-acre fee tract in the George Hampton Survey, Gregg County to Kewanee Oil and Gas Company for more than $500,000 cash was reported.

The property was purchased in fee about two decades ago for $6 an acre by Texas Pacific Coal Company which used the timber in mines operated by the concern at Thurber.

There are three completed wells on the tract and the first drilled was for several weeks conceded to be the largest producer in the East Texas Field. The acreage is in what is known as the "heart" of the field.[26]

A copy of the conveyance obtained from the office of the Gregg County Clerk reveals the land was originally purchased by TP on June 13, 1907, from W. L. Dean and wife. The conveyance revealed that the tract was one of 169 acres, not the 183 stipulated in the news story. TP did not sell it to Kewanee but instead executed an oil and gas lease for a term of one year and for so long as production was had therefrom. TP retained the usual one-eighth royalty. While Yager, Fuqua, and Moore indicate that Chairman of the Executive Committee Penn was the prime mover in the deal, the lease was signed by Edgar J. Marston, President.

According to Moody's Manual of Investments for 1933, the profit realized by the Kewanee lease was $518,160.[27] The receipts from the transaction were immediately applied to notes payable, reducing this item from $1,800,000 to $1,331,278. Although the balance owed was still daunting, bankruptcy was forestalled.

In addition to company trials, Marston himself had personal tribulations. During the Roaring Twenties, Americans had fallen in love with the get rich trick of buying stock on margin. By some accounts, more than a million Americans owned stock on margin by 1929.[28] Marston was one of those million. After the crash, his broker called to advise that the value of the stock he had bought on margin had plummeted—but this was only the beginning of his demise. He was hard pressed to deposit additional funds.

Robert C. Marston said his father "resigned in 1932, as he was suffering from bronchiectasis and had entered the early stages of emphysema. Had he not resigned, more than likely he would have been fired, as there had to be a 'fall guy' responsible for the poor corporate financial position. What better 'fall guy' than someone in poor health, who was unable to maintain his position and continue working?"[29]

Of the half dozen men who headed the company's fortunes during its life, Edgar J. Marston seems to have left the fewest footprints. He resigned as president at age forty-four and moved to Colorado Springs in 1932. In 1955, he moved to La Jolla, California. He died in La Jolla on January 8, 1962, at age seventy-four. Cremated, his ashes are interred in Evergreen Cemetery in Colorado Springs.[30]

✦

If 1932 was not the best of years for Edgar J. Marston, it was an unspeakably tragic year for Charles and Anne Morrow Lindbergh. In what has been called the crime of the century, their twenty-month old son, Charles, Jr., was kidnapped on March 1, 1932. Two months later, the baby was found, his skull fractured, in a shallow grave several miles away. Bruno Richard Hauptmann, a German immigrant carpenter, was accused of kidnapping the baby from his nursery in Hopewell, N. J. He denied the accusation. Prosecutors said Hauptmann made a ladder to reach the nursery window and that the child died when the ladder collapsed. The evidence against Hauptmann included part of the fifty thousand dollars ransom money found in his garage and a handwriting analysis that indicated that he wrote fourteen ransom notes. Hauptmann was convicted in 1935 and executed in 1936.

✦

As the year 1932 slowly unrolled, the Great Depression tightened its relentless stranglehold. Millions of persons lost every cent they owned. Banks failed, factories shut down, stores closed, and almost every business seemed paralyzed. By the end of 1930, more than six million Americans were out of work. The number rose to twelve million a year later. More than five thousand banks failed and over thirty-two thousand businesses went bankrupt. Farm prices fell lower than ever before. Desperate men sold apples on street corners, ate in "soup kitchens," and lived in clustered shacks called "Hoovervilles." Some, unable to deal with the present or face the future, shot themselves to death or, like meat packer Edward F. Swift, jumped out of tall buildings. From the 1929 high of $24, TP stock fell to $9.50. For the next six years, the stock's lows were $4, $2, $1.50, $1.50, $2.50, and $3.50. Not until 1944 would the stock rise again to the pre-crash high of $24.[31] The oil industry would be greatly affected by events occurring in 1928-33: the discovery of a huge oil field in Oklahoma City in

1928 which flooded the market; two years later the East Texas oil discovery would exacerbate the problem; and the Depression.[32]

On July 2, 1932, all TP employees, in Fort Worth, Thurber, and in the field camps, joined millions of Americans as they sat by their Philcos and heard Franklin D. Roosevelt address the Democratic National Convention in Chicago. In accepting the nomination for president, Roosevelt, in a strong, vibrant voice, fired the enthusiasm of the delegates—indeed the entire nation—"I pledge you, I pledge myself, to a new deal for the American people. Let us all here assembled constitute ourselves prophets of a new order of competence and courage. This is more than a political campaign; it is a call to arms. Give me your help, not to win votes alone, but to win in this crusade to restore America to its own people." Thus the New Deal was born.[33] The Democrats promised that if Roosevelt were elected, good times would be just around the corner.

About two months after headlines proclaimed the nomination of Roosevelt at Chicago, Texas Pacific Coal and Oil Company was the subject of a banner front-page headline in the *Fort Worth Star-Telegram* on September 13, 1932:

TWO BURNED TO DEATH IN REFINERY EXPLOSION

Two pipe fitters, Lonnie Moore, 49, and Ray Bruce, 31, had mounted a scaffold at the top of a crude oil still on September 12 to loosen a flange preparatory to cleaning it. There was a flash as an explosion sent burning gas around the two men. Moore fell to the ground and Bruce dropped to the floor of the scaffold. E. R. Lederer said the only explanation that could be offered was that gas had been blown into a pocket at the side of the still and was exploded by an exposed electric wire when one of the men dropped a wrench on a light bulb. No fire followed the explosion and the still was practically undamaged.[34]

On November 8, 1932, Franklin D. Roosevelt, promising happy days and running on a platform to repeal the eighteenth prohibition amendment, was elected President by an electoral vote of 472 to incumbent President Herbert Hoover's 59. It was a New Deal for America!

7

President Franklin D. Roosevelt, two days after his inauguration took action to snap the country out of the depression. The first step was to get the banks in order. On March 6, 1933, he ordered every bank in the country closed, and by the time he had assembled Congress in special session on 9 March, he had ready for instant passage an Emergency Banking Act. Before the day was over, the law received the president's signature, breaking all known records. This measure authorized the secretary of the treasury to call in all gold, whether coin, bullion, or gold certificates; it provided for the examination and reopening of all banks deemed sound, and for a system of conservators to take charge of all others; and it authorized an extensive issue of emergency currency to be used, if necessary, to halt runs on banks. By 13 March, banks that federal examiners found solvent began to reopen and the government's guaranty of their stability proved sufficient to restore public confidence. Only fifteen million dollars of emergency currency had to be used until the millions of dollars that the banks had paid out during the crisis to anxious depositors began to flow back. Some three thousand banks, scattered throughout the country, were either reopened under conservators or were not reopened at all, but there was no longer any reason to doubt the essential soundness of the banking structure.[1]

In his inaugural address, Roosevelt had boldly declared: "Let me assert my firm belief that the only thing we have to fear is fear itself—nameless, unreasoning, unjustified terror which paralyzes needed efforts to convert retreat into advance." But fear, nonetheless, was casting a great pall of gloom everywhere. Texas Pacific was wallowing in debt and losing money by the barrel. Operations had shown a net loss for 1930 and 1931 and bank debt reached nearly two million dollars in both those years. After Edgar J. Marston's resignation as president in 1932, no one had been elected to take his place. Tension, uncertainty, and politics ruled.

◆

In Fort Worth in February 1933, O. D. Stevens could not wait for the promised good times and happy days promised by Franklin D. Roosevelt. Impatient, he robbed the U.S. mail of seventy-two thousand dollars (nearly half a million dollars in 1997 terms). Because of the magnitude of the amount hijacked, the daring brazenness with which the foul deed was carried out, and ensuing events, the crime captured the attention not only of John R. Penn, W. K. Gordon, Dooley Yager, and all other TPers, but indeed that of all Fort Worth and Texas.

On the night of February 21, 1933, three shadows stalked out of the darkness atop the South Main underpass at the Texas & Pacific Railway depot in Fort Worth. A platform truck loaded with mail pouches containing seventy-two thousand dollars trundled away from a T&P train and down the ramp. Suddenly three masked men appeared and leveled pistols at the guards and the driver on the open truck. Throwing the pouches over their shoulders, the robbers faded into the night.

Later, two of the robbers, Jack Sturdivant of Eula and Harry Rutherford of Abilene, together with Rutherford's brother, J. D. of Dallas,[2] went to Stevens's home at 1408 Morrison in the Handley area to collect their part of the loot. There they were murdered. Their bodies, trussed in wire and weighted with concrete, were found beneath the East First Street Bridge over the Trinity River on July 12, 1933. Even though Stevens was not present at the train robbery, officers believed that he was the ringleader. In April 1934, he was sentenced to twenty-seven years in prison on the robbery charge and in June, he was found guilty of the triple murder of his fellow hoodlums and given the death penalty. On July 1, 1934, he was taken to Leavenworth Penitentiary and later transferred to Alcatraz. An appeals court found error in the murder trial and threw out the death verdict. On retrial, he was acquitted on the murder charges but still had to serve his sentence for the robbery conviction. He was paroled after seventeen years in Alcatraz and lived the rest of his life in Arkansas. One of Stevens's accomplices, W. D. May, was electrocuted in Huntsville on September 6, 1935, not for his part in the robbery, but for the murder of his confederates.

Federal agents, searching the house for the hijacked seventy-two thousand dollars, found many ingenious hiding places: secret compartments under cabinets and in the woodwork, a hidden room under a trick stairway in the basement, a gable room with no apparent means of access. About half of the loot was recovered. People still gaze in awe at the gabled native stone house, perched on a hill that overlooks Interstate 30 in Handley, and wonder if the remainder of the treasure is not hidden away in some undiscovered cache. Perhaps it is.[3]

◆

Although the five hundred thousand dollars received from the East Texas lease deal had given the company breathing room, the New York banks continued nervously watching the teetering oil company. In 1933, fearful that the company was about to be sucked into an economic black hole, they dispatched a petroleum engineer, Charles Osmond, to Fort Worth and put him on the Board of Directors, replacing in-company Director Ralph Fleckenstein, Superintendent of Production. Osmond–a graduate from Swarthmore College and Temple University who hailed from Chester

County, Pennsylvania,—operated under bank orders that every dime spent by the company must first be approved by him.

Charles E. Yager, who had been promoted to chief geologist in 1929 succeeding David Donoghue, spoke of this troubling time:

> Marston envisioned TP as an integrated oil company, and started buying in the late 20s. He bought filling stations and put them all over northwest Texas. He over-extended the company and got it into deep debt. The depression came on. . . . The company was so deep in debt that the New Yorkers sent Roderick Crandall and Charles Osmond to Fort Worth in 1933 to OK anything that anybody did. Every dime had to be cleared by them. Crandall was a famous geologist in New York. He had worked in Russia. He had some funny ideas.
>
> Any hill he saw he thought it would be an anticline. We flew out to El Paso. As we crossed over Loving County, he looked down and said, "That is a good place to buy some leases." He had a brother in Oklahoma. Any time they found a hill, they would buy royalty on it. Crandall graduated from Stanford University. He was very brilliant. Osmond was strictly a financial man.[4]

George Studdard corroborated Yager in recalling those tough times: "During the depression years, the company was on the rocks. The oil company was, so to speak, nearly out of gas. They had to borrow money from the bankers. They had to cut expenses to the bone. There was an efficiency expert sent by the bankers to Fort Worth to oversee what was taking place. His name was Charles Osmond. Everything pertaining to expenses had to pass over his desk."[5]

Osmond asked Rudolph Seibel to provide him a secretary. Seibel gave Osmond two names to choose from. One of the two was Pat Woods. Osmond chose Woods: "Working for Mr. Osmond was one of the outstanding experiences of my life. In spite of his vast experience and intelligence, he was very helpful and understanding with my youth and lack of knowledge. For instance, I had never heard of the word 'seismograph.' It sounded like 'sizable map' to me. He corrected my many goofs with patience and understanding. When my two years with him had ended, I had an education I could not have obtained otherwise. In addition to bolstering my knowledge, he boosted my self esteem."[6]

The company's gasoline and motor oil were sold under the trademark TP Aero in over five hundred service stations in Texas and Oklahoma. Marketing operations were carried on through the company's Petroleum Sales Department. The department was subdivided into four principal divisions: Tank Car (wholesale), Bulk Agency, Tire Sales (retail) and Service Stations (retail).[7] In 1993, octogenarian Henry Boykin gave a vivid glimpse of the times of the TP Aero service stations:

TP Service Station, circa 1942. Courtesy W. D. Smith, Inc. Commercial Photography, Fort Worth, Texas.

During the Great Depression which began in 1929, I had been working for $18 a week in a garage and service station when I got word in 1933 that TP needed a service station attendant at its Capps and Hemphill station, where Glen Carter was the manager. They offered me $22 a week. Man! That was a $4 a week increase. I took the job. My wife and I were so elated that we celebrated with a five-cent hamburger and a ten-cent movie.

I really worked hard for TP and Glen Carter. When word got out that the big boys were coming around to see how clean the station was, we all got busy, even Glen Carter, and made things sparkle and shine.

TP would give prizes to the station that sold the most grease for rear ends and transmissions. I, being a half-way mechanic, would tell the customers how important it was to change the grease and flush out the unit. It was no trouble to sell the job. We sold a lot of grease, and our little station won first prize for all of Fort Worth. We sold a hundred pounds more grease than did the largest and most prominent TP station in Fort Worth, the one which was located at the Camp Bowie and West Seventh intersection.[8]

Subsequent to the disastrous fire at Thurber in September 1930, the decision was made to consolidate the General Office with the Executive Office in Fort Worth, although the move did not take place for a couple of years. On July 1, 1933, approximately 120 employees made the move to the twenty-third and twenty-fourth floors of the Fort Worth National Bank Building at the northwest corner of West Seventh and Main. The company paid all moving expenses, including hotel, apartment, or other lodging expense for a month. "This increased the population of the Fort Worth office by several executives and department heads," said Pat Woods. "I remember Ray DeCordova and Wiltie Creswell. Then there was a number of female personnel—stenos and file clerks."[9]

After the transfer of employees in the General Office to Fort Worth, the process of shutting down Thurber was quickened. After 1933, most of the people still in Thurber were in the cemetery. The salvage operation was placed under the supervision of Guy J. Gentry, electrician and mechanic. Although houses had been sold and moved when the last mine was closed in 1927, there were still hundreds of homes waiting for the house mover. Gas and water lines had to be torn out. Stores had to be closed and their fixtures and stock disposed of.[10] The brick plant was torn down by a Breckenridge salvage company. Each brick was carefully cleaned, sorted, and stacked for sale. The machinery and all other iron and steel was purchased by another salvage firm, and, according to common belief, shipped to Japan as scrap iron. It would be among the last scrap iron shipped to Japan, for in September 1940, after Japanese forces moved into northern Indochina, President Roosevelt announced an embargo on scrap iron and steel to Japan.[11] Loading the iron and steel onto a gondola car, one Thurberite remarked: "Boys, we're gonna see these old wheels comin' back at us one of these days."[12]

Two dreary years had gone by without a president for TP. The New York banks preferred their man Osmond for the job while the old guard wanted Chairman of the Executive Committee John R. Penn to return. Election of the new president was scheduled for the April 18, 1934, annual meeting in Thurber. Although most of the employees had been transferred to Fort Worth in 1933, the company's by-laws provided that the annual meeting would be held in Thurber.[13] Katherine Stell, to whom E. J. Marston used to give twenty-dollar gold pieces, told this story of intrigue and corporate politics: "I had the ballots typed up to elect Osmond, but Mr. Seibel got on the bus and went over to Dallas to see Dallas banker Lang Wharton, who was on the Texas Pacific Board. He also talked with Fort Worth banker Ellison Harding. They in turn contacted other Board members. Then I was instructed to type up another set of ballots. So when the Board met at Thurber, they had two sets of ballots. I remained in Fort Worth with instructions to call Thurber on the private line in the event a telegram was received. A telegram for Mr. Osmond did arrive, and I called

Mr. Osmond in Thurber. When he stepped out of the room to take my call, the Board elected Mr. Penn President."[14]

John Roby Penn was forty-five when elected President of TP in 1920. When elected for the second time, he was fifty-eight years old. When he stepped down from the presidency in 1927, it had been the best of times. Now upon his return in 1934, it was the worst of times. He was deemed by his fellow directors to have the experience, know-how, prestige, leadership, and ability to finesse the company back from the edge of bankruptcy.

During the intervening years between his two terms with TP, he served three terms on the Fort Worth City Council. The once and future TP President was appointed to the council in 1929, and elected in 1931 and 1933. At that time, councilmen were elected by a city-wide vote and it was not unusual for top businessmen to serve. Because councilmen were elected at large, two or more often lived in the same area. In smoke-filled caucuses at the Fort Worth Club—the forerunner of what would later be called the Seventh Street Gang—Amon Carter and his lieutenants would finger a businessman and advise him that the city needed his talents on its governing council. Their ensuing election usually was pro forma.

Pat Woods, George Studdard, and Charles Yager all agreed that Charles Osmond was an able executive and gave him high marks. O. E. (Erle) Mitchell,[15] Vice President for Administration, on the other hand, flunked Osmond and gave Penn an A+:

> Mr. Penn was recalled to the presidency of the Company at the regular annual meeting of directors held in April, 1934, after he had been urged to return to active management of the Company by a group of its directors.
>
> For some time prior to Mr. Penn's election, his predecessor, Edgar J. Marston, had been absent because of illness and had tendered his resignation. During Marston's illness and absence, a firm of engineers had been in charge of the Company's affairs. This firm had been engaged (at TP's expense) by reason of pressure brought by the New York banks to which the Company was indebted.
>
> One of the engineering firm's members [Charles Osmond] was slated to become president of the Company. However, the activities of this individual in dealing with the employees and properties of the Company were such that the morale of the employees, both in Fort Worth and in the field, broke down to the extent it appeared to the directors that the Company would be placed in jeopardy if the plan were consummated to employ the said individual as president. These directors therefore communicated with the other directors of the Company and all agreed that it was to the best interests of the Company to ask Mr. Penn to return to active management of the Company, which he had relinquished in 1927.

Mr. Penn took over the president's duties reluctantly, as he was engaged in highly satisfactory personal business activities which might suffer by reason of his active participation in the management of the Company's affairs.

Mr. Penn's starting salary of $18,000 a year was nominal, particularly for a person of his experience and he accepted it largely because he felt that the Company's financial condition could not afford a higher salary. This unusually fair and conservative attitude was held by Mr. Penn throughout his tenure as president.[16]

Penn retained Woods as his secretary, sharing her with O. E. Mitchell.

That same year on May 23, seventy-two-year old W. K. Gordon was elected Chairman of TP's Board, succeeding seventy-four-year old Edgar L. Marston who resigned because of ill health. Marston's resignation brought to an end his family's active voice in the management of the company exercised since the its inception in 1888.

✦

On that same day, some 300 miles to the east at Gibsland, Louisiana, 43 miles east of Shreveport, a well-armed posse led by Texas Ranger Frank Hamer pumped 187 shells into notorious bank robbers Bonnie Parker and Clyde Barrow, killing them instantly in their car. Hamer made his laconic report: "Both of them died with their guns in their hands, but they didn't have a chance to use them."[17]

In May 1934, a dust storm rising to fifteen hundred feet extended from Texas to Canada and blew east. Dust settled on FDR's desk and on ships hundreds of miles out on the Atlantic. Crop-eating grasshoppers came like a dark cloud. The heat was oppressive. As Penn and his team pored over company ledgers and reports in unairconditioned offices, their situation was made somewhat more tolerable because of the daily ministrations of one young employee.

In 1933 and 1934, Aubrey Morgan, sixteen and just out of high school, had a ninety-dollar-a-month job at TP as an office boy. One of his jobs was to take the street car and deliver bills of lading for oil, grease and other refinery products to the various freight handlers. He had other duties as well. In the days before the blessings of central air-conditioning, office workers sweltered in the Texas summers, the oppressive heat alleviated only by ceiling fans. It was Aubrey's job to make sure that special seating was provided for Penn and other executives. The chairs of the executives were furnished with half-inch thick cushions made from a strawlike material that held little metal coils that could be slipped out and immersed in water. After the excess water was removed, the coils were reinserted into the cushions, and by the magic of evaporation, the executives could at least enjoy cool hindermosts.[18]

✦

W. K. Gordon, circa 1930s. Courtesy Mrs. W. K. Gordon, Jr.

In 1932, after having applied the proceeds from the Kewanee lease to notes payable, the company still owed the banks 1.3 million dollars (8.3 million in 1997 dollars). By the end of 1935, this indebtedness was completely eliminated. The absence of the bank loans from the balance sheet were not the only thing missing from the 1936 annual report. Conspicuous by its absence from the list of directors was the name of Charles Osmond.[19] Osmond served on the TP Board during 1934 and 1935. Although not re-elected in 1936, he remained in Fort Worth for the rest of his life. He died on January 26, 1973, and was entombed in Greenwood Mausoleum. News account of his death said that "he came to Fort Worth in 1933 to reorganize the TP Coal and Oil Co."[20]

Under the Penn-Gordon leadership TP was able to retire this huge debt in less than three years. A combination of the judicious use of operating profits and reductions in receivables and inventory was used to free up additional liquidity. Operating profits for 1934 and 1935 were $437,228 and $646,026, respectively. Receivables in 1935 were some $500,000 less than they were in 1934. Penn began to jettison outmoded properties that were siphoning off profits. In 1934 he shut down the Wynnewood refinery and sold it for salvage in 1935. In the latter part of 1935, arrangements were also made to discontinue the operation of the Fort Worth refinery. With the exception of that portion required for compounding oils and greases from Ranger crude for the company's bulk distribution, and the operation of the Fort Worth bulk sales agency, plans were made to dispose of this plant.

It was not only to major policy decisions that Penn devoted his financial wizardry. It was also matters small that he scrutinized. He was frugal when it came to company funds. He told Charles Yager in the 1930s, "Don't spend a lot of money on blue binders. Write your ideas on the back of an envelope." W. B. (Bill) Harris, Jr. remembered Penn for his famous pencil extender. In the lean years of the Depression, Penn insisted that pencils be used down to a stub. But they were not to be discarded even then. When the pencils had become too short to be held between the thumb and forefinger, they were inserted into a three-inch metal holder and used until nothing was left.[21]

Secretary Pat Woods remembered Penn's devotion to economy. "He would pay his bills by writing checks, but instead of mailing them, he would save the cost of postage by having Arthur, his chauffeur, deliver the envelopes all over town. After all, stamps cost two cents each."[22]

Penn's frugality was chronic. During the 1940s when the company was in much better financial health, Texas Pacific landman Billy Moore put in a requisition for a car radio. He was going to Montana to buy leases and wanted a radio so that he could get weather reports. Penn told Moore that he should be thankful that at least he had an enclosed car: "When I was chasing leases at Salt Creek, Wyoming, my car did not even have a heater. In fact, I did not even have side curtains on my old tin lizzie."[23]

Despite his legendary frugality, Penn also knew when not to pinch pennies. One cold winter day Henry Boykin was trying to open the lock on a gasoline pump at his TP Aero Station: "My pliers flew up and knocked my front tooth out. I was dreading having to pay the dentist, but Mr. Penn insisted on TP paying the $25 dental bill. The dentist did a good job. It lasted 60 years."[24]

John Roby Penn at the helm of Texas Pacific mirrored the philosophy of President Calvin Coolidge. In age, temperament, and habit, the two men were much alike. Coolidge was born in 1872, Penn in 1875. Both were Easterners. Both had attended the same school—Amherst College. Both dressed in conservative Ivy League style. Both were reserved and stoic, quiet and introspective, voluble only about economy. Coolidge was known as Silent Cal. Penn was anything but garrulous. Coolidge never smiled. Penn seldom smiled. "As between the two," observed Robbie Martin, whose impressions of Coolidge came from the media and news reels, but who as a 1930s TP employee knew Penn first hand, "Mr. Penn had more personality." Both men were scrupulously and conscientiously honest. Both were spartan with the dollar, stingy but never greedy.

All Texas Pacific employees, and especially those nearing retirement, took great interest in the signing by President Franklin D. Roosevelt on August 14, 1935, of the Social Security Act. The purpose of the act was to eliminate fears that any aged person in America would go without food and shelter. The program would be financed by a 2 percent payroll tax (1 percent each by employee and employer) up to three thousand dollars of wages annually. FDR did not live to see the benefits of Social Security. He died at sixty-three on April 12, 1945. John Roby Penn, seventy when Roosevelt died, lived to draw Social Security.

The day after FDR signed the Social Security Act, a tragic accident occurred in Alaska. Will Rogers, fifty-six, was killed, along with noted aviator Wiley Post, in a plane crash at Point Barrow. His death deeply affected people from all walks of life, from the White House to the poor house. It saddened fun-loving Henry Boykin as he pumped TP Aero gas into Fords and Chevys. It deeply grieved Rogers's close friend, Amon G. Carter, who would the next year sponsor the construction of the classic Will Rogers Memorial Auditorium and Coliseum in Fort Worth. In front of the Coliseum is a casting of a sculpture by Electra Waggoner Biggs—a thirteen-and-a-half foot bronze of the renowned cowboy humorist astride his favorite horse, Soapsuds.

◆

In late summer of 1935, a spectacular display of gunfire took place in Louisiana. Huey P. Long, known as the "Kingfish," was assassinated on September 8, 1935, in the thirty-four-story Capitol building in Baton Rouge. He was a U.S. Senator when he was killed at age forty-two by Dr. Carl Weiss.

✦

Shortly thereafter, in Los Angeles, on September 23, 1935, Edgar L. Marston died at age seventy-five. He had moved to Los Angeles in 1933 before resigning as Chairman of the Board in 1934. Marston had been present with Colonel Hunter at the birth of TP in a Fort Worth hotel in 1888. The two, father-in-law and son-in-law, working in close harmony with W. K. Gordon, had nurtured the fledgling company through its flowerage in the 1890s. Together in life, so in death. His imposing white sepulcher is neighbor to the Colonel's grave in St. Louis's famed Bellefontaine Cemetery.[25]

In the mid-1930s, Melvin Slagle (who later would become TP Manager of Lands and Leasing and a TP Vice-President) began his career with the company. At the time, he was a lifeguard at River Crest Country Club. For some two years, he lived in quarters on the top floor of the club. He became well acquainted with William D. Waltman, step-son of John Roby Penn. Years later, a story was to gain currency concerning Slagle and Penn's other son, John Roby Penn, Jr. One day, Bill Gupton, former TP geologist related, skylarking John Roby Penn, Jr. was breaking glasses around the swimming pool. Melvin sent him home. In about fifteen minutes, Mr. Penn came down to the club with young Roby in tow. "Why did you send him home?" he demanded. "Because he was breaking glasses around the pool. And if he does it again, I will send him home again!" Slagle said. Penn was impressed with the young lifeguard's bravado. At the end of the summer, he gave Slagle a job at Texas Pacific.

At the 1992 Christmas party of ex-TP employees, Billy Joe Moore told another version of the story. According to Moore, young John Roby came near to drowning in the River Crest pool, and alert life guard Slagle pulled him out in the nick of time. If this scenario were true, it would follow that gratitude for saving his son might have been the motivation for Penn hiring Slagle.

John Roby Penn, Jr. was dubious about both stories. According to Penn, Jr., it was Melvin's friendship with William D. Waltman (stepson of John Roby Penn) that landed Slagle a TP job in 1936: "Bill spoke to my dad about Melvin when Melvin decided he had had enough of being lifeguard."[26]

Henry Boykin remembered working for TP in the 1930s:

> Roy Naugle in 1934 was the supervisor of service stations. He was a real nice man. I did not know at that time that he was watching me, but I guess he

was, because he asked me if I would like to be the manager of the station at Jennings and Magnolia, across the street from St. Mary's Catholic Church. I told him I sure would. He said, "Your salary will be $125 a month." I spent the year of 1935 at this station. It was at this station where I met George Studdard. We became good friends. Jimmie Jay was the other attendant. He was a real good worker. We worked good together. Jimmie would wash and grease the cars, and I would tend the front. Roy Naugle would come by and say, "You men are doing a real good job." That would make us work harder. The reason our business picked up so much is we would let the churchgoers park their cars at our station. They would tell us to "fill 'em up" and check the oil. Some of them would tell us to grease their cars while they were in church.

In 1936 the company decided to lease all the stations, most of which consisted of a very small building with grease and wash racks behind and gasoline pumps out front. Jimmie Jay and I leased the station at Magnolia and Jennings, and ran it for about a year and did real good.

Then we also leased a station at Mulkey and Jennings, where I had worked in 1929. I ran this one while Jimmie ran the station at Jennings and Magnolia. Both stations sold TP products.

Roy Naugle became the TP City Salesman, and he would come by and sell us oil and grease. Wiltie Creswell was TP Credit Manager, and he would do everything possible to get a new account through for me. We became good friends, so he started trading with me. Al Purvis was the man who delivered our gas to us. Old Rip Harden took the order at the desk, and I would say, "Rip, get that gas out early so I can make a few gallons extra." So he would. The expansion on 500 gallons would be pretty good. Gas at that time, 1936, was 15 cents a gallon. I can still hear old Purvis yelling out half a block away, "Henry, here I come!"[27]

In 1936, Texas celebrated its Centennial. It had been one hundred years since General Sam Houston and his valiant band of Texans defeated Santa Anna and his Mexican army at San Jacinto. To commemorate the battle, work was begun in that year on a 570-foot marble monument, fifteen feet taller than the Washington Monument in the nation's capital. Texas Pacific employees joined in the hoopla. Everyone was singing the "Yellow Rose of Texas," "Will You Come To My Bower," and a new song "Beautiful Texas" written by flour salesman soon-to-be-governor, W. Lee O'Daniel.

While Texans were celebrating the Centennial, out in Thurber a melancholy event was marked as the post office closed. On November 30, 1936, the last postcard was mailed from the little picture-postcard town. Now Thurber's days were truly numbered.

✦

On December 11, 1936, less than a fortnight following the close of the Thurber Post Office, King Edward VIII abdicated the throne of England in favor of his

Robert Henry Ward, Josephine Lawrence Warfield, W. K. Gordon, Ella Lawrence Warfield, Mary Joseph Warfield Ward, and Col. Robert D. Hunter, circa 1899. Courtesy Mrs. W. K. Gordon, Jr.

brother, the Duke of York, who became King George VI. The reason for the abdication was the King's determination to marry an American divorcee, Wallis Warfield Simpson. *Warfield,* that name had appeared on the Thurber rolls.

Stories began to circulate that Wallis Warfield, as a girl, had visited Warfield relatives in Thurber. Regretfully, there is no proof.[28]

◆

On March 18, 1937, the *Los Angeles Evening Express* reported that Gulf Oil executive H. B. Fuqua of Fort Worth had been installed as President of the American Association of Petroleum Geologists at their L.A. convention. (A dozen years later the famed geologist would succeed J. Roby Penn as TP Chairman.) Also on that day in East Texas a horrendous explosion shook the little town of New London in Rusk County to its very foundations. It is thought that an accumulation of gas in the New London School basement was touched off by a spark when a switch was flipped in the machine shop five minutes before the end of the school day. The blast killed 296 students and teachers. Sympathy and assistance poured in from all over the nation. Most of the victims were buried in New London's Pleasant Hill Cemetery. A stranger walking through the cemetery, might wonder at the fact that so many of the headstones would give the date of death as March 18, 1937.[29]

The four-year demolition of the Thurber brick plant, commenced in 1933, had been completed except that its smokestack still stood proud and tall. On March 29, 1937, thousands of people came from miles around to witness its implosion. (This smokestack was the one erected in 1898, not to be confused with the one constructed in 1908 at the power complex and which still stands.) Reporter Dave Hall covered the degringolade for the *Fort Worth Press:* "Forty sticks of dynamite were placed in the base of the 1898 chimney under the direction of C.C. Hamilton of Mingus. Mr. Hamilton pushed a plunger. The base of the great chimney shot out with a dull roar, ballooning red dust. The giant shook, tilted and crumbled. . . . Construction of the chimney had required about 60 days. It came down in six seconds."[30]

John B. Garrett, then a twelve-year old lad, later a prominent Fort Worth attorney, was there that day. "Several of the families in Stephenville had purchased some of the fine homes in Thurber and had moved them to Stephenville. These included J. W. Heaton, who managed Texas Power & Light Company, and Coach Billy Jack Wisdom who coached the John Tarleton Agricultural College Plowboys basketball team to the longest winning streak in college history. These families, as well as many others, including my mother and father and their five children, were among those who were fortunate enough to observe the dynamiting of the old smokestack. We parked on the north side of Highway 80, just east of 'downtown'

Thurber, and watched the smokestack come tumbling down. My father and others dashed to what a minute before had been the smokestack and picked up arms full of bricks as souvenirs, and the ones my dad picked up wound up being a portion of the curb to my mother's flower beds. Every time I go west on I-20, my mind's eye recreates that eventful day."[31]

The demolition was Thurber's requiem. W. K. Gordon, who had supervised the building of the stack forty years before, was on hand to witness its destruction. Now all the houses had been moved. Only a few brick buildings and the 1908 smokestack were left.

On July 4, 1937, several hundred ex-Thurberites held a reunion and formed the Thurber Old Settlers Association. In the early 1960s the Thurber Ex-Students and Teachers Association was organized. The two organizations were merged in 1967 to become the Thurber Historical Association, a state-chartered corporation formed for the purpose of preserving Thurber's history. The association meets annually on the second Saturday in June.[32]

Writers, intrigued and inspired, often revel in Thurber's past. Consider the tale of the Phantom of the Thurber Opera as related by Frank X. Tolbert of *The Dallas Morning News:*

> I stopped for breakfast in Thurber at the Smokestack Restaurant, once called The Ghost Town Cafe. This is a ghost town, although eight inhabitants were found in the last census check.
>
> Anyway, the Smokestack is the most interesting restaurant on this stretch of Interstate 20, and when I was paying my bill, the young proprietor of the cafe, Ted DeLorme, mentioned that three of his employees had left recently because they claimed the ghost town had ghosts in residence.
>
> When I asked, DeLorme said he hadn't seen or heard any ghosts, much less the beautiful female one who, according to some supposedly sober auditors, appears on Thurber streets singing selections from Italian operas. An Italian ghost, yet! Still, hundreds of Italian miners were brought here long ago, along with workers from other European countries. Dr. Leo S. Bielinski, a descendant of Polish miners who came here almost a century ago, said that this town, in its heyday, had a big Opera House. And Thurber was a regular stop for opera companies traveling between Fort Worth-Dallas and El Paso.
>
> Bielinski spoke of Eliza Whitehead. She was one of the old-timers who claimed to see and hear the singing ghost. Back in 1955, Mrs. Whitehead told Bielinski of the musical apparition: 'I've lived here 40 years. And only once did I see and hear the singing ghost. I was just walking in downtown Thurber one night. And here came this pretty young lady singing in some foreign language. Then she just vanished in front of my eyes.'
>
> The brick walls of the Opera House have come down, and there are only ruins of the homes of mining-company executives in the once-elite New York Hill section. Still standing downtown are three stout brick buildings, one of

which houses Smokestack Restaurant, named for the dominant landmark, a very tall brick smokestack.[33]

Some sixty thousand cars a day pass by the smokestack as they cruise east and west on the Interstate. As dramatic as a 148-foot tall exclamation point, it escapes no one's attention, whether a first-time tourist or veteran truck driver familiar with the route. All have a question, a comment, a thought. One such traveler was Gordon Ramsey of Fort Worth: "It was a dark and stormy night. I was driving west to Andrews. Tatters of clouds, black like the coal dust on a miner's shirt after a 10-hour shift, flaked the sky. I saw that smokestack lit up from its base. The shadows flickered up into the clouds. I thought I was seeing a tornado." Ramsey testified that he came "real close to turning around and heading east!" [34]

In 1993 another newsman, Bud Kennedy of the *Fort Worth Star-Telegram* stopped in Thurber, albeit against his will.

I have been 38 for eight days now, and so far it stinks. I first reached this conclusion about 3:45 P.M. Wednesday, standing by my dead car in the dust and gravel alongside Interstate 20 in Thurber, Texas, which is three miles south of Mingus, Texas, which is not a likely site for an Ed Bass downtown opera hall.

I always enjoy visiting Thurber, a famous coal and oil boom town now reduced to old storefronts and a tall brick smokestack. But until Wednesday, I had never enjoyed visiting Thurber for three hours, which is long enough to memorize the entire historical marker and rewrite it as a rap hit.

I knew I was in trouble when I told the auto club call-taker where I was, and she said, "Gerber?"

"Thurber," I repeated.

She told me bluntly, "There's no such place."

I waited an hour and a half. Still no tow truck. By then, she nearly had me convinced: Maybe there's no such place.

Life was easier when I was 37, and that was only till a week ago yesterday, when I aged another year and some great friends consoled me with cake and cards and balloons and Thai hot-pepper chicken.

I figure I must have passed through some kind of Over-The-Hill looking-glass, out of reality into the haze of this West Texas ghost town.

There's no such place. I called the auto club again, and this time I really started to wonder whether I had dropped off into the West Texas Twilight Zone. I repeated my name and membership number.

"Kennedy?" she said. "There's no call by that name."

Now I'm no-call-by-that-name in no-such place.

This time I give the highway numbers: Interstate 20 at Texas 108, eastbound on the south service road.

"Yes, sir," she said politely. "What town is that close to?"

"It's in Thurber," I said. "Between Ranger and Weatherford."

"Yes, sir," she said. "What towns are *they* close to?"

By this time, it was about 3:45 P.M. The day had started as a placid drive for lunch with college journalists in Abilene, but the afternoon was dragging on toward supper and maybe an overnight bunk at Thurber's New York Hill Restaurant.

About 20 minutes later, I called the auto club again. Another call-taker answered. "Yes, sir!" he said excitedly. "We found a wrecker driver who knows where you are! He should be there in about an hour!"

Four o'clock. Four-fifteen. No tow truck. I remembered a bottle of spring water in the trunk. I turned the trunk key, raised the lid and watched as a bright balloon floated up over Interstate 20, proclaiming to all of Thurber, "Happy Birthday!"

The last time I saw the birthday balloon it was floating north into the sky, past the ghost town smokestack.

I was about to scream, or roll in the gravel and cry from frustration. But just then, out of the West Texas twilight came rumbling up in a cloud of dust: a giant red tow truck.

My car and I both got back to Fort Worth by nightfall. By then, we both needed a couple of belts. Just don't ask where we were all day Wednesday. There's no such place.[35]

Well, of course, there is a Thurber. It left its imprint indelibly upon the map of Texas. Some have even speculated that it is the Brigadoon of the Lone Star State. Brigadoon? How so? In the musical *Brigadoon,* a small long-vanished hamlet in the Scotland Highlands comes back to life for one day every 100 years. With 127,000,000 tons of coal still in place, only 12,000,000 tons having been mined over a period of thirty years, could Thurber come back to life some day? With a constantly increasing population, surging demand for more and more energy, when the world's oil has been depleted, when new technologies are developed to bring the coal to the surface, who can say that Thurber will not be reincarnated?

◆

On February 13, 1993, a springlike winter day some fifty-six years after the brickyard stack was blasted down, my wife Wanda and I were given a tour of Elk Castle Ranch by its owner, Jack Daugherty, Chairman of the Board of Cash America, who had purchased 5,500 acres of land formerly owned by Texas Pacific Coal and Oil Company and was engaged in building an Edinburgh-like castle high atop the mountain above New York Hill.[36] Daugherty pointed out to us the ruins of brick homes on New York Hill, a train trestle, walls of the brick kilns, and other detritus from Thurber's heyday. Standing atop the train trestle, I gazed northward at

The smokestack that is still standing at Thurber was part of the power complex built in 1908. Courtesy Nita Stewart Haley Memorial Library, Midland, Texas.

what had been the glory of Thurber. The most obvious surviving remnant is the 1908 smokestack. An occasional curious traveler on Interstate 20 stops for a closer look at the red relic that stands as a lonely monument to a time when black diamonds lit Thurber.

8

Texas Pacific employees of the thirties lived through many historic events occurring not only in Texas, but nationally and internationally as well.

On May 6, 1937, the dirigible *Hindenberg*, pride of the Third Reich, exploded and burned at Lakehurst, New Jersey. Two months after C. C. Hamilton pushed a plunger to bring down the brickyard smokestack in Thurber, President Franklin D. Roosevelt on May 28 pushed a button in Washington, D.C. to open the Golden Gate Bridge in San Francisco. A year before, on July 18, 1936, a lariat across the entrance to Billy Rose's fabulous Casa Manana in Fort Worth was cut via an electrical impulse touched off by Roosevelt aboard a U.S. Navy cruiser off the coast of Maine.[1]

On July 2, 1937, Amelia Earhart and her navigator, Fred Noonan, took off from Lae, New Guinea, en route to Howland Island, 2556 miles away on one of the final legs of their ambitious plan to circle the globe near the Equator. They never made it.

In 1938, song-writing flour salesman W. Lee O'Daniel confounded all observers when he was elected governor, defeating several established politicians and winning the Democratic primary without a runoff. Many believe that O'Daniel's "Beautiful Texas," which was on the lips of Texans everywhere, played an important role in his victory.

On Sunday, January 22, 1939, TP suffered a heavy loss in the death of a key executive, fifty-four-year-old Vice-President and General Counsel John Hancock. Hancock was born in Newton, Texas, on September 21, 1884, the son of John Hancock and Elizabeth Harger Hancock. He began his law career in Newton in 1910. He joined TP in 1919 at Thurber and moved to Fort Worth in 1921 as General Counsel. In 1922 he was made President of TP's pipeline subsidiary.

On Monday morning the *Fort Worth Star-Telegram* ran the story of his death on the front page complete with his picture and the headline: JOHN HANCOCK DIES AT HOME.[2] Cause of death was listed as acute coronary thrombosis. Shown on the death certificate as informant was Hancock's son-in-law, E. T. Adair. President J. R. Penn was a pallbearer. So was former President Edgar J. Marston who returned to Fort Worth from his home in Colorado Springs. On his headstone in Greenwood Memorial

Park appears no name in customary block letters, but, most proudly, Hancock's own signature.

And what were TP employees as well as the rest of the general public doing for entertainment? Through the depths of the Great Depression and beyond, they passed many an hour throwing dice in Monopoly, a game introduced in February 1935 that rewarded players for sending rivals into bankruptcy. Movies were a popular form of entertainment—in 1934 *The Thin Man,* starring William Powell and Myrna Loy was a hit. They loved Shirley Temple and her rollicking "Good Ship Lollipop," and laughed heartily at the antics of the *Little Rascals*—Spanky, Darla, Alfalfa, and the gang. In 1938 Walt Disney produced his first full-length feature film, *Snow White and the Seven Dwarfs* and in 1940 armchair travelers took their first of seven trips "on the road" with Dorothy Lamour, Bob Hope, and Bing Crosby. Many were entranced with Orson Welles's 1941 film, *Citizen Kane,* a thinly disguised portrait of publisher William Randolph Hearst.

Radio programs were also popular. In the late 1930s and early 1940s many tuned in radio commentator Walter Winchell to hear: "Good evening, Mr. and Mrs. North and South America and all the ships at sea . . . let's go to press." One of the most memorable programs was Welles's gripping 1938 broadcast that described a fictional invasion of New Jersey by Martians. The broadcast was so realistic that thousands of alarmed listeners flooded authorities with calls.

Although his days were taken up by company problems, Penn also made time to enjoy leisure activities. Pat Woods stated that he was a movie aficionado and "We were kindred spirits, literary-wise. We read the same books, and saw and discussed the same movies and plays."[3]

◆

Europe, September 1939—British Prime Minister Neville Chamberlain thought he could buy "peace in our time" by handing over the mountain defenses of Czechoslovakia to Adolf Hitler, who promised to accept a deal of land for peace. On his deathbed barely six months after his resignation as prime minister, Chamberlain said, "Everything would have been all right if Hitler hadn't lied to me."

But Hitler did lie and soon all Europe was aflame. A new word entered the language: Blitzkreig! Nothing could withstand the onslaught of Nazi Stuka dive bombers and the tread of the mighty goose-stepping German army. Poland fell in hours. Early in 1940, Denmark and Norway were vanquished. Holland and Belgium were next. Then an end run around the vaunted Maginot Line and on June 14, Paris fell. An armistice between France and Germany was signed on June 22 in a railway car (the same car, in fact, in which Germany signed its surrender in 1918) in the Compiègne Forest. On May 10, 1940, Chamberlain walked out of the House of Commons and Winston Churchill took up residence at No. 10 Downing Street. On June 4 in a speech to Parliment following the tattered British

Expeditionary Force's flight from Dunkirk, he vowed: "We shall fight on the beaches; we shall fight on the landing-grounds, we shall fight in the fields and in the streets, we shall fight in the hills; we shall never surrender."[4]

In an effort to strangle and starve England, Hitler unleashed the fury of his U-boats against American shipping in the North Atlantic. The merchant marine as well as military vessels were targeted. A U.S. destroyer, the *Reuben James*, was torpedoed and sunk on October 31, 1941, with a loss of 115 men.

◆

The question as to America's entry into the war became when, and not whether. It was obvious in the gathering storm that the American petroleum industry would be called upon to provide ever increasing quantities of oil. John Roby Penn, like oil men everywhere, did not shrink from the service to his country. With an unbounded determination to produce the oceans of petroleum that would be needed, he, as did all TP personnel, creased his brow, spit on his hands, and set to work with a will.

The worker who predicted that the machinery from the dismantled Thurber brick plant that was shipped to Japan would come back some day was right.[5] Beginning in the 1930s, Japan began an ambitious expansion program. On December 7, 1941, a surprise attack on Pearl Harbor was carried out.[6]

◆

Eight sleeping battleships—*Pennsylvania* in dry dock; *West Virginia, Tennessee, California, Arizona, Oklahoma, Maryland,* and *Nevada* all in a row like sitting ducks. For the Japanese pilots it was like shooting fish in a barrel.

The next day President Roosevelt spoke to Congress: "Yesterday, December 7, 1941—a day that will live in infamy—the United States of America was suddenly and deliberately attacked by naval and air forces of the Empire of Japan." After a somber recounting of the terrible losses inflicted in the sneak attack, the President concluded his message:

> As Commander-in-Chief of the Army and Navy, I have directed that all measures be taken for our defense. Always will we remember the character of the onslaught against us. With confidence in our armed forces, with the unbounded determination of our people, we will gain the inevitable triumph, so help us God. I ask that the Congress declare that since the unprovoked and dastardly attack by Japan on Sunday, December seventh, a state of war has existed between the United States and the Japanese Empire.[7]

America was at war. And not only with Japan. On December 11, both Germany and Italy declared war on the United States. The U.S. quickly replied in kind. It was now truly World War II.

◆

✦

Like the rest of the country, TP employees and future employees marched off to war. Those who stayed at home also served. They planted Victory Gardens. They salvaged toothpaste tubes. They endured rationing of meat, sugar, gasoline, and tires. Need a new car? Forget it. Red Jello was hard to come by. Lucky Strike Green had gone to war. They rolled up their sleeves and gave red blood. In Europe and in the Pacific, events moved on: Battle of Midway; invasion of North Africa; then Sicily and Italy and D-Day at Omaha Beach.

In 1943, J. R. Penn and the Board of Directors, wishing to supplement benefits to be provided by the eight-year-old Social Security Act, adopted a retirement plan for its employees. The company agreed to pay 100 percent of the cost for past service annuities, plus the greater part of the cost of retirement income based on future service.

The Battle of the Bulge was the final and deciding battle of World War II in Europe. In mid-December 1944, the snow lay deep and silent in the Ardennes Forest. General George S. Patton's tanks of the 10th Armored Divison, Third U.S. Army, were out of gas.[8] General Omar Bradley, commander of the Twelfth Army Group consisting of the First, Third, Ninth, and Fifteenth Armies, scrounged the fuel. Because of the efforts of the men and women of Texas Pacific Coal and Oil Company and all of the rest of the mighty petroleum industry back on the home front, gasoline flooded in on the landing beaches. In 1940, Texas Pacific produced 2,560,274 barrels of oil; in 1945, 4,407,901.[9] Gasoline and fuel oil were brought onto the continent by means of flexible pipe lines laid under the English Channel. From the beaches the gas and oil were pumped forward to main distribution points through pipe lines laid on the surface of the ground.[10] The hitch was in the inability of the supply trucks to move the gasoline up from the rear areas fast enough to keep pace with Patton's rambunctious and audacious tanks up on the spearhead three hundred miles to the north.

On April 12, 1945, FDR died of a cerebral hemorrhage in Warm Springs, Georgia, and Harry S. Truman became president.[11]

In January 1945, about three months before Roosevelt's death, Charles Yager hired Billy Joe Moore as a landman. Moore was assigned to the recently opened Breckenridge office and instructed to join the Abilene scout check.[12] Moore recalled:

> I knew nothing about land work. One Wednesday after the Abilene scout check had concluded, head landman Melvin Slagle told me to meet him in Ballinger, County Seat of Runnels. We went to the court house, and Slagle showed me how to check records. Then we drove to Lawn in Taylor County and called on Walter LaFoon who owned land in northeast Runnels County.

LaFoon accepted Slagle's offer of two dollars an acre for a ten year lease. Slagle told LaFoon that I would return the next day with a lease for him to sign.

Since this was my first deal, I did not know how to fill out the lease. Slagle told me to call Miles Hart in TP's legal department and Miles would tell me how to do it. After buying the LaFoon lease, I bought others in that general area. Whenever I ran into a land or legal question, I would call Miles Hart. Some times I would call him five or ten times a day. Hart trained me over the phone.

I drew the drafts on TP through the Fort Worth National Bank and signed them as Billy Joe Moore. When Mr. Penn reviewed the drafts that were arriving, he called Slagle in and asked, "When did you hire a woman to buy leases?" Slagle replied that he had not hired a woman landman, that Billy Joe Moore was not a woman but rather a young man working in the Breckenridge office. Mr. Penn ordered, "Have him go by Billy J. Moore hereafter." That is what I did.[13]

U.S. involvement in World War II began suddenly with a big bang surprise Japanese attack. It ended just as suddenly, 1339 days later, with an American big bang surprise attack. President Harry S. Truman authorized the deployment of the first atomic bomb to be dropped on Hiroshima on August 6, 1945, with a second shortly thereafter on Nagasaki. The Japanese on August 14 had had enough. On September 2, aboard the battleship *Missouri* in Tokyo Bay, General Douglas MacArthur accepted the surrender of the Japanese.

✦

Two years later Texas had its own never-to-be-forgotten explosion. It happened at 9:12 A.M. on April 16, 1947. The French freighter *Grandcamp,* which had taken on 2,500 tons of ammonium nitrate fertilizer, caught fire and exploded at the Gulf Coast port of Texas City. Then the nearby Monsanto chemical plant blew up. Like dominoes falling, tin smelters, gas tanks, and oil refineries caught fire along the two-mile waterfront. Finally, at 1:11 the next morning, the *High Flyer, Grandcamp's* sister ship, loaded with 900 tons of ammonium nitrate, exploded. Although the *Grandcamp* was docked at Texas City, people reported hearing the blast 150 miles away. People were blown through doors. Dead people were carted to Galveston and other points. The final death count was placed at 576. Another 4000 were injured. It was the worst industrial accident ever in the United States. It is believed that a cigarette thrown in the *Grandcamp's* hold started the fire that ignited the ammonium nitrate fertilizer.[14]

✦

During the nightmare of the Depression, it became apparent to Penn that a false turning had occurred when the company went into deep debt proliferating Texas Pacific filling stations like bluebonnets over the

John Roby Penn, circa 1950. Courtesy of John Roby Penn, Jr.

countryside. In addition to the stations, TP also owned two refineries, two gasoline plants, and one-half interest in two other plants.

The refineries, located in Fort Worth and Wynnewood, Oklahoma, had a combined daily capacity of around twelve thousand barrels. The two wholly owned gasoline plants, located near TP's Ranger Field discovery, had a daily through-put potential of six million cubic feet of natural gas with a yield of fifteen thousand gallons of liquid daily.[15] The two half-owned gasoline plants, operated by Mid-Kansas Oil & Gas Co., had a daily capability of approximately twenty-eight thousand gallons of liquids.

Penn believed that Texas Pacific should stop trying to juggle three balls—exploration-production, refining, and marketing. He believed that TP should stick to exploration-production. He made up his mind to dispose of the subsidiaries: Texas Pacific Mercantile & Manufacturing Co., Thurber Brick Company, Thurber Tank Line Company, Thurber Construction Co., the pipelines, the two refineries, and the five hundred TP Aero Service Stations, the prodigy of Edgar Jean Marston's dream of large promise and small performance.[16]

The first to go was the Wynnewood Refinery, which had been completed in June 1923, with a capacity of three thousand barrels daily. In May 1932, a vacuum-operated asphalt plant with a daily capacity of one hundred tons of asphaltic products had been placed in operation there. The Oklahoma refinery was shut down immediately after Penn's return to power in 1934. In the latter part of 1935, it was sold as salvage. At the same time, arrangements were begun to discontinue the operation of the Fort Worth Refinery which had become "practically obsolete and unprofitable."[17]

All of the service stations were sold on December 1, 1945, to Humble Oil & Refining Company (now Exxon) for $400,000. With the sale, the company's marketing department was discontinued.[18]

The Fort Worth refinery and the Thurber Pipe Line Gathering System were sold to Premier Oil Company on November 13, 1946.[19] From that date TP would be a company dedicated exclusively to the exploration for and production of black gold. It would become a favorite of investors on the New York Stock Exchange where it would be called affectionately by the pet name of Tessie because of its trading symbol, TS. But not only would it be a favorite of investors, it also would be a lure for predators.

When John Roby Penn took the reins of the company for the second time in 1934, TP stock sold for $1.25 per share on the New York Stock Exchange. In 1948, the directors declared a 100 percent stock dividend. When the torch was passed to a new leader in 1949, the stock hit a high of $28 per share. Before the stock dividend, this would have been equivalent to $56 per share. No wonder Tessie was so popular in old New York.

The TP Story paid homage to Penn's financial finesse with this benediction: "Its swift and complete emergence from this difficult period contains a tribute to the administrative genius of J. Roby Penn."[20]

By 1948, hard times were over. The war was over. Texas Pacific was healthy and wealthy. Unfortunately, John Roby Penn was not healthy. It would not be long until a successor would take his place—but who would it be? Texas Pacific employees and the industry at large assumed it would be Executive Vice-President Charles Yager. But that was not to be. The next big chief in the TP would be a man called Babe.

9

Because of the rapid growth of Texas Pacific Coal and Oil Company, the Directors had felt for some months the need to employ a Chief Executive Officer experienced in the fields of geology, geophysics, and petroleum engineering. In 1948, at the behest of TP Director Ellison Harding, President of Fort Worth National Bank, Robert Windfohr, independent oil man and a TP director, approached H. B. (Babe) Fuqua (pronounced FEW-quay), Assistant to the Vice-President of Gulf Oil Corporation in Houston, with an offer of employment. Fuqua was a board member of Harding's bank and lived in Fort Worth until transferred by Gulf to Houston in 1944. Fuqua evinced a willingness to become Chief Executive Officer of TP provided he was given a five-year contract and that two of his colleagues from the oil patch, Ernest Closuit and Sid Richardson, were placed on the board. Windfohr and Harding were agreeable.

Accordingly, Windfohr on October 8, 1948, wrote to J. Roby Penn who was having a physical check up at Johns Hopkins Hospital in Baltimore:

> As it will finally work out, Fuqua will get a contract of employment for a period of five years. Neither we nor any succeeding Board of Directors can promise that the stockholders will elect him a Director or that subsequent Boards of Directors will elect him Chairman. For this reason and because we have to amend the by-laws to allow us to make contracts of employment for a period longer than one year, we may want to enlarge the Board of Directors from twelve to fifteen.
>
> One other change is needed in the by-laws to make the Chairman the No. 1 executive officer. Gillis Johnson (Fuqua's attorney) says that if we were to make a formal contract with Babe at this time, we would be under obligation to disclose this fact fully to the stockholders in the proxy that we mail out for the special meeting, and since we do not want to tell the world at large our business, only one copy of a "memorandum of intent" has been made. I have it in my office initialed by [Park] Weaver, [Charley] Yager, [Ellison] Harding, [Erle] Mitchell and [Robert] Windfohr.
>
> While the memorandum in my office doesn't say so, as it was drawn principally for the purpose of outlining our trade with Fuqua, the understanding I have had with everyone I have talked to is that the office of Chairman of the Executive Committee will continue at your present salary.[1]

Three weeks later on October 27, Windfohr again wrote to Penn who was still at Johns Hopkins:

At this morning's meeting of the Board of Directors resolutions were approved covering two proposed changes in the by-laws: (1) increasing the Board from twelve to fifteen and (2) authorizing contracts of employment for a period of not longer than five years. At the suggestion of Gene Adair the third proposed change making the Chairman the Chief Executive Officer was postponed until the annual meeting in April, principally because of the vast number of changes needed in the by-laws, something like a dozen.

I spent yesterday morning talking to Lang Wharton in Dallas. Found he had investigated Fuqua and was entirely happy about him and every other part of the arrangement except that he is constitutionally opposed to a five-year contract. He had checked Fuqua with the President of the Magnolia and was enthusiastic about him but thought he should rely for his security of job on control of the Board of Directors. For this reason, Lang was very much in favor of increasing the Board from twelve to fifteen. Mr. [S. J.] Stuart had talked at some length with Lang by phone, and it developed this morning that both he and Lang were of the same opinion. Louie Greene, as usual, was against almost everything. After a thorough discussion, it developed that both Greene and Mr. Stuart were ready to go along with the rest of us, and Lang told me over the phone last night that he would go along, so the resolution was adopted unanimously recommending the above two changes to the stockholders at a special meeting to be held on December 22. I was very careful to state at the meeting the objection of Lang to five-year contracts and thought it desirable to say that you were only lukewarm about increasing the Board of Directors. There was no thought on the part of any of the directors in overriding anybody's wishes, and the above motions were carried unanimously, it appearing to everyone that Fuqua's best chance of security would come from controlling the Board of Directors, and that we should perhaps offer a Directorship to Jack Snyder.[2] After all, he is not an in-and-outer in the stock. He has had his present position in it for something over five years, and his family, I believe, are the largest individual stockholders. He has just recently arranged with the Trustees of Harvard University to buy 20,000 shares of the stock, so I think he has earned a place on the Board, and I hope you agree.

As to the five-year contract, Ellison made the comment after the resolution was approved for submission to the stockholders that Babe would probably not insist upon execution of the contract, accepting our willingness to make it as sufficient evidence of security.

I think the present plan is to hold a Directors' meeting as soon as the special stockholders' meeting approves the changes, say at the regular December meeting, and elect Fuqua to the Board in place of Mr. Gordon, and thereupon elect him Chairman effective January 1. You will be President, and

Yager will be Vice President until the April meeting, at which time the by-laws changes will be made allowing the Chairman to become Chief Executive Officer.

I hope the matter has been handled the way you would have had it handled. Incidentally, the agreement was general that your salary as Chairman of the Executive Committee will remain exactly what it is now [$27,000] and while you are El Presidente some of your office boys like me are going to vote against any suggestion of yours to change that.[3]

✦

Not only was Texas Pacific Coal and Oil Company in the throes of finding a new leader, but Texas in 1948 was caught up in a wild and woolly campaign to elect a new U.S. Senator to replace retiring Senator W. Lee O'Daniel. The protagonists in the senate race were conservative former Governor Coke Stevenson and liberal New Deal Congressman Lyndon B. Johnson. The race ended in a virtual tie with Johnson clinging to a hotly disputed 87 vote lead. Final tally: Johnson 494,191; Stevenson 494,104. After heated debate and some truly Texas-sized shenanigans, Johnson was declared the winner.[4]

In the presidential election of 1948, Texas was one of the Southern states where the States Rights Party was a force. Prominent in the movement were oilmen from all over the state. One of the untiring and outspoken States Righters was Arch Rowan, president of Rowan Oil Company and friend to H. B. Fuqua. The party was formed by conservative elements of the Democratic Party and had as its nominees Governor J. Strom Thurmond of South Carolina and Governor Fielding L. Wright of Mississippi. Its game plan was to win enough electoral votes that the election would be thrown into the House of Representatives. After the shouting and the tumult died, the States Rights party garnered thirty-eight electoral votes by carrying four states in the South, not enough to throw the election into the House. On November 2, 1948, Harry S. Truman was the clear winner over Thurmond and Republican Thomas E. Dewey.

✦

Ten days following the presidential election, on November 12, Windfohr wrote to Fuqua in Houston to advise him of what had transpired that morning at the TP Board of Directors meeting. He closed his letter:

> Mr. Gordon will resign in time for you to be elected a Director and Chairman at the meeting to be held December 22. It seems certain to me that Lang Wharton's place will become vacant even faster than I thought. News from there yesterday afternoon wasn't good.[5] Incidentally, you will be glad to know that there was not a dissenting voice against either Ernest or Sid.

In his letter to Fuqua, Windfohr enclosed copies of letters he wrote to Ernest Closuit, Sid Richardson, and J. T. Snyder the same day informing them that they had been approved by the TP Board as directors and that they would be recommended for election at a special stockholders' meeting to be held December 22nd. Windfohr closed his letters to Closuit and Richardson:

> This is a darn good little outfit with some $15 million of quick assets above current liabilities and with 16,000 barrels daily net production. I think you will enjoy the association, and it is going to be fun to have you, especially with Babe running the show.[6]

Not all of Windfohr's plans worked out exactly as he had envisioned. While Snyder and Fuqua sidekicks Closuit and Richardson were elected Directors at the December 22 meeting, that part of the scenario calling for the resignation of W. K. Gordon and the ensuing immediate election of Fuqua to fill the contemplated vacancy did not occur. Fuqua's five-year contract and CEO status could not be granted until after stockholder approval at the annual meeting in April.

While the company top brass was absorbed in the intrigue attendant on bringing Fuqua into the TP, efforts to recruit other oil finders were also pressed. When World War II ended, many returning veterans entered college under the GI Bill of Rights to study geology, geophysics, and petroleum engineering. Now in 1948 and 1949 as they began to graduate, oil company personnel departments paid visits to college campuses to interview and recruit the brightest minds. Once on the payroll, neophyte geologists and engineers found themselves assigned to remote areas of far West Texas and Lea and Eddy Counties, New Mexico. It was a job, and that outweighed the rigors of living in the middle of nowhere far from the civilized world. One such young geologist was W. L. Gupton, Jr., who, fresh out of college, came to work for TP in January, 1948. In the spring he was moved out to Breckenridge. Then he went to Hobbs, New Mexico, to be a well-site geologist.

These young geologists soon began to see crude pre-World War II machinery replaced with sophisticated and efficient modern equipment. Gupton described one such new device:

> TP had acreage offsetting a new wildcat discovery drilled by Amerada in northwest Lea County. The company had a standard rotary rig (owned by TP and operated by TP personnel) that was moved to the area to develop these leases in the Bagley Field.
>
> One of the ways a well-site geologist used to determine what formation might be encountered during drilling was recording the time it took to drill a foot of formation. In 1949, the method used was for the driller to take a five-foot board marked off in one-foot units, hold it next to the rotating kelly,[7] and mark off the kelly in one-foot units with pipe dope, refined oil or chalk. The driller then noted on a pad the time it took for the kelly to go down a

foot. Such measurement might be less than a minute in soft formation, and five to ten minutes in hard formation.

In most cases, an increase in drilling rate would mean a formation change, i.e., from shale to sand or lime. If the drilling rate dropped significantly, the driller would record same, drill 10 or 15 feet, stop and circulate.[8] Sometimes the circulated samples, when recovered from the mud system, would reveal a sandstone or limestone that was porous and saturated with oil. This was an important method of formation evaluation on rotary type drilling rigs.

In 1949, an Oklahoma company developed an instrument called a Geolograph which was calibrated and connected to the kelly. This instrument would make a foot mark on a drum which was turned by a clock. The driller was thereby relieved of this chore. The geologist and driller could see the time taken to drill each foot. Consequently, a more accurate and efficient way was now available. The instrument could be rented.

The drillers and geologists were happy to have the tool, and the tool was put on the company rig. Mr. R. J. Fleckenstein, the Drilling and Production Manager for TP, did not know of this new fangled machine, and while on tour visiting the rig, saw the Geolograph and said, "What the hell is that thing!" When told what it was, he said, "What's wrong with the old way?" It was an additional expense that he thought unnecessary. The tool remained on the rig, and variations of it are still in use on all active rigs today.[9]

J. Roby Penn's closeness with the dollar obviously had made an impression on TP's Drilling and Production Manager.

Amidst all the maneuvering to find a new company chairman, and two months after the burial of Lang Wharton, death came again to the TP, this time to the man who was Chairman, W. K. Gordon. Gordon died at his home in Fort Worth on Sunday, March 13, 1949. The Bigga Boss—King of Thurber and wildcatter supreme—survived Colonel Robert Dickie Hunter by forty-seven years and Edgar L. Marston by fourteen. He was present when TP's foundations were laid and the cornerstone put in place. He watched Thurber blossom and flourish from a mining camp to the most important town between Fort Worth and El Paso and then wither and perish and pass into oblivion. As discoverer of the Ranger Field in 1917, he put "oil" in TP's name and opened a vast empire to the quest for petroleum. Great builders and leaders must not only be talented, but durable and consistent. In those categories, Gordon had few equals. In his eighty-seven years—with his unflagging commitment to coal, bricks, oil, insurance, marriage, and family—he never stumbled.

On March 23, the Texas Pacific Board of Directors adopted a resolution commemorating his death:

> The deep feeling of sorrow in which we record the death of William Knox Gordon is tempered only by the memories we shall retain of a wonderful friend and associate, and of the long and useful life he led as a citizen.

Mr. Gordon, who became associated with Texas Pacific in 1889—practically from its inception—served the Company continuously until the time of his death on March 13, 1949—a period of sixty years.

He was first employed by the Company as a mining engineer, successively becoming Assistant General Manager, General Manager, Vice President and finally Chairman of the Board of Directors. Mr. Gordon was continuously a Director from January 8, 1892, and Chairman of the Board from May 23, 1934.

A man of great courage, energy, resource and vision, he was truly a Texas pioneer, who won the admiration and respect of the many. He was largely responsible for the early and successful development of the Company's mining operations, and the building of the town of Thurber, Texas. His determination led to the discovery of the Ranger oil field of Texas at a time when the nation and the state were suffering from a crude oil shortage brought on by World War I.

Mr. Gordon's kind and understanding disposition made a friend of all with whom he came in contact.[10]

On July 12, 1949, the Board of Directors of Southwestern Life Insurance Company also adopted a resolution to honor Gordon's passing which stated in part:

Next to Texas Pacific Coal and Oil Company, whose affairs he had guided so long, he loved the Southwestern Life Insurance Company. On May 1, 1903, he became one of Southwestern Life's original stockholders and during the years increased his holdings until at the time of his death, he was its largest single stockholder. In June, 1911, he became a Director of Southwestern Life and in March, 1936, a member of its Executive Committee, both of which offices he held throughout the remainder of his life.

It can truly be said of Mr. Gordon that in achieving outstanding success in the business world, he never at any time compromised the Christian ideals and high principles which governed his life nor lost that human touch and intense interest in the welfare of his fellow man which endeared him to all that knew him. We who had the pleasure of serving with him on the Board of Directors of this Company respected and relied upon his wise counsel and sound business judgment and loved him for the kindly, courteous gentleman that he was.[11]

Flowers, cards, editorials, and messages of condolence poured in from all over the country. After services at his residence, Gordon was entombed in Hillcrest Mausoleum in Dallas, alongside his wife Fay, who died the previous year, and his daughters Margie and Louise.

At the stockholders' meeting held on April 20, 1949, the by-laws were amended to allow a five-year employment contract and denominating the Chairman as Chief Executive Officer.[12]

Immediately following the stockholders' meeting, the Board met and authorized the President "to appoint a committee to assist in finding and considering candidates for employment by the Company who might qualify to supplement the Company's staff engaged in the exploration for and the production of crude oil and gas."[13]

It did not take the committee long to complete its search—by letter dated April 22, 1949, Windfohr advised Warren Scarborough, partner in the Cantey Hanger law firm, that the committee had met immediately on April 20 and that the name of H. B. Fuqua of Houston was favorably mentioned by every member of the committee. Windfohr asked Scarborough to use "his fertile legal mind" to prepare a contract to submit to Fuqua.[14]

About a month after Windfohr's directive to Scarborough to draw up a contract, twelve inches of rain fell in eight hours in Fort Worth on May 17. Trinity River levees were breached, sending dark, swirling floodwaters over a large area of the city's west side. Fort Worth's "Big One" reached the second floor of the Montgomery Ward store at 2600 West Seventh Street.

The Holly Plant of the Fort Worth Water Department was under water and the city's water supply was cut off. There was water all around, but not a drop to drink, or to flush toilets. To provide a bare minimum of water to the citizens, the city dispatched tank trucks to designated locations. TP employees, along with all other residents, trekked to these points with buckets, pails, and jars to receive their allotment. In due course the waters receded and the men and women in the Fort Worth offices of Texas Pacific returned to their desks to speculate on who would succeed J. Roby Penn as president. The odds-on favorite was Dooley Yager.

The ultimate contract drawn up by Cantey Hanger's Scarborough and Gillis Johnson was in the form of a three-page letter on Texas Pacific Coal and Oil Company letterhead dated July 6, 1949, and signed by J. R. Penn, President. The first paragraph stipulated:

> Texas Pacific Coal and Oil Company desires to secure your professional technical and engineering services. We agree to employ you, and you agree and undertake to accept and perform such employment in the field of geology, geophysics, and petroleum engineering services. The term of this employment is for five years. We agree to pay you $250,000 in the form of an annual salary of $50,000.

The letter ended:

> You may indicate your acceptance of this employment by signing and returning the extra copy herewith enclosed, and thereupon this shall form the full contract between you and Texas Pacific Coal and Oil Company.[15]

Nowhere in the letter-contract was it specified that Fuqua would be a Board Member, Chairman, or Chief Executive Officer. In a personal note dated April 22, 1949, Windfohr had advised Fuqua that "No mention can

Fort Worth flood, May 17, 1949. Building on right is Montgomery Ward. Courtesy W. D. Smith, Inc., Commercial Photography, Fort Worth, Texas.

be made of Chairmanship of the Board of Directors without invalidating contract for professional services. This point is covered and protected by the initialed memorandum in my desk."[16] Days went by. Weeks. Then on August 2, 1949, Fuqua wrote to Ellison Harding:

> In line with Mr. Penn's request, I am enclosing contract of employment with the Texas Pacific Coal and Oil Company, dated July 6, 1949. My acceptance of this contract is indicated by my signature thereon.
>
> This next week I am taking a trip to Mexico, and will be out of the country for a week or ten days. On my return I hope I can conclude all of my affairs with Gulf, and expect to be in Fort Worth on or about September 1.[17]

It is not clear why Fuqua returned the signed contract to Harding rather than to Penn or Windfohr. Pat Woods, who would become Fuqua's Executive Secretary, stated years later that it was probably because Harding was really the man behind the efforts to lure Fuqua back to Fort Worth.

The next day, August 3, Harding replied:

> Dear Babe: I am at a loss to tell you how much I appreciate your letter of the 2nd, enclosing the signed contract. When you called me Monday [August 1st] and started to talk, I had a sinking feeling because I thought you were getting ready to say "no," and I do not think I expressed my appreciation of your saying "yes" as much as I would like to have.
>
> I though it well to tell the directors who are available, and they are very much pleased over your decision. I cautioned them that there should be no public announcement for the time being. I think it is important that we get together and give an interview or statement.
>
> I hope you have a fine time at Cuernavaca. Your final decision has made me very happy, and I thank you.[18]

From Oil City, Pennsylvania, J. Roby Penn on August 9, 1949, sent a handwritten note to Fuqua:

> Just a line to assure you how pleased I am at your decision which Ellison passed along to me early last week. This feeling of satisfaction I know is shared by all of our directors, and I am sure the move will work out to the benefit of our little company as well as to your own [Gulf].
>
> Your host of friends will be more than glad to welcome you and Mrs. Fuqua back to Fort Worth.
>
> Ellison also mentioned the matter of timing of any statement in connection with the move, and I suggested that he handle to suit your wishes in this respect.
>
> Looking forward to seeing you in Fort Worth during the coming month and with best regards.[19]

Because Fuqua had lived in Fort Worth for eighteen years from 1926 to 1944 he indeed did have, as Penn mentioned, "a host of friends" in Fort Worth. Returning would be a happy homecoming.

During the discussions between Fuqua and the TP Board, Myrt Vititow and Tommy Tomlinson were pilots for Frank Wood Drilling Company of Wichita Falls. "Frank Wood and Babe Fuqua were like brothers," recalled Vititow. "In 1949 we often flew Mr. Fuqua to Fort Worth and return to Houston. I had no way of knowing that these trips had anything to do with his coming to TP from Gulf."[20] In February 1954 Vititow became TP's chief pilot. Tomlinson joined TP in May 1955.

Venerable John Roby Penn's retirement as TP President in September was the second sad event for the company in 1949, Gordon's death in March being the first. Gordon had presided at the birth of Texas Pacific as an oil company, and Penn had been largely responsible for breathing new life into it when it was gasping for breath in the dark days of the Depression. In nominating Penn in 1985 to the Hall of Fame of the Permian Basin Petroleum Museum, Fuqua wrote:

> At the time of Mr. Penn's return to the management of TP in 1934, the company had developed an indebtedness of over $400,000 and an operating loss of $250,000. The unprofitable operations included a refinery and 500 service stations. No dividends had been paid since 1929. As a result of discontinuing the refining and marketing operations and the sale of one piece of property in the East Texas oil field, all the indebtedness was cleared up. The company's earnings changed from a net loss of $250,000 in 1934 to an accumulated net profit of $7,460,000 at the end of 1948. In no year after 1934 did the company show a loss. In 1948 production amounted to 15,800 barrels daily compared to 3,578 barrels daily in 1934. Payment of dividends was resumed in 1936, at which time a total of $220,000 was paid to shareholders. Payments were increased in 1947 to $1,772,000 and in 1948 to $3,100,000. The company's net position was $1,096,000 at the end of 1934; at the end of 1948 it was $4,790,000 although cash dividends amounting to a cumulative figure of $10,234,000 had been paid from 1936 through 1948.[21]

For a quarter of a century beginning with Penn's arrival in 1920, his ideas and those of Gordon grew intertwined like two vines, so that it became difficult to separate the thinking of one from the other's. And the two were not just close business associates. They were, according to John Roby Penn, Jr., the best of friends. Almost every Sunday the families alternated having lunch at each other's home. Both men were the quintessence of politeness and courtesy. Whenever Penn addressed Gordon, it was always "Mr. Gordon." Whenever Gordon addressed Penn, it was always "Mr. Penn."

In September 1949, Penn was back in Johns Hopkins in Baltimore for further treatment. Fuqua had rapidly taken command of the ship and had his hand firmly on the wheel. On September 23 he wrote to the hospitalized Penn giving him a report of drilling activities and oil industry outlook. He closed his letter with a personal note:

> Mrs. Fuqua and I are having a very difficult time locating a satisfactory place to live, but feel confident that in due course we will find satisfactory quarters. Presently, it looks as though we will find it necessary to live at the Texas Hotel.[22]

At the Directors Meeting on September 28, Fuqua was elected to the Board and made Chairman. John Roby Penn's resignation as President was announced and Charles Yager was promoted to President. Two days later Fuqua wrote to Penn at Johns Hopkins:

> This week has been a busy one for me. There has been considerable to do in the Company and on the outside, which included moving our household effects from Houston to Fort Worth. Mrs. Fuqua will arrive here today. For the present, we plan to live at the Texas Hotel. However, we will ultimately buy or build us a home.
>
> You, of course, know that the Board had its regular monthly meeting on Wednesday, September 28th. All of the changes approved by you were acted upon favorably. It is my impression that everyone is quite pleased about the whole situation. We were all sorry you could not be here for this meeting, but will be looking forward to seeing you before too long.
>
> Bob Windfohr and Sid Richardson gave a cocktail party last night at the Fort Worth Club. Am sorry you could not have been present because you would have seen so many of your old friends at one gathering. Many people asked about you, and were told that we expect you back in Fort Worth before long, and that you were getting along fine.
>
> The various associations affiliated with the oil industry are having a deluge of conventions. The I.P.A.A. [Independent Petroleum Association of America] meets in Fort Worth this next week. The Drilling Contractors had their meeting in Dallas last week, and the Mid-Continent Oil & Gas Association and the State-Wide Proration Meeting will be in Houston on the 12th, 13th and 14th of the month. I presume all of these associations are desirable and contribute their part in the running of the industry. However, it does take a great deal of time and considerable money to keep them going.
>
> As to company drilling, it seems that anything I might say would be repetitious, since you occasionally get a copy of the drilling report, but we are encouraged over the two nice completions in the Fisher County field.[23]

So Babe Fuqua, five feet, nine inches and fifty-four years of age, soft-spoken and precise, took charge.

What about Charles Yager? Yager began his career with TP in 1922 at the Wynnewood refinery. In 1926 he was transferred to Fort Worth. This was the same year that Gulf moved Fuqua to Fort Worth. In 1929 he had been promoted to Chief Geologist. In 1939 he became Vice President and in 1945 Executive Vice President. In the years since 1929 he had been responsible for the acquisition and development of properties in the Permian Basin of West Texas and New Mexico, as well as in the Powder River Basin of Wyoming and Montana. As the strong right arm of J. Roby Penn, he had helped to lead the company. In the mid-40s, he was looked upon as heir apparent, but in the 1948-49 bandwagon enthusiasm of the draft Fuqua movement, Yager was passed over. He was made President, but President was not Number 1. As Chairman and CEO, Fuqua was Number 1, the Big Chief in the TP.

"I felt my legs had been cut off from under me," Yager told me when I interviewed him in 1991. But while he felt that life had handed him a lemon, he never betrayed his disappointment to his compatriots. He always wore a smile and he lilted when he talked. He never identified whom he felt were the ones who blocked his aspirations. He was, however, certain that J. Roby Penn had nothing to do with it.[24]

Babe Fuqua was christened Herbert Breedlove Fuqua, born December 27, 1895, to Frank and Beatrice Fuqua, in Duncan, Oklahoma, then still Indian Territory. Babe Fuqua's older brother, Nolen, had been born on March 25, 1894. The two boys were the couple's only children.

When Herbert was born, Texas Pacific Coal Company, founded in 1888, was seven years old and was working four mines, Nos. 5, 6, 7, and 8. Thurber was a beehive of activity. When the company's founder, Colonel Robert D. Hunter, died in 1902, Fuqua was almost seven years old. It was about this age that his mother affectionately started calling him Babe and the sobriquet would stick forever.

The boys attended public schools in Duncan. In 1908, when Babe was thirteen and Nolen fourteen, their mother died. That same year the power plant with its towering stack was completed at Thurber. Near its top appears the year of its birth and his mother's death: 1908. Down the corridor of time, Fuqua would act to preserve the smokestack as a historical landmark.[25]

In 1917, while a student at the University of Oklahoma, Fuqua was employed by Empire Fuel & Oil Company as a surface geologist.[26] In April 1917, America entered the First World War. When the summer was over, Fuqua enlisted in the army, and served for a period of thirteen months. Pat Woods recalled that whenever he was asked in later years what his rank was in the Army, he always replied without hesitation, "I was a very private soldier." After his discharge, he returned to the University to complete his work for a degree in geology and renewed his connection with Empire.[27]

At the University of Oklahoma, Babe met a coed from Elk City named Sarena Taylor. Sarena had transferred to the Norman campus from William Woods College in Fulton, Missouri.[28] Sarena was the daughter of

Laura and Alfred L. Taylor, western Oklahoma ranchers. Besides Sarena, there were four other daughters: Myrtle, Sally, Ruth, and Viola, as well as a son, Claud. Father Alfred, who had participated in the Oklahoma land rush, was illiterate. Laura taught Alfred to read and write. Her textbook was the Bible. Alfred acquired considerable wealth—a fine home, an interest in an Elk City bank and a ranch in San Luis Potosi, Mexico.[29]

Babe and Sarena were married in 1920—the year that John Roby Penn became TP President—and made their first of many homes in Wichita Falls, Texas. At that time the Empire Company entered into an extensive employment of geologists who had training or experience in surveying anomalous conditions in surface rock exposures.[30] The tools of the profession were the use of plane table, alidade, and Brunton compass, recording unusual dips in surface beds, as well as surface seeps of gas or oil. The magnetometer, gravity meter, and reflection seismic surveying were fully accepted in the late 1920s and 1930s after surface geology had proved the scientific method of finding oil and gas.

After a brief period of employment with Atlantic Oil Producing Company followed by a short stint as an independent geologist, Fuqua in 1922 was employed by Gulf Oil at Wichita Falls, Texas.[31] The man who hired him was Ernest Closuit, Sr. Closuit's son, Ernest, Jr., recalled:

> Dad was Chief Geologist for the Wichita Falls Division of Gulf Oil Corporation by 1922, having started in the mid to late teens with only a high school diploma. His first position had been as an assistant to a geological crew mapping surface outcrops looking for deep structures that might trap oil. Mr. Fuqua arrived sometime in 1922 looking for work and Dad signed him up with Gulf, most likely to be an "instrument man" with a mapping crew. Babe had a college degree and at least one earlier job in geology, so he didn't start as an assistant. Years later, especially if Babe was within earshot, Dad with a grin would mention the early days and those "College Boys" he hired and supervised.[32]

In 1923 Fuqua was transferred to San Angelo. In 1924 he returned to Wichita Falls. In 1926 he came to Fort Worth where he moved swiftly up the Gulf Oil ladder.[33] Although his tour in Fort Worth would prove both happy and productive, those years brought sadness as well. His father Frank died at his home in Duncan, Oklahoma, on October 23, 1932, at age eighty. Babe was thirty-seven at the time.

In Fort Worth, Fuqua *was* Gulf Oil. He was Chief Geologist for the Fort Worth Division, which included North Texas, North Central Texas, West Texas, Panhandle, and New Mexico. He played a dominant role in Gulf's leasing and drilling activities in West Texas and New Mexico during the 1920s and 1930s. The towering position held by Gulf in the Permian Basin was in large part due to Fuqua's vision and persistence.[34]

Sarena Fuqua, circa 1925. Courtesy Pat Woods.

H. B. Fuqua, circa 1935. Courtesy Blank & Stoller Corp.

In an interview years later with *News-Tribune* reporter Irvin Farman, Fuqua observed: "My most rewarding experiences were during my days with Gulf. I was practically running the company during my Fort Worth days, and the Pittsburgh office insisted that I move to Houston, which I did. Then they started this move to get me to Pittsburgh, which I knew I wasn't going to do. Have you ever seen Pittsburgh?"[35]

During his years in Fort Worth, Fuqua had begun many lifelong friendships: Publisher Amon Carter, banker Ellison Harding, attorneys Rice Tilley, Gillis Johnson, and Warren Scarborough, and oilmen John Roby Penn, Charley Yager, Neville Penrose, Arch and Charley Rowan, W. A. Moncrief, Robert F. Windfohr, and Sid Richardson. Sid was a favorite. The two often lunched together in the Fort Worth Club, which was located catty-corner to Fuqua's Gulf Oil office in the Petroleum Building at Sixth and Throckmorton.

✦

Richardson, who in the 1930s found it difficult to pay office rent, shared a small office with Frank Kelsey on the 11th floor of the Fort Worth National Bank Building. In 1934 freelance draftsman Bryan Poff went to the office to tell Sid he needed more information before he could complete a Winkler County map which Richardson had hired him to make. "That's no problem," Richardson said. "I will take you up to a place where you can get the dope."

"We ended up in the Gulf Oil Engineering Department on the eleventh floor of the Petroleum Building," said Poff. "We went back to a large room where there were about ten six-foot drawing tables. Half of them were vacant as this was during the depth of the Depression. R. L. Woodbury was head of the Department. He greeted Sid like it was his boss Babe Fuqua coming in. You could tell that Sid had free access to whatever he wanted. After a good-old boy exchange, they walked over to the map cabinet and got the map I needed. Sid left and I sat down at one of the drawing tables and transferred the data from the Gulf map to the map I was making for Sid."

In January 1938, Poff, 28, went to work as a draftsman in the Gulf Engineering Department. How did he remember Fuqua? "He was a perfectionist . . . cold, stern, seldom smiled. Passing in the hall, he might speak by nodding. Again he might not."[36]

Fuqua's friend, Sid Richardson, was a hustler. Although he made and lost more than one fortune, he would never admit defeat. He was like W. K. Gordon at Ranger a quarter of a century before. He would always try again. He would drill just a little bit further. An example: On September 15, 1942, Sid's sidekick Amon G. Carter and The Pure Oil Company commenced drilling the J. B. Walton No. 2C in Section 1, Block B-3, PSL Survey, in Winkler County, Texas. Location of the well was on the shallow producing Keystone Cattle Ranch. Sid with nearby leases had more than a passing interest in the outcome of the operation. When the Carter-

Pure well reached the Silurian formation, Amon had seen enough, but Sid and Babe Fuqua's Gulf Oil, also with leases in the immediate area, had a hunch that the big pay would be in the lower-lying Ellenberger, and, according to LeRoy Menzing, Oil Editor of the *Fort Worth Star-Telegram* at the time, agreed to pay the costs of deepening the well to that formation.[37] On June 6, 1943, the Walton hit the Ellenberger at 9524 feet, flowing at a rate of more than 6,500 barrels a day to open Winkler County's fabulous Keystone Ellenberger field.[38] Sid Richardson's "drill a little deeper" philosophy paid off. Oil reserves from this mammoth field were worth more than a billion dollars. In 1946, Sid and Amon bought the Texas Hotel in downtown Fort Worth and opened a swank club-restaurant on the lower level of the hotel. Its name? The Keystone Room.

✦

Years later Richardson's nephew Perry Bass wrote:

> My uncle, Sid Richardson, told me that it was rumored around Fort Worth that during the Depression, Texas Pacific Coal and Oil Company had $4,000,000 in the bank. Uncle Sid was broke. With four $10 bills borrowed from my mother, Ann Richardson Bass, he went to West Texas and started over. It was no problem to get blocks of several thousand acres with a promise to drill a well on that acreage. Sid Richardson sold checkerboard spreads to the major oil companies and kept a little acreage for himself to drill if the wildcat financed by the sale of acreage hit. The wells were primarily 3,000 to 3,500 foot wells, most often drilled with cable tools. Sid Richardson parlayed his sister's $40 into a fortune that enabled him to pay off all his debts. That included his sister—with interest![39]

Commenting on the large blocks of acreage put together by Sid Richardson with only a $40 outlay, Perry Bass observed in 1992: "TP could have pretty nearly bought all of West Texas with the amount of money rumored to be in its bank account."[40] But West Texas is a big place. One still had to know where to buy the leases.

Sid Richardson was not a fair-weather friend. He believed in loyalty. He was like Neville Penrose, Fort Worth independent oilman for whom I worked as a political assistant from 1947 to 1952. Penrose was always looking for ways to show his regard for his friends. What do you give someone who has everything? One of the things that Penrose liked to give was silver baby spoons to new mothers. One Christmas he gave fireplace pokers to William Fleming, Charles Yager, Arch Rowan, Fuqua, and a number of others. Each poker was custom-made at a blacksmith shop in the form of a branding iron replete with the initials of the donee on the handle. Silver spoons and fire pokers were not the only gifts that Penrose made. He also gave liquor.

On July 9, 1949, *Star-Telegram* reporter Joe Bell called Penrose at the crack of dawn to advise him that Governor Beauford H. Jester had been found dead in a Pullman car in Houston. Bell got a quote from Penrose and soon thereafter there arrived at Bell's desk a gift from Penrose—two fifths of Old Granddad.[41]

In a similar vein, according to Pat Woods, Richardson gave Fuqua an overriding royalty interest in the rich Keystone Field of Winkler County, and a bust of himself engraved: "To my friend Babe Fuqua." Fuqua prized the bust and placed it in his bedroom as a bookend.[42]

In the 1930s, Leroy Menzing, Oil Editor of the *Fort Worth Star-Telegram* would occasionally drive down to Austin with Fuqua to attend the state-wide proration hearings of the Texas Railroad Commission. Menzing recalled:

> Babe would come by and pick me up. He always had a bottle of Johnny Walker Black Label and a thermos of water. We would sip Scotch and water on the way. We never got drunk. We did not need the Scotch in Austin as there were always lots of cocktail parties going on.
>
> Babe was a nice guy. He could go into a hotel and in 30 minutes know every bell boy and his history. Coming back to Fort Worth, he would always stop at Nemeceks in West. Nemeceks was and remains today one of the most famous old style meat markets in Texas. Travelers from Dallas and Fort Worth stop to buy their famous Czech meats. Babe would lay in a supply of bacon and sausage.
>
> In 1944 Babe was transferred to Houston where he headed Gulf's south-western operations. Before his departure, he called me over to his office in the Gulf Building and introduced me to H. M. (Rusty) Bayer, who had moved in from Gulf's Midland office to take Babe's place in Fort Worth. Characteristically thoughtful, he asked me to go to Austin with Rusty and introduce him around.[43]

✦

Less than a year after Fuqua's return to Fort Worth, North Korean troops on June 25, 1950, crossed the 38th Parallel into South Korea. President Truman rushed troops to repel the invaders. So unpopular was the Korean War that Truman insisted that it was a mere "police action" or "conflict." Whatever its name, the Korean War was as horrible and difficult as any war the U.S. ever fought. Three years of fighting claimed 54,246 American lives.

✦

While still in Houston, Fuqua had since 1948 been a Director of Fort Worth's largest bank, Ellison Harding's Fort Worth National. In February 1952, now back in Fort Worth for two years, he was elected Chairman of the Board of the bank to fill the vacancy caused by Harding's death. On February 27, 1952, the TP Board of Directors passed the following resolution: "RESOLVED, that it is the opinion of the Board of Directors of the Company that the duties H. B. Fuqua may be required to fulfill as Chairman of the Board of Directors of The Fort Worth National Bank will not conflict or interfere in any way with his duties as Chairman of the Board of Directors of the Texas Pacific Coal and Oil Company or with the proper fulfillment of his employment contract with this Company."[44]

In a letter on August 1, 1952, to Roby Penn who was in Oil City, Pennsylvania, Fuqua brought Penn up to date on the progress being made on the Fort Worth National's new bank building:

> You were fortunate in leaving Fort Worth at the time you did. It has been terrifically warm. However, our offices have been most pleasant. The air conditioning is exceptionally good in our new building.
>
> Incidentally, while on the subject of our new building, Tom Byrne is progressing with the interior work in a very satisfactory manner. I think the bank will start moving August 9th and it is planned to open up for business on August 26th. Our big formalities will be Labor Day weekend.[45]

In 1952 I was offered and accepted a job as a landman by M. M. Slagle, Jr., head of the Land Department of the Texas Pacific Coal and Oil Company.[46] Now I was a landman—just like John Roby Penn had been.

Land work was only a part of my routine. In Fort Worth, the Citizens' Committee—prominent oil men, attorneys, and merchants met weekly to plan political strategy to control precinct and county conventions. I attended all of these caucuses.

✦

On a state level, these Tarrant County activists were an integral component of the conservative Democrats known in 1944 as Texas Regulars who were opposed to a fourth term by President Franklin D. Roosevelt. In 1948 they were called States Righters, opposed to the election of either Democrat Harry Truman or Republican Thomas E. Dewey and supporting Governor J. Strom Thurmond of South Carolina. In 1952 they were called Shivercrats (after Governor Allan Shivers) and in November would spurn Democrat Adlai Stevenson in favor of Republican Dwight D. Eisenhower.

✦

In his August 1, 1952 letter to Penn, Fuqua reported on local politics: "The State and County election is behind us, and we were all very disappointed about the results of our County election. The Citizens' Committee was badly scuttled by some opposition that should have been with it. I will tell you about the split-up when you return. I think our most damaging loss was Keith Kelly in the State Senator's race."[47]

Much if not most of Fuqua's influence was exercised behind the scenes and out of the public eye. An example of his modus operandi was in the 1952 State Senate race. The Conservative Democrats had gone all out to defeat Liberal Democrat State Representative Doyle Willis who was seeking to step up to the Senate by running against incumbent Conservative Democrat Keith Kelly.

Kelly wanted me, a TP landman, to devote full time to managing his campaign. Fuqua was agreeable to my running the campaign but said I couldn't be paid by TP while away from company duties. I was given a leave of absence without pay. But I had to be paid. One day W. Ridley Wheeler, a strong Fuqua ally and Treasurer of the Conservative Finance Committee, asked me to come to see him. He gave me an envelope containing several $100 bills to replace my TP salary. The campaign turned out to be a political dry hole. Willis won.[48]

◆

On August 8, 1952, Fort Worth lost one of its most famous, colorful, and controversial sons, the Reverend J. Frank Norris, pastor of the First Baptist Church. With the passing of Norris, many Texas Pacific employees lost their minister. Both revered and hated, Norris was acquitted in 1912 of burning down his own church and in 1927 of murdering wealthy lumberman Dexter Elliot Chipps the previous July in his church study.

Norris was the founder of the Baptist Fundamentalist Fellowship. Inspired by his leadership, independent Baptist churches, colleges, seminaries, and Bible schools sprang up throughout the nation. He was the spiritual father of the Christian Right movement that was to become a powerful political force in the 1980s and 1990s. The Tarrant County Democratic Party used to hold its biennial conventions in his First Baptist Church.

In the historic presidential election year of 1952, Texas Governor Allan Shivers, a Democrat, broke with the National Democratic Party over control of the Texas tidelands. The Democratic nominees, Governor Adlai Stevenson of Illinois and Senator John Sparkman of Alabama, said the tidelands belonged to the United States. Republican Eisenhower came out for Texas ownership. Under Shivers's leadership, Texas Democrats bolted the national party and formed Democrats for Eisenhower. Babe Fuqua sided with Shivers and Texas. On Election night, Texas, for the first time since 1928, had gone Republican and Dwight Eisenhower was elected 34th president of the United States. Elected vice-president was Senator Richard M. Nixon.

◆

In 1953 Texas Pacific followed the bank by moving out of the twenty-four-story Fort Worth National Bank Building into the new fifteen-story Fort Worth National Bank Building on the other side of West Seventh Street.

In 1952 Melvin Slagle, Head of TP's Land Department, had hired Lawton Gambill as a young landman just out of law school. He was sent to Baton Rouge to work with a venerable old TP landman, Jack Kennedy. Nine months later he was transferred to Midland and, after nine more months, he was moved into the Legal Department in Fort Worth under Eugene T. Adair, the company's Executive Vice-President and General Counsel. Adair was a tall, balding man. His manner was brusque and his stride was brisk. His office on the fourteenth floor of the new Fort Worth National Bank Building was at the opposite end of the block long corridor from Fuqua's. He often could be seen scurrying down the hall to confer with the Chairman. He did not merely walk. He loped. One afternoon at the end of September 1953, it was raining hard. Adair had an important visitor in his office. The man prepared to go. Adair remarked that since it was raining, he would send Lawton to get the man's car so he wouldn't get wet. The visitor protested that he had a rain coat, and he would prefer to get his own car. Adair persisted that he would send Lawton. Finally, Lawton spoke up and said that he didn't want to get wet either! The silence that ensued was deafening. The next morning, several in the company had heard of the incident. Gambill decided he would probably prefer a non-corporate type practice and later that same morning, he rode the elevator down to the sixth floor and met with Baylor Agerton and Judge B. B. Stone, partners in Bryan, Stone, Wade & Agerton, one of the leading law firms of the city. He told them he would like a job. They said they would think about it. That afternoon they called and said he was hired.[49]

In the 1940s and 1950s, there was an eccentric and introverted geologist with the company whose name was Leon English. English was a throwback to John Roby Penn's economy. Land Manager Melvin Slagle used to laugh about one of English's expense accounts following a field trip. The only item listed for which reimbursement was sought: One can of Vienna Sausage—10 cents! During 1953, Edd Riddle was assigned by H. C. Vanderpool, TP's Exploration Manager, to accompany English to map surface geology south of the Arbuckle Mountains, in Carter County, Oklahoma.

> One day during the field work, it was past noon and I told English I was hungry. He looked at his watch and agreed it was time to eat. He opened the trunk of the car and exposed a sack of peanuts which was to be lunch! I told him I needed something a bit more substantial, so we went into Woodford, Oklahoma to the Country Store for lunch.[50]

Soon after Fuqua's arrival, the company built a magnificent employee recreation camp on the shores of Big Lake at Thurber. By providing amenities for company employees, Fuqua was following in the tradition of Colonel Robert Dickie Hunter who built a library and the Opera House at Thurber for the pleasure, recreation, and improvement of the employees.

To enjoy a weekend of pleasure at this secluded resort for themselves and their families, company employees had but to make a reservation—everything was free. A little-noticed road led from Highway 80, perhaps two hundred yards, to the entrance guarded by a caretaker's cabin over which Old Glory was always unfurled. There was a landing strip for small planes. It was used primarily by Gene Adair. TPers dubbed it Adair Field. There was a boat dock with several boats and facilities to clean fish taken from the lake. Shaded, grassy picnic areas with barbecue grills bordered the lake's east side. Several redwood cabins, supplied with necessary dishes, kitchen ware, beds and furniture, dotted the grounds. Each cabin had a screened porch or veranda, cooled by breezes from off the lake. Each cabin was affixed with a name plate honoring one of the men who had quarterbacked the company: Hunter Lodge; Marston Cabin; Gordon Cabin; Penn Cabin; Fuqua Cabin. A small shelter building honored the name of an oil well—McCleskey, of course.[51]

The big white house in Thurber that had been the home of W. K. Gordon was reserved for company executives. One work day in the 1950s, several department heads and key employees were treated to an all day outing at the Gordon house. Tubs of ice cold beer were set about the veranda, while barbecue simmered over mesquite fires on grills in the front yard.

As the years rolled on, Charles Yager pondered his future at TP. Fuqua had been given a five-year contract when he came with TP in 1949. "Who could say?" mused Yager. "Maybe it wouldn't work out."[52]

But Fuqua's contract did work out. Not only did it work out, but at the end of the five-year term, Fuqua was so solidly entrenched that he advised the Directors on September 22, 1954, that he did not desire to renew the contract but preferred to continue his employment on a year-to-year basis. The Directors promptly increased his salary from fifty thousand dollars to seventy thousand dollars annually beginning October 1, 1954.

About that time multimillionaire oilman, W. H. McFadden, Board Chairman of Southland Royalty Company, came to see Yager and advised him that Fritz Aurin, President of Southland, would soon retire. McFadden wanted Yager to come over and run Southland as President and CEO. Yager, fifty-five, responded: "Mr. McFadden, I accept your offer with the proviso that I will retire when I am sixty-five years old." On December 21, 1954, Yager wrote to Fuqua:

> Dear Sir:
> I herewith tender my resignation as a Director and as President of the Texas Pacific Coal and Oil Company, to become effective at the convenience of the Board. I have given careful consideration to the step I am taking, and it

is only because I feel that the opportunity offered by the new work I am about to enter offers such an excellent future for me that I have come to the decision to sever my connection with the Company.

It is natural that I should feel deeply regretful in severing my employment with the Company after so long a period of association, which commenced on December 1, 1922. I have enjoyed my 32 years of association with the Company, its officers and other employees, and am deeply appreciative of the opportunity I had to work with them and of the cooperation they extended to me during this time.

I also want to express my appreciation to the Directors, individually and as a Board, for the many considerations they have extended to me and for the privilege of working with them as a member of the Board.

Sincerely yours,

C. E. Yager[53]

It is interesting to note that Yager did not reveal the name of his new employer. But can there be any doubt that Fuqua knew?[54]

With Yager gone, the Board gave yet another title to Chairman of the Board and CEO Fuqua: President. To replace Yager on the Board of Directors, Fuqua in April 1955 brought in Robert I. Dickey to be Vice-President of Exploration. Dickey was a native of Massachusetts, educated at Clark University in Worcester and at Johns Hopkins University. From 1934 to 1939, he was in the geological department of Stanolind Oil & Gas Company in Houston and Midland. He joined Forest Oil Corporation in 1939 as District Geologist, becoming Vice-President in 1952. For three years he directed West Texas and New Mexico operations for Forest.[55]

Bob Dickey was a large, quiet-spoken man who enjoyed fine cigars and good books. One day he came into my office in the Land Department to advise that, due to an oversight, TP had missed a drilling deadline on a TP lease in Eastland County owned by Judge L. R. Pearson of Ranger. Consequently, the valuable lease had expired. My assignment from Dickey: Go immediately to see Pearson and try to get a new lease. I called Pearson's office in Ranger but was informed he was attending a meeting at the Adolphus Hotel in Dallas. On the chance that I could catch him there and save a one hundred-mile drive to Ranger, I drove over to Dallas only to discover that he had checked out earlier. I again called his office in Ranger and told his secretary I had missed him in Dallas but that I would be in his office about 6 P.M. So I retraced my route, passing through Fort Worth, headed for Ranger. At 6 P.M. I walked into the Judge's office. We negotiated for two hours. Finally, a deal was struck. I agreed to give an extra one-sixteenth in addition to the customary one-eighth royalty. Furthermore, I committed TP to commencing a well in short order on the lease. Dickey was delighted that I had been able to get a new lease signed with only a modest extra royalty given as consideration. In a few days TP moved a rig onto the Pearson lease and I received a pay raise.

Until 1953, Amon G. Carter, legendary publisher of the *Fort Worth Star-Telegram,* was still a vigorous, active man at age seventy-three. No man could assume the throne while he lived—the Carter Administration reigned supreme in Fort Worth. Jerry Flemmons in *Amon* describes his final days: "On an early June evening in 1955, about ten o'clock, Amon went into a coma. On June 19, Father's Day, he briefly awoke to ask, 'Am I still here?,' then lapsed again into unconsciousness. Four days later, June 23, forty minutes before the morning *Star-Telegram's* two-star deadline, Herb Schultz received the telephone call. He turned to others around the city desk and announced: 'He's dead.'"[56] The most fitting recognition of Carter's influence was the rival *Fort Worth Press's* headline on the date of Carter's funeral: AMON CARTER LIES IN STATE.

In the dual role as head of Fort Worth's largest independent oil company and the largest bank in town, Babe Fuqua had amassed great economic power, and quickly became the acknowledged successor to Carter. Amon Carter and Babe Fuqua were polar opposites. Carter was a gregarious showman who loved center stage and the spotlight, whereas Fuqua was reserved and quiet and preferred working back stage. Reporters went to see Fuqua. Carter sent editors to see reporters. A white Shady Oaks Stetson was Carter's trade mark; a gray fedora with a turned-up brim was Fuqua's.

Fuqua became Carter's successor because he was a natural leader. As the years progressed, he became the commander-in-chief of a powerful conservative political organization in Fort Worth. As to City Council involvement, the organization was at first known as the Citizens' Committee, then the Good Government League, but finally came to be called The Seventh Street Gang. Actually, this was an egregious title bestowed on the organization by liberal labor opposition. Regardless, it stuck.

Besides Seventh Street Gang, there was another sobriquet—Uncle Babe. While I never heard anyone address Fuqua to his face as Uncle Babe, it was nevertheless the favorite term of affection by which TPers referred to him. The nickname also found wide currency in the media and was glibly used by members of the Seventh Street Gang.

Fuqua's power and authority were acknowledged, accepted, and hard earned. Not only did Fuqua juggle the twin roles of top oilman and banker, but he was also committed to civic and political involvement.

Among those in attendance at a 1954 meeting in the Royal Room of the Fort Worth Club were J. B. Thomas, President of Texas Electric Service Company, the great wildcatter W. A. Moncrief, Bewley Mills President W. P. Bomar, and public relations man Charles Ringler. Ringler was a past President of the Fort Worth Junior Chamber of Commerce and was representing merchant prince Marvin Leonard. Ringler reflected:

Mr. Fuqua . . . got into politics where he was responsible for selecting the right people to run for office. He was the overseer of what he felt to be best for Fort Worth. "To be a good citizen of a community," he told me, "you have to put something back into the community. Cities grow by what we put back into them. I am proud of you, Charles, for all the civic work you have contributed to our city." This was indeed high praise for a young man to receive, and coming from Mr. Fort Worth himself, it made me want to work harder and give more back to my community.[57]

In 1956 Governor Allan Shivers announced that he would not run for a fourth term. Conservatives in Texas looked with fear and foreboding on the prospect that absent a strong conservative candidate, liberal Democrat Ralph Yarborough might succeed Shivers in the governor's office. To forestall this unpalatable occurrence, Fuqua, Adair, and Arch Rowan joined with other leaders of the oil and gas establishment and prevailed upon U.S. Senator Price Daniel to run for Governor. Daniel won, but barely. Out of a total vote of 1.4 million, the margin of victory was a slim three thousand votes.

In 1956 another presidential campaign was at hand. The Republicans ran again with Eisenhower and Nixon. The Democrats stayed with Stevenson but gave him a new running mate, Senator Estes Kefauver of Tennessee. Down in the infrastructure of the precincts, the 1956 campaign provided another example of Fuqua's behind-the-scenes maneuvering. In 1956 Tarrant County Conservative Democrats[58] were supporting Dwight Eisenhower for a second term, and, with Fuqua's acquiescence, I was elected Chairman of Tarrant Democrats for Eisenhower. We were searching high and low for a candidate to run for County Chairman. The Conservatives had suffered four straight defeats for this important party post. Someone suggested that Davey O'Brien could defeat the liberal candidate. This former TCU superstar quarterback had name identification in spades.[59] That would be great on the ballot; only O'Brien knew nothing about the fine art of politics. It would take some vigorous arm-twisting to get the shy and reticent O'Brien to agree to run.

Babe invited Davey to come to his office. O'Brien, who was at the time a representative of Bum Gibbons Well Servicing Company, a well work-over outfit in Midland, replied to Fuqua's offer to back him for County Chairman as follows:

"Mr. Fuqua, I don't know anything about politics."
"Don't worry. Don Woodard will handle the office for you."
"Well, Mr. Fuqua, I don't know . . ."

Whereupon, as O'Brien laughingly told it many times in the future, Fuqua opened a desk drawer and pulled out a long list of TP wells that needed work-over jobs. The tactic worked. With O'Brien, the Conservative

Governor Shivers and friends, September 1956, [left to right] Governor Allan
Shivers, H. B. Fuqua, Warren Scarborough, Senator Price Daniel, and Arch Rowan.
Courtesy Pat Woods.

Democrats fielded a candidate for County Chairman who beat the previously unbeatable liberal incumbent by a landslide vote.[60]

Although Fuqua greatly admired O'Brien, the first Southwest Conference player to win the Heisman Trophy, and although he had gained fame and fortune in the Lone Star State; and had made his home in Wichita Falls, San Angelo, Houston, and Fort Worth, and served on the Board of Trustees of Texas Christian University, he was born and bred an Okie. His heart belonged to his Alma Mater, the University of Oklahoma. And he remained fiercely loyal to his school, and especially its famed football program.[61]

In 1957 after extensive geophysical testing, TP decided to bid one million dollars on four sections of the Navajo Indian Reservation in Arizona. I was designated to carry the check to the tribal headquarters in Window Rock, Arizona. I flew to Albuquerque, New Mexico, and rented a car to drive to Grants. At the hotel in Grants, I rendezvoused with Gene O'Connor, TP's landman in Denver. The next morning we drove to Window Rock where we dutifully handed over TP's check to the tribal authorities. The bid was successful. But the end result was not. No matter how sophisticated and expensive geophysical and geological investigation may be, the only way definitely to prove whether oil is down below is to drill. TP's well drilled on its million-dollar Navajo lease was dry. While industry statistics reveal that only one out of nine wildcats results in a producer, TP's record, despite the Navajo disappointment, was consistently higher—almost a fourth of its wildcats proved to be productive.[62]

In 1957 Fuqua, thinking it would be good stockholder and investor public relations to tell the story of Texas Pacific Coal and Oil Company, authorized the publication of a handsome twenty-four-page booklet—*The Story of Texas Pacific Coal and Oil Company*. The publication emphasized that the company had no funded debt and how well it had performed overall:

> Stockholders have profited. One of the most talked of years in our economic past is 1929. It is an interesting fact that if an investor purchased 100 shares of Texas Pacific Coal and Oil Company stock at the top price in 1929, he would have paid something like $2,400. The high was around 23 7/8. In that year, he would have received a stock dividend of 10% and 100% stock dividends in 1948 and 1955. His holdings in June, 1957, would be approximately 440 shares with an average sales price in that month of about $38 a share. The total value of his holdings would be in excess of $16,720—an appreciation of more than $14,000. Although the cash dividend rate has been conservative, the hypothetical investor would have been well rewarded for his patience.[63]

About the time that *The Story of Texas Pacific* was being sent out to stockholders and the investment community, Fuqua looked north to Canada. Edd Riddle, who in 1948 had been hired fresh out of the University of

Oklahoma's geological school for $315 a month by H. C. Vanderpool, remembered a Fuqua inspection trip in the summer of 1957:

> Mr. Fuqua made a 50-50 deal with Pure Oil Company, for a venture in Alberta. He sent me to Calgary as Exploration Manager for TP. In the summer of 1955, Mr. Fuqua and Raymond B. Kelly came to Calgary in TP's Super Beach-18 airplane. Kelly was Pure's Vice President of Production.
>
> The next day we—pilots Myrt Vititow and L.C. (Tommie) Tomlinson, Mr. Fuqua, Mr. Kelly, TP geologist Wayne Hurt and I—took off to view the geology and the oil and gas fields from the air, some of which were close and parallel to the Canadian Rocky Mountains. I was acting as a guide, telling the pilots where to fly. Shortly after we took off, Mr. Fuqua admonished me: "Don't fly too close to the mountains, Eddy!"[64]

◆

Fuqua was leery about any of his people flying in private planes other than on the company plane. Myrt Vititow was always cautious about the weather. Many a time I would wait in the hangar until he felt flying conditions were acceptable. I remember flying out to TP's Round Top Field in Fisher County one time to get an oil and gas lease signed. A dust storm was blowing in from the west. Vititow kept the engine running while I got the farmer to sign the lease. Years later, in 1960, I flew to Washington, D.C. with a private pilot and two other passengers, one of whom was Jake Pickle, who succeeded Lyndon Johnson as Texas Congressman representing the Austin District. The pilot became lost in a snow storm over Tennessee. Suddenly an opening appeared in the clouds, and directly below was the Nashville airport. We got down. After lunch, we continued our journey to Washington. Coming in to National Airport, airplanes were whizzing all around. I heard an air controller tell our pilot, "I told you to wait until it was clear for you to land. Now go over to the Masonic monument across the Potomac and circle there until I tell you to come in!"

Finally on the ground, I went immediately to the American Airlines counter to make a return reservation. When I relayed the incident to Mr. Fuqua the following Monday morning, he rubbed his chin and admonished me to stay off of private planes and always to travel on commercial airliners: "If you get killed on one of those puddle jumpers, don't expect any sympathy from me."

◆

While Fuqua loved football and was always looking to find not only a new oil field, but a possible Oklahoma quarterback as well, one did not have to be a football hero to get a job with the Texas Pacific Coal and Oil Company.[65] His bent for helping young people get a start flowed over to department heads and superintendents. Mike Reese, then nineteen, describes the life of a roustabout in a TP camp in the late 1950s:

I had never worked for more than minimum wage which as I recall was about fifty cents per hour. My soon to be father-in-law, Harless Gardenhire, worked as a pumper for the TP out of Butler Camp west of Ranger. Knowing that I was planning to marry his daughter Betty, he introduced me to Production Manager Don Bonney, who deviated from the normal "football player" mode and hired me as a roustabout in Eliasville to begin in May 1959, for the summer months.

When I told the guys in the dorm that I was going to be making $2.55 per hour, I was a local hero at Abilene Christian College. They asked me what in the world I would be doing, to which I replied, "I don't know but I would dip manure for $2.55 per hour." Little did I know that I soon would be doing just that—cleaning out a stopped up septic tank line, dipping out a liquefied version with an old coffee can so that we could get to the line to fix the problem.

There were about ten pickups leaving the camp each day to see that the wells kept pumping, etc. Not a day went by but what at least one rattlesnake was killed. I'll never forget the day when one of the pumpers drove into the yard and said, "Look at the back of my pickup." A rattlesnake's head was tied to one end of the top of the tail-gate and its tail was tied to the other side of the pickup. Its body, about the size of my leg, hung down below the bumper. We were careful where we sat when we opened our lunch boxes for a few days after that.

In the summer of '60 and '61, Bob Ratts was the "farm boss" at Eliasville. He was a stickler for rules, especially where safety was concerned. The college gang was more than willing to wear the steel hat and steel-toed boots (and they saved many a toe and noggin), but we were as tan as boot leather and saw no need for shirts.

Also, working on a rod-and-tubing pulling unit, one couldn't do a very effective job of wrenching rods wearing the cotton or leather gloves that Mr. Ratts insisted that we wear. So we would dress as we saw fit, and the person working at the top of the rig in the crow's nest would watch for the dust trailing behind Mr. Ratts's car. When he would signal, we would stop long enough to put on our shirts and gloves. It never dawned on us that Mr. Ratts could perfectly well tell what was going on when he saw clean shirts and gloves on otherwise grimy, sweaty, and oil-soaked college kids.

One of the guys (Mickey Slagle, son of M. M. Slagle, Jr. in the home office) was married and had two children who apparently kept him up late at night. He would sleep while we were assembling and getting our assignments, in the pickup on the way from the camp to the job site, and on the way back at the end of the day. At lunch, he would eat all of his lunch in three minutes and go to sleep under the rack of tubing on a pole trailer, using his steel hat as a pillow. Pranks were the order of the day, so each day we would warn Mickey that one day we were going to untie the load of tubing and let it fall on him while he slept. Then as soon as he was snoring soundly, one of us would rake our steel hat across the underside of the tubing and yell "Watch out!!" Mickey would jump straight up, slamming his head into the tubing. Then the rest of us would have to be very watchful the rest of the day as he tried to get even.

One of our wells between Trent and Sweetwater was two feet inside the barbed wire fence alongside Interstate 20. As usual, we were working sans shirts and covered in dirt, sweat, oil, and grease. One day, tourists, obviously not from the oil patch, stopped beside the road to take snapshots of "real Texas oil men." We posed proudly.[66]

Fuqua had an abiding and active interest in good government. He believed that in government, as well as in business and football, "You've got to have the right kind of people. The whole thing revolves around people. In elected officials, integrity is vital. Integrity is first, intelligence second. If your officials don't have both, you're in trouble."

He applied the same criteria to businessmen. Alan Roberts, Vice President of Fort Worth National Bank's Oil Department, recalled an incident during a meeting of the bank's Investment Committee when the Investment Officer recommended the purchase of a major company stock. "Mr. Fuqua let the official make his presentation in full, then quietly asked, 'Have you looked at their management? It stinks.' The stock was not acquired."[67]

Although he was not a 100 percent subscriber to Vince Lombardi's creed that nice guys finish last, Fuqua still played to win. Some wondered whether his initials H. B. stood for Hard Boiled. When he sent a landman to get a lease for TP, he usually got it. And on those occasions when an attempt failed, he wanted to know why.[68]

Kenneth L. Webb, a TP landman, was dispatched to call on William Fleming, prominent Fort Worth oilman and pillar of the Broadway Baptist Church, to buy an oil and gas lease from him. Fleming's predilection to seek the Lord's will in all his business dealings was well known. He once gave an address to the Baptist General Convention. In his speech he told his fellow Baptists: "If you and I were bargaining over an oil and gas lease, we would get down on our knees and pray." Here he paused before adding: "And God would tell you to give me the lease!"[69]

After Webb had outlined the Texas Pacific offer to Fleming, the devout man asked Webb to kneel in his office so the two of them could have a word of prayer about the transaction. The prayer completed, Fleming rose and signed. Returning to his office, Webb related the solemn occurrence to Fuqua who listened impatiently and then said, "I don't give a damn about that. Did you get the lease signed?"

If Fuqua conjured up in people's minds a hard-driving General Patton type, still he was a man of great compassion. He was like John Roby Penn who twenty years before insisted on TP's paying Henry Boykin's dental bill. Carolyn Vastine, the young wife of Title & Rental Clerk Bill Vastine, died as a result of child birth. Fuqua instructed Wiltie Creswell, Vastine's supervisor, to let him have as much time off from his job as he wanted before returning to work.

He stood behind his people. Alan Roberts told about an oil man who came to see him in the 1950s at the Fort Worth National Bank, desirous of acquiring an oil and gas lease on a sizable block of acreage which the bank controlled. The would-be lessee, unhappy with the terms that Roberts proposed, wagged his finger in Roberts's face with the threat, "I'm going to talk to Babe about this." Roberts looked him in the eye and asked, "Do you know where his office is?" Later Roberts went to see Fuqua about the matter. The Bank Chairman was sitting in his office, feet on his desk, cigar in hand.[70] He reassured Roberts: "Since I have been around the oil patch for fifty years, some people will try to use my name to persuade you. You know what you are doing. Trade with them . . . but don't take their britches off," he added with a trademark grin.[71]

Fuqua, the no-nonsense quintessential geologist, could, with his withering looks and pointed questions, reduce an incompetent to mumbling. TP geologist Edd Riddle observed that it was never wise for a geologist to go into Babe's office and keep answering questions if he did not know what he was talking about. "He kept asking questions until he found out just how much you really knew."[72]

Riddle liked to tell about the adventures of TP geologist Nolan Hirsch in the lion's den: "Nolan would become very nervous around Babe. When he would go into Babe's office, he would always have a cigarette in his hand. He would become so nervous that he would light another one before the prior one had been finished. This habit agitated Babe whose transparent disdain of the practice would make Nolan all the more nervous so that another cigarette would follow as predictably as night the day."[73]

Encounters of the Fuqua-Hirsch kind became the joke du jour in the TP offices and at the Petroleum Club. It was laughed that if the nervous and fidgety Hirsch did not have bad luck, he would have no luck at all.

"Whatever he did," recalled Bill Scales, "seemed to go wrong. He was an unlucky guy. One morning he went into Mr. Fuqua's office to show him a map. He put his cigarette on the ash tray and started talking to Fuqua. The cigarette rolled off and burned a hole in Mr. Fuqua's new desk.

"One day he proudly announced to Fuqua that he had bought a new home on the west side. Fuqua asked, 'Where is it?' Nolan, beaming, answered. Fuqua's droll response: 'Even an Indian would not pitch his teepee on a flood plain.' Nolan's jaw dropped."[74]

Hirsch, too, remembered those meetings with The Man:

> Mr. Fuqua was always an enigma to me. He could be as hard as nails. He would chew me and Production Vice President Reagan Teague out. His political foes said he was a merciless, hard-hearted S.O.B. But just when you thought you had him categorized as cold and unfeeling, he would change

completely. I remember one morning Reagan Teague was telling Mr. Fuqua that one of his men in the McCamey Camp was really feeling down. "He cannot come to work any more," said Teague, "and he lacks 14 months until retirement." Babe spoke up in a soft voice and said, "You keep him on the pay roll. Make sure he is there until the end regardless of whether he can make it down to work."[75]

TP Petroleum Engineer Jerry Sherrod told about a geologist who in the mid-1950s unwittingly incurred the wrath of Fuqua:

My principal contact with Mr. Fuqua was due to my responsibility to keep the company reserves up to date; new wells as well as the annual review for the auditors, etc. Walter Berger was Chairman of the Reserves Committee on the Board of Directors, and I met regularly with him to bring him up to date on the company's reserves. In addition, we would make an annual trip to the fields to give Walter a better feel for our reserve and production situation . . . .

We usually met with Mr. Fuqua monthly to update him on any developments. I will never forget that a company geologist misread an electric log on a supposedly big well in Oklahoma and had estimated a net pay that would have resulted in company reserves of over one million barrels for that well. This was communicated to Mr. Fuqua, and needless to say, he was very happy, for one million barrels was a considerable boost for the company. The geologist later reviewed the log and determined that a major portion of the net pay that he had attributed to hydrocarbons was actually water-bearing.

When the geologist told Mr. Fuqua the bad news, the people present said Mr. Fuqua's cold blue gray eyes froze the poor man in his tracks and the poor guy was never the same again.[76]

Nearly four decades later, prominent Petroleum Engineer Aaron Cawley gave additional testimony concerning Fuqua's obsession with reserves—putting a handle on reserves was like trying to grab a fistful of Jell-O: "In 1956 Jimmie Harrington and I were Petroleum Engineers for the firm of Keller & Peterson. My first assignment was a six-month evaluation of Texas Pacific Coal and Oil Company. TP also hired two other firms, Pishney & Atkinson and Walter Berger, to conduct reserve studies. In addition, TP had its own in-house study, so they had four in all. Keller & Peterson's evaluation was approximately 50 percent higher than Pishney & Atkinson's. Berger's was close to ours. Later, James A. Lewis of Dallas was hired to make a study. Theirs was approximately twice that of Keller & Peterson's."[77]

In 1956, while Fuqua was conducting reserve evaluations, Congress passed legislation providing for the financing of the Federal Interstate Highway system, a program estimated to cost in excess of fifty-six billion dollars. The federal government would pay 90 percent of the cost and the states 10 percent. To finance the program, Congress established a Highway Trust Fund. This fund receives money from taxes on motor fuel, tires, new trucks, and buses, and an annual tax on heavy vehicles. Construction or improvement of the roads is done by the states, with federal aid. The roads belong to the states or local governments which must maintain them.

Passage of this Eisenhower-era legislation elated Fuqua who came into my office the next morning to predict that the gigantic construction program would trigger much prosperity and physically unite the United States. Forty years later the magnificent Interstate Highways of the nation show that Fuqua was correct in his judgment of the merits of the program.

On February 8, 1958, John Roby Penn died. The day of his funeral, the *Fort Worth Star-Telegram* wrote a glowing editorial:

> J. Roby Penn, who died Saturday at 82, was one of that early group of city councilmen who got Fort Worth's council-manager system of government off to a good start. Adoption of this form of government in 1925 was prompted by the need to restore popular confidence in a municipal government that had become bankrupt politically and financially. In the effort to establish a city government in which businesslike operation was the foremost thought, the first city councils selected were a blue-ribbon group.
>
> Though he was not one of the original group, Mr. Penn was placed on the City Council after the first three years. For nearly seven years he served with the same quiet effectiveness which marked his operation of the Texas Pacific Coal and Oil Company, of which he was top executive for many years. Never one to expound his views at length in public, he acted on all municipal questions with a minimum of talk and a maximum of good judgment.
>
> This was a reflection of his attitude in regard to civic affairs in general. He was always ready to do his part in undertakings of public benefit, but quietly and without fanfare. Over the years, his counsel in such matters has been at least as valuable as his contributions in time and money.
>
> Mr. Penn was of that school of business men who believed that his word, once given, should be an inviolable pledge. Perhaps the highest mark of the man was the respect and regard in which he was held by his business associates and his employees.
>
> Mr. Penn was one of those who feel that the higher they rise in the business world the greater their responsibility to their community and to the men and women who work with and for them.[78]

Penn was laid to rest in Fort Worth's Greenwood Memorial Park, fifteen hundred miles west of his native Pennsylvania.

10

In the year of John R. Penn's death, 1958, under Fuqua's guidance, TP acquired the Rowan Oil Company, owned by the brothers Arch and Charles Rowan. No cash changed hands. It was a tax-free stock swap by which the Rowans received 275,400 shares of TP stock worth approximately $25 per share. The Texas Pacific 1958 Annual Report contained this passage:

> Previous reports have pointed out the many advantages of our Company's freedom from debt and our sound cash position, providing sufficient flexibility of operation to meet any situation or alteration of conditions. This past year has offered excellent evidence of that ability, as we weathered the oil industry's worst post-war year with a satisfactory profit.
>
> Specific example of this flexibility was our Company's acquisition, in July, 1958, of the Rowan Oil Company assets, whereby we substantially increased our oil and gas reserves and production rate without the usual risk of exploratory drilling. It is estimated that the properties acquired will pay out their net cost in four years, leaving us 65 per cent of the acquired assets after pay-out.[1]

The acquisition of the Rowan reserves was hailed at first as a home run for the Babe. But, as future events unfolded, it might have been better for TP had Fuqua struck out in the Rowan matter. Larger oil companies were on the move looking to buy out smaller ones—and TP was still a smaller company. In particular there was the Sinclair Oil Corporation which on August 16, 1956, had acquired 1,085,792 shares of Texas Pacific common stock. Lehman Brothers, a New York brokerage firm working with Sinclair, had acquired more than 165,000 shares. Subsequently, Sinclair bought an additional 35,900 shares, giving that company control of one third of TP's stock.[2]

Robert F. Windfohr supported the take-over. Divergent views on the issue created an unbridgeable canyon between him and Fuqua.[3] As a consequence, Windfohr, a Director since 1944, sold his TP stock and quit the Board in 1957, being replaced by Sinclair's Chairman of the Board, P. C. Spencer. The following year a second Sinclair official, Vice-President O. P. Thomas, took a seat on the board, filling the vacancy caused by the death of J. R. Penn. With Lehman Brothers partner J. R. Fell, a Director since

H. B. Fuqua and Arch Rowan with stock certificate for 275,400 shares of Texas Pacific Coal and Oil Company, 1958. Courtesy of Pat Woods.

1952, Sinclair now had three of the fifteen TP directorships. From his inside position on the TP Board, Spencer recognized a good thing when he saw it. Owning a third of TP was not enough. He wanted it all.

Windfohr, who had played a leading role in bringing Fuqua up from Houston to head TP ten years before, now became Spencer's paladin. Leroy Menzing, then Oil Editor of the *Star-Telegram,* remembered: "I will never forget when Bob Windfohr called me one night at home about 10 P.M. and told me he had a deal arranged for Sinclair to buy TP. I phoned the story in and it was in the *Star-Telegram* the next morning."[4]

> Sinclair Oil Corporation Monday submitted an offer to directors of Texas Pacific Coal and Oil Company to acquire all assets of TP. Sinclair offered to exchange one share of Sinclair stock for 1.55 shares of Texas Pacific stock. At Sinclair's present market value, the offer would place a value of approximately $40 per share on Texas Pacific stock. . . . Texas Pacific directors referred the offer to its executive committee for study and recommendations. The Sinclair offer, made by P. C. Spencer, board chairman, requested a decision by the Texas Pacific board not later than January 28. Spencer said, "We believe the proposal to be one that is not only fair in all respects but one that offers tremendous advantages and opportunities to both shareholders and employees of Texas Pacific."[5]

Menzing said, "You always knew where you stood with Babe. . . . It wasn't long before I had a call from Babe, hot and bothered. He gave me hell. He said, 'The next time you want to know anything about TP, call me.'"[6]

There was one other detail in Sinclair's strategy that was not revealed in Menzing's story. When TP had acquired Rowan Oil earlier in the year, its forty-four-year-old boy-wonder President, Hamilton Rogers, had come into TP as a Vice-President, involved primarily in stockholder relations. Sinclair through third parties now offered to make Rogers TP President if the acquisition was successful. The ploy probably had a double objective—it would put the Rowan block of 275,400 TP shares in the Sinclair camp and at the same time install as president one who would be beholden to Sinclair.[7]

To fight the buyout offer, Fuqua and Adair decided to call in their political IOUs. They prevailed upon Will Wilson, Texas Attorney General, to file suit against Sinclair. On January 26, 1959, an antitrust suit was brought in Judge Jack M. Langdon's 17th District Court by the Attorney General of Texas against Sinclair, Lehman Brothers, and Texas Pacific to halt consideration of the merger proposal. The petition pointed out that Sinclair and Texas Pacific were in competition with each other in the purchase of oil and gas leases and production of oil and gas. Wilson described Texas Pacific as a prosperous, expanding, and independent Texas oil company with assets in excess of $100,000,000. He estimated its net oil production in excess of 20,000 barrels daily. Merger of the companies, he contended, would bring about a restriction of trade and block free pursuit of oil and gas business authorized by law. The suit asked that Sinclair and Lehman Brothers be permanently enjoined from indirectly acquiring any stock or voting power in future operations of Texas Pacific. Judge Langdon issued a temporary restraining order blocking consideration of the Sinclair proposal at the regular TP board meeting scheduled to meet two days later on January 28. Hearing on the Attorney General's pleas for a temporary injunction was set for February 2.[8]

Spencer denied any wrongdoing by Sinclair in its acquisition of TP stock. He said Sinclair had not attempted to dominate or control Texas Pacific management or its board evidenced by Sinclair's execution of its proxy in favor of management for each regular or special shareholders meeting since acquiring its stock ownership. Sinclair had no more than two members of the fifteen-member board, even though it owned approximately 30 percent of the outstanding stock of the company. Sinclair did not expect special consideration of any kind but wanted its offer considered solely on its merits. As further evidence of good faith Sinclair had executed an agreement by which it vested in former Governor Allan Shivers of Austin, Ben C. Belt of Houston (formerly Fuqua's boss at Gulf Oil), and L. R. Bryan, former president of the Bank of the Southwest in Houston, the right to vote Sinclair's holdings of Texas Pacific stock according to their independent judgment in the best interest of all Texas Pacific stockholders.[9]

Texas Pacific's reaction to the turn of events was stated by Fuqua:

> While the Attorney General has made our company a party to this suit to the extent that we have been directed to take no action on the merger proposal, we are of course pleased that he, after investigation, has not asserted that Texas Pacific Coal and Oil Company has done anything wrong. The petition has emphasized that we are a strong independent Texas oil company and that there is no sound business reason why the company should be merged.[10]

At its meeting on January 28, TP Directors voted to take no action on the Sinclair offer and to comply with the order issued in 17th District Court restraining all parties from action on the offer. At the board meeting, the unpopular P. C. Spencer announced that the Sinclair offer had expired by its own terms and would not be renewed. He expressed regrets that the TP shareholders would not be afforded an opportunity to consider the proposal or possible similar proposals from other parties.

Even though the immediate threat of merger had been eliminated, Spencer's thinly veiled threat about similar proposals from other parties had not fallen on deaf ears. Fuqua sent Rogers and Adair over to confer with Arch Rowan on his Georgia plantation about strategy to deal with future hostile bids. Upon their return to Fort Worth, Fuqua, who since the resignation of Charles Yager in 1954 had served as Chairman, President, and Chief Executive Officer, decided to bolster the management team by making Rogers Executive Vice-President and Adair President.[11] The TP Board ratified his wishes and elevated both men on February 25, 1959.

The new president was born in Dalhart, Texas, August 2, 1912. He obtained a Bachelor of Arts degree from Texas Tech and his law degree from the University of Texas in 1933. In 1933 he joined the law department of the TP where his father-in-law, John Hancock, was Vice-President and General Counsel. In 1935 he entered private law practice, but returned to TP in 1941 as staff attorney. From 1942 to 1946 he served with the Air Force, and was discharged a major after service in combat intelligence on Okinawa. He returned to TP as General Attorney in 1946, in which capacity he acted until 1949, when he became General Counsel. In 1951 he was elected to the Board of Directors. In 1953, like his father-in-law before him, he was named Vice-President and General Counsel. In 1954 he became Executive Vice-President and General Counsel.[12] Wes Yarbro, then TP Financial Vice-President, thought Adair's elevation to the presidency a wise move. Although Sinclair had disengaged and withdrawn, the Attorney General's antitrust suit still pended in 17th District Court. "Adair," said Yarbro, "was a natural. He was brilliant in the political and legal arena where Sinclair was routed in only two months. He was a good friend of attorney-lobbyist Ira Butler. Adair and Butler shared friendship with officials in high places in Austin."[13]

Pat Woods, Fuqua's secretary, always went to early morning mass at St. Patrick's Cathedral before coming to work. Often she was a little late. Fuqua never seemed to mind. The morning after Adair assumed the presidency Pat arrived at work to find the new President standing in her office, tapping his foot impatiently and pointedly looking at his watch.[14]

Eight months after the Sinclair victory, Fuqua suffered a grievous loss. On September 30, 1959, his longtime friend, Sid Richardson, died on his island in the Gulf of Mexico. His funeral was held in the Broadway Baptist Church in Fort Worth, the Reverend Billy Graham officiating.[15] With Sid's death, a mighty derrick had gone down and left an awesome vacancy on the TP Board. Fuqua had lost a staunch ally. His absence would have dire implications for the company's future.

To fill Richardson's vacancy on the Texas Pacific Board, Fuqua chose TP Financial Vice-President J. Wesley Yarbro, a tax expert who had been hired in 1957 to head the TP Accounting Department. He came to TP from Southern Production Company, and prior to that had been an IRS agent. "I have no illusions as to why Babe put me on the Board," said Yarbro. "He wanted to replace his dependable ally Sid with an equally safe vote."[16]

Yarbro was a proven tax expert. In the mid 1950s, Congress amended the tax code to provide a new term, "Operating Unit." Such a unit could be adopted as an optional replacement for the term "lease" in computing statutory depletion. Yarbro recalled:

> Soon after joining TP, I was taken on a tour of the Company's field operations by Bob Hines, Production Vice President. I found them ideally suited to the "Operating Unit" concept. About 80% of the Company's producing wells were contained in district organizations closely coinciding with Treasury Department definition of an "Operating Unit."
>
> Under the rules, producers could adopt the new optional provision for the current and future years plus three prior years by filing amended returns.
>
> At the next meeting of the Board, I made a full report of my observations and conclusions and requested approval to file amended returns, claiming refunds for the three past years and future returns computed on the optional "Operating Unit" concept. Before the Board acted on my request, Gene Adair stated his approval to my filing the claims but then stated unequivocally that no part of the claim would be allowed because he and the Company's tax and accounting personnel had previously examined the new law and concluded that there was no way the Company could benefit from it. The filings were then unanimously approved by the Board, and benefits were subsequently realized in excess of $3,000,000.[17]

About a month after Richardson's death, there was a significant development in the Sinclair antitrust law suit. By judgment dated November 6, 1959, the action against Lehman Brothers was severed, and by consent of Lehman Brothers, a decree was entered compelling Lehman and its partners to dispose of all TP stock that they then owned, and providing further that neither Lehman nor any of its partners could own or vote any TP stock for a period of five years, and restraining them from attempting to cause or bring about, either directly or indirectly, a merger between Sinclair and TP. Pursuant to the decree, Lehman Brothers and its partners disposed of all of their TP stock. The Sinclair portion of the suit would pend in the court for another two years.[18]

Executive Vice-President Hamilton Rogers became ever more responsive to the concerns of stockholders. "While the Sinclair proposal and subsequent litigation were pending, we would get all of these letters from stockholders who seemed impressed with the Sinclair bid. My job was to answer these letters. Consequently, I gained a feel for the attitude of the stockholders. That's why Babe and Gene were much concerned about the possibility of future hostile bids. Every share was going to be important in battles to come. Proxies were going to be bullets."[19] Rogers would for the next three years call me to his office and hand me a stack of proxies for Dallas shareholders. I would contact these owners and get them to sign a proxy for management. None ever refused to sign.

H. B. Fuqua and Pat
Woods, November
1960. Courtesy Pat
Woods.

◆

Down a blacktop road, midway between Thurber Cemetery and Strawn's
Mount Marion Cemetery, one comes to a picturesque country graveyard right out
of Gray's *Elegy*. Situated on a knoll dotted with post oaks and blackjacks, Davidson
Cemetery with a majestic towered entrance is surrounded by a wall constructed of
dark red Thurber brick. Here in a family plot lie longtime TP Director S. J. Stuart
and his wife, Margaret. About the time I was calling on Dallas stockholders for
their proxies, I would also make occasional trips west to Strawn with an oil and gas
lease for Mrs. Stuart's signature. Her home was built in 1874 by her father-in-law,
James Nesbit Stuart. It was the first home in southwestern Palo Pinto County built
from milled lumber, and featured real window glass. The house, along with other
large homes in the twenty-three-acre Stuart compound, looks out upon a grassy
courtyard necklaced by a road paved with Thurber brick. Her husband, S. J., died
in 1951. She died on July 2, 1975. On June 14, 1997, after attending the Thurber
reunion, I drove over to Strawn and into the Stuart compound. A crowd of people
milled round the yard and sat in the shade of the trees. The house, in which W. W.
Johnson, Colonel Robert Dickie Hunter, Edgar L. Marston, and W. K. Gordon
once sat with two generations of Stuarts, had been emptied, and household treas-
ures were stacked all about the yard. I was advised that the famous old house had
been sold by Mrs. Stuart's great nephew, Bill Nemir, and would be remodeled. A
Texas historical marker posted in 1971 stood in the yard like a silent observer

while a motormouth auctioneer methodically and impassively disposed of a life-time of memories.

✦

While Fuqua was directing TP in its day to day activities in the oil fields and keeping an eye out for corporate raiders, he continued to hold sway in the political arena. In eventful 1959, a group of young city leaders, includ-ing John S. Justin, Jr., President of Justin Boot Company, was asked to come to a meeting in the Board Room of the Fort Worth National Bank. When Justin, resplendent as always in Justin boots, arrived at the bank, he was greeted by Fuqua and other prominent members of the establish-ment. They came right to the point—these young men had been drafted by the Fuqua group to run for City Council. If any one of them had any rea-son why he could not be a candidate, let him speak then or forever hold his peace. Standing in the presence of such a prestigious array of city fa-thers, Justin, try as he might, was unable to come up with any reason that would keep him from the fray. "Mr. Fuqua put the finger on me," Justin mused in 1994, "so I ran and was elected."[20]

In 1950, Bob Ratts joined TP as a trainee engineer at Odessa. By 1959 he had risen through the ranks to become district engineer in the Lawn district. "My salary was $365 a month," Ratts recalled thirty-five years later. On November 25, 1959, the company sent him to Northern Alberta to drill a well near the confluence of the Clear and Peace rivers. The well site was forty miles west of Hines Creek, population five hundred.

> The day before I left for Canada, my wife Norma went with me to the Fort Worth office where I received the final plans for drilling the well. Mr. Fuqua told Norma to call him if she needed anything while I was gone, and he would do his best to help solve her problems. I was gone for Thanksgiving, Christmas and New Year's. The wildcat, No. 1 Clear River, was dry as a bone. Nothing was found. It was plugged at 6400 feet in the Blue Sky formation. When I returned to Fort Worth the last part of January 1960, I went to the of-fice to turn in my report and logs. Mr. Fuqua walked into Production Man-ager Don Bonney's office and told me to call Norma and have her meet me in Abilene as he had asked TP's pilot, Myrt Vititow, to fly me to Abilene, the closest airport to Lawn. Mr. Fuqua was always concerned for the welfare of TP employees.[21]

In 1960 Lambuth Tomlinson, owner of the All Church Press, decided to open an account with the Fort Worth National Bank. Until that point most of his banking business had been done with Dallas banks. The day after he opened his account with a $10,000 deposit, Lambuth was flat-tered to receive thank you calls from Fuqua and Board Member Marvin Leonard. They assured Tomlinson that they were going to build a real bank for Fort Worth so businesses would not have to go to Dallas for funding. "It was not a large account but it showed that the men at the very top of the bank knew what was going on down below. That's why the bank prospered while Fuqua was in control."[22]

The year 1960 proved to be a historic one in presidential politics: the Democratic ticket of Kennedy-Johnson vs. the Republican ticket of Nixon-Lodge. In Tarrant County, the Democratic campaign was led by three stalwart allies of Lyndon Johnson: William Hunter McLean, Raymond Buck, and John Connally. On October 21, 1960, McLean, the great nephew of TP founder Colonel Robert Dickie Hunter, sent out a letter inviting local Democrats to a Democratic Rally on November 3rd. The names of dozens of prominent Tarrant County Democrats appeared on the letter as members of the General Committee. Conspicuous by its absence was that of Babe Fuqua. At heart a Republican, he wanted no truck with liberal and labor-backed Jack Kennedy or with New Deal disciple Lyndon Johnson. With the ensuing Democratic triumph, Lyndon Johnson thus had not only been elected Vice-President, but he had on the same ballot been reelected U.S. Senator from Texas over a college professor named John Tower. When LBJ resigned from the Senate following the November election, Governor Price Daniel appointed former Senator William A. Blakley of Dallas to succeed him in the Senate until a successor was chosen in a special election on April 4, 1961.[23]

◆

Seventy-one candidates filed for the April election. The top six vote getters were Republican John Tower 321,686; Democrats Bill Blakley 186,666; Jim Wright 166,776; Will Wilson 118,374; Maury Maverick 103,058 and Henry Gonzales 95,744. A run-off election between Tower and Blakley was scheduled for May 27. Blakley was considered the favorite due to incumbency and wide support from conservative and moderate Democrats.

In a watershed election on May 27, 1961, John Tower, reaping not only the Republican vote but garnering the votes of thousands of liberal Democrats determined to defeat conservative Democrat Blakley, scored a dramatic and stunning upset by polling 448,439 votes to Bill Blakley's 437,921. Liberals had reasoned that if they could administer the coup de grace to Blakley in 1961, they would have broken the stranglehold of the conservatives in the party, and they then would be masters of the house. But in a historic miscalculation, their strategy blew up in their faces. Following Blakley's defeat, disaffected and disillusioned conservative Democrats in a veritable hemorrhage crossed over into the Republican party to form a hybrid juggernaut destined to control Texas elections into the future far as the human eye could see. So began Republican hegemony in the Lone Star State.

◆

Fuqua, a Texas Christian University trustee, was vitally interested in the future of his adopted second Alma Mater. In 1961 the Fort Worth City Council called an election for September 12 on a proposal by TCU to buy the 106-acre city-owned Worth Hills Golf Course at a price of $6,500 an acre. The University wanted the land for additional dormitories. Arrayed against the TCU expansion was an army of nearby up-in-arms homeowners, vocal environmentalists and, naturally, unhappy golfers. Fuqua lumped them all together under the pejorative term "bird watchers." After a heated campaign, TCU's offer was approved by the voters. Today handsome dormitories, as well as the Lard Tennis Center, grace the spacious grounds. A large lake and many trees can still be found on the former golf course. There are jogging paths, walking trails, soccer and football fields, and baseball diamonds. One can even see an occasional golfer out practicing his drives.[24]

On October 19, 1961, TP was dismissed as a defendant in the Attorney General's Sinclair antitrust case. On October 23, 1961, an agreed judgment between the State of Texas and Sinclair was entered, under the terms of which (1) Sinclair gave assurances that its ownership of TP stock would not be used in violation of the antitrust laws of Texas and of its intention to sell or dispose of its TP stock when it could do so without loss, and (2) Sinclair was enjoined from acquiring any additional TP stock or from causing or attempting to bring about a merger between TP and Sinclair or any of its subsidiaries, or from using its TP stock for the purposes of preventing or lessening any competition in violation of the antitrust laws of the State of Texas, or creating any unlawful restrictions in trade or commerce in the oil and gas industry in Texas, or of creating or carrying out any unlawful restrictions against TP in the free pursuit of its business in Texas.

In the agreed judgment Sinclair otherwise reserved the right to vote its TP stock and to participate in the business and affairs of the company. The agreed judgment further provided that during the period while Sinclair was a substantial shareholder of TP, if the TP Board of Directors decided to seek proposals for the sale of the assets of TP, Sinclair, if it had not caused or brought about such board decision, would be permitted to bid for the assets of TP.[25]

In 1961, Aaron Cawley and Jimmie Harrington, who as young engineers for Keller & Peterson had conducted reserve evaluations for TP five years earlier, left to establish their own firm. Having known nothing but the security of a paycheck, it was a scary feeling. Cawley told of running into Fuqua in about 1962 in the lobby of the Fort Worth National Bank Building where TP had its headquarters. "In discussing our prospects, Mr. Fuqua told me: 'Well, you can't play golf all the time.'"[26]

Fuqua was never too busy to lend a helping hand to young people. One young man given a boost up the ladder by Fuqua was Thurman McGaugh who went to work for TP as a novice engineer at Levelland in 1949. When he left the company in 1959, he worked for some four years with Fort Worth Pipe & Supply Company. But then he decided to take a new tack—waterflooding. Waterflooding is the reinjecting of produced water to wash out the oil remaining after most of the oil has been brought to the surface. For the most part, the majors were not willing to spend the time, money, and effort necessary to squeeze these last drops from their wells. When production declined to a trickle, the majors sold the leases to small producers not burdened by heavy operating overhead and moved on to new areas. Waterflooding spelled opportunity for many enterprising young landmen, engineers, and geologists who were not content to spend their entire careers making money for someone else. They were not afraid of hard work and often they literally took a wrench in hand to keep things going.[27]

In 1963, McGaugh was at the Fort Worth National Bank when he ran into Fuqua in the hall:

> I told him that I had come to see John Richards, Vice-President for oil loans to see if I could borrow some money in order to start my own business. He walked down the hall with me and accompanied me into Richards' office. He said to Richards, "John, let's lend this boy some money. He will pay it back. He pays his debts."
>
> Ever afterwards, I was able to do business with the bank by phone. Babe Fuqua made me. He enabled me to borrow money when no one else would lend it to me. Mr. Fuqua was tough but he was a good banker. He knew people. He recognized people who were responsible and would pay their debts.[28]

McGaugh went on to build a successful secondary recovery operation.

"You could talk to Mr. Fuqua." said Myrt Vititow. "I was a young man with two kids. At Christmas, he and Mrs. Fuqua would have us come by their home at which time they would give us presents for us and our children. Not too many CEOs do that. He would always give me advice on what to do. He was very helpful. One time I was flying him to a golfing holiday in Palm Springs, California. He was alone. Over Abilene I went back to see how he was. 'Well, we are over the great American desert,' he said. 'We'll be over it a long time before we get to Palm Springs. I want to give you a little advice, Myrt. I know you don't make a lot of money, but regardless of how little you make, always save some of it.' I have never forgotten that."[29]

Although a court ordered armistice held uneasy sway between Sinclair and TP, dissension arose within the ranks of the victors. Certain TP board members felt that Texas Pacific's time had come and gone. They wanted to sell the grand old company; others believed the company would continue to prosper.

Arch Rowan was a strong proponent to sell. Added together, Sinclair's TP holdings of 28.5 percent and Rowan's 7 percent equaled 35.5 percent and that spelled trouble. Whereas Sinclair had been restrained by court order from aggressively pursuing a take-over at TP, it could do so if invited by the Board. Moreover, the court order specifically gave Sinclair the right to "vote its stock and participate in the business and affairs of the Company" as long as it did nothing in contravention of the antitrust laws of Texas. Sinclair Chairman Spencer, in complete conformity with the court order, was content to sit back and watch Arch Rowan lead the charge.[30]

Babe Fuqua and Arch Rowan had been the warmest of friends for thirty years, personally, politically, and business-wise. Though the two men were from diverse backgrounds, they shared common traits; Fuqua was elite, polite, reserved, proper, polished, always the gentleman, kind, gentle, considerate. Rowan, a product of the Texas oil fields was brash, rough, tough, pugnacious, "don't-tread-on-me," but also kind, gentle, and considerate.[31] But the longstanding friendship came to an abrupt end because of their divergent views over the sale of TP. From my personal recollections, as well as from conversations with contemporaries present at the time, particularly Hamilton Rogers, Pat Woods, and Wes Yarbro, a picture comes into focus of the Rowan block putting the pedal to the metal, while Fuqua was tapping on the brakes, concerned not only with obtaining the highest possible sale price for shareholders but with the welfare of TP employees as well.[32]

In the darkening and uncertain political and industry atmosphere that prevailed in the early 1960s, the doubters on the TP Board believed the company's glory days were over. Oil was more difficult and expensive to find. Certainly, in the ensuing half century, there had not been another bonanza to rank with W. K. Gordon's storied Ranger discovery in 1917. These directors were aided and abetted by institutional stockholders—the soft underbelly of all corporations—who saw in the sale of the company an opportunity to triple the value of their stock.

An atmosphere of intrigue, distrust, and suspicion began to settle over the protagonists. One morning at 6:30, TP in-house Director Wes Yarbro, received a phone call from oil man Pat Rutherford in Houston. Rutherford, a TP board member and owner of 50,100 TP shares, was aligned with the Arch Rowan pro-sale bloc. He talked to Yarbro for more than an hour, explaining to him why the company should be sold. Sensing that he had become a pawn in a titanic struggle, the uncomfortable Yarbro listened but volunteered little.

Arriving at his office, Yarbro felt it incumbent upon him to report the incident to President Gene Adair. Adair promptly loped down the long hall to Fuqua's office to inform the Chairman of the latest action by the enemy camp. From that time, the warm relationship that Yarbro had enjoyed with Fuqua suddenly soured.

Although Fuqua had lost three of his staunch supporters—John Roby Penn and Sid Richardson by death, and Arch Rowan by his stance on the sale—others stood firm. One supporter who remained was Ernest Closuit, Sr., the man who had hired Fuqua at Gulf Oil in 1922. Closuit left Gulf in

1925 to become an independent producer and subsequently moved to San Antonio, while Fuqua, steadily rising in Gulf, went to Houston. In 1949, the year that Fuqua returned to Fort Worth to head TP, Closuit also moved back to Fort Worth and opened his office in the Fort Worth National Bank Building, where TP had its offices. Fuqua put him on the TP Board. During negotiations for the sale of TP, Closuit remained a Fuqua ally, assisting Babe with recalcitrant shareholders when the sale of TP was being negotiated."[33]

Finally, the sale proponents among the Directors had their way, and venerable and historic Texas Pacific Coal and Oil Company by unanimous board vote was put on the block to be sold. Bid invitations went out to five companies: Socony-Mobil Oil Company; Standard Oil Company of California; Standard Oil Company of Ohio; Continental Oil Company; and Frankfort Oil Company, a division of Joseph E. Seagram & Sons, Inc., the giant liquor distilling firm, whose Chairman was hard-nosed Sam Bronfman.[34]

Billy Joe Moore in 1997 observed that it was not remarkable that the four oil companies appeared on the list of bid invitees, but he wondered who suggested Seagram. He thought it sounded like Fuqua and Adair's work. Having beaten back Sinclair's take-over attempt four years ago on antitrust grounds, they would have sought this time at the outset to eliminate antitrust as an issue by seeking out an invitee with minimum or no ties to the oil industry. But why Seagram? Why not some other non-oil industry giant?[35] Pat Woods postulated: "The reason Seagram got the company was because Carrol Bennett promised Gene Adair a five-year contract. At the very end, Mr. Fuqua became disillusioned with Adair."[36]

Seagram could not have been Arch Rowan's idea, for J. Roby Penn, Jr. recalled that when Sam Bronfman's name was advanced in a TP directors meeting, Rowan expostulated: "Who the hell is Sam Bronfman?" He got his answer: "His income from Seagram dividends is $1,000,000 a month."[37]

Roby Penn told about another potential buyer, Kerr-McGee Oil Corporation. At a 1962 Board meeting, Penn recalled, it was suggested there might be an antitrust implication in selling TP to another oil company. President Kennedy and the Democrats were in power in Washington. The Antitrust Division of the Justice Department might take the position that TP's acquisition by another oil and gas producer would tend not only to eliminate competition between the two companies, but it might encourage similar mergers in the oil industry. Maybe it would be good politics as well as good business to consult powerful Democratic U.S. Senator Robert S. Kerr before the news broke in the media that sale negotiations were underway. Kerr and D. A. McGee founded Kerr-McGee Oil Corporation in 1936. Fuqua and Kerr were both contemporary Oklahomans, Fuqua born in Duncan in 1895 and Kerr in Ada in 1896. They were both oil men. They were friends. Not to consult with him might offend him. It made sense that Kerr should be contacted and advised of what was coming down. This ought to ensure that TP would have a friend in the Senate if antitrust clouds should begin to gather. Not only would such a meeting identify any possible antitrust problem, but it would be a diplomatic and offhanded way to let the Senator know that a Kerr-McGee bid would not be considered unfriendly by the TP Board. It was decided that TP's President, Eugene Adair, should call on Senator Kerr. But as he prepared during the Christmas holidays to leave for Washington, Fate intervened. Senator Kerr died on New Year's Day 1963.[38]

On February 28, 1963, the deadline for bids to be submitted, Claude W. Dodgen, Jr. of Frankfort Oil Company—a Seagram subsidiary—personally delivered the Seagram bid to Fuqua.[39] The approximate Seagram bid of $70 per share included a reserved production payment to be sold to a third party in a classic ABC transaction. In so-called ABC oil transactions, three parties normally are involved. The buyer, "B," in this case Seagram, gives the seller, "A," Texas Pacific, a portion ($61,000,000) of the purchase price ($277,000,000) in cash, and a promise to pay the remainder ($216,000,000) plus interest on the money owed, out of future production revenues. A third party, "C," usually a group of financial institutions or private investors, then buys the production payment contract from "A" at its face value. "C" then collects the production payments and interest. Once the bids were opened some companies wanted to increase their offer but Fuqua said "No!" Two weeks later Seagram was notified they won the bid.

Following the announcement that Seagram was the winner, there was much legal work to accomplish. Edgar H. Keltner, Jr., a partner in the Fort Worth law firm of Hudson, Keltner, Smith, and Cunningham, worked with Fuqua and the Texas Pacific management in preparing the Proxy Statement to be submitted to the shareholders of the company for their approval of the sale. Keltner joined two other attorneys who had been engaged by the company—Maurice Purnell of the Dallas firm of Locke, Purnell, Boren, Laney & Neely, who represented the company in the negotiations and closing matters, and Ben Bird of the Fort Worth law firm of Weeks, Bird, Cannon & Appleman, who handled the tax aspects of the transaction.

◆

When Ben Bird went to New York to confer with the liquor czar Sam Bronfman about closing details, Bronfman indignantly asked Bird about a story he had heard that he had a two-inch pipeline carrying booze across the Detroit River from Windsor, Ontario. Bird confirmed that such a story was circulating in the Fort Worth Club. Bronfman supposedly retorted: "That is a damn lie! It was a four-inch pipeline!"[40]

Regardless of the diameter of the pipeline, Bronfman liquor flowed freely from Canada into the United States during the Prohibition years 1920-1933. Bronfman biographer Peter C. Newman wrote that "Speakeasies became the most popular spots in every large U.S. city. In their search for reliable sources of booze, the speakeasy operators looked northward at the long, undefended border with Canada, where imports of British brands were still legal and domestic distilleries were capable of turning out a river of quality booze available for export. The bootleggers drove into Montreal from Saranac Lake, Plattsburgh, and other northern U.S. towns to load up their Packards and Pierce-Arrows with Bronfman package goods. Out west in Saskatchewan and Manitoba, the Studebaker 'Whiskey Six' with a bulletproof gas tank was the bootleggers' favorite. Fully stripped down, with reinforced springs and upholstery removed, it could carry forty cases of whiskey, worth $2,000." By the mid-twenties, the bulk of the direct liquor traffic into the United States was flowing across the Detroit River from Windsor, Ontario. It had created a navy of small boats (as well as a temporary pipeline and a complicated rope arrangement that pulled an underwater sled into a house boat anchored off the U.S. shore) to handle the booze. U.S. Prohibition Commissioner James Doran testified before a Senate committee in 1929 that at least $100 million worth of Canadian liquor was being illegally imported through Detroit.[41]

✦

During the negotiations, Keltner was elected a Texas Pacific Vice-President and came to know Fuqua quite well. He recalled sitting in a conference room with Fuqua, Purnell, Bird, and the New York lawyer representing Seagram: "The negotiations were not particularly strenuous or strained," said Keltner, "for the simple reason that Fuqua knew what TP wanted to do, what it ought to do, and what it would not do, and his position would be expressed without leaving any doubt in anyone's mind how any particular issue would be resolved."[42]

By letter dated September 20, 1963, Fuqua and Adair informed the shareholders:

At the 1963 Annual Meeting of Shareholders, the Board reported that each of the five companies from whom proposals had been requested had tendered proposals, each upon a "cash for assets" basis and that no proposals involving a tax free "stock for assets" exchange were received. At that time the shareholders were further advised that after careful examination of the proposals received and after preliminary discussions with two of the companies, the Board of Directors by unanimous vote had selected Frankfort Oil Company, a division of Joseph E. Seagram & Sons, Inc., as having submitted the best proposal taking into consideration all of the relevant factors. Of the five proposals received, the Frankfort Oil Company proposal offered the highest price for the assets of the Company.[43]

But acquiring TP was not as simple as submitting the highest bid. The matter of antitrust laws, both state and federal, had to be considered. The 1959 abortive Sinclair take-over attempt was still fresh in mind. Simply because Seagram was not an oil company, its bid took on added luster.

Sinclair, although not barred from bidding under the terms of the 1961 agreed judgment between the State of Texas and Sinclair, did not submit a bid. Holding 1,121,692 shares of TP stock, being 28.17 percent of the shares outstanding, its profit on the sale to Seagram was $25,000,000.[44]

Seagram's successful bid was for 277 million dollars, comprised of 61 million dollars cash and a production payment of 216 million dollars. This was seventy dollars a share. In 1949, the year that Fuqua became Chairman, the highest price of TP on the New York Stock Exchange was $13.25. Thus under Fuqua's guidance, TP stock in fourteen years had more than quintupled in value.

✦

To dramatize the magnitude of the transaction, compare the 277 million dollar selling price to the 111 million dollars paid by Conrad Hilton for The Statler Hotel chain in 1954. Or consider this. In the same year of 1963 that Fort Worth's Texas Pacific sold for 277 million dollars to New Yorkers, Fort Worth's Charles Tandy purchased Boston-based Radio Shack for three hundred thousand dollars.[45]

✦

Now began the monstrous job of updating title on all of TP's producing properties. In the spring of 1963, Rogers Gideon, only recently discharged from the Navy, was hired by TP's General Attorney, Miles Hart, to order the required supplemental abstracts. The cost: almost one million dollars.[46]

The formal agreement between Texas Pacific and Seagram commenced as follows:

AGREEMENT OF SALE AND PURCHASE

This Agreement of Sale and Purchase, dated the 21st day of May, 1963, between Texas Pacific Coal and Oil Company, a Texas corporation ("Seller"), and Joseph E. Seagram & Sons, an Indiana corporation ("Buyer").[47]

Ironically, on May 21, 1888—seventy-five years ago to the day—William Whipple Johnson and Colonel Robert Dickie Hunter commenced the three quarters of a century-long Texas Pacific odyssey by signing the option for Hunter to acquire the Johnson Coal properties.

The 216 million dollar production payment was contemporaneously bought by Glanville Minerals Corp., which financed the acquisition with bank and insurance company loans.[48]

First National City Bank	$130,000,000
New York Life Insurance Company	$ 38,000,000
Mutual Life Insurance Company of New York	$ 24,000,000
Aetna Life Insurance Company	$ 7,000,000
Connecticut Gen. Life Insurance Company	$ 7,000,000
First National City Bank, Pension Trustee	$ 7,000,000
Teachers Insurance and Annuity Association	$ 3,000,000
TOTAL	$216,000,000

At the time, this was the largest production payment ever made. "First National City Bank wanted it that way," said Dodgen, "for historic and prestige purposes."[49]

Jerry Sherrod was a young petroleum engineer with Texas Pacific Coal and Oil Company in the 1950s. In June 1957, he left the company to go to New York, where he was employed by First National City Bank. Little did he dream when he left TP that he would become deeply involved in the financial negotiations that took place in the sale of the company to Seagram. Years later Sherrod shed light on those transactions:

> The structure of the $216,000,000 production loan is correct, but the bank portion is not broken down. In those days a bank could sign one note, and then participate out portions of the total loan to other banks. On the other hand, insurance companies, because of their regulations, had to have an individual note for each of their loan shares.
>
> So, First National City (the Agent bank) signed a note for the total bank portion of $130,000,000, then used participation certificates to parcel out the loan to other banks. First National City ended up with a $34,000,000 portion of the bank loan but had committed to a larger amount originally [probably $50,000,000 to $60,000,000, which was a very large bank loan in 1963]. The loan was so popular among banks that it was over-subscribed. The Agent bank then reduced its share to accommodate the participating banks.
>
> As I remember, the Chase Bank and some Texas banks were among the participating banks. There were probably between seven and 12 banks in the total $130,000,000 loan. There were not many oil patch banks with a loan limit much larger than $10 to $20 million, so the money center banks, with larger limits, were important participants. Bank groups of larger than about 15 banks were costly for the Agent bank to administer and somewhat unwieldy if decisions (needing all the banks' consent) were necessary during the loan term.
>
> The original loan term was estimated to be ten years based on projected production rates with flat oil and gas prices assumed. The loan actually paid off in 11 years. Loan payments were made "when, if and as" hydrocarbons were produced and sold. The interest rate on the $130,000,000 bank portion

of the loan was $5\frac{1}{2}$% but $5\frac{3}{4}$% on the $86,000,000 insurance portion of the loan.

Glanville Minerals was a "production payment holder" with little capital or substance. They tacked on a $\frac{1}{16}$th per cent to the interest as payment for their being the "third party borrower." Jim Glanville, who was with one of the major Wall Street brokerage firms, was a principal in the company.

I particularly remember that Mobil complained that Seagram had "over-paid" when actually the Mobil bid was within a few million of the Seagram successful bid. I remember that the top three bids were very close together, probably within 1% [$3,000,000] of each other.[50]

Some time in late September or October, 1963, Fuqua, Wes Yarbro, and Frank Martin, a TP accountant and old Thurber hand who had developed a very close relation with Fuqua, flew to New York to meet investment bankers and attorneys to iron out last minute details of the agreement. Martin had prepared a series of impressive financial charts with which to educate the New Yorkers. "Babe and I decided," said Yarbro, "that since Frank was pretty well running the show, there was no need for us to re-main, so we flew back to Fort Worth." Even though seated side by side on the plane, few words were exchanged. Finally, Yarbro, in an effort to rees-tablish communication, summoned up sufficient courage to ask Fuqua: "Why are you mad at me?" The terse response: "You know." While Yarbro did not know, he reasoned it had to do with the early morning phone call he had received months ago from Pat Rutherford.[51]

The deal was finally consummated on November 1, 1963. There were three closings. One was in Fort Worth where President Eugene T. Adair executed a General Conveyance, Assignment, and Transfer of certain as-sets from Texas Pacific to Seagram. A second closing was in Wilmington, Delaware, where Maurice Purnell represented TP at The Corporation Trust Company, 100 West Tenth Street, Wilmington, Delaware, on Octo-ber 23, 24, and 25. This closing was held in Wilmington rather than New York because of the existence of a New York City tax which would have applied had the closing been conducted there. To avoid that tax, such closings were normally held across the Hudson River in New Jersey, but because of the tremendous number of assignments and documents that had to be signed and recorded all over the oil patch in such short order, the TP closing was held in Wilmington utilizing the extensive facilities of The Corporation Trust Company.

A third closing occurred in New York City where Ed Keltner and Roy Stevenson, Vice President of the Fort Worth National Bank, were on hand at the First National City Bank to receive the Seagram $61,000,000 check plus the $216,000,000 Glanville Production Payment that flowed in from several participating banks and insurance companies. Rather than being deposited in one bank, the funds were, in the interest of safety and according to plan, placed in a number of banks around the country until disbursement could be made to the shareholders.[52]

The lenders required delivery to them of legal opinions dated November 1, 1963, the date of the closing, attesting that the title of TP in its leases was good and marketable, free and clear of all liens, charges and encumbrances. This was a herculean exercise in logistics. TP pilot Myrt Vititow picked up the executed original documents in Wilmington and flew them to various points where landmen or attorneys would file them of record in the local courthouse. The documents pertaining to West Texas and New Mexico were delivered to Billy Joe Moore in Midland. Moore had employed several landmen who were standing by to take counterparts of the documents to courthouses in the more significant counties. After records were checked to make sure nothing affecting TP leases had been filed of record, the sale documents were recorded. Moore informed TP Attorney Miles Hart in Fort Worth when the operation was completed.[53]

Shortly after the sale, Eugene T. Adair resigned as President and Director and R. I. Dickey resigned as Vice-President and Director. At the meeting approving the initial liquidating distribution to the shareholders, Jess Norman and Keltner were elected to the Board to fill the unexpired terms of Adair and Dickey. Thereafter, as the company made additional liquidating distributions, various Directors resigned and were not replaced. When the last liquidating distribution was made in March 1965, it was authorized by a board consisting only of Fuqua, Norman, and Keltner.[54]

Soon after its acquisition, Seagram proceeded to wed TP to its other oil company, Frankfort Oil, under the name of Texas Pacific Oil Company. Coal—Black Diamonds—the first jewel in the Triple Crown, was tossed out. The offices were moved to Dallas.

Eugene T. Adair secured from Seagram a five-year consulting contract, complete with salary, office, and secretary. The oil man became a cattleman. In contrast with Colonel Robert Dickie Hunter's conversion from cattle to coal in 1888, which brought fame and fortune, Adair's occupational evolution from oil to cattle was met with failure.

During Fuqua's fortnight of years with Texas Pacific, the company had a solid discovery record, better than average for the industry for both extensions to existing fields and discoveries of new fields. The daily production was approximately 32,500 barrels at the time of the sale.

✦

On November 21, just three weeks after the sale to Seagram had been formalized, Fuqua appeared in my office in the Land Department of TP. "[President] Kennedy is going to be here tomorrow and I have three tickets for the breakfast. I'm not going. I promised one to Pat Woods. Would you like to have the other two for yourself and Wanda?"

I had been a Delegate to the 1960 Democratic National Convention in Los Angeles that had nominated Kennedy and Johnson. "I certainly would," I responded. "Don't you want to go?"

His reply was vintage Fuqua: "I wouldn't walk across the street to see the son of a bitch." He missed a most historic breakfast.

At the breakfast, Raymond Buck, President of the Fort Worth Chamber of Commerce, presented Kennedy with a white Stetson hat. "Put it on!" the audience chanted. The President laughed and responded, "Come to see me Monday at the White House and I'll put it on for you."

That Friday afternoon I walked down West Seventh Street holding a transistor radio to my ear. Others also had radios. Coming up the sidewalk was Peter Gregory, prominent petroleum engineer who had fled Russia in 1920 after the Bolshevik Revolution. In the late 1920s, he had become Chairman of the Yates Pool Engineering Committee, which represented all of the producers in the Yates field. He inquired why everyone was listening to the radio.

Gregory had not heard about the assassination. Soon thereafter he was thrust into the middle of the drama. A deputized officer was dispatched to bring him to a secret motel room in Arlington to interpret for Marina Oswald, the Russian-born widow of the accused assassin, Lee Harvey Oswald.[55]

◆

A cold, dreary January day in 1964 was Fuqua's last day in his Texas Pacific office. Ralph Dahlstrom of the Clifford Mooers Estate, of which Fuqua was Executor, was present as he was clearing out his desk and credenza prior to moving to another suite on another floor in the Fort Worth National Bank Building. It was obvious that saying good-bye to Texas Pacific Coal and Oil Company was not a very happy occasion.[56]

Following the sale of the company to Seagram, Fuqua, operating from his new quarters, spent the ensuing year tying up loose ends involved in the sale of TP. To avoid federal taxation at the corporate level, Section 337 of the Internal Revenue Code of 1954 provided that a corporation must be dissolved within one year from sale, with all remaining assets distributed to shareholders, except for a contingency fund with which to meet unpaid obligations. Accordingly, Tax Attorney Ben Bird prepared a document which assigned to all stockholders their proportionate part of all of TP's remaining assets, less a contingency fund of $518,477.43. This was to be the last document Fuqua would sign as President. Fuqua asked John Roby Penn, Jr. to acknowledge receipt of such assignment on behalf of all stockholders. Fuqua signed. Penn signed. Now it was truly over.

The Fuqua-Penn document was signed on October 22, 1964. Coincidentally, on October 22, 1917, the No. 1 McCleskey blew in at Ranger, and transformed a coal company into an oil company.

BABE'S LEGACY

11

After the sale of Texas Pacific, Fuqua, then 68, became immersed in the affairs of the Fort Worth National Bank and in political and civic matters.[1] One of the causes which captured his attention and imagination was the building of the Dallas-Fort Worth International Airport. He later said that construction of the airport was "the biggest thing I was ever involved in."

Although Fort Worth had recently built Greater Southwest International Airport midway between Fort Worth and Dallas, the airlines ignored the new field, opting to use Love Field fifteen miles away in Dallas. This chapped Fort Worth air travelers who found it exceedingly inconvenient and demeaning to have to go to Dallas to catch their flights. Fort Worth leaders, knowing that Love Field was inadequate for the future, feared that Dallas would choose to replace it by building a new airport east of Big D. On September 30, 1964, the Civil Aeronautics Board (CAB), after extensive hearings at the Inn of the Six Flags in Arlington, directed Dallas and Fort Worth to develop a single airport between the two cities. Fort Worth Mayor Bayard Friedman asked Fuqua and Chamber of Commerce President J. Lee Johnson III to join him on a negotiating committee to discuss the federal mandate with Dallas.

The negotiators promptly scurried down to Austin and called on Lieutenant Governor Preston Smith to seek his assistance on a Resolution providing for a constitutional amendment permitting the creation of a Bi-County Airport Authority. Smith assured the delegation that the Resolution would have his complete support. In fact, he promised that it would be the first business introduced in the coming January 1965 session. The Legislature agreed to submit the amendment to the voters.

In May 1965, the Dallas/Fort Worth Regional Airport Board was appointed by the two city councils as an interim board. Members of that interim board included, from Dallas Mayor J. Erik Jonsson, Frank A. Hoke, Hobart Turman, and R. B. Cullum as an advisory member. Interim Board members from Fort Worth were H. B. Fuqua, J. Lee Johnson, III, and Bayard H. Friedman and, as an advisory member, Mayor Willard Barr.[2]

In 1965, the Board hired the New York engineering and architectural firm of Tippetts, Abbott, McCarthy & Stratton to select a site. Without waiting for the adoption of the constitutional amendment in a November 1966 state-wide election, the Board let its first contract for site selection on June 6, 1965. Fort Worth led the charge when its voters in October 1965 approved a $7.5 million bond issue to provide money for purchase of land. Dallas voters approved a like amount two years later in an August 1967 bond election.

The constitutional amendment won resounding approval of Texas voters on November 8, 1966. On February 16, 1967, the legislature, pursuant to the new constitutional amendment, passed and Governor John Connally signed into law a bill providing for creation of the North Central Texas Airport Authority. Then voters from Tarrant and Dallas counties petitioned their respective Commissioners Court to call an election in each county for the purpose of creating the Authority. In order for the Authority to be created, both counties had to approve it in an election, which was held on June 6, 1967. While it was contemplated that no more than 15 cents on the $100 valuation would be initially necessary to prime the pump for airport construction, the ballot, in conformance with the constitutional amendment, read:

AUTHORIZING THE LEVY OF A TAX NOT TO EXCEED 75 CENTS ON THE $100 ASSESSED VALUATION.

Tarrant County voted Aye overwhelmingly—25,160 For and 8,747 Against. But Dallas County incredibly voted Nay—26,385 Against and 24,125 For. The majority of the Nay votes came from the Dallas suburbs.

I was with Fuqua at the 82nd annual meeting of the Fort Worth Club on election night. When word came that Dallas County had turned down the proposition, gloom prevailed throughout the Club. After all, Fort Worth had already spent nearly $4 million to acquire some 4,000 acres for the airport. But Fuqua told me on that night, "That airport will be built! It is going to be!"

The dust had not even settled until rescue operations were underway. In fact, the next morning's edition of the *Fort Worth Star-Telegram* carried the results of the balloting under a big headline which announced:

DALLAS DEFEATS AUTHORITY

Under that was an even larger headline:

CITIES TO PUSH ON WITH 'PORT.

Negotiators from both cities decided they would, under provisions of a 1948 state law that permits cities to act together to build airports, push on with the project without involvement of the counties. Innumerable meetings were held to hammer out the details. At a meeting in the fall of 1967 where the representatives were working on the contract, someone mentioned that soil sampling was being done at the site of the future airport.

Doug Clarke a *Star-Telegram* city hall reporter was at that meeting and rode with Fuqua back to Fort Worth:

> As we traveled back on the Dallas-Fort Worth Toll Road, I mentioned that it seemed very early in the planning to already be doing soil sampling. Mr. Fuqua, sitting beside me in the back seat, said, "Well, I don't know why they would be sampling out there. They ran a test there in 1917 or 1918." I asked him if he had seen the results of any recent testing. He replied, "No, but I saw that 1917 report." He then proceeded to name off four or five different strata that would be found. Being a curious type, I made a list of the strata, thinking there might be some sort of story there if they found oil, dinosaur bones or a flying saucer. About six months later, I came across my notes and called the testing firm. They ran a check of the results and speaking very slowly and very loudly for the non-geology oriented reporter, confirmed Fuqua's prediction of what they would find.
>
> I was very impressed that Mr. Fuqua could so effortlessly draw on his memory of what must have been thousands of core samples he had reviewed during the past fifty years and predict exactly what the testing company would find. I remembered that Mr. Fuqua had had his hat on that day with the brim turned up. I marveled at the incongruity of such a formidable mind underneath that hat with its rustic brim.[3]

Bayard Friedman spoke of the blood, toil, tears, and sweat expended in bringing the airport into being:

> There were countless meetings with our Dallas counterparts, and Babe was very much involved. He let me do most of the table-thumping but he provided much needed maturity and wisdom. There never was a time during the entire course of the negotiations that there was a disagreement among the three of us, but when the lines were drawn between the two communities, Babe fought like a tiger for Fort Worth.
>
> I recall that at one tense point Babe threatened a prominent Dallas banker that if his folks didn't accede to the Fort Worth position, the Fort Worth banks would sever relationships with their upstream Dallas correspondents and go to Houston instead. That was typical of Babe's aggressive style when provoked. The fact of the matter is that the Dallas leadership had a great deal of respect for Babe, and he was a major player in the creation of the Dallas-Fort Worth Airport.[4]

In April 1968 the day finally came when all negotiations had been concluded and it was time to sign on the dotted line. The negotiators from Fort Worth and Dallas and representatives from the airlines met in Dallas for the formal signing and announcement.[5] The joint operating agreement established an eleven-member airport board. Because of the population difference, the board was composed of seven members from Dallas and

H. B. Fuqua portrait by Gittings, circa 1970. Courtesy Pat Woods.

four from Fort Worth. Airport financing would be provided from revenue bonds and federal grants, with the two cities providing the needed land.

Ground was broken for 17,500-acre Dallas-Fort Worth International Airport on December 15, 1968, and construction began early the next year. On September 22, 1973, after five years of building and the issuance of $750 million in bonds, with the flags of fifty-five nations waving under partly cloudy skies and the arrival of the supersonic Concorde, Dallas-Fort Worth Airport was officially dedicated. The airport became operational at 12:01 Sunday, January 13, 1974. Six minutes later an American Airlines 727, flight 341 from Little Rock, appeared from out of the midnight darkness and landed. The airport was in business.

A decade later, Bayard Friedman said: "Next to bringing the railroad here in 1873, this was the most important thing that ever happened to Fort Worth. It meant more, proportionately, to Fort Worth than to Dallas. It revived Fort Worth. Without it, many of the projects that now exist wouldn't have taken place."[6]

Today DFW Airport is an unqualified success. Projections are that before the turn of the century it will be the biggest airport in the world. In the face of defeat on the night of June 6, 1967, the Babe, figuratively speaking, stepped up to the plate and pointed to the fence, "We are going to build that airport! It is going to be!" And so it was. A grand slam home run!

✦

There is an interesting historical sidebar concerning Fuqua and the DFW Airport. In the 1968 Democratic Primary, Fuqua had pledged to support Governor John Connally's handpicked candidate, Eugene Locke, to succeed Connally as Governor.

Lieutenant Governor Preston Smith came to Fort Worth in his bid to step up to the Governor's office. He told Dr. J. D. Tomme, Jr., Smith's Tarrant County campaign manager, that he wanted to go see Babe Fuqua, although he knew that Babe was for Locke. Tomme asked me to arrange an appointment.

The three of us went to Fuqua's office in the Fort Worth National Bank on Seventh Street one late afternoon. We sat across from Fuqua behind his big desk. Blunt Preston wasted no time with formalities. He came right to the point.

"Babe, we intend to be Governor and we want your help." Smith was famous for using the royal "We."

"Well, Preston," Fuqua replied, "I would like to help you but I'm committed to Eugene Locke."

"Well, Babe," Preston countered, "you came down to Austin to see us about the airport authorization, and you wanted us to give the Resolution a low number, didn't you?"

"Well, yes, that's so."

"Well, Babe, what number did we give your Resolution?"

"No. 1," Babe answered sheepishly.

You could have heard a pin drop on the thick carpet. Tomme and I squirmed in our chairs. The incident spoke to the situation where party leaders who have supported politicians in the past and have availed themselves of aid and assistance from those politicians now find themselves in the uncomfortable position where two of them are seeking the same office. Both assumed, quid pro quo, that because of past backing they had received and favors they had bestowed, that they had earned the blessing and support of a kingmaker in their latest electoral venture. Fuqua had promised John Connally he would back Eugene Locke. But Smith thought he had earned Fuqua's support, implied or expressed. He believed that Fuqua had reneged on a commitment. Thirty years later Smith wrote: "Fuqua was a great guy but he did break a promise to me. However, it made no difference. It's easy to see how a man gets committed sometimes and things just don't work out."[7]

12

On the political stage in Fort Worth, Babe Fuqua bestrode the scene like a Colossus. This is not to say that his candidates always won, for like Babe Ruth, he sometimes struck out. His occasional political dry hole appeared conspicuous because it stood out like a tall derrick in the middle of a field of flowing oil wells. For every negative outcome in a hotly contested election, there were many more successes not only in high profile races but in quiet ones not long remembered because the Fuqua candidates were either uncontested or opposed by unknown and poorly financed opponents. If the history of all of Fuqua's victories in campaigns for city council, water board, school board, judges, sheriff, district attorney, commissioners, legislative, precinct, and county chairmen were recorded, it would require many books. It could be said that no decision of the Fort Worth establishment was ever made without Fuqua's acquiescence and involvement.

For some three decades—the 50s, 60s, and 70s, especially after the death of Amon Carter in 1955—Babe Fuqua's name was synonymous with civic leadership, hardheaded business acumen and political clout in Fort Worth.

This was the era of the "Seventh Street Gang," an appellation hung on the group of influential downtown business leaders whose base of operations was the Fort Worth Club.

Over the years, many political candidates pitched their campaigns and diatribes against Babe Fuqua and the "Seventh Street Gang," usually to no avail.

The power of the group lay in its ability to raise campaign funds for anointed candidates and to dry up the sources of money for their opponents. Traditionally, an aspiring candidate would make his way to Fuqua's office to ask for his political blessing. The plainspoken Fuqua would lay it on the line—yes or no—never leaving the supplicant unsure of where he stood.

What needs to be remembered about the "Seventh Street Gang" is that they were a vastly different breed from the corrupt, graft-ridden political machines that flourished in New York under Tammany Hall, Chicago under Mayor Richard Daley, Jersey City under Frank Hague, and Kansas City under Jim Pendergast.

The Citizens Committee in Fort Worth had as its primary motivation making the city run efficiently and harmoniously to promote new industry and growth.

Of his role as "kingmaker" of local politics, Fuqua said, "During the days we had a good city council I collected the money and paid the campaign expenses. My job was to keep City Hall straight. We kept a good council. The system worked.

"The system quit working only after single-member council districts became the law of the land, an eventuality Fuqua would deplore until the day of his death."[1]

Fuqua was opposed to single-member districts in which neighborhood politicians would be tempted to logroll for narrow interests rather than embrace policies designed to promote what was best for the entire city. He thought that single-member districts would tend to produce a council controlled by liberals and characterized by divisiveness and petty bickering. However, he was known to help qualified conservatives of both parties:[2]

Conservatism, to Babe Fuqua, meant preserving what was good about the America he grew up in. The America where people improved their lives by personal work and study, not by welfare. The America where people welcomed spiritual guidance from church and temple. The America where nearly everyone could read, write, and do sums. The America where men respected women and women did not find it shameful to be mothers and homemakers. The America where children respected their elders.[3]

In the April 1967 City Council elections, Fuqua and his establishment allies heavily backed incumbent Mayor Willard Barr, publisher of the *Labor News,* for a second term. But they had not reckoned on a feisty veteran businessman, albeit newcomer to City Council hustlings. That was colorful, inarticulate curmudgeon DeWitt McKinley, salty President of the McKinley Iron Works. Without asking Fuqua's advice or permission, he up and announced he would run for Mayor.

Fuqua left no stone unturned in his determination to defeat the audacious McKinley. His fierce combativeness even took him to Corporation Court where he obtained copies of numerous tickets and citations that had been issued to McKinley in the past for various traffic violations. These were used in the campaign to show that if McKinley could not be trusted to drive a car in a safe, sober, and legal manner, he probably could not be trusted as Mayor to sit in the driver's seat of the city. In spite of such tactics and fierce opposition, McKinley, teamed with maverick Councilman Harris Hoover, a North Side furniture dealer, upset Barr. City Council watchers were stunned.

Nevertheless, under McKinley the city survived and prospered. During his term as Mayor, McKinley used two mules pulling a slip to break ground for the new City hall.

Fuqua was tenacity incarnate. He believed that any defeat was only temporary. Two years later in 1969 McKinley was defeated in his bid for reelection by popular Councilman Sharky Stovall, who received heavy support from both the lodge and Fuqua's Seventh Street Gang.

Fuqua's influence was not confined to Seventh Street or the chandeliered banquet halls of the Fort Worth Club and the arcane cloisters of the Chamber of Commerce. The Chamber and the Fort Worth Independent School District planned a program in which business leaders would board buses and visit every school in the city. When one of the buses stopped in front of one school, the principal met the delegation at the curb with the query: "Is Mr. Fuqua on this bus?"[4]

From 1966 until 1984, Sopora Hicks was the powerful Democratic chair of Lake Como, a west Fort Worth community. She was known to be not adverse to stepping inside a voting booth to assist the occasional confused voter, a tactic that at times prompted considerable Republican irritation. Upon her death in 1984, the leadership reins passed to Viola Pitts. In time, she even surpassed Hicks in renown and influence. Pitts recalled "We called Babe Fuqua 'Mr. Seventh Street' because he ran the town."[5]

Eventful 1968 furnished another example of how Fuqua worked quietly behind the scenes. In July longtime Precinct 4 County Commissioner Rosco Minton died.[6] In Court 4, a Texas beer joint across from the court house, Assistant District Attorney Gordon Gray chanced to see County Judge Howard Green. Gray seized the day and told the Judge that he would be interested in succeeding Minton as County Commissioner. Green readily agreed to appoint him. But Gray's tenure on Commissioners Court would prove to be fleeting and ephemeral. Because Minton died subsequent to the Democratic Primary, it fell to the Precinct Chairmen in Precinct 4 to name a new nominee. And that created a problem. Liberal State Representative George "Skeet" Richardson, knowing that Minton's days were numbered, secured pledges from all of the liberal precinct chairmen to support him if a vacancy should occur.

Gray went to see Babe Fuqua. Fuqua promised him that he would call Rosco Minton's widow and ask her to endorse Gray. She complied on television. Influential attorney Berl Godfrey, Judge Jesse M. Brown, and other members of the Seventh Street Gang also were quick to pledge Gray their support. However, Richardson's pledges were enough to carry the day, and he was named by the precinct chairmen as the Democratic nominee on the fall ballot. Elected in November, he succeeded Gray on the court.[7]

A year later Commissioner Richardson headed a delegation to Austin to ask Governor Preston Smith to appoint defense lawyer Ronald Aultman to new Criminal District Court No. 4. What did the Governor do? He appointed Gordon Gray, who, some ten years later, black-robed, high and lifted up, a $75,000-a-year State District Judge, would sit in judgment on multimillionaire Cullen Davis.[8]

◆

On January 15, 1969, Fuqua's Fort Worth National Bank participated in the announcement of the largest downtown real estate transaction in the history of Fort Worth, involving the sale and leasing of the bank building and the acquisition of more than four downtown blocks as a site for a new thirty-five-story bank building with a connecting motor bank and garage. The structures were completed in late 1973 in time for the bank's 100th Anniversary.

◆

In 1970, a second skirmish over this commissioner's seat was fought when Fuqua and Green were again allies to defeat Richardson for another term. This time the Green-Fuqua candidate was Steve Murrin. They were unsuccessful and Richardson was reelected.[9]

Also in 1970 Mike Moncrief aspired to run for the State Legislature. He remembers:

> The "7th Street Gang" was a very active, viable force in Fort Worth. You simply did not seek political office without their blessing. Babe was the leader of the organization which included Amon Carter, Jr., Charles Tandy, William M. Brown, and others.
>
> Because of protocol, I went to see Babe to ask for his advice and counsel as well as his support. He told me in no uncertain terms that he would not support me, because I needed more experience at the local level. He told me to heed his advice or I would be soundly defeated.
>
> I did not choose to follow his instructions and filed for the Texas House of Representatives which in those days before the establishment of single member districts meant an expensive countywide race. I had eight opponents, Democrat and Republican. After a primary run-off victory, I defeated the Republican in the General Election.
>
> About a month after my election, I received a check from Babe along with a note congratulating me on my victory. I tore up the check and put it in an envelope along with a note stating that I did not feel comfortable accepting a post-election check to my campaign.
>
> According to sources close to Babe, when he received my note and his check in pieces, he went absolutely ballistic. Shortly afterwards, I received a phone call requesting my presence in his office—right now! Upon receiving the summons, I went to visit him. The only things on his desk were the torn check and my note. He proceeded to tell me that he never, as long as he had been in the political arena, had had anyone to refuse a contribution he had made, much less tear it up and return it.

I explained that I did not feel comfortable in accepting the money for my campaign after being elected, especially since I had requested his support prior to the election. . . .

Once Babe understood that I was dead serious about my ethics and my beliefs, we became close friends. From that day forward, Mr. Fuqua was my mentor and a man I deeply admired and loved. However, make no mistake about it, he was an individual who had the world's worst temper with the shortest fuse. These characteristics defined the man we called Babe and I called friend. [10]

Fuqua's readiness to make a post-election contribution to Moncrief was not an unheard of practice in Texas politics. Walter Mischer, Houston banker and kingmaker, is credited with coining the Texas political adage, "There's always time to buy a ticket on the late train." [11]

On January 16, 1970, a group of sixteen Fort Worth conservative and moderate Democratic leaders met with Houston businessman and former Congressman Lloyd Bentsen in the Will Rogers Suite of the Texas Hotel. Among those attending were Hamilton Rogers, Garrett Morris, David Belew, Al Komatsu, and Rice Tilley, Jr. Bentsen had announced his candidacy for Ralph Yarborough's seat in the U.S. Senate. The campaign's slogan would be "A Senator for the Seventies." All present knew that after Yarborough's defeat of Bill Blakley in 1958 and winning reelection in 1964, the entrenched liberal Senator would be exceedingly hard to oust. But all were more than willing to join the battle. It was not that everyone in attendance was all that gung ho for Bentsen and his allegiance to the Democratic party. Rather, it was an opportunity to administer the coup de grace to the ring leader of Texas liberals that energized Hamilton Rogers and Babe Fuqua (although Fuqua was not present at the meeting) and others of their quasi-Republican persuasion. [12] The grand coalition succeeded. Not only did Bentsen defeat Yarborough in the primary, but in the fall election he defeated Republican Congressman George Bush, a future President of the United States. Nineteen-seventy was a very good year for Lloyd Bentsen.

Fuqua retired as Chairman of the Board of the Fort Worth National Bank on January 19, 1971. [13] He had served in that capacity for 19 years but never took a penny of compensation. He continued to serve the bank as Honorary Chairman and Advisory Director. During the time he was Bank Chairman, Fort Worth National experienced its greatest growth. Total assets grew from $231 million to $573 million; deposits soared from $213 million to $470 million; and loans increased from $94 million to $287 million. In an interview with Irvin Farman at the time of his retirement from the bank, Fuqua declared:

A bank must have interest, understanding and dedication to make a community grow. You've got to back up your interest with your financial resources. Very often the difference is having the people who are willing to work and put up their money. To sum it all up, it comes down to a question of community pride. With it, you can't fail; without it, you can't succeed.[14]

The most important thing in the world, in Fuqua's opinion, was people. "You do things through people," he was fond of saying. Friend or foe, Fuqua knew how to work with people when something needed to be done. He knew the right buttons to push and the right levers to pull. A case in point:

In 1972 President Richard Nixon was elected to a second term, but the Democrats remained in control of Congress. The Republican administration proposed a reorganization of government so that all federal agencies would be coterminous, which would avoid the situation in which two agencies located in the same office building would be located in different districts. The Republican plan envisioned increasing the number of regions from seven to eleven and vesting each agency with more administrative control. The idea was to move government from Washington and put it closer to the people. Many federal offices staffed by Democrats took a dim view of the Republican plan. With Democrats in control of Congress, the only way a Republican administration could put such a proposal into effect would be by Executive order. The Republicans in Dallas stipulated that if new regions were created the federal offices would be in Dallas.

So the Housing & Urban Development offices were moved from the Lanham Federal Building in Fort Worth to the Cabell Federal Building in Dallas at 8 A.M. on Monday, September 10, 1973. Fuqua reacted to the move by calling R. M. (Sharky) Stovall, Mayor of Fort Worth at the time: "Fuqua never was exactly a supporter of mine, but with the HUD move, he called me. I called Jim Wright. We had a meeting in Jim's office to see what could be done to keep HUD in Fort Worth."[15] More than six years and a change of administrations were required for Fuqua and his allies to turn the dreadnought of federal bureaucracy. The ad hoc trio, a marriage of convenience, held together and tackled other problems in the future.

In 1973 there was a hotly contested race for Mayor. The candidates were incumbent Sharky Stovall and Attorney Sterling W. Steves.[16] Fuqua was the force behind the Seventh Street Gang that was backing incumbent Sharky Stovall. Clark Nowlin, a prominent, up-and-coming young realtor in Fort Worth, had promised his support to Steves. In the months leading up to the election, Nowlin, with Fuqua's behind the scenes go-ahead, had quietly assembled the properties on which the Fort Worth National built its new bank at 5th and Throckmorton Streets. When Nowlin realized Fuqua was pro-Stovall he apologized to Babe. Babe responded: "Clark, son, we all make mistakes. You should always check with your elders first."[17]

In 1973 the Fuqua organization was concerned not only with re-electing Sharky Stovall as Mayor, but also with other council races. When

Taylor Gandy announced he would not seek reelection to his Southwest Fort Worth Place 3 seat, Fuqua sent furniture dealer Watt Kemble to tell Clif Overcash that the downtown group would support him for the Place 3 seat. Overcash ran and won. Before the two-year term was over, the Fuqua-Overcash alliance would turn sour.

Babe's dislike of Overcash had its beginnings in a business deal involving Lee Goodman, Executive Director of the Downtown Fort Worth Association. Goodman and the Leonard family of Leonards Department Store agreed to put together a deal to construct a $2.5 million building in the Convention Center area to be leased to Southwestern Bell Telephone Company. In the midst of setting up the deal, the Leonards backed out. In 1971 Goodman approached Overcash who was then President of Leonards Department Store and told him if he could invest $100,000 in the venture he could do the deal himself. Overcash put up the money. Fuqua then advised Goodman that it was a conflict of interest for him to be involved in the matter because he was working for the Downtown Association. Although the actual reason the Leonards withdrew from the deal is not known, it is likely Fuqua's influence was at work. Babe and Marvin Leonard were close friends—it was the talk of the Fort Worth Club that the two conferred by telephone every morning even before arising from bed. When Marvin died in August 1970, Fuqua probably believed it was his responsibility to apprise the family of what he perceived to be an impropriety. Under pressure from Fuqua, Goodman resigned from the Downtown Association in June 1971. A year or so later in 1972, Overcash resigned from Leonards and entered a full-time partnership with Goodman. "So far as Babe's dislike for me, it was sort of guilt by association," said Overcash. Despite his choice of associates, Fuqua, believing Overcash would make a good councilman, backed him in the 1973 election.[18]

By 1975, a dozen years after the sale of Texas Pacific, Fuqua's political stature had grown to legendary proportions. But in that year rebellion was in the air. Former City Councilman Taylor Gandy was the behind-the-scenes mastermind of the revolt. Under Gandy's plan, Place 3 on the Council would be vacated by Clif Overcash who would make a last minute announcement for Mayor. Jim Bradshaw would announce for Place 3, too late for others to enter the race.

As he had done two years ago, Fuqua dispatched Watt Kemble to inform Overcash that the Seventh Street organization wanted him to run for re-election to Place 3. Overcash replied that he was going to run for Mayor. Kemble said they would not support him for mayor because they had already picked J. C. Pace, Jr. as their candidate. The next day Overcash hied himself off to see Mayor Stovall, a fellow Shriner, and told him he was going to run for Mayor whether or not he ran. "The reason Stovall would not reveal his plans," said Overcash, "is because they had a scheme. They thought if they delayed making an announcement about Sharky, I would not have enough time to crank up a campaign."

Gandy's plan clicked like a clock: Stovall did not run for Mayor. Overcash did. Bradshaw announced for Place 3. But there was one hitch. Car dealer Jack Williams and Richard Hyde, an east-side businessman, also announced for Place 3.

In the campaign, Overcash attacked Babe Fuqua and the Seventh Street Gang, but Bradshaw had a different game plan. He tried to enlist the support of Fuqua and couldn't. Overcash overcame Pace and won the mayor's race.[19]

In the race for Place 3, Bradshaw finished first but did not poll enough votes to avoid a runoff with second place finisher Jack Williams. Hyde, courted by Babe Fuqua and his friends, endorsed Jack Williams.

When Fuqua put out letters during the runoff urging support for Williams, Bradshaw switched tactics and attacked Babe.

> A radio spot was cut, and a lot of time was purchased on all of the stations. The ad used a voice that might have sounded like that of the Shadow. It said, "DID YOU GET THE WORD? FROM HIS BIG BANK'S GLASS TOWER BABE FUQUA HAS SPOKEN: WHAT DO YOU MEAN NOT ELECTING MY CANDIDATE? FORT WORTH IS MY TOWN AND JACK WILLIAMS IS MY CANDIDATE . . . NOW DO WHAT YOU'RE TOLD OR ELSE . . ."
>
> A male voice with a small town Texas accent chimed in and said, "OR ELSE WHAT? THIS IS MY TOWN, TOO! THIS BABE FUQUA AND HIS SEVENTH STREET GANG BETTER WATCH OUT BECAUSE WE HAVE A VOICE IN THIS TOWN, TOO, AND WE'RE LIABLE TO ELECT OUR OWN CANDIDATE.
>
> A Paging voice came in at the end and said, "JIM BRADSHAW, PAGING JIM BRADSHAW . . . YOU'RE WANTED ON THE CITY COUNCIL."[20]

The Sunday *Star-Telegram* preceding the runoff election on Tuesday, quoted Fuqua to the effect that a liberal coalition was forming on the City Council and that voters would be making a mistake to elect Jim Bradshaw rather than Jack Williams.

The spots and a lot of hard work put Bradshaw over on election night.[21]

Three new members who were to loom large on the local political scene were elected to the Council on the night that Overcash was elected mayor—Hugh Parmer, Woodie Woods, and Jim Bradshaw. Two of these men—Parmer and Woods—were destined to be future Mayors. As a matter of fact, it was street talk that Parmer had prepared a political time schedule that would take him to the White House. The third new Councilman—Jim Bradshaw—would be a Mayor Pro Tem and run a strong race against unbeatable Jim Wright for Congress.

Fuqua was vitally interested in civic affairs. In the early 1970s, Fuqua and attorney Tom Law, President of the Fort Worth Chamber of

Commerce, worked together in an effort to have a state mental health and mental retardation facility for children located in Fort Worth:

> Babe Fuqua was unswerving in his support of causes in which he believed. I remember one morning when he was nearing 80 years of age, he arose at 5:30 and met me at Meacham airport. We boarded a plane at 7:00, flew to Austin and conferred with Governor Preston Smith and the director of the state agency who would make the ultimate decision as to the location of the proposed facility. We were successful and the multi-million dollar Fort Worth State School was opened in 1975. Upon our return to Fort Worth later that day, he went not home or to the golf course. He went to his office. For ever after, I marveled at the single-minded determination of this almost-octogenarian, never having had children of his own, to bring this home for handicapped children to Fort Worth. Babe Fuqua never received, nor did he seek or even want, credit for his role in this endeavor. Success of his efforts in a cause in which he believed was all that mattered to him.[22]

Although Fuqua was a driving force in the development of Fort Worth, he did not see a major potential sitting right before him. After his close defeat by Skeet Richardson in the 1970 Democratic Primary for County Commissioner, Steve Murrin began to see visions of splendor for the historic stockyards on the North Side. He foresaw the district's popular tourist mecca of today. The central jewel in the diadem of his dream was the North Side Coliseum. But that city-owned structure was leased by Mrs. Elizabeth Moore, who was represented by William M. Brown, a powerful Seventh Street attorney. Murrin remembered:

> I went up to see Mr. Fuqua in early 1975, with the hope that I might be able to change the odds. Mr. Fuqua had been my big supporter when I ran against Skeet Richardson for County Commissioner in 1970. He hated Skeet Richardson more than he hated anything else in the world. I said, "Mr. Fuqua, I want to explain to you what we are trying to do in the stockyards." He said "Fine, Steve, I will let you tell me about it, but I can tell you right off I have had it with this Cowtown bullshit." I smiled and replied that we could do the "Cowtown bullshit" in the stockyards and you can remain progressive and pristine downtown. I told him that Underground Atlanta, Gaslight in St. Louis, and Old Town in Chicago all had opened in the late 60s and had great success initially and then folded because they did not have a theme and failed to keep the facilities clean and safe. I said out in the stockyards we have inherited a wonderful theme, and since it was a closed-in area, we could clean it up and make it safe. He listened to me. He nodded and smiled, and said, "Steve, that sounds fine to me, but I want to tell you again that I've had enough of the Cowtown bullshit." You always knew where Babe stood. If you didn't want to know, you didn't ask. He would declare his position. He would never hedge.[23]

For Murrin to oust the Moore interests from the Coliseum, he would have to convince the City Council to vote for him. Mayor Stovall and Council-woman Margaret Rimmer were solidly pro-Moore. In the last session of the 1973-75 Council, Murrin's hopes were dashed. The Council voted to renew the Moore lease.

The next week, the new council was seated. One of the new members was former State Representative Hugh Parmer. While Parmer was in the main roundly loathed by Fuqua's Seventh Street organization, he and Steve Murrin nevertheless were friends. Parmer's first act as a new Council member was to move to reconsider the Coliseum vote taken the previous week by the old Council. As a result, Murrin got the lease on the Coliseum and his dream became one of the modern success stories of Fort Worth, as tourists from all over the nation and indeed the world pour into the stock-yards to revel in its realistic Old West atmosphere.

Neal Hospers, who in 1975 was General Manager of the newly opened Hilton Hotel at 1701 Commerce, spoke of another incident which under-scored Fuqua's commitment to city development:

> Mr. Fuqua called me in 1975 and asked to come visit me. I really didn't know he knew me although I had met him before. So I was in shock as to why he would want to see me, and why would he not call me to his office. He came and he quickly told me what his mission was. He was there on behalf of the Fort Worth Chamber Development Corporation, landholders of the many blocks just to the east of the Hilton. Metro Hotels, owners of the Hilton, eventually bought the lot immediately east of the hotel for parking.[24]

It was irony of the first order, but unrecognized and unacknow-ledged—Fuqua, the last chairman of the Texas Pacific Coal and Oil Company, paying a business call on the manager of a hotel of the Hilton chain, a worldwide organization that arguably owes its existence to the TP McCleskey gusher at Ranger which resulted in Conrad Hilton's first hotel in Cisco more than half a century before. Did either Fuqua or Hospers grasp the irony?

In July 1975, a young, little-known Texas A&M economics professor by the name of Phil Gramm had come to town to test the winds for a possible 1976 race for Congress in the Sixth District. The only difficulty was that the incumbent Congressman was Olin E. (Tiger) Teague, the darling of the Fort Worth Conservative establishment. It was obvious that Gramm would have his work cut out for him if he decided to run against Teague.[25]

A luncheon hosted by Texas Steel President Beverly Thompson, Jr. and attended by perhaps 25 Conservative big guns was held in the Camellia room of the Fort Worth Club on July 8, 1975. It was Gramm's thirty-third birthday. At the conclusion of the professor's remarks, in answer to a question by Ed Palm, Gramm bared his ultimate goal to his audience: He wanted someday to be President. Gramm was informed at this time that if he ran against Teague he would not have the support of anyone in the room. Fuqua, flanked by Charles Tandy and Rice Tilley, spoke in a low almost inaudible whisper: "Why don't you go run against Lloyd Bentsen?" It may have been a whisper, but it was heard by all in the room including the professor.[26] As a result of that meeting and acceding to Babe Fuqua's wishes, Gramm did in fact announce for the U.S. Senate. He was roundly and predictably defeated by Bentsen.

✦

About a month after the nation celebrated its bicentennial, the curtain went up in Fort Worth on a real life Perry Mason murder mystery that would capture the intense interest of all of Fort Worth–indeed all of Texas–for a decade. At midnight on August 2, 1976, a gunman dressed in black and wearing a woman's black wig broke into Cullen Davis's $6,000,000 mansion occupied by Davis's estranged wife Priscilla. Priscilla's twelve-year old daughter, Andrea Wilborn (Cullen's stepdaughter), was shot and killed. So was Stan Farr, Priscilla's live-in boyfriend. Priscilla and Bubba Gavrel, a visitor at the mansion, were critically wounded in the shooting rampage. Gavrel's date, Beverly Bass, escaped unharmed. Davis, stoutly protesting his innocence, was arrested and charged with the murders. He was the richest man ever to be tried on murder charges. After an abortive beginning in Fort Worth, Judge Tom Cave in June 1977 moved the trial to Amarillo where it lasted for five months, the longest and costliest in Texas history. The verdict came on November 17, 1977: Not Guilty!

But there were more trials and tribulations ahead. On Sunday morning, August 20, 1978, Davis was arrested and charged with solicitation of capital murder. On September 19, on a change of venue, the trial was moved to Houston. David McCrory, an FBI informant, testified that Davis wanted 15 people killed, including the survivors of the mansion slayings and Judge Joe Eidson, the judge in his divorce case. The murder-for-hire case ended in an 8 to 4 mistrial on January 22, 1979. He was retried in Fort Worth, where a hometown jury on November 9, 1979, returned its verdict: Not guilty!

On June 22, 1987, a third mistrial occurred in the 16.5 million dollar wrongful death suit brought against Davis by Priscilla and her ex-husband Jack Wilborn for the death of their daughter Andrea. The jury deadlocked 8 to 4 in favor of the plaintiffs.

The saga of Cullen Davis was Fame and Fortune on a Texas scale. Unfortunately, however, Fame went north while Fortune went south. As a result of his monstrous legal bills and the fact that oil and real estate plummeted in the mid-1980s, Cullen was forced into bankruptcy. He became the living manifestation of a joke that was circulating around the Lone Star State at the time: How do you make a Texas millionaire? You start with a Texas billionaire.

✦

In 1977 Mayor Clif Overcash was up for reelection. His opponent—Council colleague Hugh Parmer. Remembering Overcash's attacks against him in 1975, Fuqua refused to support the Mayor. "Babe was the type of guy who never forgot anything," said Overcash. "He held grudges. If he disliked someone, he never forgot it."[27] While he gave no aid to Overcash, there was no way on earth that he would ever have had any truck with liberal Hugh Parmer. Consequently, his position in the 1977 Mayor's race was in the mode of "a plague on both your houses." Parmer received the endorsement of Woodie Woods, a fellow council member who was very popular with the people, and defeated Overcash by about 1,000 votes.

Fuqua had a major falling out with Tommy Vandergriff, Mayor of Arlington over the Dallas-Fort Worth Turnpike. In 1958 the Dallas-Fort Worth Turnpike Authority issued bonds in the amount of $58,000,000 and constructed a magnificent six-lane toll road between the two cities. The road was a hyphen, not separating but connecting two great cities. The bond covenant provided that when the bonds were redeemed, all tolls would be eliminated. However, as the date approached in 1977 when the bonds would be paid off, Dee J. Kelly, chairman of the Turnpike Authority, advanced the idea of issuing additional bonds to construct another toll road to be known as the Trinity Toll Way, located north of the Dallas-Fort Worth toll road. He contended that a short spur connecting the two roads would essentially make both projects one, and therefore allow Dallas-Fort Worth Turnpike tolls to be kept in force to pay off the additional bonds.

Fuqua and other leaders in both cities believed that a second road would be needed to carry traffic to the new but burgeoning DFW Airport. Vandergriff disagreed. He had been instrumental in the move of the American League Washington Senators to Arlington to be known thenceforth as the Texas Rangers. He had been involved in the creation of dazzlingly successful amusement park Six Flags Over Texas. He also was a prime mover for a companion amusement park known as Seven Seas which turned out to be a dog. A prime advocate and original supporter of the toll road, his goal now was to remove the tolls. And the Mayor, who in years to come would be elected to Congress and after that Tarrant County Judge, was unyielding in his stand:

> Building a toll road had not been universally accepted in the first place. A great many of us had taken a blood oath in the 50s that once the tolls paid off the bonds, the road would be turned into a freeway. The trouble was that I was one of the few who had "taken the pledge" still breathing in the 70s when suddenly the road paid off. We had thought it would be in the 90s before sufficient revenue was generated to redeem the bonds. But that did not alter the fact that I had given a pledge that if, as and when the bonds were paid off, the road would become a freeway.

Mr. Fuqua was very upset with me and he was not alone. In banking circles at both ends of the turnpike, I was personna non grata, a pariah held in low esteem and of ill repute. The banks had banded together. They were the depositories of The Turnpike Authority. Naturally, they were very sensitive to turnpike finances. I received lectures from Republic National and First National of Dallas officials as well as the officers of Mr. Fuqua's Fort Worth National. They made it very clear to me they wanted the tolls continued. Over their strenuous objections, we had to go to Austin to get legislation enacted to remove the tolls.[28]

Legislative sanction in hand, the Turnpike Authority set midnight of December 31, 1977, as the hour when the bells would toll for the tolls. Bright and early on New Year's Day of January 1978, Mayor Vandergriff arrived at the Fielder entrance in order to be among the first free riders. "There were at least twenty cars in line ahead of me waiting for the gates to open," he recalled.

Reporters noticed that during the pitched battle Vandergriff was no longer invited to Fort Worth functions and no longer served as Master of Ceremonies at important dinners as he had in the past. It was apparent that the Fuqua ice treatment had been prescribed for young Tom Vandergriff.[29]

In 1978, Congressman Tiger Teague, in failing health, elected not to seek another term. Phil Gramm, using his 1976 statewide Senate race as a launching pad, ran for the House, this time with Fuqua's support. His Tarrant County Campaign Manager was Wanda Woodard. In the first primary, there were five contenders. Well-known TV weatherman Ron Godbey finished first; Gramm was second; and Teague aide Chet Edwards third. In the ensuing runoff, Gramm came out on top by 122 votes. He was handily elected against Republican Wes Mowery in November.

Some time in late summer of 1978, City Councilman Woodie Woods went up to discuss with Babe Fuqua his plan to run for Mayor against incumbent Hugh Parmer, the man who Woods had been largely responsible for electing to that post in 1977. In the ensuing two years, the paths of Woods and Parmer had diverged. According to Woodie's wife, Jewel, Fuqua told him, "Your integrity has never been questioned." Integrity was always No. 1 with Babe Fuqua. Since Fuqua, Watt Kemble, Rice Tilley, and others admired the manner in which Wanda Woodard ran Phil Gramm's Tarrant County Campaign for Congress, Fuqua suggested to Woods that he talk to her about running his mayoral campaign.[30] Following his meeting with Fuqua, Woods met with Wanda one Saturday morning for breakfast in the Colonial Country Club where she agreed to manage his campaign. When this agreement had been released to the press, Channel 8's anchor Iola Johnson alliteratively trilled; WOODIE WOODS AND WANDA WOODARD!

One piece of the campaign's strategy was to attempt to secure the endorsement of former Mayor Clif Overcash. They did. In endorsing Woods, Overcash vowed: "We cannot afford to have a mayor in that seat who is a professional politician, and it has taken the public two years to understand this. We need a mayor who will do what is right for the city instead of what is best for himself. That is why I am for Woodie."[31]

The 1979 campaign, like the 1978 Gramm campaign, would prove successful, historic, and narrow. Narrow? It would make Gramm's 122 vote win look like a landslide. In the mayor's race, there were only two candidates, Mayor Hugh Parmer and challenger Woodie Woods. But with only two men in the race, there was a runoff! How could this be? On election night, Woodie Woods edged Parmer by 23 votes—15,572 to 15,549. Great argument arose as to whether a handful of write-in votes should be considered in the tabulation, and if so, perhaps Woods had not obtained a majority. Hugh Parmer, a few hours later, committed a grievous mistake.

At 2 A.M. Sunday morning, City Secretary Jack Green was awakened by a phone call at his home. He had just gotten to bed after finishing the vote count at City Hall. Parmer wanted to check the returns in City Hall. So at 9 A.M. on Palm Sunday, Green, Assistant City Secretary Ruth Howard and Assistant City Attorney Bill Wood met in City Hall with Parmer's representatives—Harold Hammett, Henry Simon, Art Brender, all lawyers, and Garland Lasater. George Armstrong III came later. But no representative of the Woods campaign or of the press was present. When the returns were checked and retotaled, the count remained the same.[32]

Jack Green called Wanda Woodard to let the Woods' campaign know what had just transpired. In response, Woodard with Councilman Dick Newkirk and Mayor Pro Tem Jim Bradshaw arrived at City Hall seeking an explanation.[33] Parmer later stated he was merely being thorough, leaving no stone unturned in trying to get the facts.

Tuesday morning, April 10, Parmer went to court to be sure that Woods was not declared Fort Worth's new mayor before a recheck of the election returns. Judge Walter Jordan of 48th District Court issued a restraining order and set a hearing for 9 A.M. April 18 for Parmer's application for a temporary injunction.

A canvassing board under the supervision of 322nd District Judge John Hill and County Judge Mike Moncrief was appointed by the Council. A sixteen-hour check began at 1 P.M. on Thursday, April 12, and ended at 4:30 A.M. on Friday. The recount widened Woods's lead over Parmer from 23 to 27: 15,570 votes for Woods and 15,543 for Parmer. That totaled 31,113.

The recount ended with the determination that a total of 30 write-in votes had been recorded, but only 22 of them were allowable. Eight write-ins were disqualified for two reasons: (1) One write-in had been cast for Woods and one for Parmer. The statute forbids a write-in for anyone whose name is already on the ballot. (2) Ballots could not be found to substantiate six write-ins that appeared on the returns.[34]

If all 30 write-in votes were added, the grand total would be 31,143. Half of that would be 15,571.5. Woods with 15,570 would need two more votes to avoid a runoff. If only 22 write-in votes were considered, the grand total would be 31,135. Half of that would be 15,567.5. Woods's 15,570 votes would make him Mayor without a runoff.

On Friday, April 13, the City Council met to canvas the returns. City Attorney Arthur Petersen ruled that only 22 write-in votes should be considered. In accordance with that opinion, freshman councilman Bert Williams made a motion that only 22 write-in votes should be counted. William's motion ended in a 4–4 tie, with Jim Bagsby, Shirley Johnson, Jeff Davis, and Louis Zapata voting Nay. Mayor Pro Tem Jim Bradshaw, Dick Newkirk, Bob Bolen, and Bert Williams voted Aye. Mayor Parmer had grandly announced that he would abstain, but after a brief pause to confer with his lawyers, he abruptly reversed himself and voted to break the tie. Against the advice of the City Attorney, his vote came down on the side of accepting all 30 write-in votes! A runoff election in the two-man race would be held! The *Dallas Times-Herald* would headline its story: PARMER VOTES HIMSELF INTO FORT WORTH RUNOFF.

Under provisions of the City Charter, Parmer was supposed to sign a proclamation the day after the April 13 canvas calling for a runoff on April 28. When this was not done, on Monday morning April 16, Mayor Pro Tem Jim Bradshaw went to City Hall and signed a proclamation calling for such April 28 runoff. Bradshaw maintained that he had been notified that Parmer was out of the city, and because of the necessity to get absentee balloting started, it was essential for the election proclamation to be signed forthwith.

However, a runoff election on April 28 would have provided for only a two-week interval, and Parmer apparently felt he needed more time to mount a get-out-the-vote campaign among his supporters. Parmer charged that he had not been out of town and Bradshaw's move was only a flagrant grab for power on the part of Bradshaw, Dick Newkirk, and Woodie Woods. On Monday April 16, he signed a counter proclamation calling for a May 5 runoff election under what he said was a provision of State Law which gave him as Mayor the authority to set the election any time within thirty days following the April 13 official canvas.

City Attorney Petersen, who had resigned as City Attorney because Parmer chose to follow the advice of his campaign attorneys, was still on the job. He took issue with this interpretation and acting on his own authority as provided by the City Charter, at 9 A.M. on Tuesday, April 17, made his own trip to the 48th District Court where he obtained a restraining order against Parmer's May 5 date.

At a hearing on Wednesday April 18, Judge Walter Jordan ruled against Parmer and for Bradshaw's April 28 date. As soon as the Judge had made his ruling, Assistant City Secretary Ruth Howard rushed to the telephone to instruct her deputies to commence absentee balloting.

Parmer's self-interest vote to accept 30 write-ins and improper inspection of precinct returns became the paramount issues. The Woods campaign seized on these two items and, financed by a blizzard of contributions primarily from Babe Fuqua's cohorts, radio and newspaper ads hammered away with the question: "Mr. Parmer, what were you, the Prince of Ethics, doing in City Hall in the early morning hours of Palm Sunday?" The entire city was inflamed and 54,350 voters streamed to the polls. Parmer was defeated by more than 10,000 votes: 32,525 to 21,825.

Never in Fort Worth had a City Council election, much less a runoff, produced such a staggering vote. Probably never in the history of democratic elections had a two-man race resulted in a runoff. The Woods-Parmer race was Babe Fuqua's last hurrah in the political arena.

Six years had passed since Fuqua had initiated the move to return the Housing and Urban Development offices to Fort Worth. Now in 1979 the efforts bore fruit. On November 19, 1979, HUD moved back to Fort Worth.[35]

✦

Fuqua was a member of River Crest Country Club whose golf course was just across the road from his palatial home. This was the same club where the city's elite turned out in 1921 to welcome TP officials John Roby Penn and Edgar J. Marston upon the occasion of their transfer from New York City to Fort Worth. On January 16, 1981, the Southern plantation-style club was reduced to toppled walls and charred columns when it burned to the ground.

Initially plans were made to rebuild the club house to the same size as the old. Eighty-six-year-old Fuqua waded into the debate. His arguments to cut down the size of the replacement to save money won the day. A smaller club house was built.[36]

✦

As a mark of the esteem, not to say awe, in which he was held by one and all, civic leader Jud Cramer in 1992 remarked: "In all the years I knew Mr. Fuqua and in all the civic and political projects in which I was involved with him, I never called him Mr. Fuqua or Babe. I always called him Mr. Chairman."[37]

From the 1940s through the 1960s Tarrant County had one of the most powerful political organizations in the state. It was comprised of conservative Democrats and among the leaders were Babe Fuqua, Neville Penrose, Arch Rowan, William M. Brown, Hamilton Rogers, and Rice Tilley.

Many of these conservative Democrats switched political allegiance to help form the powerful Texas Republican party of today. Through it all, Fuqua was viewed by most as the leader of the pack. And as long as he was, no one else was ever so bold as to assert: "I am in control here!"

13

On April 21, 1983, Fuqua suffered a great loss. Sarena, his wife of 63 years, died. While her husband was well known, she had remained a private person, unknown outside her own circles. Her friends declared that she sought no prominence but did her good out of the limelight. Kaye Buck McDermott said, "Mrs. Fuqua was a lady from the old school who believed in propriety and ethics and kindness. She was very small of stature but very large of image. She was a very gracious lady."[1] Marie Tarlton added, "She didn't belong to a lot of things, but she did things for so many people that nobody knew anything about. She didn't seek prominence or social things too much. That wasn't her goal in life. It was doing good. And being a wonderful friend. And being there first when you needed help."[2] At Christmas she always presented several TP employees with a box of dressed frozen pheasants that had been raised by the Fuquas' longtime friend, Frank Wood of Wichita Falls.

Although Babe would never fully recover from Sarena's loss, time heals all wounds, personal, economic, and political. Over the years Babe made amends with DeWitt McKinley. McKinley called on Babe to enlist his help when the Allen Street Bridge over the railroad tracks near St. Joseph Hospital was replaced with a new overpass. McKinley wanted the new structure named for former Councilman Edward Guinn and Babe agreed to help.[3]

Another former antagonist to whom Fuqua warmed as the years slipped by was Sterling Steves who had opposed the Seventh Street Gang in the 1973 Mayor's race:

> I used to see Babe coming up to the Fort Worth Club to have lunch. He was always unfailingly courteous and polite, but not overly friendly. I got to know him a little better after he had retired and I would walk by his house across from the River Crest Country Club golf course. Babe would walk out into the yard to get a little exercise and sunshine, and I would stop and talk to him. He was always extremely pleasant and I would talk to him about whatever was occurring. He never hesitated to give me his frank and candid opinion. I always enjoyed talking with the old man because you never doubted where he was.[4]

Sarena and Babe Fuqua, circa 1982. Courtesy Pat Woods.

Jim Bradshaw tried to make amends a number of times with Babe after the 1975 contentious election in which Bradshaw was elected to City Council. In 1980 after Bradshaw ran against Jim Wright for Congress and was defeated, Fuqua invited Bradshaw to come see him. Babe commented "Jim, you ran a damn good campaign against that son of a bitch. You kept your nose dry, you handled yourself with dignity, and you didn't lose a thing by losing. I just wanted you to know that . . . ." That was as close to letting bygones be bygones as he could give.[5]

Although Fuqua was reknowned for his forthright attitude, he always comported himself as a gentleman and was quick to lend assistance when needed.[6] He was steadfast in his concern and empathy for his friends. Odessa Nelson, a waitress at the Fort Worth Club for 35 years, was always a favorite of Babe Fuqua. "He gave me the job as Captain of the Men's Grill," she said. "All during the year he was doing things for me. Vacation and Christmas were very special. When I was sick I got notes from him. He would always want to know if anybody was giving me trouble. He went to bat for me."[7]

He was universally recognized as the most powerful man in Fort Worth. One day Rice Tilley, Jr. was riding in a Fort Worth National Bank elevator with Fuqua. Fuqua not remembering whether he had punched the button for his floor when he got on, muttered he may have missed his floor. But the elevator did stop and Fuqua got off. After the door closed, Tilley quipped to those still on the elevator: "It wouldn't dare not stop!"[8]

Fuqua had a complex personality. Certain characteristics could be seen by anyone: his granite-like integrity, his dedication to city, state, and country, his loyalty to the stockholders and employees of Texas Pacific Coal and Oil Company. I knew Babe Fuqua up close for nearly four decades in business, political, and social settings, and while he was most assuredly possessed of a sense of gravity, seriousness, competence, and self-confidence, I often saw his blue-gray eyes twinkle and the lines of his face wreathe into a smile. Others, among them H. Bryan Poff, a draftsman in the Gulf Geological Department in Fort Worth in the 1940s, claimed Fuqua did not often smile.

✦

Thirty years later a lad of about nine years of age would try to find a way to make him smile. The boy was James J. Fuqua of Vernon, Texas, the grandson of Babe's brother Nolen.

To some, my great uncle, H. B. Fuqua, was a stone cold, hard man who would drive over, around or through a problem with force if he deemed it necessary. However, I saw other sides to the man from my unique vantage point as his great nephew.

I seemed always afraid that I couldn't please my great uncle. He seemed never to smile and usually asked me questions to which I found no answer. This lack of an answer to his painfully straight forward questions always bothered me.

In 1970 when I was nine years old, I decided that I would build him a model airplane. So after long, hard hours of time, I finally finished my model. With the paint still tacky, I presented the stone hard man my gift. With that I thought I had him. There was no escape from the smile which had eluded me for so long.

He took the work of art from my hands, inspected every detail, looked backwards and forwards, and with a slight grin said, "Thank you." Again with a grin he asked me what type of plane it was, who flew it and what was its purpose. I could answer all his questions except why the Navy flew it. So, brokenhearted, I raced to my room to feel sorry for myself.

After some time, I got my airplane book out and began to read. After a while I believed I had the answer to any possible question he could ask about this darn plane. With my research completed, I returned to where he was. With a smile on my face, I answered his question, so he asked me others. I answered them all. Finally, I saw a smile that would have made Jimmy Carter proud. With that I saw what he had done for me without telling me a word. He made me force myself to learn.

When it came time for him to leave for the airport, we found after arriving for his flight that we had failed to bring the model airplane I had made for him. His flight was not ready to leave for thirty minutes, and a round trip to our house would take at least that much time. So off my Grand Prix father drove to get the plane his son had built for his uncle.

Mom and I heard them call "last boarding," and my Uncle Babe headed for the plane. After half an hour, my out-of-breath father raced in with the model airplane. When he saw that the plane had not left, he asked the attendant at the boarding gate if we could go through the gate and give the model plane to Uncle Babe.

Eyeballing the model plane and not being at all amused, she exclaimed, "That is what we are holding this plane for?"

We raced out to the plane. My great uncle got his model plane and I another big smile.[9]

Apparently this was not the only time that James ever coaxed a smile from his great uncle. When the time came for the young man to go to college, his choice was Texas A&M. Before its Kyle Field football games, it is a tradition for A&M to have a five-story-high bonfire on campus. During his years at A&M, Cadet Fuqua was always involved with the bonfires. Years later, Beth Newberry, whose husband O. P. and she were close friends of Babe and Sarena, related that when Babe was asked by friends what James was studying at A&M, he would always reply with a wide grin that he was majoring in bonfires.[10]

✦

Harold Achziger, Fort Worth National Bank Vice-President, spoke of Fuqua's temperament:

> Everyone who knew Babe Fuqua typically was addressed by him in a warm, soft, friendly tone, giving the image of a man very likeable, very nice and mild-mannered. However, on one occasion at a business meeting, one of our associates raised a question concerning a local politician. Babe's demeanor was entirely different. His voice changed from a tone that was soft, gentle and kind to one that was staccato, sharp, almost knife-like and cutting. The voice change made me think, "Hey, I never would want to cross this man because he would cut you up in little pieces and feed you to the alligators.[11]

Carl Freund echoed that sentiment: "Fuqua could be the nicest guy in the world, but he was not the kind you ever wanted to cross."[12] Sinclair's P. C. Spencer would have agreed. And so would Bob Windfohr, Charley Yager, Arch Rowan, Gene Adair, Wes Yarbro, and jittery TP geologist Nolan Hirsch.

Following his retirement from the bank, Fuqua sat in his office on the twentieth floor of the bank building and watched as the bank started down a path that would lead it into an abyss. In July 1983, Texas American Bank declined an offer from Texas Commerce bank to buy the bank for fifty dollars a share. Three years later with the oil/real estate crunch underway, shares had dropped to $23.50 a share. The stock continued to retreat. Retreat turned to rout. Two years later shares sold at twenty-eight cents.[13]

But Fuqua stayed on board. At the bitter end his 60,000 shares–in 1983 worth $50 a share for a total of $3,000,000–were liquidated for 12.5 cents a share for a total of $7,500. "He so loved the bank, that he refused to sell his stock. Like Captain Smith of the *Titanic,* he went down with his ship."[14]

✦

In the meantime, what of the fortunes of E. T. Adair who had walked away from TP a millionaire? He and his son Eugene went into purebred Brangus cattle breeding on a 500-acre ranch northwest of Weatherford.

> On a cool Saturday in 1983 near Weatherford, the tents were pitched, the landing pad readied and the beef piled high on the grills. The air smelled of hickory smoke, cattle and money. By 1 P.M., there was an auction on, and the purebred stock of E. T. Adair and the Flying A Ranch were moving briskly through the chutes and into the possession of the highest bidders. But when it was over, there was a pall on the place. It hung over Adair like the smoke from the barbecue pits drifting into the air. The auction was a disaster. Adair's registered cattle, ranked by some breeders as among the best in the state,

sold for less than one-third of their predicted worth. Though almost 200 people attended the dispersal sale, the main purebred cattle buyers, whose presence makes or breaks a cattle auction, didn't show. And while that happens to a lot of breeders, no one expected it to happen to a man such as E. T. Adair, who together with his son, Eugene, had spent well over $2 million lining the pockets of his competitors and peers while building a herd of his own. In fact, some breeders lamented that Adair's sale failed because the cattle business—considered one of the last endeavors where a promise is a promise and a handshake is enough—turned its back on one of its own. "To see this happen with a top breeder like he was, with one of the top bulls in the nation, may make people think twice about getting into this business," said B. L. Littleton, a major cattle breeder from Texarkana.[15]

That is a sad tale, but a sadder one would come less than five months from the day it ran as the *Star-Telegram*'s headline story on Sunday, October 27, 1985, for on March 6, 1986, E. T. Adair died. Like TP at its death, he was 75. Graveside services were held in the Zion Hill Cemetery north of Weatherford. In 1888, Colonel Robert D. Hunter left cattle to go into TP and coal and made a fortune. In 1963, E. T. Adair left TP and oil to go into cattle and lost a fortune. The wheel had come full circle.

◆

Not only did Babe Fuqua keep his bank stock but he was in his office in the bank tower every day. He drove himself. In the 1980s Dennis Veit, a Fort Worth National Bank officer, and his wife Marie who was Executive Secretary to oilman William M. Fuller, observed Fuqua's daily arrival and departure at the bank:

> Many mornings and evenings we would often notice a line of cars in the parking garage. Always leading the parade would be a large Cadillac creeping along from floor to floor at no more than 5 mph. Two focused eyes under a hat with a turned up brim could be observed peering out above the steering wheel. Nothing else. Once parked in its assigned slot, one could see that the wizened figure under the hat was the esteemed H. B. Fuqua.[16]

Fuqua drove his car until the very end. "Driving his own car was one of his last vestiges of independence." After an accident in 1987, Pat Woods would never let him drive alone. She always insisted on riding with him to watch out for other cars. Her concerns about his driving were hinted at to the clerk in the State Highway Department when she went with him to renew his driver's license in December of 1988. She was hoping his renewal application would be denied. After he had read the eye chart and was sent around the corner to have his picture taken, Pat said to the clerk, "He is 93. Don't you ever turn anyone down for age?" The clerk barked back at her: "HE READ THE LIST!" The license was renewed.[17]

In July 1989, two decades after Fuqua's retirement as Chairman, federal regulators seized and sold Texas American Bancshares, holding company for Fort Worth National Bank. Few of the bank's board members were braced for such a devastating and final blow. Charlie Hillard, longtime automobile dealer in Fort Worth and member of the Board of Directors of West Side Bank, which later became an affiliate of the Fort Worth National Bank saw the value of his thirty thousand shares decrease by $1.5 million. He attributed the bank's demise to bad real estate loan practices.

> Had Babe's conservative guidelines been followed, the bank would never have rushed head on into such terrible real estate loans. I borrowed $100,000 from the bank to buy a piece of property on West Seventh Street across from Trinity Park. Two years later the people I bought it from decided they would like to have it back. They asked me what I would sell it to them for. I told them $200,000. They went down to the Texas American Bank and the bank loaned them $200,000 to buy the same property that they had loaned me $100,000 for. Real estate deals like this is what killed the bank. Babe would never have stood for that.

Hillard was an ardent admirer of The Babe. While seated in the barber's chair at Colonial Country Club on May 4, 1994, nine months before his own death, the 87-year old auto king mused: "Babe was a very loveable guy. If I were to count [my friends] on the fingers of my hand, Babe Fuqua and Gil Weaver would be the first two fingers."[18]

On December 23, 1988, 93-year old Fuqua went to Vernon, Texas, to spend Christmas with his brother Nolen and Nolen's daughter-in-law Sherry Fuqua, her son, Jamie and daughter, Stacy. On Christmas Day, the brothers were to be driven to Nolen's home in Duncan, Oklahoma, by Sherry. But Babe, a suitcase in each hand, failed to notice a step-down into the garage and suffered a hard fall. It appeared that the fall had done no serious damage, although he presently became aware of a soreness in his side. Consequently, upon arriving in Duncan, Sherry drove him to the hospital. Even though X-rays revealed several cracked ribs, the trio continued on to Nolen's home where Babe called Pat Woods in Fort Worth to advise her of what had transpired but said that he felt everything would turn out all right. "I'll cross the Red River and be home in the morning," he told her.

When morning of the 26th came, his pain had so increased that Nolen took him back to the hospital where his condition gradually worsened and he slipped into a coma. He never regained consciousness and died from complications of the rib injury, December 30, 1988. The fabulous Babe was gone. Who could have known when he started out on this final trip to Duncan, Oklahoma, that, like the king salmon of the Columbia River, he was returning to his birthplace to die?[19]

In a stirring eulogy on January 3, 1989, the Reverend Robert W. Bohl, pastor of Fort Worth's First Presbyterian Church, paid tribute to Fuqua:

> Herbert Breedlove (affectionately known by his mother and us as Babe) Fuqua had a sense of high, moral principles. He had integrity and honesty. He was a consummate businessman and, behind the scenes, a consummate politician, always looking out for what would be good for this City, this State and this Nation. He knew how to weed out the nonessentials, and could get quickly at the heart of the matter. It is true that his Yes was Yes and his No was No. But he was always fair.
>
> Once I suggested to him, about two years ago, that when people assemble to remember his life upon the occasion of his death, some would probably suggest that Babe Fuqua had elements of perfection in him, and he smiled and said, "Maybe a little bit, but not enough."[20]

Babe Fuqua's grave in Greenwood Memorial Park is marked by a large North Dakota mahogany granite monument. It lies just across the road from Amon Carter's giant Georgia granite mausoleum, and about a quarter of a mile as the crow flies from the grave of John Roby Penn. He had observed his 93rd birthday only three days before he died on December 30, 1988, exactly 100 years after Texas Pacific was born.

In 1980 Seagram sold Texas Pacific Coal and Oil to Sun Oil Company of Philadelphia for 2.3 billion dollars. Sun Oil spun it off in 1988 to Sun Exploration & Production Company. In 1989 the name was changed to Oryx Energy Company. The word oryx comes from the name of a large straight-horned African antelope, which derives from the Greek word meaning "to dig." While not a bad name for an oil company, the few graying veterans who still attended the TP ex-employee Christmas parties in the 1990s would sniff, "Not as good as Texas Pacific." But Texas Pacific was gone with the wind.

NOTES

PREFACE

1. Fort Worth Petroleum Club, Historical Committee *Oil Legends of Fort Worth* (Dallas: Taylor Publishing Company, 1993).
2. William Hunter McLean, *From Ayr to Thurber* (Fort Worth: News Printing Co., 1978), 20.
3. *Sale of Texas Pacific Coal and Oil Company to Joseph E. Seagram & Sons, Inc.,* Bound Volume of Sale Documents, comp. by Edgar H. Keltner, Jr., 1963.

I: IN THE BEGINNING: WILL JOHNSON

1. Robert W. Spoede, "William Whipple Johnson" (master's thesis, Hardin-Simmons University, 1968), 9.
2. Ibid., 10.
3. Ibid., 11.
4. Ibid., 15.
5. Ibid., 20.
6. Ibid., 21.
7. Don Watson and Steve Brown, *Texas & Pacific–From Ox Teams to Eagles* (Cheltenham, Ontario: The Boston Mills Press, 1978), 34-35.
   Jon McConal, "Cemetery Lore," *Fort Worth Star-Telegram,* 7 September 1995. The town of Strawn was named for Stephen B. Strawn, who settled in the area in 1861. He served in the Confederate Army during the Civil War and is buried in Mount Marion Cemetery south of Strawn. William Johnson donated the land for the cemetery, which is named for Johnson's daughter, Marion.
8. Spoede, "W. W. Johnson," 39.
9. Ibid., 29.
10. Ibid., 30.
11. Ibid., 27.
12. Watson and Brown, *Ox Teams to Eagles,* 39.
13. Spoede, "W. W. Johnson," 33
14. Mary Jane Gentry, "Life and Death of a Texas Town" (master's thesis, University of Texas, 1946), 8.
15. Spoede, "W. W. Johnson," 43.
16. Ibid., 53.
17. Weldon B. Hardman, *Fire in a Hole* (Gordon, Tex.: Thurber Historical Association, 1975), 14.

18. Spoede, "W. W. Johnson," 48-49. In his historical novel, *The Back Road to Thurber* (Baird, Tex.: Joy Presswork Collection, 1993), Leo Bielinski postulates that F. T. Jowell was the farmer at whose well W. W. Johnson had earlier drunk and first seen coal.

19. Hardman, *Fire in a Hole,* 23.

20. Ibid., 3.

21. Ibid., 8-11.

22. Spoede, "W. W. Johnson," 54

23. Richard F. Selcer, *Hell's Half Acre* (Fort Worth: Texas Christian University Press, 1991), 212.

24. Spoede, "W. W. Johnson," 54.

25. Hardman, *Fire in a Hole,* 25-26; and Spoede, "W. W. Johnson," 54.

26. George B. Studdard, *Life of the Texas Pacific Coal & Oil Co.* (Fort Worth: [self-published], 1992), 41.

27. Spoede, "W. W. Johnson," 49.

28. Ibid., 50-52.

29. Ibid., 74.

30. Hardman, *Fire in a Hole,* 25.

2: THE MIGHTY HUNTER

1. Mary Jane Gentry, Weldon Hardman, and other authors spell Hunter's middle name *Dickey,* whereas Hunter McLean spells it *Dickie,* the maiden name of his mother. McLean, *From Ayr to Thurber,* 16, 20.

2. Robert C. Marston, interview by author, 13 March 1997. This story was often told to Marston by his great-grandmother, Jennie Colorado Hunter Marston Chapin who died in 1935. Jennie's date and place of birth were found in the family Bible.

3. McLean, *Ayr to Thurber,* 16, 17. Robert D. Hunter was twenty-eight when the war started, thirty-two when it ended. In his geneaology, Hunter McLean observed that such military titles were commonplace honorifics in those times.

4. Ibid., 17, 18.

5. Ibid., 18.

6. Hardman, *Fire in a Hole,* 18.

7. McLean, *Ayr to Thurber,* 19.

8. Ibid., 19.

9. Custer had been a general in the Civil War but after the war had been dropped back to his permanent rank of captain. Later promotions moved him up to Lieutenant Colonel which rank he held at the Last Stand.

10. McLean, *Ayr to Thurber,* 21.

11. Kelly Garbus, "Jesse James' Remains Wanted for DNA Identification," *Fort Worth Star-Telegram,* July 2, 1995.

12. McLean, *Ayr to Thurber,* 22, 30.

13. Ibid., 24.

14. Ibid., 20.

15. Ibid., 31. The site of Hunter's home at 3650 Lindell Boulevard would eventually be occupied by the library of St. Louis University. No doubt that would have

pleased Colonel Robert D. Hunter, who always was in quest for knowledge and learning. Rose and Don Fischer, letter to Don Woodard, 3 July 1993.

16. McLean, *Ayr to Thurber*, 32.

17. Spoede, "W. W. Johnson," 65.

18. Ibid., 53.

19. Watson and Brown, *Ox Teams to Eagles*, 41-43.

20. Spoede, "W. W. Johnson," 55-56.

21. *Gordon Courier Times*, 28 May 1903.

22. Spoede, "W. W. Johnson," 57, 64.

23. Ibid., 66.

24. Hardman, *Fire in a Hole*, 27.

25. TP Coal Company financial records were discovered by Janis Mills and contributed to Special Collections, University of Texas at Arlington Library, in 1995.

26. McLean, *Ayr to Thurber*, 33.

27. Spoede, "W. W. Johnson," 66-67.

28. Hardman, *Fire in a Hole*, 27. In an 1890 letter concerning the sale to his long-time confidant and attorney, Henry Taylor, Johnson referred to Hunter as "that damned villain." Johnson apparently felt that Hunter had gotten the mine while he himself had gotten the shaft.

29. Ibid., 26.

30. McLean, *Ayr to Thurber*, 22.

31. Gentry, *Life and Death*, 12.

32. Ibid., 28-29.

33. Edgar Jean Marston's son, Robert C. Marston, theorized about his father's middle name: "Jean is the French spelling for John. On our side of the Marston family there are many named John. Edgar Jean Marston was to have been a girl and named after her mother. No caring parent would name a boy Jennie; so it became Jean as Edgar John is not very euphonious." Robert C. Marston, letter to author, 6 April 1993.

34. John Sharp, "Land Legacy," *Fiscal Notes*, May 1996, 11.

35. Hardman, *Fire in a Hole*, 29.

36. Ibid., 29, 30-31. The vaunted legendary Texas Rangers were riding the iron horse to battle. Some six years prior to this event, a paean to the Rangers had declared: "Underneath his rough exterior, the Ranger hides a heart as simple and guileless as a child's and a soul whose tenderest chords are instantly touched by human misery or woe. He will share his only dollar with a man in want, and throw his last biscuit to a hungry dog. He will tackle a bunch of rustlers single-handed. He never saw the inside of a college, but he has been the advance courier of civilization, and has made life and property safe in Texas. He returns to citizens their stolen horses and cattle, brings to justice the man who robs them on the highway and guards their homes day and night." Alexander Edwin Sweet, "Texas Siftings—September 1882," *Fort Worth Star-Telegram*, 3 October 1993.

37. Hardman, *Fire in a Hole*, 31.

38. Ibid., 32.

39. Obituaries, *New York Times*, 22 July 1899.

40. Hardman, *Fire in a Hole*, 32.

Courtesy Robert Peet.

41. R. D. Hunter, *First Annual Report* (Texas & Pacific Coal Company, 1890), 3.

42. Hardman, *Fire in a Hole,* 33, 34.

43. Studdard, *Life of Texas Pacific,* 74-75.

44. Hunter, *First Annual Report,* 4.

45. Hardman, *Fire in a Hole,* 100-101.

46. Leon Hale, "Texas Chronicles," *Fort Worth Star-Telegram,* 10 October 1993.

47. Hardman, *Fire in a Hole,* 101, 103-104.

48. Ibid., 95, 97.

49. Captain B. B. Paddock, ed., *Fort Worth and the Texas Northwest,* vol. 1 (Chicago and New York: The Lewiston Publishing Company, 1922), 155-156.

50. Hardman, *Fire in a Hole,* 19.

51. Hunter, *First Annual Report,* 5

52. McLean, *Ayr to Thurber,* 39. Robert E. Beckham was Mayor of Fort Worth in 1878-1879. He was later Judge of the 17th district court, the first district court for Tarrant County. He was Judge of the court from its creation in 1884 until 1892.

53. Ibid., 40.

54. Hardman, *Fire in a Hole,* 116.

55. Ibid., 105-106.

56. McLean, *Ayr to Thurber,* 40. Ye Arlington Inn and Lake Como created by H. B. Chamberlain as attractions to his development of Arlington Heights, had a short but renowned existence. The Inn is described as a luxurious and pretentious hotel, a winter-resort commanding a splendid view of the Trinity Valley, which won recommendation "stars" of national vacation guidebooks. It stood at the northwest corner of the intersection of present day Crestline Road and Merrick Street. In 1893, just months after the Phelan-Hunter wedding, the popular four-year-old Ye Arlington Inn was destroyed by fire.

57. Contrasted to the 400th anniversary, the 500th in 1992 was barely observed. There had been expectations that the quincentennial would produce mammoth observances. Instead, it became a non-event.

58. Spoede, "W. W. Johnson," 85.

59. Dr. Robert T. Maberry, Sr., "A Time To Be Born And A Time To Die," *Fort Worth Star-Telegram,* 4 March 1990. In the 1890s only about half of Americans lived to be 65, largely because so many of the young died of diseases that are now curable or eradicated.

60. Hardman, *Fire in a Hole,* 35-38.

61. Ibid., 38-39.

62. Ibid., 38-40.

63. Ibid., 104.

64. Thomas R. Hall, *Twenty-Fifth Anniversary Souvenir,* 30 July 1913; reprinted in Studdard, *Life of Texas Pacific,* 40.

65. McLean, *Ayr to Thurber,* 39.

66. Hardman, *Fire in a Hole,* 108, 110 and Studdard, *Life of Texas Pacific,* 105.

67. Harmon Greene, letter to author, 1 December 1992.

68. Captain B. B. Paddock, ed., *Fort Worth and the Texas Northwest,* vol. 2 (Chicago and New York: The Lewiston Publishing Company, 1922), 555.

69. George Carter in his memoirs of Thurber, published in *The Palo Pinto County Star* in 1966; reprinted in Hardman, *Fire in a Hole,* 106.

70. Hardman, Ibid., 107, 109, 119.

71. Bryan's vice-presidential running mate was Adlai E. Stevenson, who had been vice-president under Grover Cleveland. Stevenson was the grandfather of Adlai E. Stevenson, twice defeated for the Presidency by General Dwight D. Eisenhower.

72. Hardman, *Fire in a Hole,* 28, 67.

73. W. K. Gordon, *Twenty-Fifth Anniversary Report,* 4 July 1913; reprinted in Studdard, *Life of Texas Pacific,* 25.

74. Reprinted in Hardman, *Fire in a Hole,* 72-77.

75. Ibid., 77.

76. Gordon, *Twenty-Fifth Anniversary Report,* 25.

77. W. K. Gordon, Jr., interview by author, 5 January 1993.

78. Dr. Fred C. Rehfeldt, address to Palo Pinto Heritage Association, 9 May 1991, 2.

79. Hardman, *Fire in a Hole,* 91-92.

80. George Will, "Dynamic Capitalism," *Fort Worth Star-Telegram,* 5 January 1993.

81. Hardman, *Fire in a Hole,* 93.

82. Ibid., 103.

83. Lillie Gibson, interview by author, 17 May 1993.

84. Hunter, *First Annual Report,* 3.

85. Cecil Johnson, *Guts: Legendary Black Rodeo Cowboy Bill Pickett* (Fort Worth: The Summit Group, 1994), 3.

86. McLean, *Ayr to Thurber,* 39.

87. Terry Lee Jones, "Little Lizard, Big Legend," *Fort Worth Star-Telegram,* 9 August 1993.

88. McLean, *Ayr to Thurber,* 38, 42.

89. TP Financial Records for 1900, Special Collections, University of Texas at Arlington Library.

90. Hardman, *Fire in a Hole,* 79.

91. Leo Bielinski, *The Demise of Thurber Cemetery,* April 1994. Thurber Historical Association.

92. Jon McConal, "Nephew's Quest Ends in Thurber Cemetery," *Fort Worth Star-Telegram,* 22 February 1993.

93. Hardman, *Fire in a Hole,* 108-109.

94. McLean, *Ayr to Thurber,* 42.

95. Studdard, *Life of Texas Pacific,* 25.

96. Hardman, *Fire in a Hole,* 91-92.

97. "Tour of Bellefontaine Cemetery," Bellefontaine Cemetery Association.

3: BOYS, YOU NOW OWN THE MINES!

1. Hardman, *Fire in a Hole,* 128.

2. Ibid., 130.

3. Ibid., 127-131.

4. Chissa Gordon, interview by author, 6 November 1994.

5. Harold F. Boss, *How Green the Grazing* (Dallas: Taylor Publishing Company, 1978), 11.

6. Ruth Allen, *History of Organized Labor in Texas,* No. 4143 of *The University of Texas Publication,* 15 November 1941, 94-95. Special Collections, University of Texas at Arlington Library.

7. Hardman, *Fire in a Hole,* 41-45.

8. Ibid., 45.

9. Hulen was born 9 September 1871. He won a Silver Star for gallantry in action in the Filipino Insurrection of 1899. Returning to the U.S., Governor Lanham on June 1, 1902, named him a Brigadier General in the Texas National Guard and appointed him Adjutant General of Texas. In 1916 he served in Mexico during the Pancho Villa trouble. When World War I broke out, he was named commander of Camp Bowie in Fort Worth, home of the 36th Division. The 36th landed in France on May 31, 1918, and saw action in the Argonne Forest until shortly before the Armistice was signed on November 11, 1918. Major General Hulen was awarded the Croix de Guerre twice by the French and the Distinguished Service Medal by the U.S. for his skillful command of the 36th's 72nd Infantry Brigade. In Fort Worth, his home was at 1221 Elizabeth Boulevard. Today a prestigious shopping mall and a busy thoroughfare in Fort Worth bear his name. In Mack Williams, *Old Fort Worth,* 106-107.

10. Hardman, *Fire in a Hole,* 46.

11. Ibid., 47.

12. Leo S. Bielinski, "The 1903 Thurber Coal Miners' Meeting At Rocky Creek Bridge," West Texas Historical Association Year Book 1995 (Hardin-Simmons University, Abilene: Rupert N. Richardson Press), 36-43. Weldon Hardman in *Fire in a Hole* described the bridge as a railroad bridge. Not so, according to Leo Bielinski. There was no railroad nearby. The little bridge over Rocky Creek was part of a county road used by ranchers and oil operators until 1995 when it was replaced by a stronger concrete one. Leo Bielinski, interview by author, 12 April 1996.

13. Hardman, *Fire in a Hole,* 47-48.

14. Reprinted in Ibid., 48-49.

15. Ibid., 49, 50.

16. Ibid., 52. It was common in that era for business executives to have private cars. His need for a private car stemmed from the fact that his home in New York was fifteen hundred miles from Thurber. Hunter never used a private car because he lived either in Thurber or Fort Worth, only seventy-five miles away.

17. Gentry, *Life and Death,* 90-92.

18. Ibid., 94.

19. It is logical to assume that operators George E. Bennett and W. H. Aston and labor leaders William Wardjon, Pete Hanraty, and J. R. Edwards are pictured. But which faces belong to them is unknown. And what about the others? Their identities also remain a mystery. And why was Gordon standing to the side of the room instead of being seated at the table with Marston and Lewis? When I interviewed Chissa Gordon on March 2, 1995, she was probably on target when she offered a pragmatic reason for her father-in-law not being seated at the table: "He did not want to show support for the proceedings by sitting with John L. Lewis." Plausible. After all, had he not at first decreed that he would not even attend the meeting?

20. During a coal mine dispute in 1937, FDR had said to the mine owners and the union leaders: "A plague on both of your houses." In response, Lewis had roundly castigated the president. In a speech on Labor Day 1937, Lewis leveled this volley at Roosevelt: "It ill behooves one who has supped at labor's table and who has been sheltered in labor's house to curse with equal fervor and fine impartiality both labor and its adversaries when they become locked in deadly embrace." Edward R. Murrow and Fred W. Friendly, *I Can Hear It Now.* Columbia Masterworks, Set MM-800, Side Two, 1933-1945.

21. Gentry, *Life and Death,* 96.

22. Hardman, *Fire in a Hole,* 125-126.

23. Hardman, *Fire in a Hole,* 55.

24. Bielinski, *Back Road,* 185-186; and telephone conversation with author, 14 January 1997.

25. McLean, *Ayr to Thurber,* 20, 42.

26. Gordon, *Twenty-Fifth Anniversary Report,* reprinted in Studdard, *Life of Texas Pacific,* 32.

27. Oliver Knight, *Fort Worth: Outpost on the Trinity* (Norman: University of Oklahoma Press, 1953), 168.

28. Minutes of Commissioners Court of Erath County, Texas, vol. H, 353. Special Collections, University of Texas at Arlington Library.

29. Hardman, *Fire in a Hole,* 96, 115.

30. Gordon, *Twenty-Fifth Anniversary Report,* reprinted in Studdard, *Life of Texas Pacific,* 32.

31. Hardman, *Fire in a Hole,* 105.

32. Studdard, *Life of Texas Pacific,* 82.

33. Edgar L. Marston, letter to S. Mims, 29 September 1908, in possession of Billy J. Moore.

34. Gordon, *Twenty-Fifth Anniversary Report,* reprinted in Studdard, *Life of Texas Pacific,* 34.

35. Hardman, *Fire in a Hole,* 103.

36. Gordon, *Twenty-Fifth Anniversary Report,* reprinted in Studdard, *Life of Texas Pacific,* 26.

37. George B. Studdard, interview by author, 23 July 1991.

38. George B. Studdard, letter to author, 4 November 1994.

39. Bill Daniels, interview by author, 28 January 1992. W. E. (Bill) Daniels, in the 1950s became Texas Pacific chief production clerk and remained with the company until his retirement. His father was A. A. Daniels.

40. Studdard, interview by author, 23 July 1991.

41. Gordon, *Twenty-Fifth Anniversary Report,* reprinted in Studdard, *Life of Texas Pacific,* 20.

42. Marston Hall was apparently built in 1911 next to the Opera House. Marston Hall does not appear in the panorama photo of Thurber square taken in December 1910. The report from which the excerpts are taken was datelined Marston Hall and covers the period 1910-1911.

43. Woman's Missionary Council, Methodist Episcopal Church, South, *First Annual Report 1910-1911,* 434-435. Courtesy Jean Traster, librarian, Eunice and James L. West Library at Texas Wesleyan University, Fort Worth.

44. Woman's Missionary Council, Methodist Episcopal Church, South, *Second Annual Report 1911-1912,* 392-393. Courtesy Jean Traster, librarian, Eunice and James L. West Library at Texas Wesleyan University, Fort Worth.

45. Woman's Missionary Council, Methodist Episcopal Church, South, *Third Annual Report 1912-1913,* 204-205. Courtesy Jean Traster, librarian, Eunice and James L. West Library at Texas Wesleyan University, Fort Worth.

46. Woman's Missionary Council, Methodist Episcopal Church, South, *Fourth Annual Report 1913-1914,* 383. Courtesy Jean Traster, librarian, Eunice and James L. West Library at Texas Wesleyan University, Fort Worth.

47. Gordon, *Twenty-Fifth Anniversary Report,* reprinted in Studdard, *Life of Texas Pacific,* 29.

48. Bielinski, *Back Road,* 7.

49. Gentry, *Life and Death,* 167-168.

50. George Will, "How Bad is 'JFK?'" *Fort Worth Star-Telegram,* 16 December 1991.

51. Spoede, "W. W. Johnson," 167.

52. Ibid., 171-172.

4: THERE'S OIL IN THE McCLESKEY!

1. Lola Spearing, interview by author, 25 September 1991.

2. Jon McConal, "Man Unearths Piece of Family's Past," *Fort Worth Star-Telegram,* 4 April 1992.

3. Ruth Sheldon Knowles, *The Greatest Gamblers* (New York: McGraw-Hill Book Company, Inc., 1959), 101.

4. Thomas R. Hall, *Twenty-Fifth Anniversary Souvenir*, reprinted in Studdard, *Life of Texas Pacific*, 46.

5. Texas Pacific Coal and Oil Company, "The Story of Texas Pacific Coal and Oil Company, 1888-1955" (n.p., 1955).

6. W. K. Gordon, letter to Ranger citizens, 8 September 1927. Gordon had enlisted Luther M. Davenport, a trusted Ranger friend, to recruit the young oil field workers who thwarted the unionists.

7. Boyce House, *Were You in Ranger?* (Dallas: Tardy Publishing Company, Inc., 1935), 7.

8. Edgar L. Marston, letter to W. K. Gordon, 27 February 1917.

9. Boyce House, *Roaring Ranger* (San Antonio: The Naylor Company, 1951), 4.

10. "Story of Texas Pacific," 6-7.

11. House, *Were You In Ranger?* 4, 7.

12. Fort Worth Petroleum Club, Historical Committee, *Oil Legends of Fort Worth*, 210. Wagner was born in 1883 in Ben Runs, West Virginia. As a boy, he worked in the oil fields in that area. After Spindletop roared in, the young man came to Texas and began drilling wells himself. He followed the train of discoveries all over Texas. From Spindletop, it was on to Petrolia, Burkburnett, and Wichita Falls where he lived until 1914. He then settled in Strawn. He was 34 years old when Gordon gave him the contract that would make him rich and famous.

13. House, *Were You in Ranger?* 4, 8-9.

14. Cable drilling was similar to an old time butter—churner-up and down, up and down. According to H. Bryan Poff, veteran wildcatter, a six-foot long bit tapered down to form a hatchet-like blade. This bit was raised and lowered to thump and pound its way through hundreds of feet of rock, shale, and sand. When the blade became dull, the bit was withdrawn and heated in a forge until it was red hot. Then a husky "tool dresser" would pummel the blade with a sledgehammer until the edge was once again sharp.

15. House, *Were You in Ranger?* 10.

16. Ibid., 10. There is some dispute over the precise date that the McCleskey roared in. I have seen dates from October 17 to October 27. On June 8, 1996, while attending the annual Thurber reunion, I thumbed through a scrapbook that had belonged to Ted Kolp and found an item from *The Thurber Journal* dated Saturday, October 27, 1917: "The Texas & Pacific Coal Company brought in an oil well on the J. H. McCleskey farm near Ranger *first of the week.*" Thus the discovery must have occurred prior to the 27th. The previous Sunday, the first day of the week, would have been October 21. Thus the well could not have been brought in on October 17. I concur with Boyce House that the discovery most likely occurred on Monday, October 22, 1917.

17. Ibid., 11.

18. Almost 79 years from the day the No. 1 J. H. McCleskey roared in, the Ranger Historical Preservation Society on September 21, 1996, dedicated a 64-foot turn-of-the-century wooden derrick which it had erected atop the actual site of the well.

19. House, *Were You in Ranger?* 12.

20. Ibid., 20. Oscar B. Colquitt was elected Governor in 1910 and 1912. In his 1912 reelection campaign, he toured the State with a large bullwhip in his hands

as a protest against the methods of punishment in the Texas prison system. An expert with the whip, he would crack it with a loud bang and cry: "Would you sustain by your ballots this implement of human torture?" Ross Phares, *The Governors of Texas* (Gretna, La.: Pelican Publishing Company, 1976), 128.

21. House, *Were You in Ranger?* 22.

22. "Story of Texas Pacific," 7.

23. Edgar L. Marston, letter to Central Trust Company, 25 April 1918. No. 368 in Haley Museum, Midland.

24. Mack Williams, *The Golden Goddess: Oil Legends of Fort Worth,* 21. Currently, the Golden Goddess can be found at the Spaghetti Warehouse Restaurant located on the site of the former offices of Swift & Company in the Fort Worth Stockyards.

25. Hardman, *Fire in a Hole,* 103.

26. Ibid., 108.

27. W. K. Gordon, Jr., interview by author, 20 January 1992.

28. Alver A. Simmans, interview by author, 8 February 1993.

29. "Story of Texas Pacific," 7.

30. John Bloom, "Old Oil: The Ranger Revival," *Texas Monthly,* February 1981, 113, 114, 197.

31. Lola Spearing, interview by author, 24 April 1994.

5: PENN FROM PENNSYLVANIA

1. Lon Tinkle, *Mr. De* (Boston, Toronto: Little, Brown and Company, 1970), 48; and Roger M. Olien and Diana D. Olien, *Easy Money: Oil Promoters and Investors in the Jazz Age* (Chapel Hill: University of North Carolina Press, 1990), 26.

2. Ed Brice, "Ford's Car Suited Americans to a T," *Fort Worth Star-Telegram,* 22 July 1996.

3. "Story of Texas Pacific." To prevent oil gluts with their ensuing price plunges, The Texas Railroad Commission has authority to regulate oil production by setting field-wide allowables, thereby prorating the volume a well can produce.

4. John Bloom, "Old Oil: The Ranger Revival," *Texas Monthly,* February 1981, 194; and Don Woodard, "The Landman," *Oil & Gas Journal,* 1957.

5. John Roby Penn, Jr., interview by author, 10 January 1991.

6. Eliot Asinof, *Eight Men Out* (New York: Henry Holt and Company, 1987), xvii.

7. W. K. Gordon, Jr., interview by author, 20 January 1992.

8. "Texas Pacific Official Retires," *Fort Worth Star-Telegram,* 30 August 1968.

9. Studdard, interview by author, 23 July 1991.

10. Raymond Rohlfs, interview by author, 4 December 1992.

11. Dwayne Holden, interview by author, 25 September 1992.

12. Gordon, *Twenty-Fifth Anniversary Report,* 26.

13. Rita Bridges, interview by author, 25 April 1997.

14. Hardman, *Fire in a Hole,* 84.

15. Studdard, interview by author, 23 July 1991.

16. Alver Simmans, interview by author, 28 May 1994.

17. Fort Worth Petroleum Club, *Oil Legends of Fort Worth* (Dallas: Taylor Publishing Company, 1993), 144.

18. Studdard, interview by author, 23 July 1991.

19. Tinkle, *Mr. De,* 28.

20. Hardman, *Fire in a Hole,* 58.

21. Associated Press, "Polio Made Roosevelt Even More Determined," *Fort Worth Star-Telegram,* 4 July 1996.

22. Spoede, "W. W. Johnson," 1, 2.

23. *Moody's Manual of Investments* (New York: Moody's Investors Service, Inc., 1932), 2422; and Studdard, *Life of Texas Pacific,* 119.

24. Ed Stephens, letter to W. K. Gordon, 11 December 1922.

25. Charles E. Yager, interview by author, 19 November 1991. Weather Bureau records show that two days before he was born (February 12, 1899), the thermometer plummeted to a minus 8 degrees Fahrenheit in Fort Worth-Dallas, the coldest temperature ever recorded in the metroplex.

26. *Abilene High School Year Book,* 1917.

27. The Wynnewood refinery produced gasoline, motor oils, and greases. In addition, because the crude oil that fed the refinery had a high asphalt base, the plant's output was also used in paving and roofing materials.

28. Gill: a quarter pint. Yager, interview by author, 19 November 1991.

29. Charles E. Yager, interview by author, 19 November 1991; *Yager Daily News,* August 3, 1923, parody tabloid sent to Gilcy Rennie by Charles E. Yager, Jr.

30. Mary Rogers, "Coffee Shop Talk," *Fort Worth Star-Telegram,* 22 June 1992.

31. Asinof, *Eight Men Out,* 5, 173.

32. Studdard, *Life of Texas Pacific,* 107.

33. Ibid., 107.

34. Knowles, *Greatest Gamblers,* 211.

35. Mrs. W. K. Gordon, Jr., interview by author, 23 April 1994.

36. The board consisted of Edgar L. Marston as Chairman, A. G. Milbank, E. C. Converse, J. C. Baldwin, Jr., E. J. Marston, all of New York; E. S. Britton, Mart Williams, W. K. Gordon and S. Mims of Thurber; and R. H. Stewart of Dallas. *Moody's Manual of Investments* (New York: Moody's Investors Service, Inc., 1919), 1886.

37. Studdard, *Life of Texas Pacific,* 74-75.

38. Kathryn Stell, interview by author, 28 December 1992.

39. Petroleum Club, *Oil Legends,* 117.

40. Jon McConal, "180-proof Tales of Prohibition," *Fort Worth Star-Telegram,* 19 January 1991.

41. Studdard, interview by author, 23 July 1991.

42. Ibid.

43. Ibid. It is amusing that Studdard would have referred to the bandleader, who was still "a one-two-threeing it" in 1991, as "Old Lawrence." Both Welk and Studdard were born in 1903, Lawrence on March 11 and George on August 1, so "Old Lawrence" was only about six months older than "Young George."

44. Lawrence Welk with Bernice McGeehan, *Wunnerful, Wunnerful!* (Santa Monica, Calif.: The Welk Group, Inc., 1971), 67-68.

45. Studdard, *Life of Texas Pacific,* 20. This tract, according to Charles E. Yager, Jr., had been bought by W. K. Gordon not for oil but in order to provide timbers to be used in the Thurber mines. That the tract was bought for timber was corroborated by Gordon himself in the chapter which he wrote in 1913 for the *Twenty-Fifth Anniversary Souvenir* booklet. He said the tract was 1,965 acres of timber land.

46. Studdard, interview by author, 23 July 1991.

47. "Texas Pacific to Open Diamond Hill Refinery," *Fort Worth Press,* 30 April 1926; Central Fort Worth Library at the Federal Writers Microfiche 6233.

48. Hamilton Rogers, interview by author, 19 August 1992. Hamilton Rogers came to TP as a Vice-President with the Rowan Oil Company acquisition in 1958. Prior to the Seagram sale, he left TP to become Board Chairman of Champlin Petroleum Company.

49. Studdard, *Life of Texas Pacific,* 58.

50. John S. Spratt, Sr., *Thurber, Texas: The Life and Death of a Company Coal Town* (Austin: University of Texas Press, 1986), 124-125.

51. Spearing, interview by author, 25 September 1991.

52. W. K. Gordon, speech to Ranger citizens, 21 October 1927.

6: FROM STAR DUST TO A NEW DEAL

1. Mack H. and Madeline C. Williams, *In Old Fort Worth,* 122. A collection of stories published in *The Fort Worth News-Tribune* in 1976 and 1977.

2. House, *Roaring Ranger,* 34-37. See also A. C. Greene's account of this event in *A Personal Country* (College Station: Texas A&M University Press, 1979), 68-69.

3. Studdard, *Life of Texas Pacific,* 101.

4. John Margolies, *Pump and Circumstance* (Boston: Little, Brown and Company, 1993), 6-10.

5. Terry Lee Jones, "Little Lizard, Big Legend," *Fort Worth Star-Telegram,* 9 August 1993; and Maybelle Trout, "Eastland to Honor Old Rip," *Fort Worth Star-Telegram,* 25 February 1995.

6. "Texas Pacific to Host Visiting Aviators," *Fort Worth Press,* 4 July 1928.

7. "Air-Rail Line Planned from Chicago," *Fort Worth Press,* 20 August 1928.

8. "Association Makes Large Gains in 1928," *Fort Worth Press,* 31 December 1928.

9. "Oil Company Backs Aviators," *Fort Worth Star-Telegram,* 26 May 1929, sec. 2, 2.

10. Lee Barnes, interview by author, 5 April 1997.

11. Robert C. Marston, interview by author, 13 March 1997.

12. David H. Poindexter, interview by author, 7 April 1997.

13. "Fuel Free as Long as Ship is Up," *Fort Worth Star-Telegram,* 26 May 1929, sec. 2, 2.

14. "Tribute Paid Robbins and Kelly at Banquet," *Fort Worth Star-Telegram,* 2 June 1929, 1.

15. Studdard, *Life of Texas Pacific,* 104.

16. Pat Woods, letter to author, 1 October 1991.

17. Studdard, *Life of Texas Pacific,* 47, 88.

18. Hardman, *Fire in a Hole,* 84.

19. "Association Makes Large Gains in 1928," *Fort Worth Press,* 31 December 1928.

20. Frank Burkett, letter to editor, *Fort Worth Star-Telegram,* 22 August 1992.

21. Studdard, letter to author, 4 November 1994.

22. Simmans, interview by author, 28 May 1994. Marston and his family lived in an impressive home at 3624 Camp Bowie Boulevard. It was located on a triangle

where Clarke angles into Camp Bowie. In 1993 Federal Judge David O. Belew, Jr., who grew up nearby at 3904 Clarke, commented that the home commanded an imposing view of the downtown skyline, similar to that today from the Amon Carter Museum of Western Art. Marston was usually driven from his home to his office by his chauffeur. Both he and Penn always had chauffeurs.

23. Studdard, *Life of Texas Pacific,* 90.

24. Yager, interview by author, 19 November 1991.

25. Billy J. Moore, interview by author, 17 December 1993.

26. "Texas Pacific Sale in East Texas Reported," *Fort Worth Star-Telegram,* 24 February 1932. Locating this company-saving tract in East Texas had been like trying to find the proverbial needle in the haystack. Many had talked about or alluded to it. This included W. K. Gordon, Charley Yager, Erle Mitchell, Babe Fuqua, George Studdard, and Billy Moore. Strangely, none had ever pinpointed its location or even given the correct name of the county. Then on March 4, 1997, I was in the Fort Worth Central Library poring over microfilm of the *Fort Worth Star-Telegram* for the year 1932 when I discovered this article.

27. *Moody's Manual of Investments* (New York: Moody's Investors Service, Inc., 1933), 2891.

28. Dave Kansas, "Peaks and Valleys," *Wall Street Journal,* reprinted in *Fort Worth Star-Telegram,* 29 May 1996. Margin refers to funds that a speculator deposits with his broker to protect the broker against loss. The deposit safeguards the broker in case the speculator loses money after he has bought stocks. It must cover the difference between the selling price of the stocks and the amount the broker can borrow from a bank, plus an amount to cover possible losses that might result from a drop in prices. The Federal Reserve sets the amount of margin required.

29. Robert C. Marston, letter to author, 6 April 1993.

30. Robert C. Marston, letter to author, 12 March 1996. At least one footprint remains. Along with J. R. Penn's, Edgar J. Marston's name is emblazoned on a honor roll heralding those members who, in 1926, purchased Second Mortgage Bonds of the Fort Worth Club. The bronze plaque hangs on the club's eleventh floor.

31. "Story of Texas Pacific," 11.

32. Tinkle, *Mr. De,* 201.

33. James A. Farley, *Jim Farley's Story: The Roosevelt Years* (New York, Toronto: Whittlesey House, McGraw-Hill Book Company, 1948), 26.

34. "Two Burned to Death in Refinery Explosion," *Fort Worth Star-Telegram,* 13 September 1932, 1.

7: I HAVE RETURNED

1. John D. Hicks and George E. Mowry, *A Short History of American Democracy* (Cambridge, Mass.: The Riverside Press, 1956), 736.

2. J. D. Rutherford played no part in the robbery but was killed in attempting to help his brother collect his part of the $72,000.

3. Blair Justice, "20-Year Old Stevens Case Remains Vivid in Memories," *Fort Worth Star-Telegram,* 22 February 1953.

4. Yager, interview by author, 19 November 1991.

5. Studdard, interview by author, 23 July 1991.

6. Pat Woods, letter to author, 1 October 1991.

7. "Story of Texas Pacific," 8.

8. Henry Boykin, letter to author, 28 December 1993; and Henry Boykin, interview by author, 10 January 1994.

9. Pat Woods, letter to author, 1 October 1994.

10. Studdard, *Life of the Texas Pacific*, 54.

11. Gordon W. Prange, *At Dawn We Slept* (New York: Penguin Books, 1981), 4, 5.

12. Hardman, *Fire in a Hole*, 84.

13. The by-laws were amended in 1934 to provide that future annual meetings would continue to be held on the third Wednesday of April but in Fort Worth.

14. Katherine Stell, interview by author, 28 December 1992.

15. David O. Belew, interview by author, 14 April 1993. O. E. (Erle) Mitchell had been one of the Thurber Old Guard. He had transferred into Fort Worth in 1929.

Federal Judge David O. Belew, who married O. E. Mitchell's daughter, Margie, recalled a vignette about his father-in-law when Mitchell worked in Thurber:

> One night when Mitchell lived at Mingus, just up the road from Thurber, he heard a noise in the backyard. Thinking that his hen house was being visited by a fox or some other critter, he sprang from his bed and grabbed his shotgun. Clad only in his drawers, the back flap of which was hanging down, he headed for the yard. Slowly and stealthily in the dark, he approached the hen house, gun barrel level and his finger on the trigger. About that time his dog, following behind, nuzzled Mitchell's hindermost with his cold nose. Startled, Mitchell fired off his shotgun and killed several of his chickens!
>
> Mitchell, born in 1889, was a gentle soul, quiet and introspective. I fondly remember that he and I shared February 16 as our birthdays. One day in 1955, he came to my office in the Land Department and sat across the desk from me to advise that the company was giving me a stock option. My last memory of Mr. Mitchell was when he died on August 11, 1958. Jess Norman, Corporate Secretary, arranged for an all-night honor vigil at his casket in the funeral home. My watch was from 2 until 4 on the morning of August 12, 1958.

16. Erle Mitchell, undated memorandum.

17. Jay Robert Nash, *Blood Letters and Bad Men* (New York: M. Evans Company, Inc., 1973), 45.

18. Aubrey Morgan became a prominent Fort Worth dentist, practicing as Dr. Douglas Morgan. Douglas Morgan, interview by author, 3 August 1996.

19. *Moody's Manual of Investments* (New York: Moody's Investors Service, Inc., 1936), 2519-2520.

20. "Retired Oil Adviser, C. H. Osmond, Dies," *Fort Worth Star-Telegram,* 27 January 1973. Osmond used to visit me occasionally in the Land Department in the 1950s. I remember him as being of average height with sandy hair and blue eyes and as being most affable and genial.

21. W. B. (Bill) Harris, interview by author, 27 April 1992. Sixty years later, Harris still treasured his Penn pencil extender.

22. Pat Woods, interview by author, 12 April 1995.

23. Billy J. Moore, interview by author, 11 December 1992.

24. Henry Boykin, letter to author, 28 December 1993.

25. McLean, *Ayr to Thurber,* 20.

26. John Roby Penn, Jr., interview by author, 24 September 1992.

27. Henry Boykin, letter to author, 28 December 1993.

28. McLean, *Ayr to Thurber,* 37-39.

Robert Henry Ward, an attorney of Washington, D.C., his wife, Mary Joseph Warfield, and their two young sons, the oldest four years of age, left Washington for Thurber in 1889. Mr. Ward was Assistant General Manager and house counsel of Texas & Pacific Coal Company.

Sometime after 1889, Mr. and Mrs. Ward were joined by her mother, Josephine Lawrence Warfield, widow of Marcellus Warfield, and Mrs. Ward's sister, Ella Lawrence Warfield, an attractive single woman. Ella lived with her mother in a Thurber house identified in the thesis of Willie M. Floyd by photograph and accompanying notation as "Home of Mrs. Warfield." This home was built before 1900. It is definite there were two mature ladies in Thurber with the surname of Warfield and a third of that maiden name. It is also certain they were well known in the Thurber community, for Mr. Ward was a company official. Mrs. Warfield's house was known as the "Warfield Home," and when Mine No. 9 was completed in 1899, it was named "Warfield," reportedly, if puzzlingly, not in honor of either of the two women bearing the surname but instead, of Mrs. Robert H. Ward.

Tracing the Wallis Warfield family history shows that Wallis Warfield was born June 19, 1896, and was related to the Thurber Warfields as a fourth cousin twice removed. That remote link, however, sparked the legend of Wallis Warfield Simpson that began with the abdication and was embellished all down the line. In the 1950s when the Duke and Duchess of Windsor were on a holiday visit to Texas and Mexico, *Dallas Morning News* columnist Frank X. Tolbert furthered the legend based on accounts of Thurber old-timers. Tolbert wrote again on December 23, 1964, as did other Texas newspapers, upon the occasion of the Duke of Windsor's heart surgery in Houston. "Summarized from those news sources," wrote Hunter McLean, "are the following impressions of Thurber's early residents. 'She was a young girl . . . was a playmate of mine when we were both around 14 . . . Col. Robert Dickie Hunter was Wallis Warfield's grandfather . . . Col. Hunter called her "Wildcat" . . . she lived both at the Colonel's house on New York Hill or at his cottage on Thurber Lake . . . we all loved her for she was a curiosity to us, would sleep in a tree all night, would strike dramatic poses while in a boat on Lake Thurber. . . was a beautiful, high-spirited "teen-ager" . . . was 16 when last seen in Thurber. . . .'"

An examination of the Robert Hunter and Wallis Warfield family trees does not show any connection. The Wards and Warfields left Thurber in 1899 so if Wallis did visit her distant relatives, she would have been at the most three years old. If she had visited the Hunters it would have had to have been prior to 1902 when he died. Furthermore, Hunter never owned a home on New York Hill. Homes were not built there until 1918. So "Who, then, was the mysterious girl the old-timers remember so well? Using the ages of 14-16 years as an indication, she, in the mid-1890s, could have been, Anita Hunter [William Hunter's daughter], niece of Col. Hunter, or after that, either of his two granddaughters, Jennifer Marston or Janet W. Phelan."

Two books by J. D. Warfield, *The Warfields of Maryland* and *Founders of Anne Arundel and Howard Counties, Maryland,* detail the genealogy and family histories of Wallis Warfield, and also the two Warfield descendants of Thurber, Mary Joseph Warfield Ward and Ella Lawrence Warfield. These sources establish the two

Warfield women in Thurber to have been fourth cousins twice removed of Wallis Warfield. These sources also show Mary Joseph Warfield Ward and R. H. Ward to have been identified with Washington, D.C., from as early as 1876 until leaving in 1889 for Thurber. The Wards then resided in Thurber, along with the Warfield mother and sister, until 1899, when Mary Joseph Warfield Ward is identified in an El Paso deed as a resident of Dallas County. The whereabouts of Mr. Ward, Ella Warfield, and Mrs. Warfield in 1899 and after have not been determined, though it is believed they also departed Thurber about that time.

Wallis Warfield was born June 19, 1896. It seems illogical that the remote cousins in distant Thurber would have known of the birth of Wallis Warfield, much less have occasion to host the infant in Thurber before their departure from Thurber three years later . . . .

Willie M. Floyd, in her master's thesis dated June 1939, reports that she wrote to the Duchess of Windsor in Badgastine, Austria, asking for confirmation of the stories of a visit to Thurber. The Duchess responded with denials.

Anita Hunter McLean was the mother of Hunter McLean.

29. Robert H. Johnson, letter to author, 1 April 1994.

30. Dave Hall, "Dynamite Topples Once-Proud Tower in Thurber Ghost Town," *Fort Worth Press*, 30 March 1937. Special Collections, University of Texas at Arlington Library.

31. John B. Garrett, letter to author, 18 January 1994.

32. Hardman, *Fire in a Hole*, 136-137.

33. Frank X. Tolbert, "Some Claim Thurber has an Operatic Ghost," *The Dallas Morning News*, 15 May 1983. The Opera House, built in 1896, was of frame construction. Frank X. Tolbert was incorrect in stating that the Opera House was built of brick. The brick plant was not built until 1897. There were no bricks in 1896.

34. Gordon Ramsey, interview by author, 17 August 1992.

35. Bud Kennedy, "At 38, Life Includes Quick Trip Through Warped Looking Glass," *Fort Worth Star-Telegram*, 27 March 1993.

36. In October 1994, Elk Castle was sold to George Privett of Dallas and Doug Bratton of Fort Worth and the name changed to Greystone Castle.

8: WAR AND PEACE

1. Mary Wynn Wayman, "Coming Up Rose's," *Fort Worth Star-Telegram*, 18 July 1996.

2. "John Hancock Dies at Home," *Fort Worth Star-Telegram*, 23 January 1939.

3. Pat Woods, letter to author, 1 October 1991.

4. Winston S. Churchill, *Their Finest Hour* (Boston: Houghton Mifflin Company, 1949), 118.

5. Hardman, *Fire in a Hole*, 84.

6. Gordon W. Prange, *At Dawn We Slept* (New York: Penguin Books, 1981), 491-502.

7. Henry Steele Commager, ed., *Documents of American History* (Englewood Cliffs, N. J.: Prentice Hall, 1973), 453.

8. Omar N. Bradley, *Bradley: A Soldier's Story* (New York: Henry Holt and Company, 1951), 402.

9. *Moody's Manual of Investments* (New York: Moody's Investors Service, Inc., 1946), 872.

10. Dwight D. Eisenhower, *Crusade in Europe* (Garden City, N.Y.: Doubleday & Company, Inc. 1948), 290, 308-309.

11. At the time of Presidential transition, I was a Yeoman aboard the Attack Transport USS *Bowie* APA-137. The *Bowie* had been participating in practice landings on the island of Maui, preparatory to the bloody storming of the beaches of Japan. On April 12, the *Bowie* was in Pearl Harbor and I had gone on liberty, riding the little train–crammed with white-uniformed sailors–that ran from Pearl into downtown Honolulu. At the depot we were greeted by newsboys hawking the *Honolulu Star Bulletin* with humongous headlines: ROOSEVELT DEAD!

12. Oil scouts work closely with landmen and geologists. Their job is to visit all wells being drilled in a designated area, ascertaining depths reached and collecting sample cuttings. Once a week the scouts meet together in a "scout check" to exchange information and bagged and tagged cuttings from wells in their district. This data is then delivered to their company officials for study.

13. Billy J. Moore, interview by author, 5 February 1996 and 28 December 1993.

14. Roger Campbell, "Memories Stir of Texas City Fire," *Fort Worth Star-Telegram,* 25 October 1989.

15. Through-put-potential: the volume which can be run through a refinery or plant in a day.

16. *Moody's Manual of Investments* (New York: Moody's Investors Service, Inc., 1934), 2731.

17. Ibid., (1936), 2519.

18. Ibid., (1947), 1577.

19. Ibid., (1948), 1854.

20. "Story of Texas Pacific," 7.

9: BABE

1. Robert F. Windfohr, letter to J. Roby Penn, 8 October 1948. In files of Don Woodard.

2. J. T. Snyder was a member of the Wall Street firm of Ingalls & Snyder.

3. Robert F. Windfohr, letter to J. Roby Penn, 27 October 1948. In files of Don Woodard.

4. Robert A. Caro, *The Years of Lyndon Johnson: Means of Ascent* (New York: Alfred A. Knopf, 1990), 317.

The event came to a head on September 14 at the State Democratic Convention at Will Rogers Auditorium in Fort Worth. The delegates were concerned with one overriding issue: Certifying which name would appear on the November ballot: Stevenson or Johnson. The convention was called to order by Chairman Robert W. Calvert who had secretly agreed in a Blackstone Hotel meeting with Johnson lieutenants the night before that he would recognize Democratic National Committeeman Byron Skelton, a Johnson loyalist, for a fiery speech and a motion to exclude the conservative delegations from Houston, Dallas, and Fort Worth for refusing to take a pledge to vote for Harry Truman in November. Skelton's rousing words to the delegates: "Take the surgeon's knife and cut this cancer from the Democratic body of Texas!"

Arch Rowan of Fort Worth, president of Rowan Oil Company and intimate friend of Babe Fuqua and Neville Penrose, rushed to the stage to defend the faith and informed the delegates that he was one of the conservatives that Skelton was denigrating. Skelton's speech touched a chord with the rural delegations and his motion carried the day. The big conservative city delegations from Harris, Dallas, and Tarrant Counties were ejected from the convention and contesting liberal delegations seated in their stead. When the Fort Worth delegates left, they took the convention's equipment, furniture, and adding machines with them. My picture appeared on page 1 of the next day's *Dallas Morning News* showing myself and delegate Worley Jones carrying out a table. I later stood side by side with Speaker Sam Rayburn in the men's room and informed the great man that I worked for Neville Penrose. His blurted response to me: "What did Neville take that furniture out for?" Penrose's defense forever after was that as the host committeeman, he had organized the convention and when he could find no one who would agree to be responsible for all the rented equipment, he issued orders for it to leave with the conservatives. The conservatives gone, the liberal loyalists did what they came to do by certifying with a shout of acclamation the winner of the senate race: Lyndon B. Johnson.

5. Windfohr assuredly had his finger on the pulse, for Lang Wharton died less than two months later on January 9, 1949.

6. Robert F. Windfohr, letter to H. B. Fuqua, 12 November 1948. In files of Don Woodard.

7. The hexagonal or square kelly, a hollow steel tube about 40 feet long set in the rotary table, screws into the drill stem. Driven by a diesel engine, the rotary table then turns the drill string.

8. Circulate: to pump up the cuttings from the bottom of the hole. Cuttings would move from the bottom at the rate of approximately 100 feet a minute.

9. Bill Gupton, letter to author, 21 October 1992.

10. Resolution adopted by Board of Directors, Texas Pacific Coal and Oil Company, 23 March 1949. Copy in files of Don Woodard.

11. Resolution adopted by Board of Directors, Southwestern Life Insurance Company, 12 July 1949. Copy in files of Don Woodard.

12. Minutes of Special Meeting of the Board of Directors of Texas Pacific Coal and Oil Company, held at Fort Worth, Texas, 16 May 1949. In files of Don Woodard.

13. Ibid.

14. Robert F. Windfohr, letter to Warren Scarborough, 22 April 1949. In files of Don Woodard.

15. J. R. Penn, letter to H. B. Fuqua, 6 July 1949. In files of Don Woodard.

16. Robert F. Windfohr, note to H. B. Fuqua, 22 April 1949.

17. H. B. Fuqua, letter to R. E. Harding, 2 August 1949. In files of Don Woodard.

18. R. E. Harding, letter to H. B. Fuqua, 3 August 1949. In files of Don Woodard.

19. J. Roby Penn, letter to H. B. Fuqua, 9 August 1949. In files of Don Woodard.

20. Myrt Vititow, interview by author, 15 April 1997.

21. H. B. Fuqua, letter to Permian Basin Petroleum Museum, 10 June 1985. Copy in files of Don Woodard. The sale of the East Texas property actually occurred in 1932 while Penn was Chairman of the Executive Committee.

22. H. B. Fuqua, letter to J. Roby Penn, 23 September 1949. In files of Don Woodard. This was the same Texas Hotel where 14 years later President John F.

Kennedy would spend his last night prior to his departure to Dallas and his rendezvous with destiny.

23. H. B. Fuqua, letter to J. Roby Penn, 30 September 1949. In files of Don Woodard.

24. Yager, interview by author, 19 November 1991.

25. Former Tarrant County Legislator, County Judge, and Treasurer Howard Green recollected in 1993 that Fuqua told him in about 1970 that he was responsible for the smokestack having been granted historical status protection. Howard Green, interview by author, 21 August 1993.

26. Empire Fuel & Oil Company later became Cities Service.

27. Pat Woods, interview by author, 1 June 1993.

28. In 1946 Winston Churchill made his famous "Iron Curtain" speech at Westminster College in Fulton, Missouri.

29. Pat Woods, interview by author, 1 June 1993.

30. "They Call Him Babe," *Energy Center: A Newsletter for Friends, Colleagues, and Industry.* Vol. 1, No. 1. April 1983. University of Oklahoma.

31. Edd Riddle, "Honorary Member," *AAPG Round Table Magazine,* September 1983.

32. Ernest Closuit, Jr., letter to author, 13 June 1996.

33. Riddle, *AAPG Round Table,* September 1983.

34. Ibid.

35. Irvin Farman, "The Last of 'The Seventh Street Gang' Bids City Farewell," *Fort Worth News-Tribune,* 6 January 1989.

36. The Fort Worth National Bank Building became Continental Life Building after the bank moved across West Seventh Street in 1952. Bryan Poff, interview by author, 23 March 1992.

37. Leroy Menzing, interview by author, 6 February 1996.

38. Nolan Hirsch, letter to author, 13 February 1997, Railroad Commission of Texas Records.

39. Perry R. Bass, letter to author, 21 January 1993.

40. Perry R. Bass, interview by author, 22 December 1992.

41. Joe Bell, interview by author, 25 July 1994. The last time I saw Governor Jester was on September 27, 1948. At four o'clock that morning, I drove to Penrose's Westover Hills mansion and picked up his ten-year-old daughter Patricia to take her to Hillsboro. President Harry S. Truman's campaign train was scheduled to make a stop in that town some ninety miles south of Fort Worth. Penrose wanted Patricia to shake hands with the President, and he felt that would not be possible when the train got to Fort Worth later in the day because of a much larger crowd. The train arrived at 10 A.M. A navy blue curtain opened on the rear car and out stepped the silver-haired President of the United States. Patricia mounted the steps of the car and Governor Jester introduced her to Truman. Patricia is today the wife of CBS Anchorman Bob Schieffer.

42. Pat Woods, interview by author, 7 January 1994.

43. Leroy Menzing, interview by author, 15 July 1994.

44. Minutes of Board of Directors Meeting, Texas Pacific Coal and Oil Company, 27 February 1952.

45. H. B. Fuqua, letter to J. Roby Penn, 1 August 1952.

46. In the four years I had worked for Penrose, oil had gotten into my blood. But so had politics. Accordingly, on February 1, 1952, I resigned from the Penrose organization to run for the Texas legislature. Not long after my announcement appeared in the papers, deciding that I could not afford to serve in the legislature for $10 a day, I accepted TP's offer of $375 a month.

47. H. B. Fuqua, letter to J. Roby Penn, 1 August 1952.

48. Myrt Vititow, interview by author, 15 April 1997.

While politics in Fort Worth were proceeding at ground level, TP pilot Myrt Vititow was seeing politics in the skies. He and Tommy Tomlinson flew quite a few politicians in those days. Two of the main principals of Texas politics in the 40s and 50s were Governor Allan Shivers and Senator Lyndon B. Johnson. Vititow had an opportunity to study both men:

> In 1952 we flew to Austin to pick up Governor Shivers and Senator Johnson at 3 P.M. and take them to Mineral Wells where they were the featured speakers at an IPAA (Independent Petroleum Association of America) meeting that night at the Baker Hotel. We frequently flew Shivers but Johnson usually was flown by Tenneco. Shivers was friendly, courteous, and thoughtful. He always knew our first names. He would say, "When you boys come down to the capitol, let me know and I will show you around." On this trip, Lyndon was not friendly when he approached the airplane nor when he left the airplane. When he got on the plane, he immediately went to the bar. Apparently, he had had several drinks already. He took a nap on the way and his chair leaned against the cockpit door, sealing it so that we were prevented from opening it and coming back to the cabin to serve refreshments or see if everything was all right. When we landed at 4 P.M., one of us went back and opened the door and let the steps down. Shivers got off and shook our hands, saying, "Thank you for the fine trip." Johnson got off with his nose in the air and walked away without a word. The Governor hollered, 'Lyndon, don't you think you should thank these boys for a fine flight?'"

49. Lawton Gambill, interview by author, 28 September 1991. From that inauspicious beginning, Gambill rose in the Fort Worth bar and upon his retirement in the 1980s was a name partner in the prestigious law firm of Law, Snakard and Gambill.

50. Edd Riddle, letter to author, 2 June 1994.

51. In the 1990s, the camp was still there, pretty much as it had been since its creation—cabins, lodge, Big Lake, and all. It was then owned by Stephenville investors who rented it to the public as a family resort. A color brochure advertised it as "Texas's Best Kept Secret."

52. Yager, interview by author, 19 November 1991.

53. Charles E. Yager, letter to H. B. Fuqua, 21 December 1954.

54. When I began writing this history, I kept telling myself that I should go see Charley Yager. I knew that he would be a veritable gold mine of Texas Pacificana. I greatly admired him in my days at TP. The first day I went to work as a landman for TP—March 11, 1952—he walked into my office and advised me that he had authorized my starting $375 a month salary, and laughed in reflecting that that was a good deal more than he made when he came to TP back in 1922. On November 19, 1991, I called him on impulse. I told him I would like to talk with him

about the TP history I was writing. "Sure, Don, when do you want to come?" The hospitality and friendliness in his voice prompted me to say, "I will come over right now." How fortunate that I did. I drove over to his Monticello-area white stucco Spanish-style home bejeweled by driveway and walks paved with red Thurber brick! He was delighted to recall his years at TP, supplying a great deal of information which only he could. Nine days later–Thanksgiving Day, November 28, 1991—Charles E. Yager, Jr. died. He was cremated and his ashes buried in Greenwood Memorial Park in Fort Worth.

55. "Story of Texas Pacific," 23.

56. Jerry Flemmons, *Amon, The Life of Amon G. Carter of Texas* (Austin: Jenkins Publishing Company, 1978), 500.

57. Charles Ringler, interview by author, 27 May 1994.

58. Most prominent businessmen and civic leaders in those pre-John Tower days were Conservative Democrats.

59. Davey O'Brien had quarterbacked the 1938 TCU Horned Frogs to a 10-0 season and the national championship. He was the first Southwest Conference player to win the Heisman Trophy and went on to become the first team quarterback on the National Football League's 1939 All-Star Team. After a two-year career with the Philadelphia Eagles, O'Brien joined the Federal Bureau of Investigation.

60. Don Looney, interview by author, 20 January 1992. Don Looney, who had played football with O'Brien, first met Fuqua in 1936. A freshman at TCU, Looney attended a party at the Blackstone Hotel that year in honor of the mother of Perry Bass, who was the sister of famed wildcatter Sid Richardson. He recalled: "I was not invited to the party. It was my date, the daughter of a prominent Dallas physician, who was the invitee. The first businessman I met in Fort Worth was at that function. It was Babe Fuqua. He was Mr. Gulf in Fort Worth. The only other important man I knew in Fort Worth at the time was TCU Coach Dutch Meyer. Mr. Fuqua was a wonderful man and a great friend to me for the rest of his life. When it came out in the papers that O'Brien was a candidate for Democratic County Chairman, I asked him why in the world he was doing this. Davey's laconic reply was: "Mr. Fuqua asked me to."

61. Jerry Sherrod, letter to author, 10 June 1993.

> Mr. Fuqua thought I was a graduate of Oklahoma University when actually I was a University of Tulsa graduate. He would call me into his office and say, "Jerry, I understand you are going to West Texas next week." I would reply, "Yes, sir, Mr. Fuqua, I am going west." He would pull out a piece of paper with the name and address of a football prospect. It was usually one of those good football towns like Ranger or Breckenridge. He would say, "Jerry, why don't you stop and tell him about Oklahoma and our football program?" Of course, I was not going to tell him that I was a TU grad because he had always thought that I was a Oklahoma University graduate. I wasn't sure how he would react to the truth. In any case, I would take the name and dutifully stop and visit the young man and his family. Of course, I just visited with them and never mentioned football. When I got back to the office the following Monday, Mr. Fuqua would always call me in and want to know if I called on the boy and what I thought about him. I always said, "Mr. Fuqua, he is a real nice boy and has a nice family."

62. "Story of Texas Pacific," 15.

63. Ibid., 9, 10.

64. Edd Riddle, letter to author, 27 July 1993.

65. How surprised and honored I was when in 1957 Fuqua came into my office in the TP Land Department to extend his congratulations upon my receipt of a degree in English and Humanities from TCU after thirteen years in the Evening College.

66. H. Michael Reese, letter to author, 1 July 1993.

67. Alan Roberts, letter to author, 21 December 1993.

68. Blake Hamman, Jr., interview by author, 14 September 1993. Blake Hamman, Jr., lounging back in his chair, feet on the desk, remembered:

> Babe was like a god to us young landmen in the 1950s when we were starting out in the oil business. He had been there. He knew it. He was well-respected. He was honest. He had integrity. He was frank and fair. And besides that, he was a hell of a fine fellow. But boy, in a few words he would tell you what he thought.

69 Ted Roe, interview by author, 15 June 1994.

70. In Fuqua's early years at TP, his secretary, Pat Woods, would go across the street to the Texas Hotel to purchase panatelas for him. In later years, he quit smoking altogether. Pat Woods, interview by author, 25 June 1996.

71. Alan Roberts, letter to author, 21 December 1993.

72. Petroleum Club, *Oil Legends of Fort Worth* (Dallas: Taylor Publishing Company, 1993), 131.

73. Edd Riddle, interview by author, 4 January 1994.

74. Bill Scales, interview by author, 30 August 1996. Nolan Hirsch's luck would change. In later life, he became a very successful independent producer in West Texas.

75. Nolan Hirsch, interview by author, 6 January 1994.

76. Jerry Sherrod, letter to author, 10 June 1993.

77. Aaron Cawley, interview by author, 8 June 1993.

78. "J. Roby Penn," *Fort Worth Star-Telegram,* Editorial, 11 February 1958.

10: THAT IS A DAMN LIE!

1. *Texas Pacific Coal and Oil Company Annual Report,* 1958

2. Leroy Menzing, "Sinclair Denies Law Violation," *Fort Worth Star-Telegram,* 27 January 1959.

3. Hamilton Rogers, interview by author, 17 August 1991.

4. Leroy Menzing, interview by author, 15 July 1994.

5. Leroy Menzing, "Sinclair Offers to Take TP Stock," *Fort Worth Star-Telegram,* 25 November 1958.

6. Menzing, interview by author, 15 July 1994.

7. Hamilton Rogers, interview by author, 7 May 1992. "Babe called in Gene Adair and asked me to repeat the story. I felt like I was being recorded."

Pat Woods, interview by author, 30 August 1991. He probably was. Pat Woods divulged that Fuqua and Adair kept a tape recorder and recorded all important incoming telephone calls and office visits. Pat's job was to activate the system. The recorder was kept in Bob Dickey's closet which was next to Fuqua's office.

8. Leroy Menzing, "Sinclair Denies Law Violation," *Fort Worth Star-Telegram,* 27 January 1959.

Langdon died in 1987. On his tombstone is inscribed: "Jack Langdon believed in justice most of all, in the right of every person to be free and in the absolute duty of every institution to be fair. He was a man at home wherever he was—humor and wit were his constant companions."

9. Leroy Menzing, "Sinclair Denies Law Violation," *Fort Worth Star-Telegram,* 27 January 1959, and "Sinclair Merger Offer Expires as Texas Pacific Obeys Court," *Fort Worth Star-Telegram,* 29 January 1959.

10. Leroy Menzing, "Sinclair Denies Law Violation," *Fort Worth Star-Telegram,* 27 January 1959.

11. Hamilton Rogers, interview by author, 7 May 1992.

12. "The Story of Texas Pacific," 1959 ed., 12.

13. Wes Yarbro, interview by author, 7 February 1996.

Adair flew his own plane to Austin regularly. Adair had been taught to fly by TP's pilot Myrt Vititow: "I had taught Gene Adair to fly TP's Beech Bonanza and the twin Beech. In 1957 we had flown to Santa Fe in the twin Beech and were returning via Roswell to visit the law firm of Governor Jack Campbell that did a lot of legal work for TP. En route, Adair decided he wanted to fly the twin. I told him that if we got into any problem that he was to take his hands and feet off the controls immediately. Unlike a Bonanza with its tricycle-type landing gear, the twin Beech is a tail dragger. When you land, you lose rudder control and you depend on your brakes. While Adair had no problem landing a Bonanza, he had had no experience with landing a tail-dragging twin Beech. As soon as we hit the ground at Roswell, the plane lurched sideways and I immediately said, 'I have control!' I hit the brakes. The skid marks may still be on that runway. It scared him and he never flew it after that." Myrt Vititow, interview by author, 15 April 1997.

14. Pat Woods, interview by author, 19 October 1994.

15. Petroleum Club, *Oil Legends of Fort Worth,* 188.

16. Wes Yarbro, interview by author, 7 February 1996.

17. Wes Yarbro, letter to author, 8 February 1996.

18. Texas Pacific Coal and Oil Company Proxy Statement, 20 September 1963, 15. Keltner File, Nos. 45-46.

19. Hamilton Rogers, interview by author, 17 August 1991.

20. John Justin, interview by author, 21 March 1994. Two years later Justin was elected Mayor by the City Council.

21. Robert V. Ratts, letter to author, 7 December 1994.

22. Lambuth Tomlinson, interview by author, 5 May 1992.

23. Blakley is the only man to occupy both Texas seats in the U.S. Senate. On January 15, 1957, immediately following Daniel's resignation from the Senate, Allan Shivers, in his last act as Governor, had catapulted the relatively unknown Dallas billionaire rancher and owner of Braniff Airways into the history books by appointing him as an interim Senator. New Governor Daniel promptly set April 2, 1957, as the date of a special election to fill the remaining two years of his Senate term. From the outset, Blakley had announced that he would not be a candidate.

Perennial candidate Yarborough ran and won with 37 percent of the vote in a sudden death election. Conservative Democrat Congressman Martin Dies received 30 percent and Republican Thad Hutcheson received 24 percent. As he retired from the Senate, Blakley addressed his Senate colleagues and Vice-President Richard Nixon: "The duty of this body is to protect the rights and privileges of the people against the possibility of a dictatorship or a totalitarian form of government. I bid you farewell. I will soon go back to my boots and saddle and once more will ride into the western sunset. May God be with you forever."

Two years later in the regular 1958 Senate election, Blakley ran but in a bitter campaign was defeated by Yarborough in the Democratic primary on July 26. The vote was 628,972 to 453,329. The primary win, as usual, was tantamount to election in Democratic Texas, and Republican nominee Roy Whittenburg proved to be no obstacle in November.

After his second appointment to the Senate, Blakley on December 15, 1960, sent an emissary, Jim Blundell, to see me. Blakley wanted me to be his Administrative Assistant in Washington. Being a great admirer of Bill Blakley, I was willing. The next morning I reported Blakley's offer to President Adair. Adair promptly scurried down the long corridor to confer with the Chairman. Both Fuqua and Adair admired Bill Blakley but, nevertheless, they were indebted to Attorney General Wilson, their staunch ally in the yet unsettled Sinclair fight, who had also announced his intention to seek the Senate seat. In their combined wisdom, it would not be seemly for a TP landman to be sitting on Blakley's right hand in the Senate while Will Wilson was also a candidate for the seat. Their decision: "You can go after Blakley is elected."

24. Although Fuqua held a geology degree from the University of Oklahoma, his interest in education was by no means confined to his Alma Mater at Norman. He served on the Texas Christian University Board of Trustees for many years, and was a proponent of the University's acquisition of the Worth Hills Golf Course to allow for new dormitory construction. In May 1973, TCU awarded him an honorary doctorate.

25. Texas Pacific Coal and Oil Company Proxy Statement, 20 September 1963, 15. Keltner File, 45-46.

26. Aaron Cawley, interview by author, 8 June 1993.

27. Chris Callaway, *The Second Generation of Oil Men,* private paper dated 27 January 1994.

28. T. E. McGaugh, interview by author, 24 September 1991.

29. Myrt Vititow, interview by author, 15 April 1997.

30. While both sides were preparing for battle, Arch Rowan suffered a personal tragedy. On August 6, 1962, his thirty-two-year old son, Arch, Jr., was burned critically when a kerosene can exploded in his hands. The accident occurred in the backyard of his ranch-style home west of Fort Worth as he prepared to charcoal steaks. Young Rowan was pouring kerosene from a five-gallon can on the lighted coals of a charcoal burner when flames flashed back in his face and set his clothes afire. He died the next day. Jack Tinsley, "Oil Operator Badly Burned in Explosion," *Fort Worth Star-Telegram,* 7 August 1962.

31. "Funeral Services for Fort Worth Oilman," *Fort Worth Star-Telegram,* 20 January 1975.

I always liked Mr. Arch. I admired and respected him as an oil man par excellence. "I've been an independent oil producer since 1927 and in the drilling business since 1923, working primarily for major oil companies, but never have I lost sight of the fact that independent oil people are a necessary segment of our industry," he once said. His soaring love of country would have made the founding fathers proud. In World War I, he served in the Marine Corps as a regimental sergeant major. He was a presidential elector in 1944 on the Democratic ticket. He was one of the organizers of the States Rights Party in 1948. From 1953 to 1959, he was Vice-Chairman of the Texas Turnpike Authority which built the toll road, now Interstate 30, between Dallas and Fort Worth. He was a longtime student of law pertaining to the oil business, and in 1962 received an honorary doctor of law degree from Bethany College in Bethany, West Virginia. Over coffee at the Petroleum Club, I once boasted to him about a contract I had drawn up covering a TP farmout. I told him it was airtight. The old digger smiled at me and said, "Don, there is no contract a lawyer can write that can hold a son of a bitch if he wants to get out of it."

32. One day at lunch I asked Rogers, "Was there something which developed in those years, a rift between Babe and Arch?" "Yeh," he answered. I responded: "I have heard as much, but I never really knew what happened."

"Well," he answered, "Arch was interested in trying to make a deal for TP, and Babe was in a way, but really bucking against it. But Arch had a contact with Mobil, and Mobil wanted to buy it. And Arch presented it. Babe wouldn't consider it. Gene Adair opposed it. So that deal fell through. And that is where the rift began." Hamilton Rogers, interview by author, 17 August 1991.

33. Ernest Closuit, Jr., letter to author, 13 June 1996. The younger Closuit, always called Buck, spoke of the friendship which existed between his father and Fuqua:

> I met Babe when I was a young boy and my oldest memories are of Babe's big after dinner cigar when Babe and Sarena dined at our home. You could smell the pungent odor the next day. He didn't really smoke it, but used it for the jaunty sport of it, like a walking cane you don't really need.
>
> After college I had several engineering jobs but eventually returned to work with Dad in the business. I reviewed several investments in petroleum and mining from 1965 to 1970 in which he and Babe were participants. Babe and some of his friends supported one of my wildcat prospects in King County, Texas, which resulted in a marginal producer. Babe called such a poor well a "stinker" which meant you didn't know what to do with it—plug it or offset it hoping to hit a winner.

34. Edgar H. Keltner, Jr., interview by author, 8 September 1994.
35. Billy Joe Moore, interview by author, 18 June 1997.
36. Pat Woods, interview by author, 29 April 1994.
37. John Roby Penn, Jr., interview by author, 29 April 1994.

In 1962, many architects considered Park Avenue's Seagram Building, designed by Mies van der Rohe and Philip Johnson, to be the most beautiful building in America. Bronze-sheathed and thrusting out of a fountained plaza, the 38-story Seagram Building cost $36 million, more than twice as much as if it had been constructed to usual standards. The New York City Tax Commission thought it so expensively elegant that it taxed it on the basis about 50% higher than the bleak glass boxes surrounding it. "Cosmetic Architecture–Prestige Value," *Time,* 7 June 1963, 49.

38. John Roby Penn, Jr., interview by author, 29 April 1994.

39. Claude W. Dodgen, Jr., interview by author, 20 September 1991. "Pat Woods, Fuqua's secretary," said Dodgen, "took me and Carrol Bennett back to the Holy of Holies. Babe was standing in the door. We handed him the envelope. Then Carrol and I went to Shady Oaks Country Club for lunch. After the bids were opened and the magnitude of the Seagram production payment was revealed, some of the companies wanted to increase their offer."

40. Hamilton Rogers, interview by author, 17 August 1991.

41. Peter C. Newman, *King of the Castle* (New York: Athenaeum, 1979), 74, 80, 103, 179.

42. Edgar H. Keltner, Jr., interview by author, 10 September 1993.

43. Texas Pacific Coal and Oil Company, letter to shareholders, 20 September 1963. Keltner File, 39.

44. Texas Pacific Coal and Oil Company Proxy Statement, 20 September 1963, 14. Keltner File, No. 45A.

45. Conrad N. Hilton, *Be My Guest* (New York: Prentice Hall, 1987), 250-251, and Irvin Farman, *Tandy's Money Machine* (Chicago: The Mobium Press, 1992), 122.

46. Rogers Gideon, letter to author, 22 April 1996.

47. Agreement of Sale and Purchase, Keltner File, 53.

48. Loan Agreement, Keltner File, 191.

49. Claude W. Dodgen, Jr., interview by author, 20 September 1991.

50. Jerry Sherrod, letter to author, 10 June 1993.

51. Wes Yarbro, interview by author, 25 November 1991. As fate would have it, some time after the TP sale, Fuqua and Yarbro would again find themselves seatmates on board a plane. Both were going to Corpus Christi on personal business. The palpable and electric animus that Yarbro had sensed in the previous months was no longer present: "Babe was most genial and affable," said Yarbro.

52. Edgar H. Keltner, Jr., interview by author, 17 March 1992.

53. Billy Joe Moore, interview by author, 10 June 1997.

54. Edgar H. Keltner, Jr., interview by author, 17 March 1992.

55. Mike Cochran, "Guarding the Oswalds," *Fort Worth Star-Telegram,* 23 November 1993.

56. Ralph Dahlstrom, letter to author, 1 September 1993.

11: THAT AIRPORT WILL BE BUILT!

1. When it became known that the headquarters of the new company would be in Dallas, I resigned effective February 1, 1964, and on November 1 joined Texas Electric Service Company as Assistant to the President. TESCO was the electric utility which served Fort Worth and much of North and West Texas. But I still remembered the oil patch and the Texas Pacific Coal and Oil Company. In December, I wrote a letter to all former TP employees and invited them to a Christmas luncheon at the Petroleum Club. Over 200 attended the dutch affair. Fuqua was one of them. The group voted to make the Christmas party an annual event.

I was elected Chair in 1964 and so acted for several years. In the 1980s Kay Capps, who had been in the Title and Rental Department, became Chair for life. The TP Exes continued to come, with mortality and infirmity taking their inevitable tolls as the years rolled by. At each Christmas party, the lilt and laughter of another familiar voice was heard no more. By 1997 the attendees had dwindled to a mere 25. There was no depletion allowance for TP exes.

2. Bayard Friedman, letter to author, 15 March 1996.

The Exchange Club of Fort Worth honored all three Fort Worth members of the Airport Board at its Golden Deeds banquet on May 5, 1966. Lewis H. Bond, President of the Fort Worth National Bank, elicited a sustained, knowing laugh in his introduction: "Will Rogers once said, 'I never met a man I didn't like' . . . [pause]. Babe Fuqua has—several times. And they know it—but so do those he counts as friends. And this number includes an unusually large proportion of young men. Nothing pleases Babe Fuqua more than helping a young man with advice and opportunity." Dallas/Fort Worth Airport Official Dedication Program, 21.

3. Doug Clarke, interview by author, 22 September 1992.

"After the meeting, my photographer friend had returned to Fort Worth and I was without transportation back to the paper. I told Bob Bain, another *Star-Telegram* reporter that I needed a ride back to Fort Worth. Bain replied that, he, too, needed a ride and said, 'let's ask Bayard Friedman for a lift.' Friedman, former Fort Worth Mayor, said he would gladly give us a ride, but 'Babe's riding with me. Let me ask him.' As can be seen, Mr. Fuqua was deferred to in all things of overwhelming importance. Mr. Fuqua assented, and we had a ride to downtown Fort Worth.

"In telling this story to Jim Vachule, one of the editors at the *Star-Telegram*, he spoke of Mr. Fuqua in near reverential tones and admonished me, 'You never want to get the Babe mad at you.'"

Bayard Friedman echoed Vachule's reverence: "As a young lawyer, I was aware of Mr. Fuqua being one of the leaders of the business community, but I really didn't get to know him until I became a member of the City Council. My mentor, Gene Cagle, was an admirer of his, and I soon learned that he and Marvin Leonard were among a handful of top citizens who supported sound, clean government with no expectation of any favors.

"In time Babe became sort of a father confessor to me. I recall one day at Shady Oaks Country Club when The Man called me to his table. He could see that I was worried. He said, 'Those newsboys have got you down, haven't they?' I admitted that was the case. He observed that I had an option I hadn't considered. When I asked what that was, he said, 'You can keep your mouth shut,' As a 37-year-old mayor, I had never thought about that, but it was good advice.

"On another occasion when I was concerned about some Council matter, I asked him what he would do. 'How many people are on the Council?' he inquired. 'Nine,' I said. 'How many votes can you count on?' 'Five.' 'Bayard, let your opponents talk all they want to. Don't say a word. When they finish, you say, "Vote," and that will be the end of that.'

"Fuqua was fearless to the point of recklessness and honest and frank to a fault. He may have been the only man I have ever known who absolutely didn't care about anyone's opinion of him as long as he remained true to his convictions which he invariably did." Bayard Friedman, letter to author, 16 March 1996.

4. Bayard Friedman, letter to author, 16 March 1996.

5. J. Lee Johnson, III, interview by author, 22 January 1996.

"Babe Fuqua—I always called him Mr. Fuqua—and I were close and good friends. When I was President of the Fort Worth Chamber of Commerce in 1964-65, a lot of important economic decisions were made. Mr. Fuqua and Mr. M. J. Neeley were of tremendous help in these matters. I shared most of Mr. Fuqua's ideas. He was for Fort Worth in the finest sense of citizenship.

"The Fort Worth and Dallas negotiating teams and the airlines had wrapped up our agreement and we were in Dallas for the announcement and signing. There was a delay that afternoon while things were set up for the proceedings. I had made some good friends on the Dallas team, and several of us decided to go to the bar upstairs to have a drink and celebrate. Mr. Fuqua had been tracking my where-abouts for two years and knew my modus operandi. So just as we were served, I was delivered his message to get to the signing immediately. I did that, of course, and Mr. Fuqua said, 'J. Lee, you stay here and don't you dare wander off again.' What a guy!"

6. Julius Karash, "Window to World," *Fort Worth Star-Telegram,* 8 January 1984.

7. Preston Smith, letter to author, 27 May 1997.

12: I HAVE HAD A FEW ENEMIES IN MY TIME

1. Irvin Farman, *The Fort Worth Club: A Centennial Story* (Fort Worth: Motheral Printing Company, 1985), 57.

Farman had been at one time a reporter for the *Star-Telegram* and *News-Tribune* and a Vice-President of the Fort Worth National Bank.

2. Besides liberals there was another element of the body politic to which he was not prepared to hand the reins of government—African-Americans. In the 1950s before the coming to Fort Worth of single member City Council districts, two African-Americans ran for the Council. Enroute to the Texas Hotel, waiting for the light to change at Eighth and Main, Lee Barnes exchanged pleasantries with Fuqua. Barnes asked the Babe what he thought about those candidates. Fuqua's quiet, crisp reply was, "I am not ready for that." They were not elected. Lee Barnes, interview by author, 28 August 1993.

3. Mack Williams, letter to author, 18 April 1993.

4. Lester Strother, interview by author, 18 May 1994.

5. Viola Pitts, letter to author, 25 October 1994.

6. Rosco Minton's brother Sherman Minton served on the U.S. Supreme Court from 1949 to 1956.

7. Gordon Gray, interview by author, 14 May 1996.

8. About the time of his meeting with Preston Smith during the Governor's race in 1968, Fuqua had another visitor, Kenneth W. Davis, Chairman of Mid-Continent Supply Company and an 85-company conglomerate known as Ken-davis Industries International. The purpose of Davis's visit was neither business nor politics. Although only a month older than Fuqua, Davis was worried about his health and concerned about how his corporate empire would fare as a triumvirate under his three sons, Ken, Jr., Cullen, and Bill. He asked Fuqua if he would look out for them. On August 29, 1968, Ken Davis died. Some time in the winter that

followed, the door to Fuqua's suite opened and in walked a young man clad in an expensive-looking black wool overcoat. He smiled at Pat Woods and asked if he could see Mr. Fuqua. The man was Ken Davis's second son, 35-year-old millionaire T. Cullen Davis. Pat promptly escorted him into Fuqua's office. Whether he was there to see Fuqua by invitation or whether he had come on his own is not known, nor did Pat know the subject of their conversation. Regardless, eight years later trouble would beset the rich young man, and he would become infamous, the subject of TV movies and best-selling books. Pat Woods, letter to author, 20 March 1995.

9. Howard Green, interview by author, 21 August 1993.

"I was talking to Mr. Fuqua and I said, 'It is going to be rough seated there on Commissioners Court every Monday with that guy.' Fuqua said, 'Let me tell you something, Green. I have had a few enemies in my time, and I will tell you how to handle them. I will tell you what to do. Don't ever speak to him. You just look right through him and don't speak. You will drive him mad, and he will come around. That is how I handled Arch Rowan.'

"I followed Mr. Fuqua's advice. One day Commissioner-elect Jerry Mebus told me that Richardson asked him who was going to swear him (Mebus) in. Mebus told him that I was because I was County Judge. Skeet replied to Mebus, 'I wish he would swear me in, but he won't even speak to me. Would you ask him, Jerry?'

"Mebus called and asked if I would swear Skeet in. I said, 'I would be delighted to. I will be honored to swear in any member of Commissioners Court.' After Mebus conveyed my attitude to Skeet, he called me and said, 'This thing has gone far enough. If you and I work together, we can do a lot for this county. I would like for you to swear me in.'

"The Fuqua freeze had worked. Skeet just could not stand being ignored. So on January 1, 1971, I swore in both Jerry and Skeet. I must say, however, that the treatment lasted for about only four months. Then Skeet got mad about an appointment and jumped on me again." Using gasoline to ignite tree branches at his Keller home on July 15, 1996, Richardson suffered severe burns to his hand and face. He died on July 28 from complications of the burns.

10. Mike Moncrief, letter to author, 3 September 1993.

11. Sandy Sheehy, *Texas Big Rich* (New York: William Morrow and Company, 1990), 80.

12. Author's personal files.

13. Some time following his retirement from the bank's chairmanship, Fuqua began an aggressive personal investment program concentrating on tax-free municipal bonds. The purchases were handled through Bill W. Lucas, Vice-President of the Fort Worth National Bank and its successors. Years later Lucas recalled: "Mr. Fuqua began to buy municipals from me for his personal account and as Trustee for the Clifford Mooers Estate.

"Through the years he and I discussed bonds of several hundred Texas municipalities. I was amazed at his knowledge of these entities. He was especially fine tuned to those areas where a county, city or school district had significant mineral values in the tax base. He had very firm ideas about the credit worthiness of a given entity." Bill W. Lucas, letter to author, 22 June 1995.

14. Irvin Farman, "The Last of 'The Seventh Street Gang' Bids City Farewell," *Fort Worth News-Tribune,* 6 January 1989.

15. R. M. (Sharky) Stovall, interview by author, 15 November 1991. Stovall was Mayor of Fort Worth 1969-1975.

16. Sterling W. Steves, letter to author, 19 July 1994.

"The reason I ran against Sharky Stovall was that I became aware that he was not a very good representative for the City of Fort Worth. There had been a lot of complaints about his lack of sobriety. I thought Fort Worth needed some new leadership that was not necessarily tied to the Old Guard. Babe said of Sharky at that time, 'You know, Sharky can make a pretty good business deal when he's sober.' That was probably true.

"Mr. Fuqua leaned on some of my close friends, such as Byron Searcy, who was helping me in the campaign. Mr. Fuqua conferred with Byron because they were close friends, both being alumni of Oklahoma University where Byron had been an All American tackle. Byron resisted Mr. Fuqua's efforts to discourage him from supporting me.

"I always had a lot of respect for Babe Fuqua, because he meant well and thought that he was doing right even when he was not. That's a lot better than someone who does wrong and knows he is doing wrong. At least, Mr. Fuqua thought he was doing right for the city."

17. Lew McNiel, interview by author, 6 May 1994.

18. Clif Overcash, interview by author, 12 July 1994.

19. Clif Overcash, interview by author, 12 July 1994; Jim Bradshaw, interview by author, 20 June 1994. The last At-Large election for City Council was in 1975. In 1977 all members with the exception of Mayor were for the first time elected from single-member districts. Overcash was unable to participate in the victory celebration at City Hall on election night. He was in Bad Neustadt, West Germany, to attend the funeral of his mother-in-law.

20. Jim Bradshaw, interview by author, 20 June 1994.

21. Jim Bradshaw, interview by author, 20 June 1994. "In the midst of a jubilant celebration with a few spirited drinks," he recalled, "I accompanied my grandmother, wife and kids and went to City Hall and proclaimed victory. When asked by the press what I thought this meant to Babe Fuqua's influence, I said, 'He's like a propeller airplane in a jet age.'"

22. Tom Law, letter to author, 11 June 1997.

23. Steve Murrin, interview by author, 30 June 1994. Murrin, who was elected to the City Council in 1968, described Fuqua as someone who was like an old mossback rattlesnake: "You think he is too old to move. You have not seen him move in a month. He is holed up in a dark, cool place in the shade. You walk past him a jillion times and you say he is over the hill, and you think about kicking him. Don't ever do that! He has been watching. You walk past one time too many and he bites you." Interview by author, 21 June 1994.

24. Neal Hospers, interview by author, 18 July 1994.

25. Tiger Teague was the living embodiment of Fuqua's dictum about integrity. Like Grover Cleveland, he believed: "A public office is a public trust." On the wall behind his desk in the Rayburn House Office Building was a plaque which proclaimed: "I sacrificed no principle to gain this office and I will sacrifice no principle to keep it." Babe Fuqua liked that.

Tiger Teague, the old soldier, had lost his ankle and two inches of his left leg in the Battle of the Siegfried Line. Outfitted in a specially made left shoe resembling an army boot, Teague slowly learned to walk again. With four Purple Hearts, three Silver Stars, three Bronze Stars, Combat Infantry Badge, Presidential Unit Citation, the French Croix de Guerre with palm and French Fouragerre, he was the most highly decorated veteran in Congress. He was Chairman of the Veterans Affairs Committee for 17 years, while at the same time serving as Chairman of the Manned Space Flight Subcommittee. The Astronauts thought Tiger hung the moon.

To further enhance his communications with the Fort Worth establishment, in 1973 Teague had placed me on his staff as his Special Representative in Fort Worth.

26. Author's personal files.

27. Clif Overcash, interview by author, 12 July 1994.

28. Tom Vandergriff, interview by author, 15 April 1994.

29. Carl Freund, interview by author, 7 April 1994. Freund was a reporter for the old *Fort Worth Press* and later for the *Dallas Morning News*. Fuqua never called him by his name, either first or last. He always called him Mr. Reporter.

30. Jewel Woods, interview by author, 20 June 1994. Wanda Woodard is the wife of Don Woodard.

31. Joe Bell, "Overcash Backs Woods in Race Against Parmer," *Fort Worth Star-Telegram,* 24 February 1979, 1.

32. Z. Joe Thornton, "Woods Nips Mayor Parmer," *Fort Worth Star-Telegram,* 8 April 1979, 1; and Joe Bell, "Woods, Parmer, Green Agree on Mistake, but not the Blame," *Fort Worth Star-Telegram,* 20 April 1979, 1B.

33. Tracey Smith (Channel 4 Reporter), interview by author, 18 July 1994.

34. Official Minutes of Fort Worth City Council. Recessed City Council Meeting. 13 April 1979.

35. Vernon Mayfield, interview by author, 20 June 1994.

36. Stan Jones and Tom Anderson, "Club Fire Continues to Smolder," *Fort Worth Star-Telegram,* 17 January 1981, 1; and Joe Lydick, letter to author, 15 October 1993.

37. Jud Cramer, interview by author, 7 July 1992.

13: SUNSET AND EVENING STAR

1. "Sarena Fuqua Dies at Age 87," *Fort Worth Star-Telegram,* 21 April 1983. Kaye Buck McDermott is a prominent Fort Worth socialite and staunch Democrat. Her father, Raymond E. Buck, 1963 President of the Fort Worth Chamber of Commerce, presented President John F. Kennedy at the historic Texas Hotel Last Breakfast on 22 November 1963.

2. Ibid. Marie Tarlton was the wife of Fort Worth Attorney Lawrence Tarlton. On 15 October 1952, she presented General Dwight Eisenhower, Republican candidate for President, to a large early morning crowd at the Texas & Pacific passenger station.

3. Pat Woods, letter to author, 28 September 1993.

4. Sterling W. Steves, letter to author, 19 July 1994.

5. Jim Bradshaw, interview by author, 20 June 1994.

6. Maurine Nailon testified not only to Fuqua's smile but to his alacrity in distress: "In 1970 I had just gone to work for an oil and gas company in Fort Worth

and was tracing some title work on a lease when I ran up against a major oil and gas company. When this happens, a person can literally spend months on the telephone or writing letters just to get a name to talk to.

"I was telling my problem to the secretary in the Sid Richardson Foundation office when the door opened, a man walked in and heard the end of my story. He asked the name of the major oil company, and when I told him he said, 'That's no problem,' picked up the phone, called the president of the company and within five minutes my problem was solved.

"From that day on, whenever I passed him in the hall or on the street, he was never too busy to smile, wave and occasionally stop for a short chat. It was much later that I found out just how influential and powerful a man he was in Fort Worth." Maurine Nailon, letter to author, 5 August 1993.

Attorney Randall Kressler was in complete agreement with Maurine Nailon: "Although most of my exposure to Mr. Fuqua was in the form of observation, I always enjoyed the opportunity for short visits with him and respected his knowledgeable opinions. The first impression which comes to my mind is that he was always the gentleman's gentleman. Although never appearing to be forceful, his appearance was always that of a proud, caring and respected individual. From the first time I ever saw Mr. Fuqua, I knew that he was a powerful man, but he never tried to verbally impress me or others in my presence with his stature or accomplishments. He was one of the last of the old gentlemen types." Randall L. Kressler, letter to author, 17 August 1993.

7. Odessa Nelson, letter to author, 3 September 1993.

8. Tilley's quip was in reference to an incident that was known about Air Force General Curtis LeMay. In the 1960s cigar-smoking LeMay visited Fort Worth's Carswell Air Force Base. A lieutenant expressed to a sergeant his fear that the General's cigar could cause a bomb-laden B-52 to explode. The sergeant reassured the lieutenant: "It wouldn't dare!"

9. James J. Fuqua, letter to author, 5 January 1992.

10. Beth Newberry, interview by author, 21 May 1993.

11. Harold Achziger, interview by author, 29 November 1991.

12. Carl Freund, interview by author, 7 April 1994.

13. David Poindexter, interview by author, 22 July 1993.

14. Beth Newberry, interview by author, 24 May 1993.

15. Stan Jones, "Cattle Breeding: Boom or Bust," *Fort Worth Star-Telegram,* 27 October 1985, 1.

16. Dennis C. Veit, letter to author, 23 April 1995.

17. Pat Woods, letter to author, 2 May 1995.

18. Charlie Hillard, interview by author, 4 May 1994. Galbraith McFadden Weaver, (always called Gil), was retired Board Chairman of Southland Royalty Company.

19. Nolen Fuqua died in Duncan Regional Hospital 7 July 1992 at age 98. His and Babe's father, Frank, was Duncan's first mayor, and Nolen followed in his footsteps, serving two terms as mayor from 1964 to 1970. Nolen married Ruth Mildred Jones on 21 January 1921. She died 30 March 1991. They had one son, Frank J., who died in 1978.

20. Reverend Robert W. Bohl, 3 January 1989.

BIBLIOGRAPHY

ADDRESSES

Bohl, Reverend Robert W. Funeral Oration, 3 January 1989.
Bond, Lewis. Remarks to Golden Deeds Banquet, 5 May 1966.
Gordon, W. K. speech to Ranger citizens, 21 October 1927.
Holmes, Oliver Wendell, Jr., Radio address on his 90th birthday, 8 March 1921.
Rehfeldt, Fred C. Address to Palo Pinto Heritage Association, 9 May 1991.

BOOKS

Abilene High School Year Book, 1917.
Allen, Ruth. *History of Organized Labor in Texas,* number 4143. Arlington: University of Texas, 1941.
Asinof, Eliot. *Eight Men Out.* New York: Henry Holt and Company, 1987.
Bielinski, Leo S. *The Back Road to Thurber.* Baird, Tex.: Joy Presswork Collection, 1993.
———. "The 1903 Thurber Coal Miners' Meeting At Rocky Creek Bridge." *West Texas Historical Association Year Book.* Abilene: Hardin-Simmons University, 1995.
Boss, Harold F. *How Green the Grazing.* Dallas: Taylor Publishing Company, 1978.
Bradley, Omar N. *A Soldier's Story.* New York: Henry Holt and Company, 1951.
Caro, Robert A. *The Years of Lyndon Johnson: Means of Ascent.* New York: Alfred A. Knopf, 1990.
Churchill, Winston S. *Their Finest Hour.* Boston: Houghton Mifflin Company, 1949.
Commager, Henry Steele. *Documents of American History.* Englewood Cliffs, N. J.: Prentice Hall, 1973.
Eisenhower, Dwight D. *Crusade in Europe.* Garden City, N.Y.: Doubleday & Company, 1948.
Farley, James A. *Jim Farley's Story: The Roosevelt Years.* New York, Toronto: Whittlesey House, McGraw-Hill Book Company, 1948.
Farman, Irvin. *Tandy's Money Machine.* Chicago: The Mobium Press, 1992.
———. *The Fort Worth Club.* Fort Worth: Motheral Printing Company, 1985.
Flemmons, Jerry. *Amon: The Life of Amon G. Carter of Texas.* Austin: Jenkins Publishing Company, 1978.
Greene, A. C. *A Personal Country.* College Station and London: Texas A&M University Press, 1979.

Hardman, Weldon B. *Fire In A Hole*. Gordon, Tex.: Thurber Historical Association, 1975.

Hicks, John D., and George E. Mowry. *A Short History of American Democracy*. Cambridge, Mass.: The Riverside Press, 1956.

Hilton, Conrad N. *Be My Guest*. New York: Prentice Hall, 1987.

The Historical Committee of The Fort Worth Petroleum Club. *Oil Legends of Fort Worth*. Dallas: Taylor Publishing Company, 1993.

House, Boyce. *Roaring Ranger*. San Antonio: The Naylor Company, 1951.

——. *Were You In Ranger?* Dallas: Tardy Publishing Company, Inc., 1935.

Johnson, Cecil. *Guts: Legendary Black Rodeo Cowboy Bill Pickett*. Fort Worth: The Summit Group, 1994.

Knight, Oliver. *Fort Worth: Outpost on the Trinity*. Norman: University of Oklahoma Press, 1953.

Knowles, Ruth Sheldon. *The Greatest Gamblers*. New York: McGraw-Hill Book Company, 1959.

McLean, William Hunter. *From Ayr to Thurber: Three Hunter Brothers and the Winning of the West*. Fort Worth: News Printing Company, 1978.

Margolies, John. *Pump and Circumstance*. Boston: Little, Brown and Company, 1993.

Nash, Jay Robert. *Blood Letters and Bad Men*. New York: M. Evans Company, 1973.

Newman, Peter C. *King of the Castle*. New York: Athenaeum, 1979.

Olien, Roger M., and Diana D. Olien. *Easy Money: Oil Promoters and Investors in the Jazz Age*. Chapel Hill: University of North Carolina Press, 1990.

Moody's Manual of Investments. New York: Moody's Investors Service, Inc.

Paddock, B. B. *Fort Worth and the Texas Northwest*. Volumes 1-2. Chicago and New York: The Lewiston Publishing Company, 1922.

Phares, Ross. *The Governors of Texas*. Gretna, La.: Pelican Publishing Company, 1976.

Prange, Gordon W. *At Dawn We Slept*. New York: Penguin Books, 1981.

Selcer, Richard F. *Hell's Half Acre*. Fort Worth: Texas Christian University Press, 1991.

Sheehy, Sandy. *Texas Big Rich*. William Morrow and Company, New York, 1990.

Spratt, John S., Sr. *Thurber, Texas: The Life and Death of a Company Coal Town*. Austin: University of Texas Press, 1986.

Studdard, George B. *Life of the Texas Pacific Coal and Oil Company*. Fort Worth: [self-published], 1992.

Tinkle, Lon. *Mr. De: A Biography of Everette Lee DeGolyer*. Boston and Toronto: Little, Brown and Company, 1970.

Watson, Don, and Steve Brown. *Texas & Pacific—From Ox Teams to Eagles*. Cheltenham, Ontario: The Boston Mills Press, 1978.

Welk, Lawrence, with Bernice McGeehan. *Wunnerful! Wunnerful!* Santa Monica, Calif.: The Welk Group, Inc., 1971.

White, William Allen. *Masks In A Pageant.* New York: The MacMillan Company, 1928.

Williams, Mack. "The Golden Goddess." In *Oil Legends of Fort Worth,* The Historical Committee of the Fort Worth Petroleum Club. Dallas: Taylor Publishing Company, 1993.

Williams, Mack, and Madeline Williams. *In Old Fort Worth.* Fort Worth: The Fort Worth News Tribune Company, 1977.

DOCUMENTS

Agreement of Sale and Purchase, Keltner File No. 53.

Bellefontaine Cemetery Association. "Tour of Bellefontaine Cemetery."

Bielinski, Leo S. *The Demise of Thurber Cemetery.* Thurber Historical Association, April 1994.

City of Fort Worth: Official Minutes of Recessed City Council Meeting, 13 April 1979.

Dallas-Fort Worth Airport Official Dedication Program.

Gordon, W. K., *Twenty-Fifth Anniversary Report,* reprinted in *Life of the Texas Pacific Coal and Oil Company* by George B. Studdard, 1992.

Hall, Thomas R., *Twenty-Fifth Anniversary Souvenir,* reprinted in *Life of the Texas Pacific Coal and Oil Company* by George B. Studdard, 1992.

Hunter, R. D., First Annual Report. Texas & Pacific Coal Company, 1890.

Loan Agreement, Keltner File No. 191.

Minutes of Commissioners Court of Erath County, Texas, vol. H, 353.

Sale of Texas Pacific Coal and Oil Company to Joseph E. Seagram & Sons, Inc. Bound Volume of Sale Documents compiled by Edgar H. Keltner, Jr., 1963.

Southwestern Life Insurance Company resolution, 12 July 1949.

Texas Pacific Coal and Oil Company Annual Report, 1958

Texas Pacific Coal and Oil Company resolution, 23 March 1949.

Texas Pacific Coal and Oil Company special meeting minutes, 16 May 1949.

Texas Pacific Coal and Oil Company Board of Directors minutes, 27 February 1952.

Texas Pacific Coal and Oil Company letter to shareholders, 20 September 1963, Keltner File No. 39.

Texas Pacific Coal and Oil Company Proxy Statement, 20 September 1963, Keltner File Nos. 45-46.

Yarborough, Ralph W., campaign ad, *Fort Worth Star-Telegram,* 23 July 1958.

MANUSCRIPTS

Callaway, Chris. "The Second Generation of Oil Men," private paper dated 27 January 1994.

Texas Pacific Coal and Oil Company, "The Story of Texas Pacific Coal and Oil Company 1888-1955." Official publication of the company, n.p., 1955 and 1959 editions.

Gentry, Mary Jane. "The Life and Death of a Texas Town." Master's thesis, University of Texas, 1946.

Spoede, Robert W. "William Whipple Johnson." Master's thesis, Hardin-Simmons University, 1968.

INTERVIEWS

Achziger, Harold, 29 November 1991.

Barnes, Lee, 28 August 1993, 5 April 1997.

Bass, Perry R., 22 December 1992.

Belew, David O. 14 April 1993.

Bell, Joe, 25 July 1994.

Boykin, Henry, 10 January 1994.

Bradshaw, Jim, 20 June 1994.

Bridges, Rita, 25 April 1997.

Cawley, Aaron, 8 June 1993.

Clarke, Doug, 22 September 1992.

Cramer, Jud, 7 July 1992.

Daniels, Bill, 28 January 1992.

Dodgen, Claude W., Jr., 20 September 1991.

Freund, Carl, 7 April 1994.

Gambill, Lawton, 28 September 1991.

Gibson, Lillie, 17 May 1993.

Gordon, W. K., Jr., 5 January 1993.

Gordon, W. K., Jr., and Chissa Gordon, 20 January 1992.

Gordon, Chissa, 23 April 1994, 6 November 1994.

Gray, Gordon, 14 May 1996.

Green, Howard, 21 August 1993.

Hamman, Blake, 14 September 1993.

Harris, W. B. (Bill), 27 April 1992.

Hillard, Charlie, 4 May 1994.

Hirsch, Nolan, 6 January 1994.

Holden, Dwayne, 25 September 1992.

Hospers, Neal, 18 July 1994.

Johnson, J. Lee, III, 22 January 1996.

Justin, John, 21 March 1994.

Keltner, Edgar H., Jr., 17 March 1992, 10 September 1993, 8 September 1994.

Leonard, Paul, 7 May 1997.

Looney, Don, 20 January 1992.

McGaugh, T. E., 24 September 1991.

McNiel, Lew, 6 May 1994.

Marston, Robert C., 13 March 1997.

Mayfield, Vernon, 29 April 1993, 20 June 1994.

Menzing, Leroy, 15 July 1994, 6 February 1996.

Moore, Billy J., 11 December 1992, 17 December 1993, 28 December 1993, 5 February 1996, 10 June 1997, 18 June 1997.

Morgan, Douglas, 3 August 1996.

Murrin, Steve, 21 June 1994, 30 June 1994.

Nelson, Odessa, 3 September 1993.

Newberry, Beth, 21 May 1993, 24 May 1993.

Overcash, Clif, 12 July 1994.

Penn, John Roby, Jr., 10 January 1991, 24 September 1992, 29 April 1994.

Poindexter, David, 22 July 1993, 7 April 1997.

Ramsey, Gordon, 17 August 1992.

Riddle, Edd, 4 January 1994.

Ringler, Charles, 27 May 1994.

Roe, Ted, 15 June 1994.

Rogers, Hamilton, 17 August 1991, 7 May 1992, 19 August 1992.

Rohlfs, Raymond, 4 December 1992.

Scales, Bill, 30 August 1996.

Simmans, Alver, 8 February 1993, 28 May 1994.

Smith, Tracey, 18 July 1994.

Spearing, Lola, 25 September 1991, 24 April 1994.

Stell, Katherine, 28 December 1992.

Stovall, R. M. (Sharky), 15 November 1991.

Studdard, George and Ruby Studdard, 23 July 1991.

Tomlinson, Lambuth, 5 May 1992.

Vandergriff, Tom, 15 April 1994.

Vititow, Myrt, 15 April 1997.

Woods, Jewel, 20 June 1994.

Woods, Pat, 30 August 1991, 1 June 1993, 2 May 1994, 7 January 1994, 29 April 1994, 19 October 1994, 12 April 1995, 25 June 1996.

Yager, Charles E., 19 November 1991.

Yarbro, Wes, 25 November 1991, 7 February 1996.

LETTERS

Bass, Perry R. to author, 21 January 1993.

Boykin, Henry to author, 28 December 1993.

Burkett, Frank, to *Fort Worth Star-Telegram,* 22 August 1992.

Closuit, Ernest, Jr., to author, 13 June 1996.

Dahlstrom, Ralph to author, 1 September 1993.

Friedman, Bayard to author, 16 March 1996.

Fuqua, H. B. to R. Ellison Harding, 2 August 1949.

Fuqua, H. B. to J. Roby Penn, 23 September 1949, 30 September 1949, 1 August 1952.

Fuqua, H.B. to Permian Basin Petroleum Museum, 10 June 1985.

Fuqua, James to author, 5 January 1992.

Garrett, John B. to author, 18 January 1994.

Gideon, Rogers to author, 22 April 1996.

Gordon, W. K. to Ranger citizens, 8 September 1927.

Greene, Harmon to author, 1 December 1992.

Gupton, Bill to author, 21 October 1992.

Harding, R. Ellison to H. B. Fuqua, 3 August 1949.

Hirsch, Nolan to author, 13 February 1997.

Johnson, Robert H. to author, 1 April 1994.

Jones, Worley to author, 1 August 1994.

Kressler, Randall to author, 17 August 1993.

Law, Tom to author, 11 June 1997.

Lucas, Bill to author, 22 June 1995.

Lydick, Joe to author, 15 October 1993.

Marston, Edgar L. to S. Mims, 29 September 1908.

Marston, Edgar L. to Central Trust Company, 25 April 1918.

Marston, Edgar L. to W. K. Gordon, 27 February 1917.

Marston, Robert C. to author, 19 March 1993, 23 March 1993, 6 April 1993, 12
     March 1996.

Moncrief, Mike to author, 3 September 1993.

Nailon, Maurine to author, 5 August 1993.

Nelson, Odessa to author, 3 September 1993.

Penn, J. Roby to H. B. Fuqua, 6 July 1949, 9 August 1949.

Pitts, Viola to author, 25 October 1994.

Ratts, Robert V. to author, 7 December 1994.

Reese, H. Michael to author, 1 July 1993.

Riddle, Edd to author, 27 July 1993, 2 June 1994.

Roberts, Alan to author, 21 December 1993.

Sherrod, Jerry to author, 10 June 1993.

Smith, Preston to author, 27 May 1997.

Spoede, Robert W. to author, 27 March 1993.

Stephens, Ed to W. K. Gordon, 11 December 1922.

Steves, Sterling to author, 19 July 1994.

Strother, Lester to author, 6 May 1994.

Studdard, George B. letter to author, 4 November 1994.

Tilley, Rice, Jr., to author, 22 April 1993.

Veit, Dennis C. to author, 23 April 1995.

Williams, Mack to author, 18 April 1993.

Windfohr, Robert F. to J. Roby Penn, 8 October 1948, 27 October 1948.

Windfohr, Robert F. to H. B. Fuqua, 12 November 1948, 22 April 1949.

Windfohr, Robert F. to Warren Scarborough, 22 April 1949.

Woods, Pat to author, 1 October 1991, 28 September 1993, 1 October 1994, 20
     March 1995, 2 May 1995.

Yager, Charles E. to Gilcy Rennie, 3 August 1923.

Yager, Charles E. to H. B. Fuqua, 21 December 1954.
Yarbro, Wes to author, 8 February 1996.

PERIODICALS

"Air-Rail Line Planned From Chicago." *Fort Worth Press*, 20 August 1928.
Associated Press. "Polio Made Roosevelt Even More Determined." *Fort Worth Star-Telegram*, 4 July 1996. "Association Makes Large Gains in 1928," *Fort Worth Press*, 31 December 1928.
"Association Makes Large Gains in 1928," *Fort Worth Star-Telegram*, 31 December 1928.
Bell, Joe. "Election Date Battle Turns into Legal Duel." *Fort Worth Star-Telegram*, 18 April 1979.
———. "Overcash Backs Woods in Race Against Parmer." *Fort Worth Star-Telegram*, 24 February 1979.
———. "Woods, Parmer, Green agree on mistake, but not the blame." *Fort Worth Star-Telegram*, 20 April 1979.
Bloom, John. "Old Oil: The Ranger Revival." *Texas Monthly*, February 1981.
Brice, Ed. "Ford's Car Suited Americans to a T." *Fort Worth Star-Telegram*, 22 July 1966.
Campbell, Roger. "Memories Stir of Texas City Fire." *Fort Worth Star-Telegram*, 25 October 1989.
"Charles Osmond Dies." *Fort Worth Star-Telegram*, 27 January 1973.
"'Coalition' is Cited by Fuqua." *Fort Worth News-Tribune*, 20 April 1975.
Cochran, Mike. "Guarding the Oswalds." *Fort Worth Star-Telegram*, 23 November 1993.
"Cosmetic Architecture—Prestige Value," *Time* (7 June 1963): 49.
Farman, Irvin. "The Last of 'The Seventh Street Gang' Bids City Farewell." *Fort Worth News-Tribune*, 6 January 1989.
"Fuel Free As Long As Ship is Up." *Fort Worth Star-Telegram*, 26 May 1929.
"Funeral Services for Fort Worth Oilman." *Fort Worth Star-Telegram*, 20 January 1975.
Garbus, Kelly. "Jesse James Remains Wanted for DNA Identification." *Kansas City Star*. Reprinted in *Fort Worth Star-Telegram*, 2 July 1995.
Hale, Leon. "Texas Chronicles." *Fort Worth Star-Telegram*, 10 October 1993.
Hall, Dave. "Dynamite Topples Once-Proud Tower in Thurber Ghost Town." *Fort Worth Press*, 30 March 1937. Special Colections, University of Texas at Arlington Library.
Hand, Martha. "Opening Day Ceremonies." *Fort Worth Star-Telegram*, 13 January 1974.
"J. Frank Norris Dead." *Fort Worth Star-Telegram*, 21 August 1952.
"J. Roby Penn," *Fort Worth Star-Telegram*, 11 February 1958.
"John Hancock Dies At Home." *Fort Worth Star-Telegram*, 23 January 1939.

Jones, Stan. "Cattle Breeding: Boom or Bust." *Fort Worth Star-Telegram,* 27 October 1985.

Jones, Stan and Tom Anderson. "Club Fire Continues to Smolder." *Fort Worth Star-Telegram,* 17 January 1981.

Jones, Terry Lee. "Little Lizard, Big Legend." *Fort Worth Star-Telegram,* 9 August 1993.

Justice, Blair. "20-Year Old Stevens Case Remains Vivid in Memories." *Fort Worth Star-Telegram,* 22 February 1953.

Kansas, Dave. "Peaks and Valleys." *Wall Street Journal.* Reprinted in *Fort Worth Star-Telegram,* 29 May 1996.

Karash, Julius. "Window to World." *Fort Worth Star-Telegram,* 8 January 1984.

Kennedy, Bud. "At 38, Life Includes Quick Trip Through Warped Looking Glass." *Fort Worth Star-Telegram,* 27 March 1993.

McConal, Jon. "Cemetery Lore." *Fort Worth Star-Telegram,* 7 September 1995.

——. "180-Proof Tales of Prohibition." *Fort Worth Star-Telegram,* 19 January 1991.

——. "Man Unearths Piece of Family's Past." *Fort Worth Star-Telegram,* 4 April 1992.

——. "Nephew's Quest Ends in Thurber Cemetery." *Fort Worth Star-Telegram,* 22 February 1993.

Maberry, Dr. Robert T., Sr. "A Time To Be Born And A Time To Die." *Fort Worth Star-Telegram,* 4 March 1990.

Menzing, Leroy. "Sinclair Denies Law Violation." *Fort Worth Star-Telegram,* 27 January 1959.

——. "Sinclair Merger Offer Expires as Texas Pacific Obeys Court." *Fort Worth Star-Telegram,* 29 January 1959.

——. "Sinclair Offers To Take TP Stock." *Fort Worth Star-Telegram,* 25 November 1958.

Obituary, *Gordon Courier Times,* 28 May 1903.

Obituaries, *New York Times,* 22 July 1899.

"Oil Company Backs Aviators." *Fort Worth Star-Telegram,* 26 May 1929.

"Retired Oil Adviser, C. H. Osmond, Dies," *Fort Worth Star-Telegram,* 27 January 1973.

Riddle, Edd. "Honorary Member." *AAPG Round Table Magazine,* September 1983.

——. "They Call Him Babe." *Energy Center,* 1, no. 1 (April 1983), University of Oklahoma.

Rogers, Mary. "Coffee Shop Talk." *Fort Worth Star-Telegram,* 22 June 1992.

"Sarena Fuqua Dies at Age 87." *Fort Worth Star-Telegram,* 21 April 1983.

Svacina, Pat. "Judge Overrules Parmer, Schedules April 28 Runoff." *Dallas Morning News,* 19 April 1979.

"Texas Pacific Sale in East Texas Reported." *Fort Worth Star-Telegram,* 24 February 1932.

"Texas Pacific Official Retires," *Fort Worth Star-Telegram,* 30 August 1968.

"Texas Pacific to Open Diamond Hill Refinery." *Fort Worth Press,* 30 April 1926.

"Texas Pacific to Host Visiting Aviators." *Fort Worth Press,* 4 July 1928.

"They Call Him Babe," *Energy Center: A Newsletter for Friends, Colleagues, and Industry.* University of Oklahoma, April 1983.

Thornton, Z. Joe. "Woods Nips Mayor Parmer." *Fort Worth Star-Telegram,* 8 April 1979.

Timmons, Bascom. "Senator Blakley Bids Colleagues Farewell." *Fort Worth Star-Telegram,* 5 April 1957.

Tinsley, Jack. "Oil Operator Badly Burned in Explosion." *Fort Worth Star-Telegram,* 7 August 1962.

Tolbert, Frank X. "Some Claim Thurber Has an Operatic Ghost." *Dallas Morning News,* 15 May 1983.

TP Voice, 2, no. 3 (May-June 1966). Official Employee Magazine.

"Tribute Paid Robbins and Kelly at Banquet." *Fort Worth Star-Telegram,* 2 June 1929.

Trout, Maybelle. "Eastland to Honor Old Rip." *Fort Worth Star-Telegram,* 25 February 1995.

"Two Burned to Death in Refinery Explosion," *Fort Worth Star-Telegram,* 13 September 1932.

Wayman, Mary Wynn. "Coming Up Rose's." *Fort Worth Star-Telegram,* 18 July 1996.

Will, George. "Dynamic Capitalism." *Fort Worth Star-Telegram,* 5 January 1993.

——. "How Bd is 'JFK'?'" *Fort Worth Star-Telegram,* 16 December 1991.

Woodard, Don. "The Landman." *Oil and Gas Journal,* 1957.

Woodard, Don. Letter to Editor. "Last of the Political Greats." *Fort Worth Star-Telegram,* 21 April 1990.

Wysatta, George. "Parmer Votes Himself into FW Runoff." *Dallas Times Herald,* 14 April 1979.

INDEX

Page numbers in italics refer to photographs or illustrations

Bradshaw, Jim, 247, 248, 254, 255, 256, 261, 298
Brender, Art, 254
Brewer, Floyd, 108
Bridier, O. B., 99-100
Brice, Ed, 278
Bridges, Rita, 278
Britton, Ed S., 33, 69, 131, *132*
Britton, Grude, 47, 48
Bronfman, Sam, 225, 226-27
Brookman, Ben, 58
Brookman, Harry, 58
Brown, Jesse M., 243
Brown, John C., 23, 24-25
Brown, William M., 244, 249, 256
Bruce, Ray, 152
Bryan, L. R., 216
Bryan, William Jennings, 55, 89
Buck, Raymond, 221, 232
Burkett, Frank, 147
Burnett, Burk, 87
Burnett, Samuel, 65
Burroughs, William S., 70
Burrows, James, 11
Burrows, Reuben, 11
Busch, Adolphus, 70
Bush, George, 245

C

Callaway, Chris, 292
Campbell, Fannie, 6
Campbell, W. C., 6
Capps, Kay, 294
Carlowitz, J. Von, 146
Carolina Central, 38
Carter, A. M., 26
Carter, Amon G., 124, 162, 194-95, 202, 244
Carter, George, 52
Cattle Barons Row (Quality Hill), 48
Cave, Tom, 251
Cawley, Aaron, 210, 222
Central Pacific Railroad, 17
Champion, Frank, 106, 107
Chapin, Howard Church, 86
Chapin, Janet Webster Phelan, 85, 86
Chapman, A. C., 67

Chapman, Eva, 67
Chapman, W. T., 67
Chipps, Dexter Elliot, 198
Chisholm Trail, 16
Chisum, John, 17-18
Cicotte, Eddie, 130
Cisco, Texas, 140-41
Clark, William, 70
Clarke, Doug, 237
Clayton Mountain, 10
Cleveland, Grover, 39, 41
Closuit, Ernest, Jr., 287, 293
Closuit, Ernest, Sr., 179, 182, 191, 224-25
Coal and Mineral Railway, 38
Coalville, 10
Cogdell, D. C., 85
Coleman, Jed, 49, 52
Colquitt, Oscar B., 108, 277-78
Connally, John, 221, 236
Connors, Harry, 77
Contri, Renaldo, *96*
Coolidge, Calvin, 129, 139, 142, 162
Corsicana, Texas, 6
Coulson, Karen, 3
Coulson, Tom, 58, 59
Cramer, Jud, 256
Crandall, Roderick, 155
Crawford, Don, x
Crawford, Don, Sr., 5
Creswell, Wiltie, 157, 164, 208
Crocker, Cornelia, 3, 97
Cullum, R. B., 235
Custer, George Armstrong, 18-19, 270
Czolgoz, Leon, 69

D

Dahlstrom, Ralph, 232
Daisy Bradford No. 3, 149
Daley, Richard, 241
Dallas-Fort Worth International Airport, 235-39
Daniel, Price, 203, *204,* 221
Daniels, A. A., 90
Daniels, W. E., 276
Daugherty, Jack, 169
Davenport, Luther M., 102, 103, 138